CONTENTS

*I am standing on the Pont des Arts in Paris. On one side of the Seine is
the harmonious, reasonable façade of the Institute of France, built as
a college in about 1670. On the other bank is the Louvre, built continu-
ously from the Middle Ages to the nineteenth century: classical architecture at its most splendid and assured. Just visible upstream is the
Cathedral of Notre-Dame — not perhaps the most lovable of cathedrals, but the most rigorously intellectual façade in the whole of
Gothic art. The houses that line the banks of the river are also a
humane and reasonable solution of what town architecture should
be...*

Kenneth Clark: Civilisation

John Murray (Publishers) Ltd/BBC Publications/Harper and Row Ltd

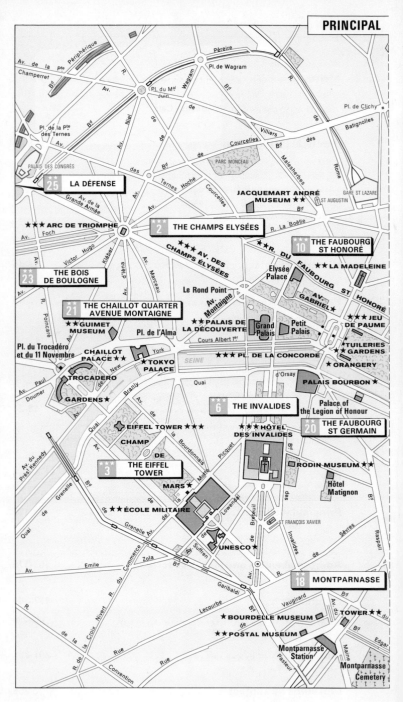

Map labels:
25 LA DÉFENSE · 2 THE CHAMPS ELYSÉES · 10 THE FAUBOURG ST HONORÉ · ★★★ ARC DE TRIOMPHE · ★★★ AV. DES CHAMPS ÉLYSÉES · 23 THE BOIS DE BOULOGNE · ★★ LA MADELEINE · Elysée Palace · AV. GABRIEL · 21 THE CHAILLOT QUARTER AVENUE MONTAIGNE · Le Rond Point · ★★★ JEU DE PAUME · ★★ GUIMET MUSEUM · ★★ PALAIS DE LA DÉCOUVERTE · Grand Palais · Petit Palais · Pl. du Trocadéro et du 11 Novembre · CHAILLOT PALACE ★★ · ★ TOKYO PALACE · ★★★ PL. DE LA CONCORDE · ★ TUILERIES GARDENS · ★ ORANGERY · ★ TROCADÉRO · PALAIS BOURBON ★ · GARDENS ★ · Palace of the Legion of Honour · ★ EIFFEL TOWER ★★★ · 6 THE INVALIDES · ★★★ HÔTEL DES INVALIDES · 20 THE FAUBOURG ST GERMAIN · CHAMP DE · 3 THE EIFFEL TOWER · ★ RODIN MUSEUM ★★ · Hôtel Matignon · MARS ■ · ★★ ÉCOLE MILITAIRE · ★ UNESCO ★ · 18 MONTPARNASSE · TOWER ★★ · ★ BOURDELLE MUSEUM · ★★ POSTAL MUSEUM · Montparnasse Station · Montparnasse Cemetery · JACQUEMART ANDRÉ MUSEUM ★★ · PARC MONCEAU

MÉTRO

Tickets. – Tickets are obtainable in booklets of ten for 26.50F – second class (40F first class) and are valid also on buses. Booklets *(carnets)* can be purchased in *métro* booking halls (also single tickets, price: 4.40F second class; 6.50F first class), on buses, at tobacco counters and at shops with the sign R.A.T.P. outside.

Most journeys, apart from those on the Sceaux spur and the R.E.R., require the flat rate of one ticket no matter how long or short they are. Insert your ticket in the slot of the machine and keep it with you until you have left the *métro*.

Tourist tickets "Paris-Sésame" can be bought on production of a passport, in larger *métro* stations and at Services Touristiques de la R.A.T.P., 53 bis Quai des Grands Augustins, 6ᵉ as well as in London, SNCF (Bureau officiel); price: 53F, 80F and 133F for unlimited journeys for 2, 4 or 7 days respectively in first class cars.

Construction. – Parisians first took the *métro* on 19 July 1900, 37 years after Londoners first took the tube (1863), 32 years after New Yorkers had begun riding on the elevated railway (1868). Since then other capitals and major cities have followed suit: Berlin (1902), Madrid (1919), Tokyo (1927), Moscow (1935), Rome (1955), Lisbon (1959). The first Paris line was on the Right Bank, from the Porte de Vincennes to the Porte Maillot; the engineer responsible was Fulgence Bienvenüe and the architect for what became the standard *métro* entrance *(illustration p 19)*, that master of the "noodle" style, Guimard.

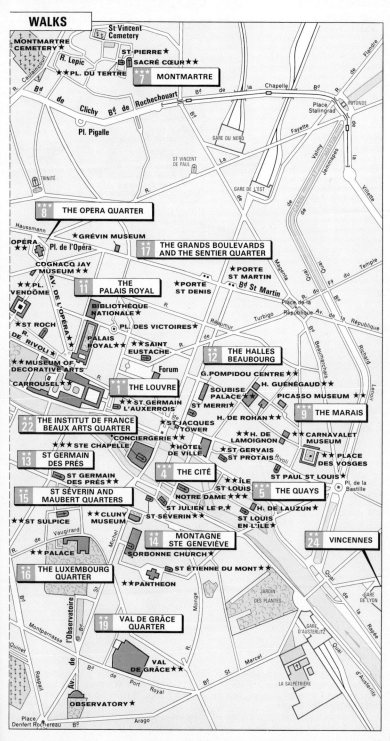

WALKS

Facts and figures. – There are 197 km – 122 miles of track for the 15 lines, apart from the R.E.R., and 365 stations of which 55 are interchanges. No point in the capital is more than 500 m – 550 yds from a métro station.

Some 4 million Parisians are transported daily – 1 200 million in 1984 – in 3 500 cars. In rush hours trains run every 95 seconds. 15 000 are employed in the métro service.

Modernization. – The system is being modernized technically and aesthetically to make it more efficient: moving walkways and escalators are being installed, tyres fitted to reduce noise and improve suspension. Stations are being decorated with window displays and glass mosaics (Franklin-Roosevelt), good reproductions (Louvre, Varenne, St-Denis-Basilique) and photographs (St-Germain-des-Prés, Hôtel-de-Ville).

The RER. – The Regional Express Network includes three lines: the A line from St-Germain-en-Laye to Boissy-St-Léger and Torcy; the B line from Robinson and St-Rémy-les-Chevreuse to Roissy and Mitry-Claye and the C line linking Versailles (south bank) and St-Quentin-en-Yvelines to Dourdan and Etampes. A line to link up the RER and suburban lines of the north and southeast will eventually serve more than 200 stations.

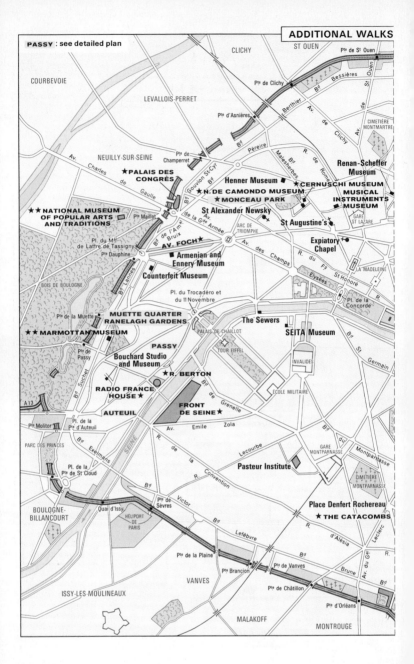

BUSES

Tickets. – Tickets are obtainable in booklets of ten for 26.50F and are valid on the *métro*. Booklets *(carnets)* can be purchased in *métro* booking halls, at tobacco counters, shops with the R.A.T.P. sign outside and on certain buses. Single tickets (4.40F) may be purchased on the buses.

Journeys are divided into stages – 1 ticket takes you two stages, 2 tickets almost any journey within the capital. Do not punch your tourist ticket *(p 4)* on the buses.

Hours. – All buses run from 7am to 8.30pm with some lines continuing later. Services may be reduced or suspended on Sundays and public holidays.

History. – In the mid 17C, on the initiative of the philosopher Pascal, there operated in Paris a network of carriages known as *fiacres* for which the fare charged was 5 *sols* or a few pence. The system worked well but eventually died, only returning in 1828 under the Restoration. In 1855 carriages known as Joséphines, Gazelles, Dames Réunies, Carolines, Hirondelles or Sylphides, and seen in all parts of Paris speeding along the streets, were united to form the General Omnibus Company. Horses were replaced in time by trams and buses. After 1918 all the road companies combined and in 1942 this joint company amalgamated with the underground. The present R.A.T.P. – Independent Paris Transport Authority – came into being in 1949.

The present problem. – In 1984, 56 routes in Paris covered 510 km – 317 miles of public thoroughfare and transported more than 294 million passengers. In order to cope with bottlenecks, all buses are linked by radio with local traffic centres and there are special lanes reserved for buses and taxis covering 111 km – 69 miles of main roads in Paris.

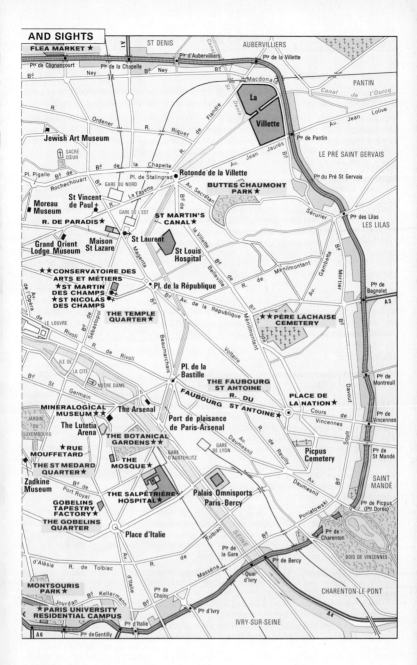

AND SIGHTS

FLEA MARKET ★

ST DENIS   AUBERVILLIERS

Pte de Clignancourt   Pte d'Aubervilliers   Pte de la Villette
Bd   Ney   Pte de la Chapelle   Bd   Ney

Macdonald   PANTIN
Canal   de   l'Ourcq

La
Villette

Ordener   R.   Riquet   de   Flandre   Av.   Jean   Lolive

Jewish Art Museum   Pte de Pantin

SACRÉ
CŒUR   LE PRÉ SAINT GERVAIS

Pl. Pigalle   Bd   de   la   Chapelle   Av.   Jean   Jaurès
Rochechouart   Pl. de Stalingrad   Rotonde de la Villette   Pte du Pré St Gervais

Moreau   St Vincent   GARE DU NORD   BUTTES CHAUMONT
Museum   de Paul ✝   La Fayette   PARK ★

R. DE PARADIS ★   GARE DE L'EST   ST MARTIN'S   Sérurier   Pte des Lilas
CANAL   LES LILAS

Grand Orient   Maison   St Laurent
Lodge Museum   St Lazare   St Louis
Hospital   Ménilmontant   Pte de
Bagnolet

★★CONSERVATOIRE DES   A3
ARTS ET MÉTIERS
★ST MARTIN   Pl. de la République
DES CHAMPS
★ST NICOLAS
DES CHAMPS   Av. de la République   ★★PÈRE LACHAISE
CEMETERY

THE TEMPLE
QUARTER ★

de Rivoli   ILE DE
LA CITÉ   Pl. de la
Bastille   Pte de
Montreuil

NOTRE DAME   THE FAUBOURG
ST ANTOINE   PLACE DE
FAUBOURG ST ANTOINE   R. DU   LA NATION

MINERALOGICAL   The Arsenal   Port de plaisance   Pte de
MUSEUM ★★★   de Paris-Arsenal   Vincennes

JARDIN
DU   The Lutetia
LUXEMBOURG   Arena   GARE
DE LYON   Picpus   Pte de
Cemetery   St Mandé

★RUE   THE BOTANICAL   GARE
MOUFFETARD   GARDENS ★★   D'AUSTERLITZ   SAINT
★THE ST MEDARD   THE   MANDÉ
QUARTER ★   MOSQUE ★

Zadkine   Palais Omnisports   Pte de Picpus
Museum   THE SALPÊTRIÈRE   Paris-Bercy   (Pte Dorée)
GOBELINS   HOSPITAL ★
TAPESTRY
FACTORY ★   Pte de
THE GOBELINS   Place d'Italie   Charenton   BOIS DE VINCENNES
QUARTER

d'Alésia   R. de Tolbiac   Pte de   Pte de Bercy   CHARENTON-LE-PONT
la Gare

MONTSOURIS   Quai
PARK ★   Masséna   d'Ivry

★PARIS UNIVERSITY   Jourdan   Pte de
RESIDENTIAL CAMPUS   Choisy   Pte d'Ivry   IVRY-SUR-SEINE

A6   Pte de Gentilly   Pte d'Italie   A4

TAXIS

There are some 14 300 taxis in Paris, cruising the streets day and night and parked in ranks alongside the kerb close to road junctions and other frequented points beneath signs labelled *Tête de Station*.

The hiring charge is 8.50F and the approximate rate 2.44F per km (1/2 mile). A supplementary charge of 3.80F is made for taxis from station forecourts, air terminals, at racecourses, and 2.70F for baggage etc. Prices are clocked up on a meter clearly visible below the centre of the dashboard. Add a 15 % tip.

PRIVATE CARS

There are about 1 000 000 private cars in Paris and an average of 90 000 cars drive along the Champs-Elysées and 95 000 along the Tuileries Quay – which explains the bottlenecks, particularly as offices close in the evening. There are only 1 200 km – 750 miles of highway and so any holdups have major repercussions. To try and alleviate the problem, road works have been and continue to be undertaken.

A west to east expressway (George Pompidou expressway, 13 km – 8 miles) along the Right Bank has been created to speed up the flow of cars as well as a ring road (*boulevard périphérique*, 35 km – 22 miles) running parallel to the outer boulevards; parking sites have been built near the outlying stations to promote the use of public transport. In the city, a blue zone *(zone bleue)* has been created with controlled parking only; also a grey zone *(zone grise)* with parking meters.

Obey the one-way and other signs, parking regulations etc with great care: the Paris police and meter maids are strict and show no particular leniency to tourists!

7

PRACTICAL INFORMATION

BEFORE LEAVING

The French Government Tourist Office at 178 Piccadilly, London WIV OAL, ☎ 491.7622 and 610 Fifth Avenue, New York, ☎ 757.1125 will provide information and literature.

When to go. – In winter the streets are bright with Christmas illuminations, the shop windows brilliant; in summer you can sit beneath the trees or an awning with a long cool drink between seeing the sights or idle away an evening on a café terrace, or go on an open boat on the Seine; in the autumn Parisians are back from their own holidays and there is an air of energy and bustle; and Paris in the spring...

Where to stay. – There are hundreds of hotels and restaurants in Paris. Hotels range from the sumptuous to modest family *pensions;* restaurants equally can provide luxurious fare at frightening prices and very good food at reasonable cost – and the great advantage with French restaurants is that the menu, with prices, is displayed outside. For a comprehensive list including prices of hotels and restaurants look in the Michelin Booklet Paris and environs (an extract from the Michelin Red Guide France).

There are several youth and student organizations – apply to the French Government Tourist Office *(address above),* the French Embassy Office, 22 Wilton Crescent, London SW1, ☎ 235.80.80 or the Central Bureau for Educational Visits and Exchanges, 44 Baker Street, London W1M 2 HJ, ☎ 487.59.61.

How to get there. – You can go from London and several other major cities in the United Kingdom directly by scheduled national airlines, by package tour flights, possibly with a rail or coach link-up or you can go by cross-channel ferry or by hovercraft and on by car or train. Enquire at any good travel agent – and remember, if you are going in the holiday season or at Christmas, Easter or Whitsun, to book well in advance.

CUSTOMS AND OTHER FORMALITIES

Papers and other documents. – A valid British Passport or other national passport or British Visitor's Passport is all that is required.

For the car a UK Driving Licence or an International Driving Licence, and International Insurance Certificate if you wish comprehensive insurance, otherwise your own policy gives you third party cover, car registration papers (log-book) and GB or other national plates (measuring not less than 175 mm wide and 115 mm high). The minimum age for driving in France is 18 years.

There are no customs formalities for holidaymakers importing their caravans into France for a stay of less than 6 months. Cars towing caravans are not allowed in Paris.

Assistance provided by the Motoring Organizations. – The AA, RAC and Routiers (354 Fulham Road, London SW10 9UH) run accident insurance and breakdown service schemes for their members.

Hiring a car. – There are agents at airports, the air terminal, railway stations and on the main streets. Hotels, travel agents, etc. will put you in touch. You require an International Driving Licence. There are restricted and paying parking zones (blue and grey zones) – beware where you leave your car! In an effort to clear traffic congestion, the Paris police and meter maids are strict, even with tourists.

Post and Telephone. – *Poste restante* mail should be addressed in your name, and then as follows: Poste restante, 52 rue du Louvre, 75100 Paris RP, ☎ 42.33.71.60. Take your passport as identification when collecting your mail.

The French telephone numbering system changed in October 1985. The country is now divided into two zones: the French provinces and Paris and its region. All **customers numbers** now have 8 digits. For the provinces add the area code to the digits of the old number. For the outer Paris region (Val-d'Oise, Yvelines, Essonne and Seine-et-Marne) the zone code becomes 1 and the area codes (3 or 6) must be added to the customer's number. Inner Paris (Ville de Paris, Hauts-de-Seine, Seine-Saint-Denis and Val-de-Marne) retains the 1 as zone code but is an exception in that the area code changes from 1 to 4.

Calling within France. – When calling within either of the two main zones dial only the 8 digit customer's number. From Paris to the provinces dial 16 + 8 digit number. From the provinces to Paris dial 16 + 1 + 8 digit number.

Calling from abroad. – For Paris the country code 33 + 1 + 8 digit number. For the provinces the country code 33 + 8 digit number.

Public phones using pre-paid plastic cards or phone cards are now in operation in some areas of Paris. The phone cards come in units of 40 or 120 and are available from post offices. The cards can be used for inland and international calls.

Telephone rates from a public telephone at any time are: Paris – London: about 19.45F for 3 minutes; Paris – New York: 54F for 3 minutes. Delays during daytime hours are usual and often lengthy – try to book your call in advance.

Health Insurance. – Even with the form E 111 you can get from a British social security office and which will save you a big percentage of doctor's or hospital bills in France, it is advisable to insure against medical expenses as, if you should require medical attention, you will have to be treated privately. Most insurance companies, travel agencies and motoring organizations have schemes at low premiums.

Nationals of non Common Market countries should make inquiries of their insurance company before leaving to see if they require a special policy, as conditions vary from company to company and policy to policy. The American Hospital in Paris *(p 10)* is a Blue Cross Member. For treatment in French hospitals or clinics it is necessary to pay the bill. Reimbursement can then be negotiated with your own insurer according to the policy held.

Currency. – There are no customs restrictions on what you take into France in the way of currency. To facilitate the export of currency in foreign bank notes, superior to the given allocation, visitors are advised to complete a currency declaration form on arrival.

Carry your money in Travellers' Cheques, obtainable from Cooks, American Express or your bank and exchangeable at banks *(hours: 9.30am to 4.30pm on weekdays)*, exchange offices *(bureaux de change)* always found at air terminals, airports, and the larger railway stations, and in some hotels and shops – you need your passport both when buying and cashing cheques. Take a small amount of local currency for expenses on the first day.

Customs. – Going into France from the UK: your personal luggage may include, 1 bottle of spirits, 300 cigarettes or 75 cigars or 400 grammes of tobacco for those over 17; 2 cameras, 10 rolls of film per camera, a portable radio, record player (and 10 records) and a musical instrument. Returning to the UK: you may bring back duty free purchases to the value of £10, 300 cigarettes or 175 small cigars or 75 cigars or 400 grammes of tobacco, 1 bottle of spirits, 2 litres of wine. See also note above on currency.

DULY ARRIVED

To get the "feel", the atmosphere, of Paris, besides seeing the sights described on pages 23-200 you will want to sit at a café table on the pavement, sipping a drink, go in one of the boats on the Seine, which enables you to see many of the major buildings from an unusual angle and rest at the same time, go, one week-end, to the Flea Market *(p 160)*.

Boat trips. – There are three types of boat:

Bateaux-Mouches: embarkation – Alma Bridge, Right Bank, ℡ 42.25.96.10.

Vedettes Paris-Tour Eiffel: embarkation – Iéna Bridge, Left Bank, ℡ 45.51.33.08.

Vedettes du Pont-Neuf: embarkation – Vert-Galant Square, ℡ 46.33.98.38.

Many of the boats have glass roofs – you can sightsee spectacularly in the worst thunderstorm.

Sightseeing tours. – *Apply to travel agencies.*

Helicopter tours. – *Apply for information to ℡ 45.54.95.11.*

(Photo P. Ronchon/Explorer)

Galerie Vivienne

Entertainment. – Look in the *Officiel des Spectacles (2F)*, *Une Semaine de Paris-Pariscope (3F)* and *7 à Paris (2.50F)* published weekly on Wednesdays and available at newspaper kiosks for a full programme of what's on in the theatre, cinema, nightclubs and for sporting and athletic fixtures, exhibitions, flower shows etc. Agencies and hotels will give full details of the sumptuous reviews and music-hall entertainments at the Folies-Bergère, the Lido, the Casino de Paris, the Paradis Latin, the Crazy Horse Saloon, the Moulin Rouge, Olympia and Bobino's.

A Theatre Ticket Booth *(open Tuesdays to Sundays 12.30-8 pm)* is situated in the Place de la Madeleine, to the west of the church of the same name. Half-price theatre tickets (if available) are sold for same day performances.

For children there are play areas in several parks, a Punch and Judy Show in the Luxembourg Palace Gardens and the Champs-Elysées. Boulogne and Vincennes both have excellent adventure playgrounds and a variety of other facilities for children. They will also enjoy a visit to the Grévin Waxworks Museum. The Georges Pompidou Centre has both a workshop and library especially for children.

Exhibitions. – Some 80 museums, 200 art galleries, numerous temporary exhibitions and the Georges Pompidou Centre keep up Paris' international reputation as a cultural and artistic centre. All national museums are closed on Tuesdays and all those belonging to the City of Paris on Mondays.

Opening times and admission prices. – The visiting times indicate the hours of opening and closing and it is important to remember that many museums, churches etc refuse admittance from up to an hour before the actual closing time.

When guided tours are indicated, the departure time for the last tour of the morning or afternoon will once again be prior to the given closing time. Most tours are conducted by French speaking guides but in some cases the term guided tour may cover group visiting with recorded commentaries. Some of the larger and more frequented museums or monuments offer guided tours in other languages. Enquire at the ticket or book stalls. Other aids for foreign tourists are notes, pamphlets or audio guides.

The admission prices indicated are for adults, however reductions for children, students and parties are common. In some cases admission is free on certain days, eg Wednesdays, Sundays or public holidays.

Churches are often closed between noon and 2pm. Tourists should also refrain from visits when services are being held.

Shops and shopping. – The big stores and larger shops are open from Monday to Saturday from 9.30am to 6.30pm. (A list of the department stores is to be found in the Michelin Guide Paris Atlas No Ⅲ.) Smaller, individual shops may close during the lunch hour. Food shops – grocers, wine merchants and bakeries – are often closed on Mondays.

Paris still has a vast number of individually owned small shops, which make every street a window-shoppers paradise: for the luxurious, exotic and fashion houses Avenue Montaigne, the Champs-Elysées, Place and Avenue de l'Opera, Rue Tronchet, Rue Royale and the Rue du Faubourg St-Honoré. The great names among jewellers are found in the Rue de la Paix and Place Vendôme. For those looking for a particular item: shoes, hand bags and leather goods (Rue St-Lazare and Boulevard St-Michel) off-the-peg French fashion (Rue de Passy and Rue de Sèvres), furniture (Rue du Faubourg St-Antoine) and crystal, glass and fine china (Rue Paradis). Antique and fine art shops are grouped in the Louvre des Antiquaires, Village Suisse, Carré Rive Gauche and the Flea Market. The Forum des Halles provides a varied selection of fashion boutiques for the young, the avant-garde and chain stores.

There are also lively street markets in every quarter.

Comparative sizes, weights and measures. – Clothing: women's dresses and suits – British 34, Continental *40;* 36, *42;* 38, *44;* 40, *46,* etc; men's suits and overcoats – British 36, Continental *46;* 38, *48;* 40, *50,* etc; shirts and collars – British 14, Continental *36; 14 1/2, 37;* 15, *38,* etc.

Weight: *1 kg* = 2 lb 3 oz; *100 grammes* = 3 1/2 oz. Length: *1 cm* = just under 1/2 inch; *1 mètre* = 39 inches; *1 km* = 5/8 mile. Volume: *1 litre* = 1 3/4 pints; *50 litres* = 11 gallons (13.21 US gal).

Temperature: *21°C* = 70°F; *15.5°C* = 60°F; *10°C* = 50°F; –98,4°F *i.e.* normal body temperature = *37°C.*

USEFUL ADDRESSES

Accueil de France, 127 Avenue des Champs-Élysées, 8ᵉ – ☎ 47.23.61.72.
Accueil de la Ville de Paris, Hôtel de Ville, 29 Rue de Rivoli, 4ᵉ – ☎ 42.76.43.43
American Express, 11 Rue Scribe, 9ᵉ – ☎ 42.66.09.99.
British Rail (Britrail Voyages), 55-57 Rue Saint-Roch, 1ᵉʳ - ☎ 42.61.85.40.

Embassies

Australia, 4 Rue Jean-Rey, 15ᵉ – ☎ 45.75.62.00.
Canada, 35 Avenue Montaigne, 8ᵉ – ☎ 47.23.01.01
Great Britain, 35 Rue du Faubourg St-Honoré, 8ᵉ – 42.66.91.42.
   Visas: 2 cité du Retiro, 8ᵉ – ☎ 42.66.38.10.
Ireland, 4 Rue Rude, 16ᵉ - ☎ 45.00.20.87.
New Zealand, 7 *ter* Rue Léonard-de-Vinci, 16ᵉ – ☎ 45.00.24.11.
South Africa, 59 Quai d'Orsay, 7ᵉ – ☎ 45.55.92.37.
United States, 2 Avenue Gabriel, 8ᵉ – ☎ 42.96.12.02.
   Visas: 2 Rue St-Florentin, 1ᵉʳ - ☎ 42.96.12.02.

Hospitals

American Hospital, 63 Bd Victor-Hugo, 92 Neuilly-sur-Seine (7.5 km – 5 miles – from central Paris) – ☎ 47.47.53.00.
British Hospital, 48 Rue de Villiers, 92 Levallois-Perret (7.5 km – 5 miles) – ☎ 47.57.24.10.

Books in English

Brentano's, 37 Avenue de l'Opéra, 2ᵉ – ☎ 42.61.52.50.
Galignani, 224 Rue de Rivoli, 1ᵉʳ – ☎ 42.60.76.07.
Nouveau Quartier Latin, 78 Bd St-Michel, 6ᵉ – ☎ 43.26.42.70.
Shakespeare and Co, 37 Rue de la Bûcherie, 5ᵉ.
W.H. Smith, 248 Rue de Rivoli, 1ᵉʳ (English Tea Room upstairs) – ☎ 42.60.37.97.

Air Terminals, Airports, Airline Main offices

Aérogare de Paris, Les Invalides
   ☎ 43.23.97.10 (Information, coach connection with Orly, left luggage etc.).
Aérogare de Paris, Porte Maillot, 2nd underground level
   ☎ 42.99.20.18. (Coach connection with Charles de Gaulle).
Charles de Gaulle Airport, Autoroute du Nord
   ☎ 48.62.22.80 (27 km – 17 miles – from central Paris).
Orly Airport, Autoroute du Sud – ☎ 48.84.32.10 (16 km – 10 miles).
Air France, 119 Avenue des Champs-Élysées, 8ᵉ – ☎ 42.99.23.64.
Air Canada, 24 Boulevard des Capucines, 9ᵉ – ☎ 47.42.21.21.
Air Lingus, 47 Avenue de l'Opéra, 2ᵉ – ☎ 47.42.12.50.
British Airways, Tour Winterthur, 102 Quartier Boieldieu, La Défense – ☎ 47.76.86.86.
British Caledonian Airways, 5 Rue de la Paix, 2ᵉ – ☎ 42.61.50.21.
Pan Am, 1 Rue Scribe, 9ᵉ – ☎ 42.66.45.45.
Qantas, 7 Rue Scribe, 9ᵉ – ☎ 42.66.52.00.
T.W.A., 101 Avenue des Champs-Élysées, 8ᵉ – ☎ 47.20.62.11.

Other **MICHELIN** Green Guides available in English

Brittany	*Austria*	*New York City*
Châteaux of the Loire	*Canada*	*Portugal*
Dordogne	*England: The West Country*	*Rome*
French Riviera	*Germany*	*Scotland*
Normandy	*Italy*	*Spain*
Provence	*London*	*Switzerland*
	New England	

Churches, Synagogues

American Church, 65 Quai d'Orsay, 7ᵉ – ℡ 47.05.07.99.
American Cathedral in Paris, 23 Avenue George-V, 8ᵉ – ℡ 47.20.17.92.
Christian Science, 36 Bd St-Jacques, 14ᵉ – ℡ 47.07.26.60.
St. Michael's English Church, 5 Rue d'Aguesseau, 8ᵉ – ℡ 47.42.70.88.
Church of Scotland, 17 Rue Bayard, 8ᵉ – ℡ 48.78.47.94.
St. George's (Anglican), 7 Rue Auguste-Vacquerie, 16ᵉ – ℡ 47.20.22.51.
Liberal Synagogue, 24 Rue Copernic, 16ᵉ – ℡ 47.27.25.76.
Great Synagogue, 44 Rue de la Victoire, 9ᵉ – ℡ 42.85.71.09.

Public Holidays in France.
– The following are days when museums and other monuments may be closed or may vary their hours of admission.

New Year's Day
Easter Sunday and Monday
May Day (1 May)
Fête de la Libération (8 May)
Ascension Day
Whit Sunday and Monday

France's National Day (14 July)
Assumption Day (15 August)
All Saints' Day (1 November)
Armistice Day (11 November)
Christmas Day

Prices and tipping (mid 1986).
– In shops and on menus, items are clearly marked; small extras cost approximately the following:

English newspapers (dailies)	8F
American newspapers (dailies, printed in France)	6.50F
Petrol (per litre)	4.87F
Petrol-Super (per litre)	4.99F
English cigarettes	8.10 to 9.70F
American cigarettes	7.65 to 8F
French cigarettes	6.10 to 6.95F
Postage: to UK	letter 2.50F; card 1.80F
to USA - Airmail	Aerogramme 3.70F; card 3.15F
Coffee - un café (black espresso)	3.05 to 9.50F
Coffee and milk - un café au lait	6.20 to 12.50F
Fresh lemon or orange juice - citron pressé, orange pressée	8.30 to 15F
A beer (bottled) - une bière bouteille	8.30 to 16.50F
A beer (draught) - une bière pression	5.20 to 14F

Service is often included on the bill; if in doubt ask; if it is not, add on 15 %.

During the season, it is difficult to find hotel accommodation in Paris.
It is wise to book your hotel in advance by letter or by telephone.
Or, apply to Accueil de France,
127, Champs-Élysées, 8ᵉ, Tel: 47.23.61.72

BOOKS TO READ

Artistic, architectural, historical and general background:

Paris – JOHN RUSSELL *(Thames & Hudson)*
The Sun King – NANCY MITFORD *(Hamish Hamilton)*
The French – THEODORE ZELDIN *(Collins)*
A Moveable Feast – ERNEST HEMINGWAY *(Granada Paperbacks)*
Access in Paris (Disabled Tourist's Guide) – *Obtainable from Pauline Hephaistos Survey Projects, 39 Bradley Gardens, West Ealing, London W5*

Five English and American fiction classics:

CHARLES DICKENS – **The Tale of Two Cities**
BARONESS ORCZY – **The Scarlet Pimpernel**
ARNOLD BENNETT – **The Old Wives' Tale** (the 1870/71 siege)
HELEN WADDELL – **Peter Abelard**
ELIOT PAUL – **A Narrow Street**

There are English translations of the works of the major authors mentioned on p 21. There are also about 150 works of fiction with Paris as their setting which make amusing holiday or post-holiday reading. They range from the semi-biographical, semi-factual to light romances and fast moving detective stories – you will find them listed in the Cumulative Fiction volumes.

*To choose a hotel or restaurant, use the small, **MICHELIN** Red Guide:*
PARIS, Hotels and restaurants,
*an extract from the current **MICHELIN** Guide FRANCE.*

January
CNIT (La Défense) . . . . Boat Show

Last Sunday in January
Vincennes racecourse . . . . . America Stakes

February
CNIT (La Défense) . . . . World Trade Fair on Tourism and Travel

Early March
Parc des Expositions . . . Agricultural Show

March
CNIT (La Défense) . Audio-visual Exhibition

Palm Sunday
Auteuil racecourse . Pres. of the Republique Stakes

Palm Sunday to end of May
Vincennes (Reuilly Lawn) . . . . . . Throne Fair

April
Bagatelle (Bois de Boulogne) . . . . . . Azaleas

Late April - eary June
Floral Garden (Vincennes) . Rhododendrons

Late April - eary May
Parc des Expositions . . . . Paris Fair

Late April - late October
Invalides . . . . Son et Lumière (in English)

May - June
Floral Garden (Vincennes) . . . . Tulips

Late May - early June
Roland Garros Courts . . French Open Tennis Championships

Between April and June
Parc des Princes Stadium - Football Cup Final

Early June *(odd years)*
Le Bourget Airport . . . . Paris Air Show

Whit Monday
St-Cloud racecourse . . . Spring Grand Prix

Last Fortnight in June
Auteuil racecourse . . . . Paris Race Meeting

Third Sunday in June
Auteuil racecourse . . . . Paris Grand Steeple Chase

Last Sunday in June
Longchamp racecourse . . . . Paris Grand Prix

June - July
Marais Quarter . Music and Drama Festival

June - July
Bagatelle (Parc Floral) . . . . Roses

June - September
L'Hay-les-Roses . . . . Roses

14 July
Military march-past, open air celebrations, fireworks

Mid - July
Champs-Élysées . . . . Finish of the Tour de France cycle race

July - October
Sceaux Orangery . . Chamber Music Festival

July - September
Paris Summer Festival

September
Vincennes racecourse . . Summer Grand Prix

September
CNIT (La Défense) . . . . SICOB: Office Automation and Computing Fair

September - October
Floral Garden (Vincennes) . . . . Dahlias

Mid. September - Mid. December
Autumn Festival

Early October *(even years)*
Parc des Expositions . . . . Motor Show

Early October *(odd years)*
Parc des Expositions . . . . Cycle and Motorcycle Show

First Saturday in October
Montmartre . . . . Wine Harvest Festival

First Sunday in October
Longchamp racecourse . . . . Arc de Triomphe Grand Prix

First or second Sunday in October
Seine . . . . 6 hour Power Boat Race

Second Sunday in October
Rue Lepic . . . . Veteran cars hill race

Last fortnight in October
Municipal Flower Garden (Boulogne) . . . . Chrysanthemum

October - November
CNIT (La Défense) . . . . D.I.Y.

1 November or nearest Sunday
Auteuil racecourse . . . . . Autumn Grand Prix

11 November (Remembrance Sunday)
Arc de Triomphe . . . . Military Parade

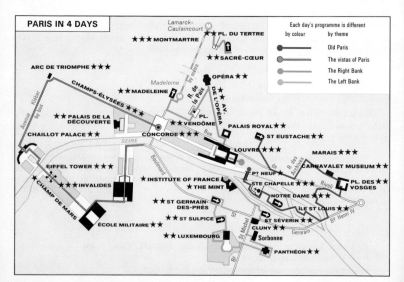

PARIS IN 4 DAYS

Each day's programme is different
by colour — by theme
Old Paris
The vistas of Paris
The Right Bank
The Left Bank

ON A FINE DAY

Monuments

Arc de Triomphe - 19C
Place de la Concorde - 18C
The Invalides - 17C

The Louvre - 14-19C
Notre-Dame - 12-14C
The Eiffel Tower - 19C

Vistas, views

Arc de Triomphe (Platform)
Montparnasse (Tower)
Notre-Dame (Towers)
Sacré-Cœur (Dome)
The Eiffel Tower (3rd floor)
Georges Pompidou Centre

Alexandre III Bridge
Place de la Concorde
Orléans Quay
Chaillot Palace (Terrace)
Tournelle Bridge
Viviani Square

Recreation areas

Bagatelle, Pré Catelan (Bois de Boulogne)
Luxembourg Gardens

Botanical Gardens
Floral Garden (Bois de Vincennes)

Open-air markets

Flowers (Place L.-Lépine)
Birds (Quai de la Mégisserie)

Stamps, post cards (Avenue de Marigny)
Book stalls (The quays)

Attractions for children

Aquarium (tropical fish) (Museum of African Art)
Amusement Park (Bois de Boulogne)

Zoo, vivarium (Botanical Gardens)
Zoo (Bois de Vincennes)

ON A RAINY DAY

Principal museums

Louvre (Paintings, sculpture)
Modern Art (Modern paintings)
Army (Arms, uniforms)
Decorative Arts (Furnishings, applied arts)
Popular Art and Traditions (Crafts)
Carnavalet (History of Paris)
Cluny (Medieval trades and crafts, tapestries)
Conciergerie (Historic prison)

Palais de la Découverte (Scientific discoveries)
Guimet (Oriental art)
Mankind (History and characteristics or man)
Jacquemart-André (Furniture, paintings)
Maritime (Naval history, navigation)
French Monuments (Plaster casts, murals)
Rodin (Sculpture by Rodin)

Religious art

Ste-Chapelle (Stained glass windows)
St-Germain-l'Auxerrois (Stained glass, altarpiece, pew)

St-Étienne-du-Mont (Roodscreen)
St-Sulpice (Organ loft, murals)

Antiquarian shops

Cour des Antiquaires
Louvre des Antiquaires

Flea Market
Village Suisse

Shopping centres, galleries, arcades

Forum des Halles
Centre Beaugrenelle
Palais des Congrès
Centre Maine-Montparnasse

Quatre-Temps, La Defense
Champs-Élysées Arcades
Palais-Royal Arcades
Rivoli Arcades

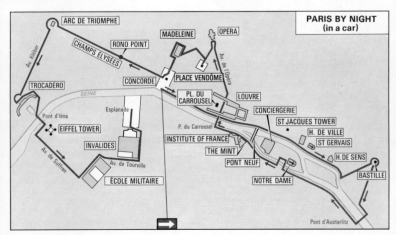

PARIS BY NIGHT (in a car)

All the year round: *Sundays to Fridays, sunset (5.15 to 10.20pm) to midnight (1am Saturdays and days before a holiday).*

In summer *some boat companies give tours on the Seine (details p 9).*

HISTORICAL FACTS

GALLO ROMAN PERIOD

3rdC BC	The Parisii settle on the Ile de la Cité.
52 BC	Labienus, Caesar's lieutenant defeats the Gauls under Camulogenes, who set alight and then abandon the Ile de la Cité.
1C AD	The Gallo Romans build the city of Lutetia.
c 250	St Denis, first Bishop of Paris, is martyred *(pp 76, 182)*.
280	Lutetia destroyed by the Barbarians.
360	Julian the Apostate, prefect of the Gauls, is proclaimed by his soldiers Emperor of Rome when in the Cité. Lutetia becomes Paris.

EARLY MIDDLE AGES

451	St Genevieve turns Attila away from Paris *(p 54)*.
508	Clovis makes Paris his capital and settles in the Cité.
8C	Charlemagne makes Aix-la-Chapelle (Aachen) his foremost city. Paris, abandoned, declines.
885	Paris besieged by the Northmen for the fifth time, is defended by Count Eudes who is elected King of France in 888 *(p 54)*.

THE CAPETIANS

Early 12C	Abelard, first studies, then teaches, in Paris. Suger, Abbot of St-Denis and minister under Louis VI and Louis VII, rebuilds the abbey.
1163	Maurice of Sully undertakes the construction of Notre-Dame.
1180-1223	Philippe Auguste erects a wall around Paris and builds the Louvre.
1215	Foundation of the University of Paris.
1226-1270	Reign of St Louis : Pierre of Montreuil builds the Sainte-Chapelle, works on Notre-Dame and St-Denis. The king dispenses justice at Vincennes.
1253	Foundation of Sorbon College *(p 109)*.
1260	The dean of the Merchants' Guild becomes Provost of Paris *(p 67)*.
1307	Philip the Fair dissolves the Order of the Knights Templar *(p 175)*.

THE VALOIS

1358	Uprising under Étienne Marcel *(pp 58, 67)*. The monarchy moves to the Marais and the Louvre.
1364-1380	Charles V builds the Bastille and a new wall round Paris *(p 16)*.
1407	Duke Louis of Orleans is assassinated on the orders of John the Fearless *(p 89)*.
1408-1420	Fighting between the Armagnacs and Burgundians. Paris handed over to the English.
1429	Charles VII besieges Paris in vain; Joan of Arc is wounded *(p 98)*.
1430	Henry VI of England is crowned King of France in Notre-Dame.
1437	Charles VII recaptures Paris.
1469	The first French printing works opens in the Sorbonne.
1530	François I founds the Collège de France.
1534	Ignatius Loyola founds the Society of Jesus in Montmartre *(p 77)*.
1559	Henri II is fatally wounded in a tourney *(p 83)*.
1572	Massacre of St Bartholomew *(p 68)*.
1578-1604	Construction of the Pont Neuf *(p 70)*.
1588	The Catholic League turns against Henri III who is forced to flee Paris, after the Day of the Barricades (12 May).
1589	Paris is invested by Henri III and Henri of Navarre. The former is assassinated at St-Cloud.

THE BOURBONS

1594	Henri IV is converted to Catholicism; Paris opens her gates to him.
1605	Creation of the Place des Vosges.
14 May 1610	Henri IV is mortally wounded by Ravaillac *(p 103)*.
1615-1625	Marie dei Medici has the Luxembourg Palace built.
1622	Paris becomes an episcopal see.
1627-1664	Development of the Ile St-Louis.
1635	Richelieu founds the French Academy.
1648-1653	Paris disturbed by the Fronde.
1661	Mazarin founds the College of Four Nations, the future Institut de France *(p 140)*
1667	Colbert establishes the Observatory *(p 132)* and reorganizes Gobelins Tapestry Works *(p 162)*.
17C	Construction of Versailles *(p 188)*; development of the Marais.
Late 17C	Erection of the Louvre Colonnade and the Invalides.
Early 18C	Construction of the Place Vendôme and development of the Faubourg St-Germain.
1717-1720	John Law's Bank *(p 103)*.
1722	Creation of the first Fire Brigade.
1727-1732	End of the Jansenist crisis; the St. Medard "Convulsionnaires".
c 1760	Louis XV has the École Militaire, the Pantheon and the Place de la Concorde constructed.
1783	Ascent of the balloonists Pilâtre de Rozier *(p 160)*, and Charles and Robert *(p 40)*.
1784-1791	Erection of the Farmers General Wall *(p 16)* including the gateways and toll-houses by Ledoux.

THE REVOLUTION AND THE FIRST EMPIRE

14 July 1789	Taking of the Bastille *(p 155)*.
17 July 1789	Louis XVI at the Hôtel de Ville; adoption of the tricolour.
14 July 1790	Festival of Federation *(p 51)*.
20 June 1792	The mob invades the Tuileries *(p 24)*.
10 Aug. 1792	Taking of the Tuileries and the fall of the monarchy *(pp 24, 40)*.
2-4 Sept. 1792	September Massacres *(p 107)*.
21 Sept. 1792	Proclamation of the Republic *(p 96)*.
21 Jan. 1793	Execution of Louis XVI *(pp 43, 159)*.
1793	Opening of the Louvre Museum.
1793-1794	The Terror *(pp 43, 61, 159, 170)*.
8 June 1794	Festival of the Supreme Being *(pp 40, 51)*.
5 Oct. 1795	Royalist uprising suppressed by Napoleon *(p 97)*.
9-10 Nov. 1799	Fall of the Directory *(p 181)*.
1800	Bonaparte creates the offices of Prefect of the Seine and of the Police.
2 Dec. 1804	Napoleon's coronation at Notre-Dame *(p 55)*.
1806-1814	Napoleon continues construction of the Louvre and erects the Arc de Triomphe and Vendôme Column. Stay at Malmaison.
31 March 1814	The Allies occupy Paris.

THE RESTORATION

1815	Waterloo. Restoration of the Bourbons.
1821-1825	Construction of the Ourcq, St Denis and St Martin Canals.
1830	Fall of Charles X; flight to the Palace of Holyroodhouse.
1832	A cholera epidemic kills 19 000 Parisians.
1837	The first French railway line, Paris – St-Germain is opened.
1840	Return of Napoleon's body from St. Helena *(p 71)*.
1841-1845	Construction of the Thiers fortifications *(p 16)*.
February 1848	Fall of Louis-Philippe *(p 80)*.
	Proclamation of the Second Republic *(p 67)*.

FROM 1848 TO 1870

June 1848	The suppression of the national workshops creates disturbances in the Faubourg St-Antoine *(p 160)*.
1852-1870	Gigantic town planning undertakings by Baron Haussmann: the Halles, railway stations, Buttes-Chaumont, Bois de Boulogne and Vincennes, the Opera, the sewers, completion of the Louvre, laying of the boulevards through the old quarters of the city. Paris is divided into 20 *arrondissements*.
1855, 1867	World Exhibitions.
4 Sept. 1870	The Third Republic is proclaimed at the Hôtel de Ville *(p 67)*.

THE THIRD REPUBLIC

Winter 1870-1871	Paris is besieged by the Prussians and capitulates *(p 67)*. St-Cloud Château is burnt to the ground. Napoleon III goes into exile in England.
March-May 1871	The Paris Commune is finally suppressed by the Men of Versailles during the Bloody Week (21-28 May); fire, destruction (Tuileries, Old Auditor General's Office, Hôtel de Ville, Vendôme Column) and massacres *(p 170)*.
1885	State funeral of Victor Hugo.
1889	World Exhibition at the foot of the new Eiffel Tower *(p 48)*.
1900	First *métro* line opened: Maillot – Vincennes. Construction of the Grand and Petit Palais *(p 45)*; Cubism is born at the Bateau-Lavoir *(p 77)*. The Sacré-Cœur Basilica is erected on the Butte Montmartre *(p 78)*.
1914-1918	Paris under threat of German attack is saved by the Battle of the Marne. A shell hits the Church of St-Gervais – St-Protais *(p 66)*.
1920	Interment of the Unknown Soldier *(p 47)*.
February 1934	Rioting in the vicinity of the Chamber of Deputies.
June 1940	Paris is bombed then occupied by the Germans. Hostages and resistance fighters detained at Mount Valérien *(p 178)*.
August 1944	Liberation of Paris: week of 19-26 *(pp 45, 96)*.

SINCE 1945

1950	Opening of the downstream port of Gennevilliers.
1958-1963	Construction of UNESCO, CNIT and ORTF buildings (now Radio-France House).
1964	Reorganization of departments of the Paris region: Nanterre, Créteil and Bobigny become prefectures.
1965	Paris region Town and Development Plan published.
May 1968	Strikes and demonstrations: Nanterre, Latin Quarter, the Boulevards, the Champs-Élysées.
1969	Transfer of the Halles Market to Rungis.
1970	Regional express *métro* system inaugurated. Thirteen autonomous universities created in the Paris Region.
1973	Completion of the ring road and Montparnasse Tower.
February 1974	Opening of the Paris Conference Centre.
March 1977	Election of the first mayor of Paris since 1871 (1789-1871: 11 appointed mayors).
May-June 1980	Pope John Paul II on an official visit to Paris.

The construction of Notre-Dame, which began after that of St-Denis and Sens in about 1140, heralded the age of great Gothic cathedrals in France: Strasbourg (c. 1176), Bourges (c. 1185), Chartres (c. 1194), Rouen (1200), Reims (1211), Amiens (1220), Beauvais (1247).

The capital's site was carved out of the limestone and Tertiary sands by the Seine at the centre of what is now the Paris Basin. At that time the river flowed at a level of 35 m – 100 ft – above its present course.

The Gallo-Roman Wall: 1. – The Parisii, taking advantage of the *Pax romana,* emerged from Lutetia, built by the Gauls and defended by the river and surrounding swamps, to settle along the Left Bank of the river *(p 109)*. The Barbarians, however, forced them to retreat, in about 276, to the Cité. On the island, they built houses, fortifications and a rampart wall to defend themselves against future invasions.

The Philippe Auguste Wall: 2. – Between the 6 and 10C, the swamps were drained and cultivated, monasteries founded and a river harbour established near the Place de Grève. Between 1180 and 1210 Philippe Auguste commanded that a massive wall be built *(pp 91, 114)* reinforced upstream by a chain barrage across the river and downstream by the Louvre Fortress and Nesle Tower.

The Charles V Rampart: 3. – The Town, which was on the Right Bank (as opposed to the University on the Left Bank, and the Cité), prospered as roads were built connecting it with Montmartre, St-Denis, the Knights Templar Commandery, Vincennes Castle. By the end of the 14C, Charles V had erected new fortifications, supported in the east by the Bastille. The ramparts enclosed a Paris of just under 440 ha – 1 3/4 sq miles – and 150 000 inhabitants.

The Louis XIII Wall: 4. – In the 16C the Catholic League, Wars of Religion, the siege by Henri of Navarre kept up the pressure on the city so that Charles IX and Louis XIII extended the 14C wall westward to include the Louvre Palace.

The Farmers General Wall: 5. – The monarchy moved to Versailles. Paris now 500 000 strong, saw the erection of the Invalides, the Observatory, the Salpêtrière and the St-Denis and St-Martin Gates. The enclosed city was too small so a new wall (1784-1791) complete with 57 **tollhouses** by Ledoux was constructed *(p 163)*. "The wall, walling in Paris", it was said, however, "makes Parisians wail".

The Thiers Fortifications: 6. – Under the Revolution properties were broken up but little was built; under the Empire, Paris began to know problems of overcrowding and supply; gas lighting appeared during the Restoration; industry, railways and economic development brought growth to outlying villages (Austerlitz, Montrouge, Vaugirard, Passy, Montmartre, Belleville) which Thiers had enclosed in a further wall (1841-45), reinforced at a cannonball's distance by 16 bastions – these became the capital's official limits from 1859. Twenty *arrondissements* were created in the 7 800 ha – 30 sq miles – as Haussmann began his transformation of the city (Population – 1846: 1 050 000; 1866: 1 800 000).

The present limits: 7. – The forts remained intact (Mount Valérien, Romainville, Ivry, Bagneux...), but the walls after serving in the city's defence in 1871, were razed by the Third Republic in 1919.

Paris' limits were defined between 1925 and 1930 as including the Bois de Boulogne and Vincennes and not extending elsewhere beyond a narrow circular belt; the area equalled 10 540 ha – 40 3/4 sq miles – and the population, in 1945, 2 700 000.

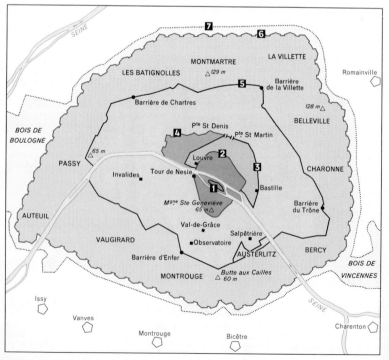

PARIS TODAY

Paris' centrifugal attraction dates from the First Empire; since then it has developed, pell mell, as the pivot of France's political, administrative, economic and cultural life. A century after Haussmann a plan was adopted in 1960 to resolve, at least, the capital's physical problems. 1965 saw the publication of a development plan.

Local government. – Since March 1977, the **Mairie de Paris** has had an elected mayor, chosen by the 163 councillors of the municipal council. With the exception of the police force, headed by a *préfet*, the mayor has the status and powers of mayors of other municipalities.

The municipal authority works closely with the primary units of Paris local government, the town halls of the 20 arrondissements, which are responsible for local problems. Paris being both a commune and a department its Council sits as a municipal authority and a general or departmental council.

(After photo Seal's Department, Archives Nationales)

Seal of the
Watermen's Guild (1210)

The city's coat of arms features the boat motif from the armorial bearings of the watermen's guild whose members were appointed by St Louis *(p 67)* in 1260 to administer the township. In the 16C the device was complemented by the motto *Fluctuat nec mergitur* – she is buffetted by the waves but does not sink. The **Ile-de-France Region** comprises eight departments (Paris, Seine-et-Marne, Yvelines, Essonne, Hauts-de-Seine, Seine-St-Denis, Val-de-Marne and Val-d'Oise), each with their own prefecture, and covers a total area of 12 011 km^2 – 4 637 sq miles with a total population of 10 073 053 (Paris: 105 km^2 – 40 sq miles; 2 176 243). The Regional Council – drawn from local authorities – is paralleled by an Economic and Social Committee. Since the 1982 decentralisation act the Regional Council is no longer headed by the *Préfet*. The latter now known as Commissioner of the Republic also exercises the same role for the department of Paris.

Metamorphosis. – Paris' historic, architectural and archeological treasures stand out in all their glory once more thanks to the enlightened policy of André Malraux who instituted a programme of cleaning, restoration, revitalising even whole areas such as the Marais.

Engineers and planners wrestle with today's problems – highways and transport (the ring road, expressway, RER), supply (Rungis, Garonor), cultural centre (Georges Pompidou Centre), sports facilities (Palais Omnisports de Bercy), office expansion (Défense, Front de Seine, Maine-Montparnasse), and urban renewal (Place d'Italie, Belleville, Bercy). The emphasis is now on the preservation and restoration of the historic heritage.

Major cultural projects include the City of Science and Industry and Music Centre at La Villette, the Museum of 19C Art in the Gare d'Orsay, a new Opera House at La Bastille and the International Communication Centre of La Défense.

The departure of the Halles, the explosion of the University into thirteen autonomous universities, the decentralisation of the Higher Schools of learning, have contributed in relieving congestion at the centre. Modern hospitals, both public and private, have been erected. Green spaces have been created, aged parks and gardens refurbished...

Future prospects. – The future of the city and of the Paris region is based on the development of new business centres in suburban areas (La Défense, St-Denis, Créteil...), the creation of new towns equipped with the necessary infrastructure (jobs, schools, transport) and on maintaining the level of population and employment in the city.

Population. – The 1974 figures showed the Paris Region as being populated by more than 10 000 000 inhabitants or 18.8 % of the total population of France. This concentration lives in 2.2 % of the land area producing a density in the City of Paris of 21 900 to the km^2 – 56 100 to the square mile and 820 in the outer region.

While the population of Paris proper is slightly decreasing, new inhabitants arrive every day to settle in the suburbs. Paris has, therefore, become the home of men and women from Brittany to Corsica, of strangers from abroad who congregate in certain areas: Jews in the Marais, White Russians in Montparnasse, Spaniards in Passy, North Africans in Clignancourt, La Villette, Aubervilliers... The true Parisian, however, remains easily identifiable among the cosmopolitan crowd: hurried, tense, protesting, frivolous, mocking, quick witted, punning – personified in the cabaret singer, the barrow boy, the urchin.

Paris quarters. – Some quarters have kept their association with a mediaeval craft or trade and retain something of the atmosphere of past centuries: Quai de la Mégisserie – seed merchants; the Odéon area – publishing houses and bookshops; the Faubourg St-Antoine – cabinet-makers; the Temple and Sentier quarters – secondhand dealers, particularly of clothes; the Rues Bonaparte and La Boëtie – antique dealers; Avenue Matignon and Faubourg St-Honoré – art galleries; Faubourg St-Honoré, Avenue Montaigne and Rue François-Ier – fashion houses; Opéra quarter – luxury shops; Rue de Rome – stringed instrument makers; Rue de Paradis – porcelain and glassmakers; Rue de la Paix and Place Vendôme – jewellers' shops.

There are, in addition, the streets lined with government offices (Rue de Grenelle, Chaillot), commercial organisations (Bourse, Opéra, Champs-Élysées, La Défense...), the big stores and schools. And between all these is a mosaic of workshops, warehouses and small shops which, with the many large undertakings, make up Paris' infinitely various economy.

17

ARCHITECTURE

Gothic architecture. – Gothic is the true style of Paris' older buildings. **Gallo-Roman** is virtually non-existent apart from a few cradle vaulted arches still standing in the Roman baths at the Hôtel de Cluny and such heavily restored remains as the Lutetia arena; **Romanesque,** known in England as Norman, and better represented elsewhere in France, can only be seen as features in a larger whole – the small chancel columns and belfry-porch in St-Germain-des-Prés, the apse of St-Martin-des-Champs, the St-Denis Cathedral crypt, and the capitals in St. Peter's, Montmartre and St-Aignan Chapel.

Gothic, however, was born in the region, arising from the combined requirements of height and increased light. An ogival style evolved, characterised inside by broken arch vaulting (St-Denis narthex and ambulatory) and outside by buttressing. These supports, it was soon discovered, could be hollowed out without diminishing their strength, and so appeared the flying buttress.

The outstanding example of Gothic development between the 12 and early 14C is to be found in Paris' greatest monument Notre-Dame Cathedral: the vast chancel, the only slightly projecting transept, the sombre galleries at the back of the triforium are typical of **early Gothic** while firmly localizing the whole are the decorative carvings on the capitals of plants and flowers native to the Paris region. Light inside was very limited still, passing only through small narrow windows in the nave surmounted by equally small round windows or oculi, an arrangement still to be seen in the cathedral transept.

Gothic skill reached its greatest heights in the reign of St. Louis with the architect Pierre of Montreuil who, with awe-inspiring daring, replaced solid side walls by vast windows, letting the light pour in. Slender column walls only between the glass supported the roof, reinforced outside by unobtrusive buttresses or flying buttresses (the St-Martin-des-Champs refectory). The new lightness and window space inspired the glassmakers in their craft.

With the construction of its greatest masterpieces, the east end of Notre-Dame, the Sainte-Chapelle in the Cité, the Royal Chapel at Vincennes, the **radiant Gothic style** had, perhaps, reached its climax when building generally was interrupted by the outbreak of the unrest and fighting, later known as the Hundred years War (1337-1453). The rising provoked by Étienne Marcel, the civil strife between the Burgundians and the Armagnacs explain the reason for such architecture as existed in the period being massive and sombre, almost feudal in style, epitomised by the Bastille and Men at Arms Hall in the Conciergerie.

Gothic continued into the 15C but was considerably marred by exaggerated interior decoration: purely decorative arches – liernes and tiercerons – segmented vaulting (St. Merry transept, St-Germain-l'Auxerrois porch), window tracery with a flame motif, pillars, unadorned by capitals, rising in a single sweep to span out directly beneath the roof (St-Séverin ambulatory) from which hung monumental keystones (St-Étienne-du-Mont).

Examples of this **Flamboyant Gothic style** are the St-Jacques Tower, the Billettes Cloister and the contemporary Hôtel de Sens and Hôtel de Cluny. In these mansions, the defensive features – turrets, crenelations, wicket gates – are trimmed with richly sculptured decorations – balustrades, mullioned dormer windows – in the same way as the early châteaux of the Loire.

The Renaissance. – War with Italy introduced those who went there to the Antique style and the profane in decoration. Pointed arches gave place to cradle vaulting or coffered ceilings (St-Nicolas-des-Champs), rounded bays (St-Eustache) descended on to Ionic or Corinthian capitals topping fluted columns (St-Médard). The roodscreen at St-Étienne-du-Mont is the finest example of interior decoration which elsewhere included mythological or commonplace motifs (St-Gervais stalls).

Pierre Lescot adopted the Italian style of a uniform façade broken by advanced bays crowned by rounded pediments for the Cour Carrée in the Louvre and for the hôtel Lamoignon. Statues decorated the niches between fluted columns; cornices and a frieze surmount the doors and each floor. Inside, the ceilings are frequently coffered and decorated as above the Henri II staircase in the Clock Pavilion again in the Louvre.

Classical Architecture. – At the end of the Wars of Religion, the influence of Antiquity increased, the king once more asserted his power – events symbolised in the solidly constructed Pont Neuf.

Religious architecture turned to the Classical, a style which was to continue throughout the 17 and 18C and be characterised by a profusion of exterior columns, pediments, statues and cupolas reminiscent of the churches of Rome.

The Jesuit style of the Counter-Reformation produced the multiplicity of domes to be seen in the Sorbonne Church, the Val-de-Grâce and St-Paul-St-Louis. But this typically Baroque feature was soon modified by the architects of Louis XIV and XV – Hardouin-Mansart (The Invalides), Libéral-Bruand (Salpêtrière), Le Vau (St-Louis-en-L'Ile), Soufflot (Pantheon).

Contemporary civil constructions were characterized, in imitation of Versailles, by Classical symmetry and simplification. The Place des Vosges and Place Dauphine are true Louis XIII with the alternating use of brick and stone while the Luxembourg Palace by Salomon de Brosse has a mixture of both French and Italian elements. Immediately after came the Mansarts, Androuet Du Cerceau, Delamair and Le Muet, evolving in the Marais, a new style of architecture with their designs for the town house.

Classical architecture reached its climax between 1650 and 1750 with the majestic constructions of Perrault in the Louvre Colonnade, Le Vau, the Institute, and Gabriel, the Place de la Concorde and École Militaire.

The Antique simplicity of the Louis XVI style can be seen in the Palace of the Legion of Honour and the Farmers General Wall pavilions by Ledoux.

The 19C. – The Empire and Restoration had little to show as regards architectural achievements: the Madeleine, Arc de Triomphe, Carrousel Arch are classical pastiches lacking any particular originality. The Second Empire, however, brought a fantastic new impetus to planning in the person of Baron Haussmann. A new style was rapidly imprinted on the capital – the iron and metalwork style exemplified by Baltard in St. Augustine's and the Halles, Labrouste in the Bibliothèque Ste-Geneviève, Hittorff in the Gare du Nord and by Gustave Eiffel in the Eiffel Tower.

While Garnier's Opera was being built, a construction in stone which was not only one of the most successful of the period but bears comparison with larger scale edifices such as the Louvre, the Hôtel de Ville and the Hôtel-Dieu, industrial development, the discovery of new materials and techniques and the ascendancy of domestic over monumental architecture, were inaugurating close collaboration between architects and civil engineers.

The 20C. – Just as the Grand and Petit Palais, the Alexandre III Bridge and Sacré-Cœur Basilica mark a certain attachment to the past, Baudot in St. John's in Montmartre and the Perret brothers in the Champs-Élysées Theatre, were discovering the possibilities of reinforced concrete which were demonstrated fully in 1937 in the Chaillot and Tokyo Palaces.

Since 1945, under the influence of Le Corbusier, of whose actual work the only examples in Paris are some of the University City halls, architectural design has undergone a fundamental reappraisal. The result is the wide variety of styles to be seen in the circular Radio-France House, the upraised UNESCO, the sweeping roof lines of the CNIT, the glass and aluminium façades at Orly, the new glass façades of the GAN and Manhattan Towers and Georges Pompidou Centre, whereas Charles de Gaulle airport illustrates the "concrete style". Currently architecture is viewed within the wider context of town planning; buildings are designed to fit into a scheme and sometimes as part of a plan for the renovation of an area (Maine-Montparnasse, Les Halles) or the creation of a new area (La Défense) or of a new town (Créteil).

(Photo Barry/Pix)

A Tower at La Défense.

SCULPTURE

The Gallo-Roman pillar of the Paris boatmen now at the Cluny Museum *(p 118)*, the capital's oldest sculpture, was followed 1 000 years later by low reliefs and statues carved by highly skilled but equally anonymous craftsmen for Notre-Dame and other churches.

From the Renaissance and for the following three centuries, the monarchy decorated the city with sumptuous religious and civil constructions which were then adorned by the sculptors to the Court: Jean Goujon (Innocents' Fountain), Germain Pilon (St-Denis), Girardon (Richelieu's tomb), Coysevox (Tuileries Gardens), Coustou (The Marly Horses), Robert Le Lorrain (Hôtel de Rohan), Bouchardon (Four Seasons Fountain) and Pigalle.

It was, however, during the mid and late 19C that Paris was gradually transformed into an open air museum with statues, particularly, multiplying in parks, gardens and streets: Carpeaux (Observatory Fountain) and Rude *(Marshal Ney)* were followed by Rodin *(Balzac, Victor Hugo)*, Dalou (Place de la Nation), Bourdelle (Tokyo Palace, Champs-Élysées Theatre), Maillol (Carrousel Gardens) and Landowski *(Ste-Geneviève)*.

Hector Guimard epitomized the style of 1900 in his famous wrought-iron *métro* entrances as Calder's mobile *(p 53)*, Zadkine's bronzes (Père-Lachaise cemetery) and Louis Leygue, Agam (La Défense) and Arman's (St-Lazare Station) sculptures symbolize the work of the 20C abstractionists now appearing in parks and in new architectural schemes.

(Photo D. Clément/Explorer)

Métro Station

PAINTING

Until the late 16C, early 17C, Paris remained largely unrepresented pictorially apart from the incidental scenes depicted by miniaturists, painters, engravers and illuminators such as the Limbourg brothers, who included Paris backgrounds in the *Very Rich Hours* of the Duke de Berry, and Jean Fouquet in the *Book of Hours* he painted for Étienne Chevalier. In the 17C landscape interest in the capital began to awaken, particularly in the Pont Neuf and the Louvre and the countryside surrounding the Invalides and the Observatory. J.-B. Raguenet, Hubert Robert, Antoine de Machy and later, Bouhot and Georges Michel, and finally Méryon with his deeply toned water colours, developed a descriptive tradition which bridges the period to the late 19C when the Impressionists emerged and made Paris the world art centre.

Corot, who painted the Paris quaysides and Ville d'Avray a few miles away, was followed by Jongkind, Lépine, Monet *(St-Germain-l'Auxerrois, Gare St-Lazare)*, Renoir *(Moulin de la Galette, Moulin Rouge)*, Sisley *(Ile St-Louis, Auteuil Viaduct)* and Pissarro *(The Pont Neuf)*, who depicted light effects in the capital at all hours and in all seasons. Paris also played an important part in the work of Seurat *(The Eiffel Tower)*, Gauguin *(The Seine by the Pont d'Iéna)*, Cézanne and Van Gogh (Montmartre scenes). Later, and more gently, Vuillard painted the peace of Paris squares and gardens.

Toulouse-Lautrec, sketching with wit and intimacy cabaret artists before and behind the footlights, presented a totally different appreciation of the Paris scene. Equally keen of eye were André Gill, Forain, Willette and Poulbot *(p 78)* again portraying not Paris but the Parisian whether he be music-hall artist, politician *pierrot* or street urchin.

At the beginning of the 20C Paris was at its height with the Paris School (Derain, Vlaminck, Bonnard, Braque, Dufy, Matisse...) the inspiration of all, and the Bateau-Lavoir *(p 77)* and the Ruche *(p 127)*, the centres of good talk, night long discussion and revolution. The painters of that time who devoted most of their work to the Paris scene were Marquet and Maurice Utrillo.

Poulbot drawing

The modern lanscape of Paris has become familiar, particularly, through the widely reproduced paintings of the present day artists, Yves Brayer and Bernard Buffet.

MUSIC

Yesterday. – Music, in France, as elsewhere, developed most elaborately first in the church: by the end of the 12C a school of polyphony had been established in Notre-Dame, expressing in harmony the deep religious faith of the period. The Hundred Years War interrupted its development and it was only with François I that attention turned once more to the art – this time in the form of court songs and airs accompanied on the lute. In 1571, the poet, Baïf founded the Academy of Music and Poetry, to re-establish the harmony of Antiquity in poetry and music.

"That most noble and gallant art" developed naturally at the royal court, first at the Louvre, and, later, at Versailles where sovereigns, their consorts and companions disported themselves in ballets, allegorical dances, recitals, opera and comedy.

The Royal Academy of Music (1672), dominated by the personality of Lulli, encouraged sacred music to new heights in Notre-Dame (with Campra), St-Gervais and the Sainte-Chapelle (with the Couperins), St-Paul-St-Louis (Charpentier) and Notre-Dame-des-Victoires (with Lulli himself).

The Regency saw the birth of comic opera (Mouret and Monsigny) and the revitalising of opera proper by Rameau (1683-1764). Not long after, Gluck, Parisian by adoption, produced his mature operas: *Orpheus and Eurydice, Iphigenia in Aulis* and *Alcestis* (1774-1779).

Composition, since the Revolution, has centred round the National Conservatory, founded in 1795. It was there that the young Romantic school grew up with Cherubini, Auber and Berlioz who created his *Fantastic Symphony* while at the Conservatory in 1830. These were followed by César Franck, Massenet, Fauré. Paris became the international musical capital, drawing the Italians Rossini and Donizetti, the Polish Chopin *(p 89)*, the Hungarian Liszt and the Germans Wagner *(p 100)* and Offenbach, to come and stay, often for years.

1870 and the years that followed saw activity with Bizet, Saint-Saëns, Charpentier and Dukas, Parisians by birth or adoption, bringing new life to symphony and opera, d'Indy founding the Schola Cantorum *(p 131)* and Debussy and Ravel co-operating with Diaghilev's Russian Ballet *(p 138)*. Finally came the Group of Six Honegger, Tailleferre, Auric, Milhaud, Poulenc, Durey) and the rival Arcueil School of Satie and Sauguet.

Today. – Today Paris musical life is reflected in a plethora of performances by large orchestras in fine concert halls, of chamber music and organ recitals.

Quite different are the clubs, cellars and *boîtes* or night-clubs scattered throughout the Latin Quarter, along the Champs-Élysées, in Montmartre and Montparnasse.

Among the best are the Trois Mailletz *(56 Rue Galande, 5ᵉ)*, Le Caveau de la Huchette *(5 Rue de la Huchette, 5ᵉ)*, Le Slow Club *(130 Rue de Rivoli, 1ᵉʳ)*, La Louisiane *(176 Rue Montmartre, 2ᵉ)*.

LETTERS

Paris, the inspiration of poets and novelists and the setting for so many works, has occupied a central place in French literature since the 13C when the University was founded and the Parisian dialect was adopted as the language of the court.

The people of the streets appear, at this time, in epic poems and Mystery plays *(p 55);* individual characters and daily life in the poems of Rutebœuf and Villon (15C). Rabelais criticized Paris, but nevertheless sent Gargantua and Pantagruel to the Sorbonne and ended living in the Marais *(c 1553 – p 91).*

As the capital grew and attracted men of letters amongst others, it inspired a devotion in many equal to their native soil: Montaigne, Guillaume Budé, who founded the Collège de France, Ronsard and the Pléiade poets *(p 110)* and Agrippa d'Aubigné who bore witness to the religious conflicts which engulfed Paris and the rest of the country at the end of the 16C.

The 17 and 18C. – As Paris underwent alternately embellishment, under Henri IV and Louis XIII, and disruption, by the Fronde at the time of Louis XIV's minority, writers, intellectuals, wits and lesser mortals developed what was to be a uniquely French cultural phenomenon, the cultivated philosophic conversation of the *salons,* first at the Hôtel de Rambouillet (17C) and later at the houses of the Marquise de Lambert, Madame du Deffand, Madame Geoffrin (18C).

In contrast to the exploration and discussion of new ideas in the *salons,* the French Academy, founded by Richelieu in 1635, sought to exert a restraining influence on all branches of literature – Saint-Amand was, meanwhile, writing satire, Boileau burlesque and Madame de Sévigné her *Letters* on daily life.

In the 18C cafés – Procope, La Régence ... – developed as centres of discussion and debate; Marivaux and Beaumarchais were presenting light comedies on the capital's life style and the provincial, Rousseau, expressing his disdain of the "noisy, smoke filled, muddy" city!

It is Voltaire, outstanding in story telling, history, correspondence and memoirs, however, who, many would say, epitomises the 18C and the Paris writer at his best, with his irony and wit, light touch and perfect turn of phrase.

The Encyclopaedists typified Paris in the Age of Enlightenment as clearly as Restif de la Bretonne's *Nights of Paris* and Sébastien Mercier's *Portrait of Paris* described the daily scene in the capital.

The 19 and 20C. – The two major writers on Paris, Hugo and Balzac, were, in fact, born in the provinces. Both, in *Les Misérables* and the *Human Comedy* respectively, portrayed Paris as a character in its own right, suffering moods, influencing others... Beside these two giants, Dumas the Younger, Musset, the song-writer Béranger, Eugène Sue *(Mysteries of Paris),* Murger *(Scenes of Bohemian Life),* Nerval and others, pale into the background.

To the new Paris of Baron Haussmann came Baudelaire and the Parnassian and Symbolist poets and Émile Zola.

Montmartre remains transfixed in the songs of Bruant (1851-1925), the novels of Carco (1886-1958) and Marcel Aymé (1902-1967), Montparnasse in the poems of Max Jacob (1876-1944) and Léon-Paul Fargue (1876-1947). More generally descriptive are the works of Colette and Cocteau, Simenon, Montherlant, Louise de Vilmorin, Aragon, Prévert, Sacha Guitry, Éluard, Sartre, Simone de Beauvoir...

PARIS AND THE ENGLISH

Paris conjures up an image in the mind of every man and woman in Britain – the association goes back so far, the distance is so small, the atmosphere so different, the streets so wide, the buildings so massive, the landmarks so familiar from posters, pictures and films. Political exchanges have been continuous, ending in agreements to differ or often in treaties – 1763, terminating the Seven Year's War, 1814 and 1815 ending the Napoleonic era, 1856 in alliance at the end of the Crimean War, 1904 – 1910 commercial treaties which concluded in the Entente Cordiale, 1919 the Treaty of Versailles.

From the time of William the Conqueror families have intermarried; since 1420 and the recognition of Henri V as King of England and France, the English have at times penetrated to the capital.

By the 17C, aristocrats and the wealthy were completing their education with the Grand Tour of Europe with Paris as the first stop; by the mid 19C, Thomas Cook was organising group visits, since, as he stated in Cook's Excursionist and Advertiser of 15 May 1863, "We would have every class of British subjects visit Paris, that they may emulate its excellencies, and shun the vices and errors which detract from the glory of the French capital. In matters of taste and courtesy we have much to learn from Parisians..."

It was the Continental Sunday, above all, that shocked Thomas Cook, and later the Bohemianism of Montmartre and Montparnasse. But it was just this that attracted and has continued to attract many visitors from Britain ever since! A first visit to Paris for many, therefore, becomes a desire to get a kaleidescopic view of the Eiffel Tower and the Moulin Rouge, to eat in a *bistro* and walk up the Champs-Élysées, to see the Bastille – which they can't! – and visit Versailles – which they can.

With second and third and later visits – for every Briton, once having been to Paris, surely desires to return – comes a growing interest.

Observation of what Lawrence Durrell has called "the national characteristics... the restless metaphysical curiosity, the tenderness of good living and the passionate individualism. This is the invisible constant in a place with which the ordinary tourist can get in touch just by sitting quite quietly over a glass of wine in a Paris bistro". Comparisons with London; how much is the same and, therefore, familiar – children and adults sailing model yachts on the ponds in the Tuileries and Kensington Gardens – and yet just different enough to make you feel on holiday, how much is unique. The following pages, we hope, will help you in your discoveries.

KEY

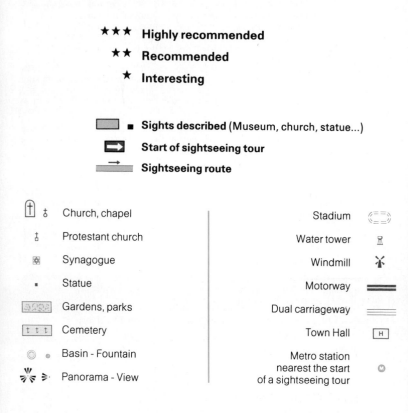

★★★ **Highly recommended**

★★ **Recommended**

★ **Interesting**

▪ **Sights described** (Museum, church, statue...)

➡ **Start of sightseeing tour**

→ **Sightseeing route**

⛪ ᵟ	Church, chapel	Stadium	⬭
ᵻ	Protestant church	Water tower	⏧
✡	Synagogue	Windmill	✳
▪	Statue	Motorway	▬
	Gardens, parks	Dual carriageway	═
t t t	Cemetery	Town Hall	H
◎ ◦	Basin - Fountain	Metro station nearest the start of a sightseeing tour	Ⓜ
☼ ⍦	Panorama - View		

PRINCIPAL WALKS

Description of walks 1 to 25.

(Photo Christiane Olivier, Nice)

Place de la Concorde by night.

THE LOUVRE

Michelin plan ⚏ - fold 31: H 13

Louvre métro station.

France's and, in fact, the world's largest royal palace is now famous above all as a museum. This walk is of great historical, architectural and artistic interest.

HISTORICAL NOTES

The original fortress. – The Louvre was constructed as a fortress on the banks of the Seine by Philippe Auguste in 1200 to protect the weakest point in his new city perimeter. It stood on less than a quarter of the space now occupied by the Cour Carrée and was used as treasurehouse, arsenal and archive. In the 14C the fortress ceased its military function with the erection of a new perimeter and Charles V converted it into a residence, installing his famous library in one of the towers.

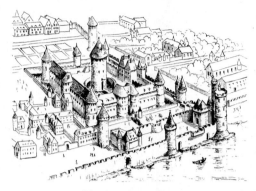

(After documents in the Carnavalet Museum)

The Louvre of Charles V.

A half Gothic, half Renaissance palace. – For 150 years after Charles V, France's kings preferred other palaces, until, in 1527, François I announced that he was going to take up residence in the Louvre. Rebuilding began with the razing of the keep, the knocking down of the advanced defences and the laying of a garden in their place. Only in 1546, was an architect, Pierre Lescot, commissioned to build a new royal palace.

François I died the following year when the foundations were scarcely showing but building continued until the outbreak of the Wars of Religion. By this time what came to be known as the Old Louvre consisted of the great Renaissance southwest façade of the Cour Carrée, and west and south wings with two Gothic and two Renaissance façades. All these constructions it was to retain until the reign of Louis XIV.

Construction of the Tuileries. – On the tragic death of Henri II *(p 83)*, his widow, Catherine dei Medici decided to move, with the young king, François II, to the Louvre. She did not wish to live in the palace itself, however, and in 1563 commissioned Philibert Delorme to build her a residence 500 m away in an area known as the Tuileries. Suddenly, in 1572, all work stopped when an astrologer frightened the queen into believing she would die on the site. Twenty-two years later it was resumed; Henri IV built the Flore wing; Louis XIV the Marsan; the harmony of the Delorme building was impaired by remodelling. The Tuileries, nevertheless, remained empty of royalty until Louis XV.

The Bord de l'Eau Gallery. – Catherine also planned a covered way between the Louvre and the Tuileries following the line of the Seine. This Galerie du Bord de l'Eau, as it is called, was completed by Henri IV who added an upper storey.

The ground floor was occupied, at first, by shops and workshops; Richelieu installed the Royal Mint and printers there; Louis XIV gave rooms as studios to well known painters, sculptors, cabinet makers and architects. Living quarters were on the *entresol* and a corridor on the first floor, where five times a year the king passed to bless and touch the sick.

Construction of the Cour Carrée. – Louis XIII decided to quadruple the old Louvre since the court had become horribly cramped. Le Mercier, architect of the Sorbonne, built the Horloge Pavilion and extended it by an exact replica of Pierre Lescot's edifice. In 1659 Louis XIV commissioned Le Vau to work on the palace: the Apollo wing *(p 38)* was rebuilt and the first two floors completed (1664). Then the Sun King decided that his palace required a grandly regal exterior and he summoned the greatest architect of the time, Bernini. The Italian's ideas, however, which began with the razing of the existing palace, proved unacceptable and alternative plans, therefore, were drawn up by Le Vau, Le Brun and Claude Perrault. Perrault who is thought to have created the Colonnade (1667-1673), removed the Gothic wings from the Cour Carrée and replaced them with north and south façades in harmony with his colonnade. However, in 1682 the court left the Louvre for Versailles and building stopped once more.

Years of Neglect. – The palace apartments, left empty by the departed court, were let to tenants: an artists' colony including Coustou, Bouchardon, Coypel, Boucher, settled in the galleries; the colonnade was divided into dwellings; stove chimneys stuck out in rows from the wonderful façade. Taverns and entertainers' shanties were built up against the walls until by 1750 the whole building had become so dilapidated it seemed in danger of being pulled down. Marigny, Minister to Louis XVI, came to its rescue.

Years of Turmoil. – On 20 June 1791 the royal family fled from the Tuileries, were arrested and returned, to be seized one year later to the day, by the Paris mob. Invading the palace the rabble pulled a red bonnet over the king's ears and made him pledge his loyalty to the nation in a toast. There followed the bloody 10 August when 600 of the Swiss Guard were massacred by the mob before the palace was sacked.

The Convention and Directory installed themselves in the opera house and apartments.

Construction and destruction. – Bonaparte expelled the last trespassers from the Louvre and began its repair. He enlarged the Carrousel Square and, on his escape from a royalist attack in the nearby street of St-Nicaise on Christmas eve 1800, erected a triumphal arch as monumental entrance to the palace forecourt. The imperial architects, Percier and Fontaine completed the Cour Carrée, reordered and decorated the royal apartments and began work on the great North Gallery along the new Rue de Rivoli. In 1810, in the Salon Carré, Napoleon III married Marie-Louise.

Work on the palace stopped at the Restoration. Louis XVIII, the only king to die in the Tuileries, was succeeded by Charles X and Louis-Philippe, both of whom were expelled by the Paris mob who subsequently pillaged the royal residence.

Finally, in 1852, Napoleon III decided to complete the Louvre. While Haussmann cleared the area around the Place du Carrousel, Visconti and, later Lefuel, finished the North Gallery and constructed monumental additions to the palace's existing wings as well as providing it with north and south gates. After three centuries the Louvre, the biggest palace in the world, was finished.

During the blood soaked week of the Paris Commune of May 1871, the Tuileries was set on fire by the insurgents but the main building was saved. The Third Republic commissioned Lefuel to rebuild the Marsan and Flore pavilions. In 1965, the base of Perrault's Colonnade was disengaged to give the columns their full height.

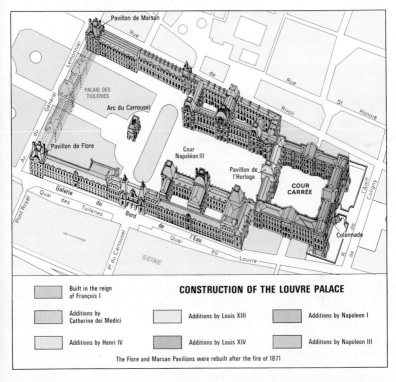

CONSTRUCTION OF THE LOUVRE PALACE

Built in the reign of François I

Additions by Catherine dei Medici

Additions by Henri IV

Additions by Louis XIII

Additions by Louis XIV

Additions by Napoleon I

Additions by Napoleon III

The Flore and Marsan Pavilions were rebuilt after the fire of 1871

The museum through the centuries. – The dispersal of Charles V's rich library left the palace empty of treasure until François I began a new collection with twelve paintings by great masters including Titian, Raphaël, Leonardo da Vinci – the *Mona Lisa* – and antique casts brought back from Italy. By Louis XIII's reign the Cabinet du Roi contained some two hundred pictures. Colbert added generously to the collection as did others, so that by the death of Louis XIV, the king's paintings numbered 2 500 scattered throughout the royal palaces. The Louvre, meanwhile, became the centre for the annual exhibition of the Academy of Painting and Sculpture. The idea of a museum, which had been envisaged by Louis XVI, was finally realised by the Convention which, on 10 August 1793, opened the doors of the Grande Gallery to the public. Napoleon made the Louvre the world's richest museum by exacting a "tribute" in works of art from every country he conquered – but in 1815 the Allies took back what had been theirs.

Louis XVIII, Charles X and Louis-Philippe added to the Louvre collection which already incorporated the Museum of French Monuments *(p 140)* created by Lenoir. The *Venus de Milo* had scarcely been rediscovered on the Island of Melos in 1820 before she was purchased by the French Government for 6 000 F and brought to Paris; further Greek, Egyptian, Assyrian antiquities were collected and transported.

In 1947, the Impressionist paintings were transferred to the Jeu de Paume museum *(p 42)*. Further gifts, legacies and acquisitions have augmented the collections so that the catalogue now lists nearly 300 000 entries.

The New Louvre. - The museum is at present engaged in a vast programme of extensions and reorganisation. Extensions will include the wing formerly occupied by the Finance Ministry. One of the more controversial aspects of the architect, Ieoh Ming Pei's overall project is the giant glass pyramid in the Cour Napoléon, to give light to the new underground reception area and main entrance.

TOUR OF THE EXTERIOR

Before starting along Rue de Rivoli, admire the Colonnade.

Colonnade★★. – *(Entrance to museum only)* Perrault produced in the Louvre colonnade a work of considerable grandeur although it bears no relation to the rest of the building. Louis XIV's cypher of two coupled Ls marks the edifice; the central pediment, carved by Lemot at the time of the Empire, centred on a bust of Napoleon, replaced at the Restoration, by one of the Sun King.

Leave the Rue de Rivoli to enter the Cour Carrée by the Marengo entrance.

Cour Carrée★★. – The courtyard is the most impressive part of the Old Louvre to remain. On the right is the Pierre Lescot façade – a Renaissance delight in proportion, balance and decoration to which the sculptor, Jean Goujon, gave his all. In the centre of this west side is the Le Mercier Horloge or Clock Pavilion and further over a Classical replica of the Lescot façade. The three remaining sides, although harmonizing with the west, are not identical with it and all lack the grace of the Lescot Renaissance work. The period of each building is marked with emblazoned monograms: H interlaced with a double C and forming a D on the Lescot face are for Henri II, Catherine dei Medici and the king's favourite, Diane de Poitiers; K, H, HDB and HG on the south side, for Charles IX, Henri III, Henri IV (Henri of Bourbon) and Henri (IV) and Gabrielle d'Estrées; right of the Horloge Pavilion, LA, LB, LMT for Louis XIII and Anne of Austria, Louis of Bourbon, Louis XIV and Marie-Thérèse.

The Old Louvre. – Recent excavations have uncovered remains of Philippe Auguste's keep and Charles V's palace. The archaeological crypt *(underground: not open before 1988)* will give visitors a chance to see the former.

Embankment Façade★. – From the embankment can be seen the majestic Perrault façade and beyond, the Bord de l'Eau Gallery on which the frieze of cherubs mounted on monsters introduces a delightful, lighter note. The area after the Carrousel entrance is the part rebuilt following the 1871 fire *(p 25)*.

Cour Napoléon. – *Closed to the public.* Future site of the glass pyramid *(p 25)* and main entrance.

The two arms of the Louvre. – The two arms of the palace today enclose a formal garden. It was in the 17C that the ground, crowded and vivid with military parades, tourneys and royal masques was named, after particularly brilliant celebrations in 1662, the Place du Carrousel. The palace is impressive from the gardens but an even grander vista★★★ is through the line of the Carrousel Arch, across the Place de la Concorde and, centring on the obelisk, up the Champs-Élysées, to the Arc de Triomphe.

The Carrousel Triumphal Arch★★. – The Carrousel, a delightful pastiche of a Roman arch with eight great rose marble columns from the Old Château at Meudon, was erected between 1806 and 1808 in celebration of the Napoleonic victories of 1805. The decoration, at one time, included the four gilded bronze horses from St. Mark's Venice and originally from Constantinople, which Napoleon had brought back to France (returned 1815).

The Parterres★. – The flowerbeds, laid out in 1909 and decorated with **statues★** by Maillol, mark the site of the Tuileries Palace which linked the Flore and Marsan Pavilions.

Cross to the Pont Royal to look below the great allegory on the south wall at the high relief by Carpeaux, **Flora's Triumph★**, after which the corner pavilion is named.

■ THE LOUVRE MUSEUM★★★

Open 9.45am to 6.30pm central area (5pm, the rest of the museum). Closed Tuesdays and holidays; 20F - free on Sundays.

Guided lecture tours (10F extra), except Sundays, start from the information desk, Salle du Manège. They are planned to include some of the most outstanding works of art. Other guided tours on a specific collection, school or period are also organized. For further details ☎ 42.60.39.26.

Some galleries may be temporarily closed for rearrangement. Other areas are closed from 11.30am to 2pm. Moreover large-scale reorganization sometimes changes the location of certain works of art, therefore the following descriptions are subject to verification. For fuller details enquire at the information desk (main entrance, Salle du Manège) — ☎ 42.60.39.26 extension 3588, or at the other information desks in the museum.

Temporary exhibitions. – Collections of delicate works are shown in rotation; this applies particularly to drawings and pastels. Major paintings from reserve collections may be seen in the Flore gallery on the second floor.

In the adjoining rooms special exhibitions (sketches and complementary documentation) are mounted to highlight the value and influence of a particular masterpiece or artist.

The museum's arrangement. – As in all museums of value nowadays, rearrangement in the Louvre is a continuing process. The Grande Gallery, extending from the Apollo Gallery to the Flore Pavilion is, at 300 m – 350 yds, the longest in the world. The gallery itself *(1st floor)* contains paintings; below is sculpture, arranged, in each case by school and period (some areas still being hung). Antiquities are arranged around the Cour Carrée *(ground and 1st floors)* with paintings from the French School above *(2nd floor)*.

Familiar paintings. – You will, of course, know many of the paintings in the Louvre from reproductions. Others bear a striking resemblance to original paintings you are familiar with in the National Gallery in London or other galleries elsewhere. An artist, preoccupied by a certain theme over perhaps a period of years, will illustrate it on several occasions with, possibly, only slight variations – such as did Leonardo da Vinci in the two versions of the *Virgin on the Rocks* now in the Louvre and London. Again the theme, by the same artist, of the Virgin, St. Anne and the Infant Christ appears as a painting in Paris (the cartoon has been lost) and as a cartoon in London (the picture has disappeared).

On the other hand the portraits of *Cardinal Richelieu* by Philippe de Champaigne are almost identical in London and in Paris.

Another occurrence is where an artist painted a series of pictures on a changing scene and the paintings have got separated as have Uccello's *Battle of San Romano*, of which one is in the Louvre, one in the National Gallery and one in the Uffizi Museum in Florence. There are many others...

ORIENTAL ANTIQUITIES

The Mesopotamian collection will be on display in the Rivoli Wing, from 1988, following refurbishment. The Far Eastern part of the collection is displayed in the Guimet Museum (p 138).

Major works displayed in this department	
(see text below and plan p 28)	
Stele of the Vultures	Statue of the Intendant Ebih-il
Stele of Naram-Sin	Code of Hammurabi
Statues of Gudea and	Frieze of the Archers
his son Ur-Ningirsu	Assyrian low-reliefs

Mesopotamian civilizations. – The art of Mesopotamia, the heart of the Orient in Antiquity, is the complex expression of conflicting and successive trends.

Gallery I. – Dating from 2450 BC, the **stele of the Vultures** commemorates the victory of a Sumerian king at Lagash (Telloh). Other examples of Sumerian art include the Ur-Nanshe low-relief, busts of men at prayer and a great silver vase.

Gallery II. – The semitic dynasty of Akkad (2340-2200 BC) is highlighted by the admirable **stele of Naram-Sin** (2250) in rose coloured sandstone. It shows the king towering above the defeated enemy soldiers and climbing a mountain.

Masterpieces of Sumerian art, the **statues of Prince Gudea** and his son Ur-Ningirsu *(the latter is exhibited every three years at the Metropolitan Museum, New York)* carved at Lagash around 2150 BC, are impressive.

Gallery III. – Statuettes of worshippers were found in the temple of Ishtar (the goddess of war and love) in the town of Mari on the middle Euphrates. The loveliest is that of the **Intendant Ebih-il** (mid-3rd millenium BC) with a full skirt in a hairy material and with staring inlaid blue eyes. Also from Mari are the mural paintings of the Royal Palace and the fiercesome lion which used to guard the entrance to the Temple of Dagan.

Gallery IV. – At the beginning of the second millenium BC, the Babylonian Empire made its mark upon history: its ruler destroyed Mari and conquered Mesopotamia. The famous **Code of Hammurabi** (1792-1750 BC) is a black basalt stele 2.50 m – 8 ft high, inscribed with 282 laws in the Akkad language. The king is shown receiving the laws from the god of Justice. The Old Babylonian Empire was followed by the Assyrian Empire *(p 30)* in the 8-7C BC and after Nebuchadnezzar (the Neo-Babylonian Empire), by the Persian Empire which extended from the eastern shores of the Mediterranean to India.

Iranian Art. – Its refinement is expressed mainly in painted ceramic and metalwork.

Gallery V. – From the end of the fifth millenium BC, its pottery is noteworthy for its fineness and decoration. The Elamite period (Susa was the capital of Elam) produced as from the 2nd millenium delicate works: gold and silver bracelets and beakers in the central glass case. From 6-4C BC, Susa was at the peak of its glory with the Achaemenid kings. The gold and silver plate was exceptionally fine.

Gallery VI. – This gallery is devoted to the Elamite civilization. In the 13-12C BC the art of metalworking was at its zenith: statues of Queen Napir Asu and praying figures.

Gallery VII. – The great capital of

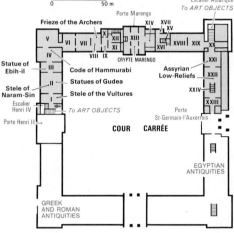

Darius evokes the vast palaces of the Achaemenid rulers. On the walls of Galleries **VIII, IX** and **XI** (Luristan bronzes) are the celebrated enamelled brick friezes from Darius' palace at Susa including the **Frieze of the Archers** (Persian art, 6C BC); there are also griffins and lions. After Alexander's conquest, Parthian and Seleucid art were influenced by Hellenism. Finally in **Gallery XII**, mosaics from Shapur's palace (3C AD) and Islamic ceramics (7-13C) mark the transition to Moslem art.

Levantine Art. – In the Near East, at the confluence of the great civilizations, the various influences existed side by side or coalesced.

Marengo Crypt (Crypte Marengo) (**Galleries XIII-XV**). – Among the Phoenician tombs the mummiform sarcophagus of a king of Sidon (5C BC) testifies to the Egyptian influence in Syria. There are sculptures from the Temple of Mithras.

Gallery XVI. – Phoenician art influenced by the Greek and Roman civilizations. Bronzes from Baalbek evoke the cult of Jupiter of Heliopolis in the Lebanon in the Roman era.

Gallery XVIII. – It contains the richest collections. Excavations at Ugarit and Byblos revealed precious information on Phoenicia which was at the cross-roads of the Antique world. Note the Ugarit tablet where for the first time around 1300 BC a written script using cuneiform symbols replaced syllabic language.

The stele of Baal with his thunderbolt and a hunting cup are the principal exhibits.

Gallery XIX. – Rich collection of carved and chased objects from Cyprus which was open to all influences, including a great limestone vase from Amathus.

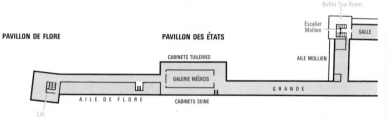

On pp 27-39 we outline six visits to particular departments in the museum which help to trace the chronological link and the relative importance of the principal works on display.

On the following plans the museum is presented by departments.

If time allows only a short visit, we list at the beginning of each visit some of the works described; these are the Louvre's most famous treasures and they are indicated on the relevant plan.

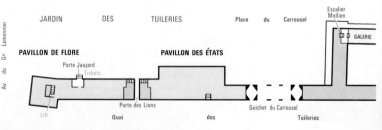

THE DEPARTMENTS OF THE LOUVRE

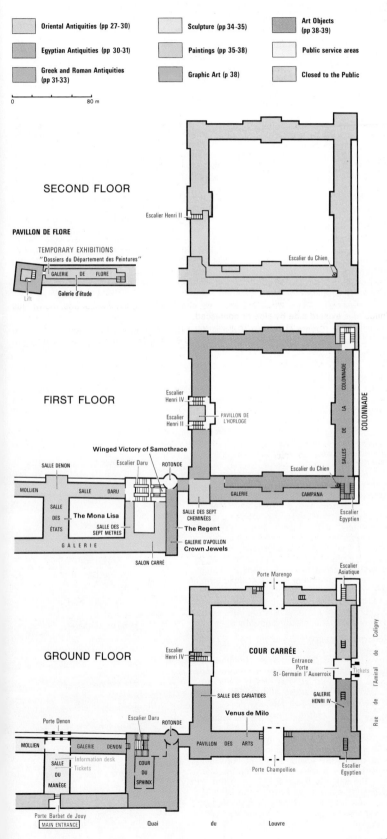

Oriental Antiquities (pp 27-30)

Egyptian Antiquities (pp 30-31)

Greek and Roman Antiquities (pp 31-33)

Sculpture (pp 34-35)

Paintings (pp 35-38)

Graphic Art (p 38)

Art Objects (pp 38-39)

Public service areas

Closed to the Public

0   80 m

SECOND FLOOR

PAVILLON DE FLORE

TEMPORARY EXHIBITIONS
"Dossiers du Département des Peintures"

GALERIE   DE   FLORE

Galerie d'étude

Lift

Escalier Henri II

Escalier du Chien

FIRST FLOOR

Escalier Henri IV

Escalier Henri II

PAVILLON DE L'HORLOGE

COLONNADE

SALLES   DE   LA   COLONNADE

Winged Victory of Samothrace

SALLE DENON

Escalier Daru

ROTONDE

MOLLIEN

SALLE   DARU

SALLE
DES
ÉTATS

The Mona Lisa

SALLE DES
SEPT METRES

G A L E R I E

SALON CARRÉ

SALLE DES SEPT
CHEMINÉES

The Regent

GALERIE D'APOLLON
Crown Jewels

Escalier du Chien

GALERIE   CAMPANA

Escalier
Egyptien

GROUND FLOOR

Porte Marengo

Escalier
Asiatique

COUR CARRÉE

Escalier
Henri IV

Entrance
Porte
St-Germain l'Auxerrois

Tickets

SALLE DES CARIATIDES

Venus de Milo

GALERIE
HENRI IV

Rue   de   l'Amiral   de   Coligny

Porte Denon

Escalier Daru

ROTONDE

MOLLIEN

GALERIE   DENON

Information desk

SALLE
DU
MANÈGE

Tickets

COUR
DU
SPHINX

PAVILLON   DES   ARTS

Porte Champollion

Escalier
Egyptien

Porte Barbet de Jouy
MAIN ENTRANCE

Quai   du   Louvre

Assyrian Art. — Galleries XXI to XXIV contain the great **Assyrian low-reliefs** from the palaces of King Ashurbanipal at Nineveh and of Sargon at Khorsabad; the giant sculptures (the five-legged winged bulls which guarded the palace entrance and the hero Gilgamesh strangling a lion...) proclaim Assyrian glory and cult of force.

EGYPTIAN ANTIQUITIES

Major works displayed in this department

(see text below and plans p 31)

Akhout-Hetep's Mastaba	and of the goddess Hathor
Gebel-el-Arak knife	Bust of Amenophis IV
The Seated Scribe	Jewels of Ramses II
Low relief of Sethi I	Statue of Queen Karomama

Ground floor. – In the **Sphinx Crypt** (Crypte du Sphinx) **(Passage des Arts)** the great sphinx in pink granite framed by the low reliefs showing Ramses II offering incense to the Giza sphinx evokes the glory of ancient Egypt. The following rooms are devoted to the sober and powerful works of the early dynasties and of the Old Kingdom.

Akhout-Hetep's Mastaba (Gallery 2), the funeral chapel of a 5th dynasty (*c* 2350 BC) tomb, was used for the cult of the deceased: the inner walls are decorated with carved and painted scenes of everyday life.

In **Gallery 3** the **Gebel-el-Arak knife** has a flint blade typical of the prehistoric period and a delicately carved ivory handle showing the origins of the art of low relief carving. Opposite, the Serpent King's stele, a masterpiece of the Thinite (Archaic) period portrays a falcon symbolizing the god Horus. The two statues of Sepa and Nesa (3rd dynasty) are early examples of civil statuary and its development can be traced in the hieratic figures (head of King Didoufri-4th dynasty, contemporary with the great pyramids) on view in **Gallery 4** and in the famous **Seated Scribe** (5th dynasty), an incredibly realistic work **(Gallery 5)**. In the adjoining passage note the giant statue of the pharaoh Ramses II (Middle Kingdom). The celebrated lintel and the highly expressive statues of Sesostris III **(Gallery 7)** date from the Middle Kingdom and have a certain gravity.

The painted sarcophagi, opposite, are also characteristic of this period.

In **Gallery 9**, the glass case at the bottom of the stairs contains silver and lapis-lazuli objects from the temple at Tod, while the paintings alongside are from the funeral chapel at Ounsou.

The **Galerie Henri IV** has been arranged to resemble an Egyptian temple: the courtyard is lined with an impressive series of statues of the lion-headed goddess Sekhmet; carved doorways and columns and the group of four baboons worshipping the sun, carved from a single block of granite which orginally adorned the base of an obelisk at Luxor. At the far end are the tabernacles reserved for the gods of the temple. Two monuments originate from tombs in the Valley of the Kings: the great vat-shaped granite sarcophagus of Ramses III and the splendid low relief in painted limestone of **King Seth I and the goddess Hathor.**

The **Osiris Crypt** (Crypte de l'Osiris) evokes the important role played by Osiris in all funerary rites. The Roman period Zodiac on the ceiling came from the temple at Denderah.

Return to the bottom of the stairs: to the right is the **Coptic art** section. With the gradual spread of Christianity Egyptian art drew its inspiration from both the Hellenistic Mediterranean world and Byzantium. **Gallery 1** contains a mummy, painted with a portrait of the deceased and the veil of Antinoüs portraying scenes from the myth of Dionysus. Items (textiles, sculpture) of Coptic art from the 5-7C AD are displayed in **Gallery 2**. **Gallery 3** demonstrates the evolution of a more stylised form of art under Islamic influence which prevailed until the 12C: reconstruction of the monastic church at Baouit and the double portrait showing Christ and the Abbot Mena.

Return and go up the Egyptian Stairway which is lined with canopic urns and sphinxes from the temple of Serapeum at Memphis, the burial place of the sacred bulls. On the upper landing, **the bust of Amenophis IV** *(see p 31, gallery C)* is a realistic and refined masterpiece which came from Karnak.

First floor. – The exhibits are presented in chronological order.

In **Gallery A** are displayed objects From Middle Kingdom tombs: models of a granary and boats, the lovely statue of Nakhti and several blue glazed terracotta hippopotami.

The items in **Gallery B** belong to the 18th dynasty the height of Egyptian civilization in the New Kingdom. Under these settled and prosperous conditions art flourished as testified by the statue of the royal couple, Sennefer

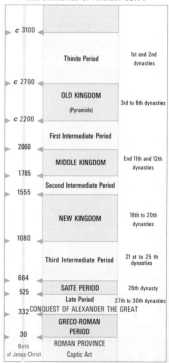

THE DYNASTIES OF ANCIENT EGYPT

c 3100	Thinite Period	1st and 2nd dynasties
c 2700	OLD KINGDOM (Pyramids)	3rd to 6th dynasties
c 2200	First Intermediate Period	
2060	MIDDLE KINGDOM	End 11th and 12th dynasties
1785	Second Intermediate Period	
1555	NEW KINGDOM	18th to 20th dynasties
1080	Third Intermediate Period	21 st to 25 th dynasties
664	SAITE PERIOD	26th dynasty
525	Late Period	27th to 30th dynasties
332	CONQUEST OF ALEXANDER THE GREAT	
30	GRECO-ROMAN PERIOD	
Birth of Jesus-Christ	ROMAN PROVINCE Coptic Art	

and Hatshepsut. In one of the show cases are small spoons in the form of wooden figures of swimming girls and others carved with delicate floral motifs.

Gallery C illustrates many aspects of daily life during the New Kingdom: dwellings, furnishings, utensils, pastimes, fishing and hunting. Towards the end of the 18th dynasty Amenophis IV, the heretical Akenaten, abandoned the religion of his predecessors and during his brief rule the Amarna style flourished. Examples in **Gallery D** include the bust of this gentle looking king, statuettes of the king and Nefertiti, the head of a princess and splendid female torso of red quartz.

Gallery E has works from the 19th and 20th dynasties, known also as the Ramesside period. The collection of texts and drawings on papyrus or limestone flakes, was the work of the stonemasons who lived in the village of Deir el-Medineh and worked on the tombs in the Valley of Kings. The jewellery case contains delightful examples of this art from all periods.

During the Third Intermediate Period (**Gallery F**) bronze craftsmen produced such masterpieces as the **Satue of Queen Karomama.** One of the funerary customs was the painted decoration of wooden coffins. The small blue statuettes of servants *(shawabti)* were included in burials to accompany the deceased on his journey to the eternal world.

The Saite Period (**Gallery G**) and the later dynasties maintained the high traditions of Egyptian sculpture. Good examples are the array of Ancient Egyptian deities.

The influence of the Greek world made itself felt in the Ptolemaic period, following Alexander the Great's conquest of Egypt, before becoming part of the Roman Empire (**Gallery H**). The funerary practices of the Ancient Egyptians are well illustrated: embalming, mummification, funeral processions...

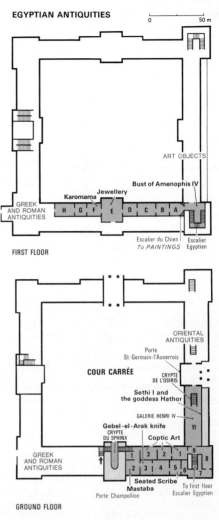

EGYPTIAN ANTIQUITIES

0 _____ 50 m

ART OBJECTS

Bust of Amenophis IV

Karomama   Jewellery

GREEK AND ROMAN ANTIQUITIES

H | G | F | E | D | C | B | A

Escalier du Chien
To PAINTINGS   Escalier Egyptien

FIRST FLOOR

ORIENTAL ANTIQUITIES

Porte St-Germain-l'Auxerrois

COUR CARRÉE   CRYPTE DE L'OSIRIS

Sethi I and the goddess Hathor

GALERIE HENRI IV

Gebel-el-Arak knife
CRYPTE DU SPHINX   Coptic Art

GREEK AND ROMAN ANTIQUITIES

11

1 | 3 | 2 | 1
2 | 3 | 4 | 5 | 6
9
8
7

Seated Scribe
Mastaba   To first floor
Porte Champollion   Escalier Egyptien

GROUND FLOOR

Major works displayed in this department

(see text below and plans p 33)

The Lady of Auxerre	The Cerveteri Sarcophagus
Hera of Samos	Winged Victory of Samothrace
The Horseman Rampin	Athlete of Benevento
Apollo of Piombino	Ephebe of Agde
The Parthenon Fragments	Tanagra Figurines
Venus de Milo	

Ground floor. – From the main entrance pass to the Denon Gallery with its display of 2 and 3C sarcophagi and 1 and 2C statuary.

Room 1. - Orientalizing style and Archaic period 7-6C BC. In the midst of the great painted vases and decorated jars (7C BC) in the geometric style, the **Lady of Auxerre** is one of the earliest examples of Greek sculpture: its rigid stance and frontality (face in line with the body) is typical of the austere Dorian style.

The **Hera of Samos** although only two generations later, shows an Ionian influence. The statue of the **Horseman Rampin** is an Attic work of the mid 6C BC. Note the delicate smile and the angular line of the body which marks a departure from the early frontal pose.

Room 2. – Early 5C BC. The works show how with the transition from Archaism to early Classicism, Greek artists freed themselves from the conventions of the former. The bronze statue of the **Apollo of Piombino** is an outstanding example of pre-Classical art. Other works include the Torso from Miletus, the Exaltation of the Flower, reliefs from the Passage of the Theoria, on the island of Thasos, and the Amphora by Myson.

Room 3. – *Reorganization in progress.* The principal exhibit will be the sculptured marble metopes from the Temple of Zeus (Olympia), depicting the Labours of Herakles.

Rooms 4 and 5. – Late 5C BC and early 4C BC originals. The various **fragments from the Parthenon marbles** clearly illustrate the mastery of Phidias. The fragments include the admirable frieze showing a procession of Athenians, the head of a horseman, the metope portraying centaurs, a male head and from one of the frontons the lovely female head known as the Laborde Head. The two running figures most probably came from the temple at Phigalia, near the Arcadian city of Bassae. The figures are the work of Ictinus one of the co-architects of the Parthenon. The steles are proof of a renewal of artistic inspiration in the art of mid-5C BC Attica and the spread of the decorative traditions of the Parthenon as far as Macedonia.

Rooms 6 and 7. – 4C BC originals. The exhibits are essentially funerary: two handled vases *(loutro-phores)*, ceramic vases *(lekythos)* and steles. Greek tombs were decorated with symbolic animal figures such as the lion, offered by a French admiral to Charles X.

Room 8. – 3C BC originals. The numerous portraits are of the Ptolemaic dynasty which ruled Egypt from 323 BC. The founder Ptolemy I Soter, the son of the Macedonian nobleman Lagus, was a friend and general of Alexander the Great.

Room 9. – 2C BC originals. The **Venus de Milo** is a masterpiece of the late Hellenistic period and demonstrates a return to Classicism. The balanced and graceful figure has a serene beauty and naturalness, a perfect example of ancient art. Alongside are copies after Praxiteles (2C BC): the Kaufmann Head, named after the former owner and the Cnidian Aphrodite from the sanctuary of this Asian Minor city. The large bust, known as Inopos, may be a portrait of Mithradates VI Eupator ruler of Pontus. His features have been idealized to resemble Alexander the Great.

(Photo Musées Nationaux)
The Lady of Auxerre.

Room 10. – 2C and 1C BC originals. Lysippus and his school may have provided the influence for the warrior known as the Borghese Gladiator by Agasias of Ephesus (*c* 100 BC).

Room 11. – Replicas of 5C and 4C BC works. Examples of the Severe style: Athena by Myron and the torso of a discus thrower. This gallery highlights the works of two famous sculptors Polyclitus (Wounded Amazon which was badly restored in the 17C and the Diadumenos) and Phidias (an Apollo similar to the Cassel version and an Athena resembling his great cult image of Athena Parthenos).

Room 12. – Replicas of 5C and 4C BC works. Classicism shows a greater search for freedom. The attitude of the Borghese Ares is typical of Polyclitus' atheletes but there is a superficial attempt at elegence and more realism in the facial expression. The late 5C BC Adonis or Narcissus is a precursor of the work of Praxiteles. The fullness of the human form is apparent under the drapes, which were once so stylised. The early 4C BC Discus Thrower by Naucydes from Argos and the Athena of Peace break with the traditions of pure Classicism and demonstrate a new striving for realism.

Room 13. – Replicas of 4C BC works. Apart from the muse, Melpomene from the theatre at Pompeii (IC BC) in her 19C niche, all the other sculptures are replicas of Praxiteles work (fl 370-330 BC). This master sculptor perfected the balance and rhythm of Polyclitus' athletes producing such graceful works as the Satyr Pouring or the Satyr Asleep. The Apollo Sauroctonus, Diana of Gabies, the Cnidian Aphrodite and the Arles Aphrodite are all full of grace.

Room 14 — Caryatid Gallery (Salle des Cariatides). – Replicas of 4C BC and Hellenistic works. This the former great hall of the Old Louvre Palace was built for Henri II by Pierre Lescot and takes its name from the four monumental statues carved by Jean Goujon which uphold the minstrels' balcony. The late Classical period was dominated by Lysippus, who was temperamentally quite different from his equally famous contemporary, Praxiteles. Lysippus' figures were generally muscular and full of movement but he innovated by giving them more slender proportions. Typical of his style is Hermes Fastening his Sandal, a composition full of fluidity and movement. As sculptor to Alexander the Great, Lysippus did many portraits of the emperor: the Azara Head is an excellent replica of Alexander with a Lance.

The art of the 3C BC is characterized by a change of subject matter. The muscular athlete and aloof beauty are forsaken for the portrayal of old age, infancy (the Child with a Goose is a lively composition), emotion, pain (the Wounded Galatian) and pathos (the Satyr Marsyas).

Rooms 16 and 17. – Etruscan antiquities. The great 6C BC terracotta **Cerveteri Sarcophagus** is adorned with beautiful and realistic carvings of a married couple serenely enjoying a divine banquet.

Rooms 18 to 21. – In Anne of Austria's suite are a succession of portraits from the Republican era: the Julio-Claudian, Flavian, Antonine and Severan dynasties.

Room 22. – 3 and 4C. Later imperial portraits cover the pillars of a portico from Salonika: Gallienus, Gordian III, Julian the Apostate and Theodosius.

Room 23. – The mosaic on the far wall is from the Hiram tomb near the Phoenician seaport of Tyre on the coast of southern Lebanon.

Room 24. – These mosaics are from Christian buildings in North Africa.

Room 25. – Syrian mosaics and several objects in basalt (pillar-column of St Simeon the Stylite, reliquary and tomb doors) are the main items.

Room 26. – Fragments of frescoes from Pompeii and mosaics give some idea of the colourful interior decoration of Roman houses at the time of the Empire.

Room 27. – **Sphinx Court** (Cour du Sphinx). The art of low-relief is exemplified by the great frieze of the Temple of Artemis depicting a battle between Greeks and Amazons.

Take the Daru Stairway up to the first floor.

The **Winged Victory of Samothrace** (3C BC) seems to defy space. The wide, soaring movement in victory is striking. Note the hand of the statue in a small display case.

First floor. – Beyond the Apollo rotunda is the **Jewel Room** (Salle des Bijoux) with frescoes from Herculaneum and silver ware from Boscoreale.

Go through the Henri II gallery (salle Henri II) – note the ceiling decorated by Braque in 1953 – to reach the **Room of Antique Bronzes** (salle des Bronzes Antiques) ranging from Greek archaism (Case 1), Classical (head of the **Athlete of Benevento** which is among the finest in Antiquity) and Hellenistic art (Case 3) to Roman specimens. The magnificent bronze statue of the **Ephebe of Agde** was found in the former Greek port of Agde in 1964.

Figurative art (3rd case right) of the Gallo-Roman period is more interesting than the great gilded statue of Apollo from Lillebonne. There are precious gold jewels in cases between the windows.

Greek Pottery. – Go through the **Clarac Gallery** (Salle Clarac) which contains Minoan pottery and Cycladic idols in an abstract style, to reach the **Campana Gallery** (Galerie Campana) on the right. After the decline of Crete and Mycenae, the geometric style (10-8C BC) evolved towards a decorated frieze. Corinth and Eastern Greece produced vases in new designs: figures in action **(Room 3)**. The same technique is used by the Master of the Caere hydria **(Room 4)** and artist of Amasis **(Room 5)**. About 530 BC Andokides adopted a new style: figures in red against a glazed black background **(Room 6)**. Around 500 BC Eurphronios' pure style **(Rooms 6 and 7)** and Douris' graceful paintings **(Room 7)** illustrate this art at its zenith. At the time of the building of the Parthenon (447-432), Classical pottery flourished **(Rooms 8 and 9)**. From the 4C BC painted scenes became very ornate: exhibits from Apulia and Lucania **(Room 10)**. The **Tanagra figurines (Room 11)** are full of life, marvels of grace and delicacy.

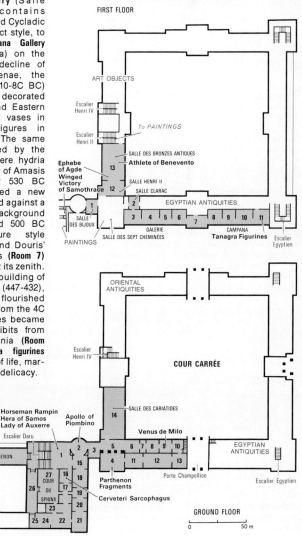

GREEK AND ROMAN ANTIQUITIES

FIRST FLOOR

ART OBJECTS

Escalier Henri IV

Escalier Henri II

To PAINTINGS

SALLE DES BRONZES ANTIQUES

Ephebe of Agde 13 **Athlete of Benevento**

Winged Victory of Samothrace 12 SALLE HENRI II

SALLE CLARAC

1 2 EGYPTIAN ANTIQUITIES

3 4 5 6 7 8 9 10 11

SALLE DES BIJOUX

GALERIE CAMPANA

SALLE DES SEPT CHEMINÉES **Tanagra Figurines**

PAINTINGS

Escalier Egyptien

ORIENTAL ANTIQUITIES

Escalier Henri IV

COUR CARRÉE

SALLE DES CARIATIDES

Horseman Rampin
Hera of Samos
Lady of Auxerre

Apollo of Piombino

14

Venus de Milo

Porte Denon Escalier Daru

GALERIE DENON

1 2 3 5 6 7 8 9 10

SALLE DU MANÈGE

15 4 11 12 13

Porte Champollion

EGYPTIAN ANTIQUITIES

27 COUR DU SPHINX

16 18

17 19

26

Parthenon Fragments

Escalier Egyptien

20

23

Cerveteri Sarcophagus

25 24 22 21

GROUND FLOOR

0 50 m

Porte Barbet de Jouy

SCULPTURE

Major works displayed in this department
(see text plan and below)

Virgin of Isenheim	Virgin and Child (Donatello)
Diana of Anet	Busts by Houdon
The Three Graces (Pilon)	Psyche revived by the Kiss of Cupid (Canova)
Nymphs from the Fountain	La Danse by Carpeaux
of the Innocents (Jean Goujon)	The Slaves by Michelangelo

Pavillon de Flore

Enter by the Porte Jaujard – Start in Room 1

French Romanesque. – Room 1: With the development of Romanesque architecture, sculpture flourished and various local schools evolved. The Head of Christ from Lavaudieu (Haute-Loire) shows an advanced technique as early as the 12C. The capital of the old Church of Ste-Geneviève in Paris (in first window recess) from an earlier period and in a rougher style is nonetheless very moving. Other outstanding works include St. Michael and the Dragon from Nevers – a remarkable triangular composition; the head of St. Peter from Autun; a severe looking Virgin from Auvergne; a great Burgundian Cross; and the doorway from the priory of Estagel (Gard).

French Gothic. – Room 2: The rigid spirituality of the late Gothic period is evident in a retable from Carrières and statue-columns from Notre-Dame de Corbeil.

Room 3: In the 13-14C Gothic art flourished with faces illustrating regional characteristics: from Poissy, three graceful angels; from Maubuisson, two recumbent royal figures; from Rheims, three magnificent heads on either side of the entrance; several Madonnas and Child from Ile-de-France and Burgundy; from Paris two more royal figures, Charles V and Jeanne of Bourbon.

Upper Gallery (9): Two angels and the Virgin of Abbeville in a pose typical of the late 13C (2nd alcove) are featured with the smiling countenance characteristic of Rheims. There is an elegant St. John from Loche to illustrate the style of Touraine.

Northern European Gothic. – The spirituality of the Middle Ages is reflected in the **Virgin of Isenheim** (on the wall to the right). The intricate drapery is reminiscent of Alsatian art in the 15C. The other alcoves of the upper gallery **(10)** are devoted to foreign Gothic schools. Opposite a painted wooden statue of Mary Magdalene (second alcove from the end) stands a Virgin in painted marble which evokes the art of the Franconian master Riemenschneider. Scenes from the Bible, Virgins, angels and saints in gilded and painted wood are the favourite themes of Flemish, Bavarian and Rhenish artists.

French late Gothic and Renaissance (15-16C). – Room 4 contains two recumbent figures in marble portraying Pierre d'Evreux-Navarre and Catherine d'Alençon. In **Room 5** at the back, great 15C masterpieces are exhibited at the foot of mutilated carvings from the rood-screen of Bourges Cathedral (mid-13C) and include the striking tomb of Philippe Pot, the seneschal of Burgundy, surrounded by hooded mourning figures; the recumbent figure of Anne of Burgundy; against the far wall a Mary Magdalene from Champagne and a Virgin from Montigny in pure Burgundian style. In **Room 6** is displayed a famous low-relief of St. George fighting the dragon by Michel Colombe. The Virgin of Olivet and the tomb of Louis de Poncher are also early 16C.

In **Room 7** the **Diana of Anet** stands in the midst of Renaissance masterpieces expressing the sensitivity and aesthetic sense of the period and combining Classical Antiquity, Italian art and French tradition: strength and antique poses of Pierre Bontemps (Admiral Chabot to the left along the wall); power and mastery of Germain Pilon (along the far wall from left to right: effigies of the Chancellor of Birague and his wife Valentine Balbiani, the Resurrection, a funerary monument for the heart of Henri II and the **Three Graces**); grace and refinement of Jean Goujon's low-reliefs (**Nymphs from the Fountain of the Innocents** in Paris); elegance of the funeral monuments of the Montmorency family by Barthélemy Prieur. The latter is characteristic of Renaissance humanism in France as the spiritual quest of the Middle Ages gave way to the anatomical study of Classical Antiquity.

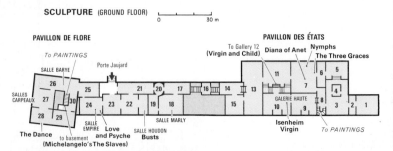

SCULPTURE (GROUND FLOOR) 0 30 m

Italian Sculpture. – In the 13C Italian sculpture had become stereotyped as evidenced by the Virgin from Ravenna to the right of the stairway **(Lower Gallery 12)**. In the 14C Pisa witnessed a new awakening (graceful Virgin by Nino Pisano) which peaked at the beginning of the 15C in Sienna with Jacopo della Quercia (seated Madonna at the far end of the gallery) and especially in Florence with the incomparable Donatello (**bas-relief of the Madonna and Child** in the second alcove next to two delightful small angels by Verrocchio). In the third alcove the painted, gilded bust of a woman is a remarkable example of Florentine art; to the left is a lovely, delicate medallion by Desiderio da Settignano. In the fourth alcove is displayed the bust of a Princess of Aragon by Francesco Laurana.

At the end of the 15C Florentine art developed a more mannered style which is illustrated by a low-relief by Agostino di Duccio (left wall of gallery) and great enamelled terracottas by the Della Robbias.

On the ground floor **(Room 11)** note above the doorway the Nymph of Fontainebleau, a bronze low-relief by Benvenuto Cellini. Provisionally on display in this room are Coustou's Marly Horses and Coysevox' Winged Horses.

17C. – **Rooms 13, 14, 15:** under Henri IV and Louis XIII, French sculpture came to a standstill: note the mannerism of Francheville *(The Slaves)* and the early classical *(The Saracen)*. On the other hand, the reign of Louis XIV saw the advent of several master sculptors including Puget *(Milo of Crotone)*, Girardon, Coysevox and Anguier.

18C. – **Room 17** contains examples of garden statuary from royal and princely palaces such as Versailles, Marly and Petit-Bourg (Louis XIV as Jupiter and Maria Leczinska as Juno by the Coustou brothers). The Regency period is represented by works by artists such as J.B. Lemoyne, P.A. Slodtz and G. Coustou.

Room 18: There are several allegorical and mythological statues by Antoine Coysevox and Nicolas Coustou from the magnificent Grande Cascade and park at Marly, the last mementoes of J. Hardouin-Mansart's impressive creation.

Room 19: In contrast with the pompous statues which were officially commissioned (models by Lemoyne, Pigalle) a more flexible style evolved: busts (G. Coustou and Lemoyne) and smaller pieces for interior decoration (graceful *Bather* by Falconet).

Statuary reached a turning point with Bouchardon: Cupid cutting his bow from Hercules' club **(Rotunda 20)**.

Room 21: The monumental sculptures from the former châteaux of Bellevue, Choisy, Louveciennes enhance the charm of the small allegories by Falconet *(the Threatening Cupid)*, the expressiveness of the statue of Voltaire by Pigalle and the nobility of works inspired from Antiquity *(Psyche abandoned* by Pajou).

Room 22 *(to the left,* works by **Houdon).** – Displayed around the statue of Diana in a slightly rigid stance although portrayed in action are an outstanding series of lifelike **busts** of the Encyclopaedists and other contemporaries ranging from Voltaire's ugly smiling face to the youthful countenance of the Brongniart children, which illustrate Houdon's keen sense of observation. The realism of Julien's *Dying Gladiator* and the delicate busts by Caffieri and terracottas by Clodion are also noteworthy.

19C. – **Room 24 (Empire):** The classical severity of the effigies of Napoleon (statue by Ramey and bust by Chaudet) makes a striking contrast with the languid poses of Pradier's mythological figures and the tenderness of feeling of the group **'Psyche revived by the Kiss of Cupid'** by Canova. *Peace* by Chaudet is a monumental work carved in silver.

Room 25: The Neo-Classical style of Bosio and Pradier contrasts with the vigour of the medallions of David of Angers, the force and energy of the *Marseillaise* by Rude and the charm of his *Young Neapolitan Fisherman* and of the *Dancing Fisherman* by Duret.

Room 26 (Barye): Bronzes, sketches and models of monuments illustrate Barye's wide-ranging style showing great realism and vitality. His great knowledge of the animal kingdom is evident in his groups of animals in combat.

Rooms 27, 28 (Carpeaux) and **29:** *(closed for reorganization; the sculptures will be on display in the Orsay Museum from the end of 1986).* – Carpeaux was the official sculptor of the Second Empire. The works displayed are dominated by his masterpiece **La Danse** *(p 81).* The exuberance and joy which emanate from this whirl of figures contrast sharply with the group of Ugolin and his children which heralds Rodin's bronzes.

Note Daumier's busts of celebrities and other late 19C works (Rodin, Frémiet).

Foreign Sculpture. – **The Slaves** of Michelangelo are displayed in the basement. These masterpieces of controlled strength and profound emotion were carved between 1513 and 1520 and were intended for the tomb of Pope Julius II.

PAINTINGS

How to find the different Schools of Painting *(Second floor, p 29)*

French	14C	Salle Duchatel
	15-16C	Salon Carré
	17-18C	Grande Galerie – Aile Mollien
	19C	Salles Mollien, Denon, Daru – Second Floor South
	Beistegui Collection	Aile de Flore (First Floor)
Italian	Primitives	Grande Galerie
	16C	Salle des États
	17C	Salle des Sept Cheminées *(plan p 29)*
	17-18C	Aile de Flore (First Floor)
Flemish and Dutch	Primitives	Cabinets Seine
	16-17C	Cabinets Tuileries
	17C	Salle Van Dyck – Galerie Médicis – Salle des Sept Mètres
Spanish	14-18C	Pavillon de Flore (First Floor)
German	15-16C	Cabinets Seine
English	17-19C	Second Floor West

Major works displayed in this department
(see text and plan pp 36-38)

Avignon Pietà
François I (Jean Clouet)
Embarkation for the
Island of Cythera (Watteau)
Gilles (Watteau)
Coronation of Napoleon (David)
The Turkish Bath (Ingres)
Scenes of the Massacres of Chios
(Delacroix)
The Raft of Medusa (Géricault)
Virgin and Angels (Cimabue)
St. Francis of Assisi (Giotto)
Coronation of the Virgin
(Fra Angelico)
St. Sebastian (Mantegna)
Mona Lisa (Leonardo da Vinci)

Virgin and Infant Jesus
with St. Anne (L. da Vinci)
Suzanna Bathing (Tintoretto)
Wedding at Cana (Veronese)
Death of the Virgin (Caravaggio)
Christ Crucified (El Greco)
The Club Foot (Ribera)
The Young Beggar (Murillo)
Madonna with Chancellor Rolin
(J. Van Eyck)
Charles I of England (Van Dyck)
Scenes from the Life
of Marie dei Medici (Rubens)
The Bohemian Girl (Frans Hals)
Self-Portraits by Rembrandt
Pilgrims of Emmaüs (Rembrandt)

French School

14C. – In a period when religious subjects were the rule the painting of Jean le Bon against the traditional gold background is the first real portrait (1360) of a French king. The Altar-Cloth of Narbonne with fine Gothic decorations on silk is of the same period.

15C. – The **Avignon Pietà** (1), a masterpiece of early French painting, is a composition of great simplicity and poignancy. Christ's broken body is set off by heads bowed in sorrow. There are lifelike portraits *(Charles VII, Guillaume Jouvenel des Ursins)* by Jean Fouquet, the greatest contemporary painter.

16C. – As Renaissance humanism grew, religion and nature were superseded by man as the main theme in art. The portraits of Jean Clouet (**François I** - 2), of his son François *(Pierre Cuthe)* and of François Quesnel *(Henri III)* show great care for detail. The works of Corneille de Lyon *(Clément Marot)* are in a small room overlooking the Seine.

(Photo Musées Nationaux)

Madame Chardin, pastel by Chardin.

17C. – The Grande Galerie opens with early works of the Great Classical period. The cold but harmonious landscapes and the sombre mythological subjects reminiscent of the Renaissance *(Orpheus and Eurydice, The Four Seasons)* of Poussin (left) are in contrast to the golden hazes of Claude Lorraine *(Cleopatra landing)*.

The canvases of Simon Vouet and Le Sueur show the Baroque influence. Note the social realism of Le Nain *(Meal of the Peasants)*, the accurate observation of contemporary society of Philippe de Champaigne *(The Magistrates of Paris* in contrasting red and black), and the light effects of La Tour. Compare his *Adoration of the Shepherds* with Le Brun's interpretation. The formality and solemnity of court life are apparent in the larger paintings: *Chancellor Séguier* by Le Brun and *Louis XIV* by Rigaud.

18C. – During the Regency period and in the reign of Louis XV reaction set in and styles changed: attitudes became less formal (Largillière: *Self-Portrait*), style more realistic (Chardin: *The Skate*). The Age of Enlightenment is aptly evoked in the dreamy quality of Watteau's **Embarkation for the Island of Cythera** (3), a harmonious composition with figures set in an ethereal decor. The relaxed 18C way of life is reflected in lighthearted (Lancret: *Innocence*) and comedy scenes (Watteau: **Gilles** - 4). Shortly before the Revolution, Hubert Robert brought ruins into fashion *(The Pont du Gard)*.

In Aile Mollien are exhibited the small 18C canvases: Fragonard *(Music, Inspiration –* evocative and colourful figures). The works of Greuze have a more serious moral tone *(The Paternal Curse)*.

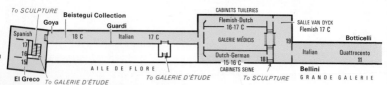

19C. – The stiff Neo-Classical style of the Empire is best seen in the vast historic canvas by David of the **Coronation of Napoleon** (5) facing which is his portrait of Madame Récamier in a classic pose. His nude antique scenes celebrating the human form are a prelude to the nude paintings of Girodet *(The Deluge)* and Ingres *(The Spring,* the voluptuous *Grande Odalisque,* the **Turkish Bath** – *2nd floor, Cour Carrée – plan p 29).* The latter attached great importance to line and draughtsmanship and was totally opposed to the Romantic movement which evolved with Géricault and Delacroix's experiments with colour and light effects. The stormy skies, the violent death and war scenes full of colour (Delacroix – **Scenes of the Massacres of Chios** – 6, *Death of Sardanapalus, Liberty leading the People*) reached a climax with Géricault's poignant shipwreck scene **Raft of Medusa** (7): only one of the figures is depicted full face. Courbet rejected this trend as can be seen from his rigid compositions *(The Artist's Studio)* and the stark resignation of the *Burial at Ornans* and marked the transition to Romanticism. With Corot's picturesque *Views of the Roman Countryside* nature gained in popularity. The Barbizon School favoured muted tones (Millet: *The Angelus,* Rousseau: *Oak-trees).* The new theories of the Impressionists *(p 42)* were countered by the cold Neo-Realism of Puvis de Chavannes. *The latter works are exhibited on the second floor of the Cour Carrée.*

Italian School

Primitives. – The works of the Italian schools of the 14 (Trecento) and 15C (Quattro-cento), the precursors of the Renaissance, are displayed in the Grande Galerie. Cima-bue's **Virgin and Angels** (8) *(c* 1280) faces Giotto's **St. Francis of Assisi** (9) which is one of the first paintings to include authentic landscape and a living person as subject.

At a time when art drew its themes from religion, the vivid colours on the traditional gold background are striking. Note the predominance of blue in Fra Angelico's **Coronation of the Virgin** (10), the rose pink of Sassetta's *Triptych of St. John.* Then the themes, expressions and attitudes became freer. The Virgin and Child remained a favourite subject (Fra Filippo Lippi, Botticelli, Perugino) but portraits became more expressive: *Sigismondo Malatesta* by Piero della Francesca, **Saint Sebastian** (11) by Mantegna, *Christ in Benediction* by Bellini, *Portrait of an Old Man* and *The Visitation* by Ghirlandaio.

16C. – *Salle des États.* There was a smooth transition to the Renaissance as the Holy Family and Venus, studies of Christ and contemporary portraits were painted alternately. The **Mona Lisa** with her rather melancholic expression, the most famous work of art in the world, holds pride of place. The smoky backcloth enhances the dark colours and mystery. The enigmatic smile of the Mona Lisa, the wife of a rich Florentine del Giocondo, is reflected in the next group of the **Virgin and Infant Jesus with Saint Anne** (12).

In addition to careful modelling, the Venetians added a profusion of colour and life to their works: Titian's *Open Air Concert,* portraits by Tintoretto (**Suzanna Bathing** – 13) and Titian (*François I, Woman at her Toilet*) are characterised by their intensity of expression, a feature which culminated with Veronese's vast painting, **Wedding at Cana** (14).

In this evangelical scene the artist depicts the Golden Age of Venice, its luminous skies, its majestic architecture and its splendid life style. Most of the 130 portraits are of contemporary figures: Christ appears beside the Emperor Charles V, Suleiman the Magnificent, 16C Venetian high society and the artist as a cello player.

17C. – *Salle des Sept Cheminées.* The artists of the Baroque style experimented with subtle lighting: Guido Reni's light and shade effects, blue and white harmony in Guerchi-no's *Raising of Lazarus,* Giordano's supernatural glow in his *Adoration of the Shepherds,* the intense luminosity of Piazzetta's *Assumption of the Virgin* and the contrasts of Caravaggio (**The Death of the Virgin** – *see plan p 29*) which anticipate the *chiaroscuro* technique. Domenichino's landscapes are reminiscent of Poussin's classical scenes.

18C. – *Aile de Flore.* The lavishness of the Age of Enlightenment is illustrated by Panini *(Concert)* and principally in Venice by Guardi *(Venetian Festivities)* and Tiepolo whose bright mythological and religious scenes are not as evocative as his street scenes *(Carnival Scene, The Charlatan).* The canvas, *Woman with a Flea,* by the Bolognese artist G.M. Crespi recalls the Dutch school.

Spanish School

The golden age of Spanish painting which encompasses many contrasting styles is preceded by the work of some 15C primitive artists including an expressive canvas of a *Man with a glass of wine* of the Portuguese school.

Ribera's *St Paul the Hermit* with his ravaged face and worn body, stands out amid the livid, almost transfigured portraits of El Greco (**Crucifixion** – 15).

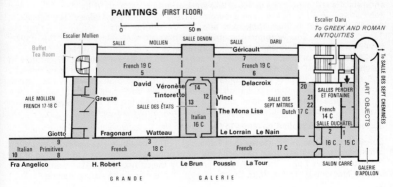

PAINTINGS (FIRST FLOOR)

The realism of Ribera's **The Club Foot** (16) with his sad smile and of Murillo's **Young Beggar** (17) with its effective indirect lighting contrasts with the mystical works of Zurbaran and Baroque exaltation of Carreno de Miranda *(The Foundation of the Trinitarian Order)* and the stiff portraits of the Spanish Court by Velasquez. The delightful Madonnas by Murillo painted in muted colours have a pastel-like quality. The Beistegui Collection (Aile de Flore) contains Goya's masterpiece of portraiture, *The Solana.*

Dutch and Flemish Schools

15, 16 and 17C. – *Cabinets Seine and Tuileries.* The works of the Flemish Primitives are characterised by the oval face, the carefully draped garments and the familiar details: Van der Weyden *(Greeting of the Angel),* Jan Van Eyck (**Madonna with Chancellor Rolin** – **18** – outstanding for the candid expressions, the detailed backcloth and crown), Memling, Quentin Metsys *(The Moneylender and his Wife).* A certain realism appears in the works of Hieronymus Bosch (*The Ship of Fools*) and Breugel the Elder *(The Beggars).*

The peaceful paintings *(Earth, Air)* of Jan Breugel, son of the above and known as Velvet Breugel, precede the small genre canvases of bourgeois life of the period by Teniers, Terborch and Vermeer with his exquisite *The Lacemaker.*

Flanders 17C. – *Salle Van Dyck.* While Jordaens achieved a vigorous style bursting with realism and colour *(The Four Evangelists),* Van Dyck dominated the period with his extremely elegant paintings (**Charles I of England**-**19**, *Madonna with Donors*).

Even in his religious works, Rubens expresses his celebration of life in his richness of colour *(Adoration of the Magi, The Village Fair),* intensity of expression (charming *Portrait of Hélène Fourment,* his second wife), sensual human forms, luxurious garments as in the 21 vast paintings of the **Life of Marie dei Medici** *(Galerie Médicis).*

Holland 17C. – *Salle des Sept Mètres.* The dark still-lifes by Snyders and the sombre portraits by Frans Hals in which a white collar brings the only bright note (**The Gypsy** – **20** – full of life and spontaneity is the only exception) make a striking contrast with Van Honthorst's riot of colour *(The Concert).* In his four celebrated **Self-Portraits** (21) and the two watchful portraits of his companion, Rembrandt, the master of the *chiaroscuro* technique, uses a limited colour range with great mastery. His paintings are bathed in an ethereal golden glow which exudes intense feeling (**Pilgrims at Emmaüs** – **22**).

2nd floor, Cour Carrée, West side. Landscapes by Jacob Ruysdael, the charming *Five Senses* by Palamedesz and *Skating scenes* by Van Goyen.

German School – *Cabinet Seine I*

The German Renaissance is represented by a few important works: a fine, solemn *Self-Portrait* of Dürer as a young man holding a thistle; a colourful allegory, *A Knight, a Young Woman and Death,* by Hans Baldung Grien, a *Venus* by Lucas Cranach; and a remarkable portrait of the humanist *Erasmus* by Holbein the Younger.

English School – *2nd floor, Cour Carrée, by the Henri II stairway.*

Apart from Hans Holbein and Van Dyck, who were official painters to the English Court, the English School is represented by 18C works in the great tradition of English portrait and landscape painting: Lawrence *(Sir Thomas Bell),* Reynolds (the delightful *Master Hare*) and Gainsborough *(Lady Alston, Conversation in a Park).* In addition there are also examples of the work of Constable, Turner and Burne-Jones.

GRAPHIC ART

Gallery. – *2nd floor, Pavillon de Flore.* The 90 000 drawings, engravings, watercolours and pastels are shown in rotation by school, period and theme.

ART OBJECTS

Major works displayed in this department
(see text, plan p 29 and plan p 39)

Crown Jewels (The Regent)
Harbaville Triptych
Ivory Virgin from the Ste-Chapelle
The Maximilian Tapestries

The Boulle Cabinets
Monkey Commode by Crescent
"Loves of the Gods" Tapestries

Apollo Gallery★★★ **(Galerie d'Apollon).** – *1st floor (plan p 29).* Built in the reign of Henri IV and remodelled after a fire in 1661, this stateroom is royal both in its dimensions and decoration. Le Brun worked there before leaving to paint the Galerie des Glaces at Versailles. Delacroix then took over and the decoration was completed during the Second Empire. The wrought iron grille (1650) is from Maisons-Lafitte. The gallery provides a Grand Siècle setting for all that remains of the royal treasures.

Besides the priceless **Crown Jewels** which include the **Regent** diamond (137 carats and purchased by the Duke of Orleans in 1717 from England) and the Côte de Bretagne ruby (105 carats), the display cases contain the most precious mementoes of the French monarchy especially the Coronation ornaments, gold and silver ware (including the porphyry vase mounted in silver gilt as an eagle presented by Abbot Suger) chased reliquaries, jasper vessels, rock-crystal ewers, finely mounted gems.

Go through the Egyptian galleries to the right to the Egyptian stairway.

Colonnade Galleries★★ **(Salles de la Colonnade).** – The Vestibule has splendid panelling taken from the Château Neuf of Vincennes and contains four ceremonial mantles of the Order of the Holy Spirit. The King's Bedchamber in the Louvre is reconstructed in a room with an alcove next to the State Chamber with its panelling and carved ceiling.

Middle Ages. – In **Gallery 4** works from Christian Rome (porphyry columns from the original basilica of St. Peter, Barberini Ivory) are shown alongside those from Byzantium (10C **Harbaville ivory triptych**) and Carolingian objets d'art (ivories, bronze statuette of Charlemagne) are offset by Romanesque items (*champlevé* enamels).

Gallery 5: Shrine of St. Potentin from the Rhineland. The religious inspiration of 13C Parisian artists is apparent in the Gothic treasures: precious **Ivory Virgin from the Ste-Chapelle,** moving Descent from the Cross. The mastery of the Limousin enamellers can be admired in the reliquaries, shrines, crosses, pyxes and the admirable ciborium by the master enameller Alpais. A stained glass window illustrates the art of the stained glass masters. In the 14 and 15C Gothic art works became more expressive and more skilled (Embriachi retable in wood and ivory).

Renaissance. – Decorators and artists in all fields were imbued with the humanist spirit.

Gallery 6: Bronzes from Padua (Riccio), Florence and Venice and fine medals by Pisanello illustrate the new trend which originated in Italy.

Gallery 7: Examples of Limousin enamels made famous by the Limosins, Reymond and Pénicaud. The masterpieces of Italian potters are noteworthy: ornate decoration from Faenza, warm hues of Urbino, reddish highlights from Deruta and glazed faience from Gubbio. In France Bernard Palissy produced elaborately coloured pottery. The walls are hung with a magnificent set of 12 tapestries entitled ''The Hunts of Maximilian'' woven in 1535 for the Emperor Charles V by the Brussels workshops at the height of their fame.

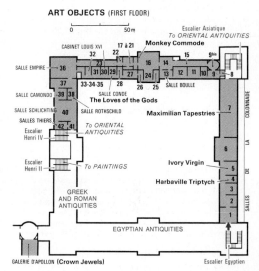

ART OBJECTS (FIRST FLOOR)

Gallery 10: Original jewellery from Spain and Italy, watches and clocks from France and Germany show the refinement of European life.

The Golden Age. – Marshal d'Effiat's room **(gallery 12)** gives a perfect example of the severe Louis XIII style of furniture. The tapestry *Moses in the Bulrushes* **(gallery 11)** is from the Louvre workshop which preceded the Gobelins, whose work included the famous series on Fable Themes (Coronation of Psyche – **gallery 16**). From 1660 onwards the majesty of Louis XIV's reign influenced the decorative arts. At the time when Le Vau and Le Brun decorated the Apollo Gallery, the royal cabinetmaker **Boulle** created his first pieces of furniture in ebony (splendid **cabinets**) inlaid with pewter, tortoiseshell and copper and ornamented with gilded bronze mounts **(galleries 13 to 16).**

The Age of Enlightenment. – The Regency signalled a relaxation in art and morals. Fantasy reigned, decoration became daintier with the curvilinear forms of the Rococo style. **Cressent** was a brilliant exponent of this trend: cabinets, the famous **Monkey Commode** in bronze, clocks, bureau **(gallery 16).** After 1750 a purer style evolved with simpler forms.

The art of the French gold and silversmiths is illustrated by the works of Roettiers, Germain and Auguste **(galleries 9 bis and 15)**. Note Marie Leczinska's dressing case in silver gilt. The Seasons' rotunda **(gallery 17)**, rooms devoted to Rouen and Moustiers faiences **(galleries 18-19)** precede the porcelain room **(gallery 20)** with its fine panelling displaying a Sèvres collection, and the snuff-box section **(gallery 23).**

There are examples of the works of the greatest cabinetmakers including Cressent, Carel (lacquer commode), B. Van Risen Burgh, Dubois, Migeon **(galleries 24 to 27)**. Oeben's distinctive marquetry design **(gallery 28)** and Leleu's elegant commodes with straight lines **(gallery 29)** are noteworthy. A roll-top desk by Riesener stands next to Benneman's splendid bureau **(gallery 30)** used by Napoleon at the Tuileries. Chairs by Jacob and lacquered furniture by Carlin are displayed in the Chinese room **(gallery 32)**. Marie-Antoinette's furniture at the Tuileries **(gallery 31)** and her travelling-case **(gallery 35)** are also by Riesener.

Wonderful Gobelins tapestries on a rose background known as **The Loves of the Gods** after Boucher **(gallery 29)**, Chinese wall hanging **(gallery 30)**, torches, clocks, consoles, escritoires and occasional furniture show the creativity and refinement of this elegant period.

19C. – Magnificent pieces evoke the Empire: Napoleon's throne with its lion claws and heads of Hercules, jewel-case by Jacob-Desmalter, the King of Rome's cradle and a silver-gilt nécessaire by Biennais **(gallery 36).**

The Restoration is illustrated by Charles X's bed **(gallery 37).**

The Rothschild, Camondo, Schlichting and Thiers galleries display comprehensive collections gifted by 19C collectors.

In the Schlichting gallery **(40)** the more ornate pieces make a striking contrast with a massive desk attributed to Roentgen.

Michelin plan 🔟 - folds 16, 17, 29 and 30: from F 8 to H 12.

Total distance: 6.5 km – 4 miles – Time: 5 1/2 hours. Start from the Tuileries métro station.

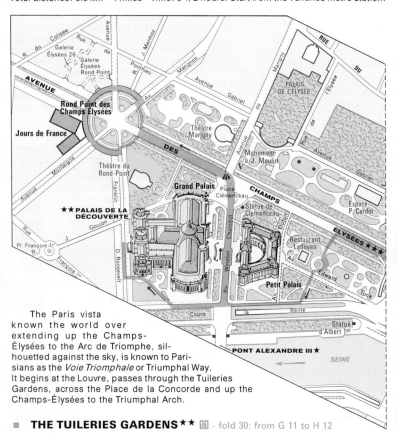

The Paris vista known the world over extending up the Champs-Élysées to the Arc de Triomphe, silhouetted against the sky, is known to Parisians as the *Voie Triomphale* or Triumphal Way. It begins at the Louvre, passes through the Tuileries Gardens, across the Place de la Concorde and up the Champs-Élysées to the Triumphal Arch.

■ THE TUILERIES GARDENS★★ 🔟 - fold 30: from G 11 to H 12

The gardens, the Jardin des Tuileries, beautifully situated beside the Seine, epitomise the formal French style of design.

The first garden. – In the 15C the area was used as a rubbish tip by butchers and tawers of the Châtelet district, the clay soil for making tiles – *tuiles* – hence the name: Tuileries.

When, in 1563, the Queen Mother, Catherine dei Medici, decided to build a château next to the Louvre *(p 24)*, she bought land from the Tuileries for an Italian style park. This included fountains, a maze, a grotto, decorated with terracotta figures by Bernard Palissy, and a menagerie and silkworm farm.

The park became the fashionable airing place and as such broke new ground, for hitherto fashion and elegance had always been displayed indoors.

Le Nôtre French Garden. – By 1664 the gardens required attention: Colbert entrusted the embellishment to Le Nôtre, born near the Marsan Pavilion and a gardener at the Tuileries, like his father and grandfather before him. He raised two terraces lengthways and of unequal height to level the sloping ground; created the magnificent central alley vista; hollowed out the pools; designed the formal flowerbeds, quincunxes and slopes.

Colbert was so delighted that he wanted the gardens kept for the royal family but was persuaded by the writer, Charles Perrault, to allow the public to enjoy them also.

In the 18C the gardens' appeal was increased by such attractions as chairs being available for hire and toilets being built.

In 1783 the physicist, Charles, and the engineer, Robert, made an early balloon flight from the gardens.

The Revolution. – On 10 August 1792, Louis XVI and his family fled the Tuileries Palace, crossed the gardens and sought refuge with the Legislative Assembly. The Swiss Guards also tried to escape but two thirds of them were slaughtered in the gardens by the mob.

The Festival of the Supreme Being, organised by the painter David on 8 June 1794, opened in the gardens before proceeding to the Champ-de-Mars *(p 51)*.

The Tuileries today. – The part of the Tuileries designed by Le Nôtre remains unaltered although the effect of his positioning of occasional statues has been jeopardized by less satisfactory additions, apart from those by Maillol (between the two wings of the Louvre) which are outstanding.

TOUR

The modern area of the Tuileries, between the wings of the Louvre and the Carrousel Arch, is described on p 26. Start from the Flore Pavilion, where the Avenue du Général-Lemonnier meets the quay and two sphinxes, brought back after the capture of Sebastopol in 1855, stand guard.

The Bord de l'Eau Terrace. – Walk up the steps to the waterside terrace from which there is a **view**★★ overlooking the gardens, the Seine and, in the background, the Louvre. This was the playground of royal princes and the sons of Napoleon I and III.

An underground passage beneath the terrace, communicating with the Place de la Concorde, enabled Louis-Philippe to escape from the palace in 1848. The bronze group *The Sons of Cain* is by Landowski.

Walk towards the formal gardens.

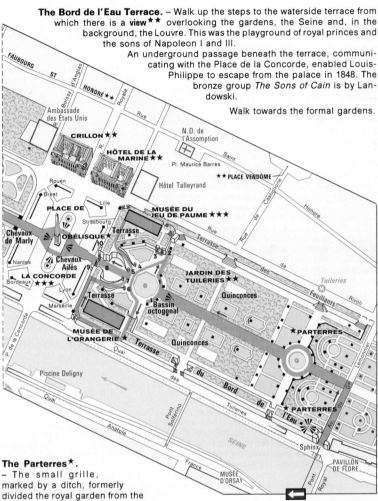

The Parterres★.
– The small grille, marked by a ditch, formerly divided the royal garden from the public area. The paths are lined with copies of statues from Antiquity and decorative vases. Towards the eastern end are works by Le Pautre, Auguste Cain and Rodin.

Quincunxes (Quinconces). – The central alley affords a magnificent **vista**★★★. On either side are areas of greenery with 19 and 20C statues: Autumn, Winter and Night.

The Octagonal Basin (Bassin octogonal) and Terraces (terrasses). – The huge octagonal basin and the adjoining statues, terraces, slopes, stairways were designed as a single architectural composition.

1) The Seasons (N. Coustou and Van Clève)
2) Arches from the Tuileries Palace
3) Bust of Le Nôtre (Coysevox). The original is in St-Roch *(p 97)*
4) The Tiber in the Antique manner
5) The Rhône and the Saône (G. Coustou)
6) The Nile in the Antique Manner
7) The Rhine and Moselle (Van Clève)
8) Commemorative tablet of the balloon ascent of Robert and Charles in 1783
9) Fame on a winged horse (after Coysevox)
10) Mercury on a winged horse (after Coysevox). Originals in the Louvre.

Until 1716 there was no exit from this end of the Tuileries, the moat at the foot of the Louis XIII wall cutting it off from the Esplanade or future Place de la Concorde. A swing bridge was constructed over the moat and ornamented in 1719 by Coysevox's winged horses (Chevaux Ailés) which were brought for the purpose from Marly. The bridge disappeared when Louis-Philippe had the Place de la Concorde redesigned.

Steps and ramps afford access at several points to the terraces *(the Feuillants on the north side, the Bord de l'Eau on the south)* which run the length of the gardens and culminate in the Jeu de Paume and Orangery Museums.

The two pavilions, the **Orangery** (Orangerie) and the **Jeu de Paume**, were built at the time of the Second Empire and have served as art galleries since the beginning of the 20C.

■ JEU DE PAUME MUSEUM ★★★ ▢▢ - fold 30: G 11

*Open 9.45am to 5.15pm; closed Tuesdays and holidays; 20F – Sundays: 10F.
☎ 42.60.12.07. The collections are to be transferred to the Orsay Museum in 1986.*
The Jeu de Paume houses the Louvre's collections of Impressionist Paintings.

Impressionism. – The Barbizon School (Th. Rousseau, Millet), which followed Corot,
favoured the dark tones of trees and the night. By contrast other artists endeavoured to
put on canvas the vibration of light, the colours of impression. Early criticism of
Claude Monet's celebrated *Impression-Sunrise* as a mere impression gave rise to the
name "impressionists". For them light was all – they analysed it, they watched its play.
Their observation made them turn to sunlit gardens, snow, mist, and flesh tints. Paint was
applied in small brightly coloured dabs to give the fleeting, unstable effect of light.

The school was born at Honfleur where the young **Claude Monet** (1840-1926) and **Sisley**
(1839-1899) studied light effects under Boudin and the Dutchman, Jongkind. On their
return to Paris, they rejoined **Pissarro** (1830-1903) and **Edouard Manet** (1832-1883) and with
their fellow artists **Cézanne** (1839-1906) and **Bazille** (1841-1870), formed an active group in
opposition to the established art circles of the day. **Degas** (1834-1917), meanwhile,
although originally a follower of Ingres, held himself apart and continued to do so until
the end of the Second Empire. **Berthe Morisot** (1841-1895) and **Fantin-Latour** (1836-1904)
exhibited regularly with the others.

Around 1875, **Renoir** (1841-1919) was introduced to Impressionism by Monet.

Although dispersed after 1880, the Impressionists remained faithful to the painting of
light: Sisley at Moret-sur-Loing, Monet in the Seine Valley and Cézanne at Aix-en-Pro-
vence. **Gauguin** (1848-1903) painted first at Pont-Aven in Brittany before setting out for the
South Seas where his work became typified by flat planes of colour surrounded by dark
outlines; Henri Rousseau, known as the **Douanier Rousseau** (1844-1910), brought a very
personal expression of light in his naïve and allegorical pictures; the Dutchman, **Van Gogh**
(1853-1890), discovered the special quality of light in Provence, although it was not
enough to save him from the ravages of his own temperament and suicide at Auvers-sur-
Oise. His canvases, with their vigorous strokes of pure colour, can now be seen as the
early forerunners of Fauvism. Finally there was **Toulouse-Lau-
trec** (1864-1901) who was primarily interested in the theatre
and its bizarre lighting effects.

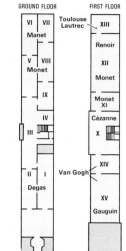

TOUR

Galleries I and II (Camondo). – Shown are Degas' portraits and
horse racing scenes; his ballet dancers reveal his concern
for movement. In *The Glass of Absinthe* the juxtaposition of
the figures on the canvas communicates pathos.

Gallery III. – The *Hommage to Delacroix* and the *Studio in
the Batignolles* by Fantin-Latour.

Gallery V (Bazille). – Note the *Women in a Garden* by Monet
and *The Cradle* by B. Morisot.

Galleries VI (Manet) and VII (Moreau-Nélaton). – The rooms
contain works by Manet: the cool *Olympia* (1864) with its
vividly contrasting colours; *Déjeuner sur l'herbe,* which
caused a scandal at the 1863 exhibition due to the originality of the composition and the permissiveness of the subject matter – it became the group's public manifesto; the
Portrait of Emile Zola; and the *Fifer* where the lone young
figure, uncluttered by details communicates a feeling of
immediacy.

Gallery VIII. – Featured by Monet are two canvases: the *Wild
Poppies* and *Peace Beneath the Lilac Trees.* Sisley's
Barges at Bougival Lock reveals his sensitivity to nature.

Gallery X (Cézanne). – *First floor.* Cézanne's works include *The Suicide's House, Woman
with Coffeepot, Still Life with Apples and Oranges* and the *Cardplayers.*

Gallery XI. – Five canvases of the *Rouen Cathedral* by Monet reveal, by their unique colour
sequence, the school's originality. The artist rented a room facing the west door and
painted more than twenty versions of the same scene, clearly exemplifying the group's
theory of ever changing light effects, at different times of day and seasons of the year,
even on a subject so apparently inert as cathedral stone.

Gallery XII (Caillebotte). – Renoir with his shimmering palette evokes a joy of living: *Le
Moulin de la Galette, Young Girls at the Piano* and the *Bathers.*

Gallery XIII (Personnaz). – Painting of *Jane Avril* dancing by Toulouse-Lautrec.

Gallery XIV (Gachet) and XV (Gauguin). – Van Gogh through his contact with the Impressionists lightened his palette as shown in the Church of Auvers. Gauguin's vigorous style
illustrates a different world: *Women of Tahiti, Le Repas* and the *White Horse.*

■ ORANGERY ★ ▢▢ - fold 30: H 11

*Open 9.45am to 5.15pm; closed Tuesdays and holidays; 15F – Sundays 8F.
☎ 42.97.48.16.* The horseshoe staircase with wrought ironwork by Raymond Subes leads
to the first floor galleries, where the Walter-Guillaume collection (Impressionists to 1930)
is on display. There are good examples of canvases by Soutine, Cezanne, Renoir, Derain
and Douanier Rousseau. The two oval rooms on the ground floor are the setting for the
series of paintings made by Monet in the garden of his house at Giverny in Normandy
(1883-1926) of water-lilies and known as the **Nymphéas ★.**

THE PLACE DE LA CONCORDE ★★★ ▣ - fold 30: G 11

See also photos pp 23 and 82.

Everything – the site, the size, the general elegance of the square – combines to impress.

Paris aldermen, wanting to find favour with Louis XV, commissioned Bouchardon to sculpt an equestrian statue of the Well Beloved, as he was known, and organised a competition to find an architect for the square. Servandoni, Soufflot, Gabriel and others all submitted plans.

The winner was Gabriel who designed an octagon with an area of nearly 84 000 m² – 21 acres – bordered by a dry moat and balustrade. Eight massive pedestals, in pairs and intended later to support statues, were to mark the oblique corners. Twin edifices with fine colonnades were to be constructed to flank the opening of the Rue Royale. Work began in 1755 and continued until 1775.

In 1770, at a firework display to celebrate the marriage of the Dauphin and Marie-Antoinette, the crowd panicked and 133 people were crushed to death in the moat. In 1792 the royal statue was toppled and Louis XV Square became the Square of the Revolution.

On Sunday 21 January 1793 a guillotine was erected near where the Brest statue now stands, to perform the execution of Louis XVI. Beginning on 13 May, the "nation's razor", by now installed near the grille to the Tuileries, cut the necks of a further 1 343 victims including Marie-Antoinette, Mme du Barry, Charlotte Corday, the Girondins, Danton and his friends, Mme Roland, Robespierre and his confederates *(p 61)*. Only after two years, in 1795, did the sound of the fall of the blade of the guillotine cease to be heard in the square. The Directory, in hope of a better future, renamed the blood soaked area, Concorde.

The Concorde Bridge was opened in 1790 and the square's decoration completed in the reign of Louis-Philippe by the architect Hittorff. The king decided against a central statue which all too easily might become an object of contention with any change in regime and selected, instead, an entirely non-political monument, an obelisk. Two fountains were added similar to those in St. Peter's Square in Rome. The north fountain represents river navigation and the south fountain maritime navigation. Eight statues of towns of France were commissioned for the pedestals provided by Gabriel. Cortot sculpted Brest and Rouen, Pradier Lille and Strasbourg. It was at the foot of this last figure, executed after the actress, Juliette Drouet, that the poet-politician, Déroulède, rallied patriots after 1870 when the town of Strasbourg was under German rule.

Obelisk★ (Obélisque). – The obelisk comes from the ruins of the temple at Luxor. It was offered by Mohammed Ali, Viceroy of Egypt, to Charles X in 1829 when seeking French support, but only reached Paris four years later, in the reign of Louis-Philippe. The monument in pink granite, 3 300 years old, is covered in hieroglyphics; it is 23 m tall – 75 ft – and weighs more than 220 tons. The base depicts the apparatus and stratagems used in its transport and erection on the square *(Maritime Museum p 50)* – Cleopatra's Needle in London, offered by the same ruler to Queen Victoria, comes from Heliopolis and is 2 m shorter -6 ft 6 in.

Views★★★. – The best point from which to get a view of the Champs-Élysées – Triumphal Way is the obelisk. The view is framed by the Marly Horses as you look up the avenue towards the Arc de Triomphe, and by the Winged Horses of the Tuileries towards the Louvre. Both sets are replicas. There are good vistas also, north to the Madeleine and, south, to the Palais-Bourbon.

(Biblio. Hist. Ville de Paris)

Place de la Concorde by Champin, 19C.

The two mansions★★. – Gabriel's colossal mansions on either side of the opening to the Rue Royale are impressive without being overbearing; the colonnades inspired by that at the Louvre are even more elegant than the original and the mansions themselves, among the finest examples of Louis XVI style.

The right pavilion, the **Hôtel de la Marine,** was originally the royal furniture store, until 1792 when it became the Admiralty Office. Today it houses the Navy Headquarters.

The pavilion, across the street, was at first occupied by four noblemen. It is now divided between the French Automobile Club and the **Hôtel Crillon,** a world famous luxury hotel. It was in this building on 6 February 1778 that the Treaty of Friendship and Trade between the King, Louis XVI and the 13 independent States of America was signed. Benjamin Franklin was among the signatories for the States. On the Rue Royale side, a plaque in English and French commemorates this treaty by which France officially recognized the independence of the U.S.A.

The two mansions on their far sides from the Rue Royale are bordered respectively by the American Embassy *(on the left)* and the Hôtel Talleyrand, designed in the 18C by Chalgrin for the Duc de la Vrillière, and where Talleyrand died in 1838.

■ **THE CHAMPS-ÉLYSÉES ★★★** ▥ – **folds 16, 17, 29 and 30: from F 8 to G 11**

The Champs-Élysées, the most famous thoroughfare in Paris, is at once an avenue with a spectacular view, a place of entertainment and a street of luxurious and smart shops.

Origin. – In the time of Henri IV there were only fields and marshlands in the area; in 1616 Marie dei Medici created the Cours-la-Reine, a long avenue which began at the Tuileries and followed the line of the Seine to the present Alma Square. The tree-lined route, in time, became the fashionable carriage ride.

In 1667 Le Nôtre extended the Tuileries vista by planting trees in rows on the plain known as the Grand Cours. The calm shades were renamed the Elysian Fields – Champs-Élysées – in 1709. In 1724 the Duke of Antin, Director of the Royal Gardens, extended the avenue to the Chaillot Mound – the present Étoile; his successor, the Marquis of Marigny, prolonged it in 1772 to the Neuilly Bridge. Two years later Soufflot, reduced the road gradient by lopping the mound by more than 5 m – 16 ft – the surplus rubble being dumped and producing the still apparent rise in the Rue Balzac.

The fashion. – At the end of the 18C the Champs-Élysées were still wild, deserted, unknown and only six private mansions

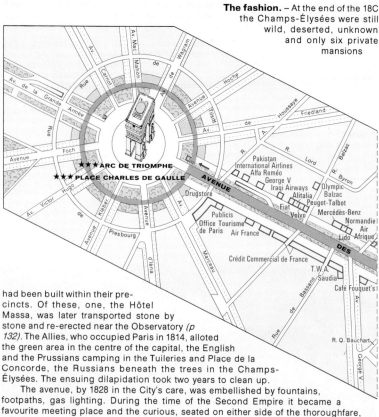

had been built within their pre-cincts. Of these, one, the Hôtel Massa, was later transported stone by stone and re-erected near the Observatory *(p 132)*. The Allies, who occupied Paris in 1814, alloted the green area in the centre of the capital, the English and the Prussians camping in the Tuileries and Place de la Concorde, the Russians beneath the trees in the Champs-Élysées. The ensuing dilapidation took two years to clean up.

The avenue, by 1828 in the City's care, was embellished by fountains, footpaths, gas lighting. During the time of the Second Empire it became a favourite meeting place and the curious, seated on either side of the thoroughfare, might see cavaliers and their escorts riding side-saddle, tilburies and broughams, eight abreast in a cloud of dust. Café orchestras (the Alcazar rebuilt by Hittorff in 1840), restaurants, panoramas, circuses attracted the elegant who swelled in number when there were race meetings at Longchamp or the great world exhibitions (1844, 1855, 1867, 1900...). In the gallant Widows' Alley, now the Avenue Montaigne, crowds gathered to dance beneath the three thousand blinding gas flares as Olivier Metra conducted polkas and mazurkas with gay abandon or in the nearby Winter Garden, to listen to Sax, the musician playing his new instrument, the saxophone.

The heart of the nation. – Today there is little that is aristocratic about the avenue, but it still sparkles, it still appeals to all.

On 14 July, military processions with bands playing used to draw immense numbers. At times of great national emotion, the triumphal avenue is the spontaneous rallying point for the people of Paris: the procession of the Liberation (26 August 1944), the manifestation of 30 May 1968, the silent march in honour of General de Gaulle on 12 November 1970.

From Place de la Concorde to the Rond-Point *see plan pp 40 and 41*

The Champs-Élysées, in this area, is planted with trees, landscaped, bordered with grand old chestnut alleys, dotted with occasional pavilions and even a small children's funfair.

The Marly Horses (Chevaux de Marly). – Replicas now replace the two original marble groups *(Africans Mastering the Numidian Horses)* which were commissioned from Guillaume Coustou for Marly, Louis XIV's superb château near Versailles. Following Marly's destruction during the Revolution a special trailer drawn by sixteen horses brought the marbles to their present site in 1795. The originals are now in the Louvre.

Go through the gardens to the left to Cours-la-Reine. In Louis XVI's time the Ledoyen Restaurant was a modest country inn where passers-by paused to drink fresh milk drawn from the cows grazing outside.

To the south, the **Alexandre III Bridge**★, was built for the 1900 World Exhibition and is another example of the popular steel architecture of the 19C and of the ornate style of the period. It has a splendid single-span, surbased arch and it affords a fine view of the Invalides.

The Petit Palais and the Grand Palais. – The halls were also built for the 1900 World Exhibition. The palaces' stone, steel and skylight architecture and very varied exterior decoration have always had critics as well as admirers but the constructions, nevertheless, have gradually come to be admitted as part of the Paris urban scene.

The **Petit Palais** houses the **Museum of Fine Arts of the City of Paris**★ *(open 10am to 5.40pm; closed Mondays and holidays; 9F, free on Sundays; special visiting times and charges for temporary exhibitions; ☏ 42.65.12.73).*

The museum is divided into the Dutuit (antiques, mediaeval and Renaissance art objects, paintings, drawings, books, enamels, porcelain), Tuck (18C furniture and art objects) and City of Paris 19C collections (Géricault, Ingres, Delacroix, Carpeaux, Corot, Courbet, Dalou, Barbizon school, Impressionists, O. Redon, Vuillard, *Art Nouveau* and 1900 Art).

An Ionic colonnade before a mosaic frieze forms the façade of the **Grand Palais** along its entire length. Enormous quadrigae crown the corners; elsewhere the decoration is 1900 "modern style". Inside, the single hall space is covered by a flat glass dome.

The Grand Palais, long the home of annual exhibitions and shows (cars, domestic equipment, etc.), has been entirely remodelled. It now comprises conference rooms with attendant facilities, a library, closed-circuit television, an exhibition area of nearly 5 000 m² – 6 000 sq yds – known as the National Galleries of the Grand Palais *(entrance: Avenue du Général Eisenhower)* and is now a cultural centre where temporary exhibitions are held.

An area on the west side has been given to the Palais de la Découverte *(p 46)* and a further area on the south side to the Paris IV University.

The statue on the left is La Fayette.

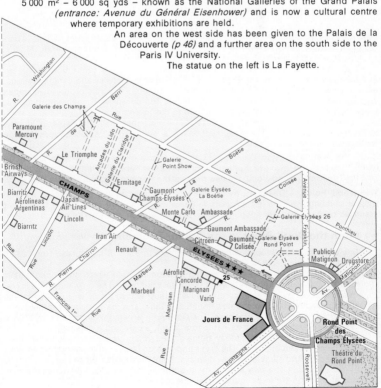

MEZZANINE

PALAIS DE LA DÉCOUVERTE

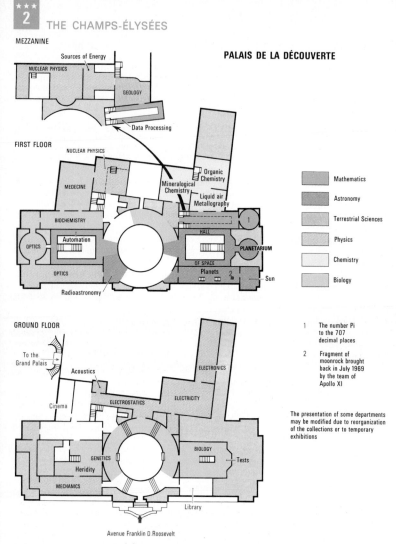

Sources of Energy

NUCLEAR PHYSICS

GEOLOGY

Data Processing

FIRST FLOOR

NUCLEAR PHYSICS

MEDECINE

Mineralogical Chemistry

Organic Chemistry

Liquid air Metallography

BIOCHEMISTRY

Automation

HALL

OPTICS

PLANETARIUM

OPTICS

OF SPACE

Planets

Sun

Radioastronomy

	Mathematics
	Astronomy
	Terrestrial Sciences
	Physics
	Chemistry
	Biology

GROUND FLOOR

To the Grand Palais

Acoustics

ELECTRONICS

ELECTROSTATICS

ELECTRICITY

Cinema

1 The number Pi to the 707 decimal places

2 Fragment of moonrock brought back in July 1969 by the team of Apollo XI

BIOLOGY

GENETICS

Heridity

Tests

MECHANICS

Library

The presentation of some departments may be modified due to reorganization of the collections or to temporary exhibitions

Avenue Franklin D.Roosevelt

Palais de la Découverte ★★. – *Avenue Franklin-Roosevelt. Open 10am to 6pm: 4 planetarium lectures daily; time: 3/4 hour. Closed Mondays, 1 January, 1 May, 14 July, 15 August and 25 December. 11F (10F for the planetarium).* ☏ *43.59.18.21.*

This museum of scientific discoveries, founded in 1937, is a centre both for higher scientific study and for popular enlightenment. Diagrams, lectures and demonstrations, experiments, documentary films and temporary exhibitions illustrate progressive stages and the most recent discoveries in the sciences. The **planetarium ★**, beneath its dome, presents a clear and fascinating introduction to the heavens.

In Place Clemenceau stands a bronze statue of Clemenceau, The Father of Victory, by François Cogné (1932). The monument on the far side of the Champs-Élysées is to the Resistance leader, Jean Moulin.

Cross the Avenue Winston Churchill. From the centre of the avenue there is a good **view ★★** towards the Invalides. Further along, the former Panorama later a skating-rink, is now the Théâtre du Rond-Point, the new home of the Renaud-Barrault Theatre Company.

The Rond-Point. – Designed by Le Nôtre, it has retained the surrounding Second Empire buildings: on the left the **Jours de France** magazine and on the right the former premises of the Figaro newspaper now a shopping arcade, but with its original façade.

From the Rond-Point to the Arc de Triomphe *see plan pp 44 and 45*

This section is the second widest thoroughfare in Paris, it measures 71 m – 233 ft overall. (Avenue Foch: 120 m – 394 ft).

The Second Empire private houses and amusement halls which once lined it have vanished so the avenue appears without historical memories. The only exception is No. **25,** a mansion built by La Païva, a Polish adventuress, whose house was famous for the dinners attended by the philosophers Renan and Taine and the Goncourt brothers, and for its probably unique onyx staircase. The Coliseum, an amphitheatre built in 1770 to hold 40 000 spectators, has left its name to a street, a café and a cinema.

Along the Champs-Élysées today airline offices, motorcar showrooms, banks alternate with cinemas and big cafés. The dress and fashion houses of the shopping arcades provide attractive and elegant window displays. Point Show at No. 68 and Les Champs at No. 84 are examples of a new style of multi-purpose centres where pubs, restaurants, cinemas and shops are to be found under one roof.

■ THE ARC DE TRIOMPHE ★★★ ⬚⬚ - fold 16: F 8

The arch and the **Place Charles-de-Gaulle** ★★★ which surrounds it, together form one of Paris' most famous landmarks. Twelve avenues radiate from the arch which, in that it commemorates Napoleon's victories, evokes at the same time, imperial glory and the fate of the Unknown Soldier whose tomb lies beneath. A Remembrance Ceremony is held on 11 November and attended by the French President.

Historical Notes. – By the end of the 18C the square was already star shaped although only five roads so far led off it. At the centre was a semicircular lawn.

1806: Napoleon commissioned the construction of a giant arch in honour of the French fighting services. Chalgrin was appointed architect.

1810: With the new Empress Marie-Louise due to make her triumphal entry along the Champs-Élysées and the arch only a few feet above ground, owing to two years of difficulty in laying the foundations, Chalgrin had to erect a dummy arch of painted canvas mounted on scaffolding, to preserve appearances.

1832-1836: Construction, abandoned during the Restoration, was completed under Louis-Philippe.

1840: The chariot bearing the Emperor's body passed beneath the arch.

1854: Haussmann redesigned the square, creating a further seven radiating avenues, while Hittorff planned the uniform façades which surround it.

1885: Victor Hugo's body lay in state for a night beneath the arch, draped in crape for the occasion, before being transported in a pauper's hearse to the Pantheon.

1919: On 14 July the victorious Allied armies, led by the marshals, marched in procession through the arch.

1920: 11 November, the Unknown Soldier began his vigil.

1923: 11 November, the flame of remembrance was kindled for the first time over the tomb of the Unknown Soldier.

1944: 26 August, Paris, liberated from German occupation, acclaimed General de Gaulle.

Circling the Arch. – It is suggested that first you walk round the square to see from a distance the arch's proportions and the relative scale of the sculpture.

Chalgrin's undertaking, inspired by Antiquity, is truly colossal, measuring 50 m high by 45 m wide – 164 × 148 ft – with massive high reliefs. Unfortunately Etex and Cortot intrigued with Thiers against their fellow artist Rude and succeeded in cornering three of the four groups of sculpture – Rude's is the only group with a hint of inspiration. Pradier filled the cornerstones of the principal faces with four figures sounding trumpets. A frieze of hundreds of figures, each 2 m tall – 6 ft – encircles the arch in a remarkable crowded composition; above, a line of shields rings the coping.

Facing the Champs-Élysées; 1) The Departure of the Volunteers in 1792, commonly called The Marseillaise, Rude's sublime masterpiece. – 2) General Marceau's funeral. – 3) The Triumph of 1810 (by Cortot) in celebration of the Treaty of Vienna. – 4) The Battle of Aboukir.

Facing the Avenue Wagram: 5) The Battle of Austerlitz.

Facing the Avenue de la Grande-Armée: 6) Resistance (by Etex). – 7) The Passage of the Bridge of Arcola. – 8) Peace (by Etex). – 9) The capture of Alexandria.

Facing the Avenue Kléber: 10) The Battle of Jemmapes.

On reaching the Champs-Élysées once more, take the underground passage which starts from the right pavement to the arch.

The names of the greatest victories won during the Revolution and the Empire appear upon the shields at the summit. Beneath the monument, the Unknown Soldier rests under a plain slab; the flame of remembrance is rekindled each evening at 6.30 pm.

Lesser victories are engraved on the arch's inner walls together with the names of 558 generals – the names of those who died in the field are underlined.

The Arch Platform. – *Access: 10 am to 5.30pm; closed 1 January, 1 and 8 May, 1 and 11 November, 25 December; 20F April to September, 9F the rest of the year; children 3F.*

There is an excellent **view** ★★★ of the capital generally from the platform and, in the foreground, of the twelve avenues radiating from the square. Standing on the arch you find yourself halfway between the Louvre and the La Défense Quarter *(p 151)*, at the apex of the Champs-Élysées – Triumphal Way.

Assembled in a small museum in the arch are mementoes of its construction and the celebratory and funerary ceremonies with which it has been associated. A documentary film traces the highlights of the monument.

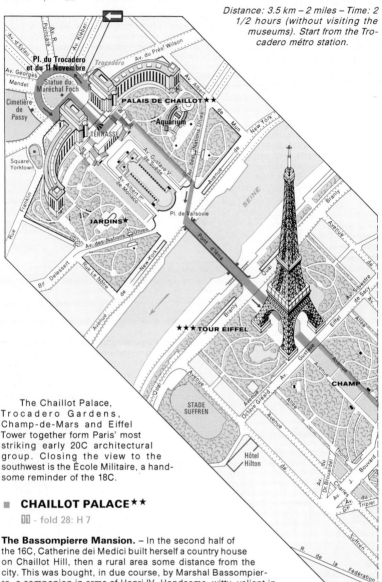

Distance: 3.5 km – 2 miles – Time: 2 1/2 hours (without visiting the museums). Start from the Trocadero métro station.

The Chaillot Palace, Trocadero Gardens, Champ-de-Mars and Eiffel Tower together form Paris' most striking early 20C architectural group. Closing the view to the southwest is the École Militaire, a handsome reminder of the 18C.

■ CHAILLOT PALACE★★

🔢 - fold 28: H 7

The Bassompierre Mansion. – In the second half of the 16C, Catherine dei Medici built herself a country house on Chaillot Hill, then a rural area some distance from the city. This was bought, in due course, by Marshal Bassompierre, a companion in arms of Henri IV. Handsome, witty, valiant in the field, he lived life to the full and was also a reckless gambler. He eventually offended Richelieu and in 1631 was sent to the Bastille – first gallantly burning 6 000 love letters it was said.

The Convent of the Visitation. – Queen Henrietta of England, wife of Philip of Orleans, took over the mansion on Bassompierre's death, and founded a Convent of the Visitation of Holy Mary – Parisians happily referred to the nuns as the Sisters of Bassompierre!

The convent became known for great preachers: Bossuet, Bourdaloue and Massillon, and as a place of retreat for great ladies of the court: Marie Mancini, Mazarin's niece, Mlle de la Vallière – for both of whom it seemed politic to withdraw from the attentions of Louis XIV.

Grandiloquent projects. – Napoleon chose Chaillot as the site for a palace for his son, the King of Rome. Stupendous plans were drawn up by Percier and Fontaine; the convent was razed; the top of the hill levelled; the slope lessened; the Iéna Bridge built – then the Empire fell. Blücher demanded that the bridge be destroyed since it commemorated a Prussian defeat but Louis XVIII interposed, saying that he would sit in the centre in his sedan and be blown up with it.

The Trocadero. – The name Trocadero was given to the area in 1827 after a military tournament on the site had re-enacted the French capture four years previously of Fort Trocadero, near Cadiz.

The square, the Place du Trocadéro, was laid out in 1858; twenty years later, at the time of the 1878 Exhibition an edifice, said to be Moorish inspired, was erected upon it. In 1937 this was replaced by the present Chaillot Palace.

TOUR

The Place du Trocadéro-et-du-11-Novembre. – The semicircular square, dominated by an equestrian statue of Marshal Foch, is a centre point from which major roads radiate to the Alma Bridge, the Étoile, the Bois de Boulogne and the Passy quarter – the wall at the corner of Avenue Georges-Mandel marks the boundary of Passy cemetery *(p 169)*.

Chaillot Palace (Palais de Chaillot). – The spectacular, low-lying palace of white stone, consisting of twin pavilions linked by a portico and extended by wings curving to frame the wide terrace, was the design of architects Carlu, Boileau and Azéma. The palace's horizontal lines along the brow of the hill make a splendid foil to the vertical sweep of the Eiffel Tower when seen from the Champ-de-Mars or from almost any of the capital's viewpoints. The pavilion copings, back and front, bear inscriptions in letters of gold by the poet Paul Valéry. Low reliefs and sculptures by forty artists adorn the wings and steps to the gardens, bronze gilt statues the terrace.

Looking across to the Champ-de-Mars, you get a wonderful **view**★★★, in the foreground, of the Seine and the Left Bank, and beyond dominating all, the Eiffel Tower. Beyond again, in the far distance is the École Militaire.

Beneath the palace terrace is one of the capital's largest theatres *(access through the hall in the left pavilion)*. Under skilled directors and talented actors, it became the home of the Peoples National Theatre – Théâtre National Populaire, the T.N.P. Known now as the **Chaillot National Theatre** this modernized theatre serves as a multi-purpose cultural centre, seating 1 200. On the left below the steps to the gardens is the small Gémier Theatre erected in 1966 as an experimental playhouse.

The Gardens★ **(Jardins).** – Beyond the walls on either side of the long rectangular pool in direct line with the Iéna Bridge, the final slopes of Chaillot Hill lead down, beneath flowering trees, to the banks of the Seine.

The pool, bordered by stone and bronze gilt statues, is at its most **spectacular**★★ at night when the powerful fountains are floodlit.

The **Trocadero Aquarium** contains freshwater fish *(closed, renovation work in progress)*.

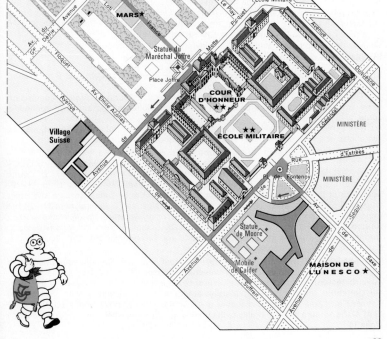

■ THE MUSEUMS

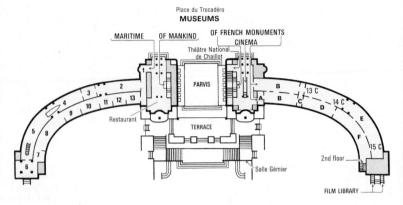

Place du Trocadéro
MUSEUMS

Maritime Museum★★. – *Open 10am to 6pm; closed Tuesdays and holidays; 14F.
℡ 45.53.31.70.*
The museum, founded in 1827 by order of Charles X, displays scale models and artefacts originating mostly from the naval dockyards. Prows, pictures, dioramas, and mementoes of naval heroes add interest to the displays.
The great hall is devoted to naval art and maritime history from the 17C. The side gallery overlooking the Trocadero gardens deals with the scientific, technical and traditional aspects of the evolution of navigation.

1) **Ocean** – late 18C ship.
2) 17 and 18C vessels: The **Louis XV** (an educational toy for the young king), The **Royal** and the **Louis le Grand.** Fine group of galleys dominated by The **Reale** (its decoration is attributed to Puget).
3) The Ports of France, a series of canvases by the 18C artist, Joseph Vernet. The **Royal Louis,** a rare model from the Louis XV period, remains of the vessel, **Le Juste,** lost in 1759. Stern of Marie-Antoinette's barge at Versailles.
4) The Revolution and the 1st Empire. The **Emperor's Barge** (1811). The **Belle Poule** in which Napoleon's body was returned from St.Helena in 1840.
5) The Restoration, the 2nd Empire and the 3rd Republic. The **Valmy,** modelled in ebony, ivory and silver, the Navy's last sailing ship. The **Gloire,** the first armour-plated vessel in the world (1859). Dioramas of the dismantling, transportation and erection of the Luxor obelisk (1831).
6) The modern navy. Reconstruction of a gun-boat bridge.
7) Underwater exploration, hydrography, life saving and diving.
8) Fishing and maritime traditions.
9) Model of an early steamship (Jouffroy d'Abbans). Restoration of models.
10) History of merchant shipping.
11) Wooden boats (18-19C). The great explorations. The **Astrolabe,** the sloop of the 19C navigator and Antarctic explorer, Dumont d'Urville. Bow of Marie-Antoinette's barge at Versailles. Wreckage from the ships of the 18C navigator La Pérouse, which were lost on a voyage of exploration in the Pacific.
12) Maritime maps and navigation instruments.
13) Temporary exhibitions.

Museum of French Monuments★★. – *Open 9.45am to 12.30pm and 2 to 5.15pm;
closed Tuesdays and holidays; 12F – Sundays: 6F. ℡ 47.27.35.74.*
This museum of the monumental art and mural painting of France comprising casts and reproductions was based on an idea of Viollet-le-Duc and was opened in about 1880.
The exhibits are grouped by geographical region, by school and by period, making evolutions of style, geographical and other influences, easy to follow.

Sculpture *(left-double gallery on the ground floor): Room 1* – **A.** Early Romanesque art – *Rooms 2 to 6* – **B.** Romanesque sculpture and tympana from Moissac, Vézelay, Autun – *Room 7* – **C.** Military architecture of the Crusade Campaigns. – *Rooms 8 to 11* – **D.** Gothic cathedral statuary (Chartres, Amiens, Rheims, Notre-Dame). – *Rooms 12 to 18* – **E.** Sculpture of the 13 and 14C (recumbent figures from the St-Denis Basilica and other churches) and 15C (palace ornaments, fountains, Calvaries). – *Rooms 19 to 21* – **F.** The Renaissance (tombs from Tours and Nantes). *2nd floor: Rooms 22 to 24:* Works by Jean Goujon, Ligier Richier, Germain Pilon. *Room 25:* Sculpture from the Versailles park. *Rooms 26 to 28:* Busts and small works of the 18 and 19C (Pigalle, Houdon, Rude, Barye, Carpeaux...). *Room 29:* Models.

Mural painting *(right-pavilion upper floors):* the most important Romanesque and Gothic frescoes are reproduced on lifesize architectural replicas: the crypt of St-Germain Abbey, Auxerre (featuring the oldest frescoes in France), the vault, porch and gallery of St-Savin-sur-Gartempe, the chancel of St. Martin's at Vic, the apse of Berzé-la-Ville, the dome of Cahors Cathedral, the dance macabre of La Chaise-Dieu Abbey Church, etc. The richness of the colours and the vitality of the figures are amazing when seen so unexpectedly close to.

Museum of Mankind★★ **(Musée de l'Homme)**. – *Open 9.45am to 5.15pm, closed Tuesdays and holidays; 14F.* ☎ *45.53.70.60.*

The subject of the museum is the races of man and his way of life.

On the first floor are an anthropological gallery and a palaeontological gallery where human characteristics are compared by means of fossils (examples include the skeleton of Menton man discovered on the French Riviera in 1872 and the mammoth ivory Lespugue Venus) and from Africa, fine collections on prehistory (frescoes from the Ahaggar area in the Sahara), ethnography (costumes, tools, arms) and art (mediaeval Abyssinian art, Central African sculpture). The European Gallery is at the end.

On the 2nd floor are displays from the Arctic regions (Eskimo crafts, masks from Greenland) and the Near and Far East and the Pacific (Easter Island, New Guinea). The Continental America galleries are rich in pre-Columbian, Maya and Atzec art (beautiful rock crystal skull and statues of the god Quetzalcoatl).

Henri Langlois Cinema Museum★. – *Guided tours at 10 and 11am, 2, 3 and 4pm; closed Tuesdays; 15F.* ☎ *45.53.21.86.*

The history of motion pictures, from the very beginning of photography, is evoked in a series of sixty galleries. Reynaud's *théâtre optique* (1888), Marey's photographic rifle, Edison's kinetoscope, the Lumière brothers' kinematograph and photorama, posters, models (some of them were executed by the Russian director Eisenstein), settings (the robot of Fritz Lang's *Metropolis*), costumes and dresses worn by film stars (Rudolph Valentino, Greta Garbo) illustrate the film world. Over 3 000 objects show the evolution of the technical aspects of filming: shooting, staging, projection. Film excerpts complete this picture of the cinema world.

Film Library **(Cinémathèque)**. – *Trocadero Gardens, Albert-de-Mun side.* This film library, one of the richest in the world, has a total of 50 000 films. As many as 3 to 4 films are shown daily. It is a meeting place for the professionals and amateurs of the film world. *Programmes at the box office and in the press. 15F; closed Mondays.* ☎ *47.04.24.24.*

Cross the Iéna Bridge to reach the Champ-de-Mars.

■ THE CHAMP-DE-MARS★ 🗺 - fold 28: J 8

The Champ-de-Mars is now a vast formal garden closed at one end by the École Militaire and at the other by Chaillot Hill. Bestriding it is the Eiffel Tower.

The parade ground. – When Gabriel had completed the École Militaire, he replaced the surrounding market gardens which ran down to the Seine by a parade ground or Champ-de-Mars – Martian Field (1765-1767). The public was first admitted in 1780.

In 1783 the physicist, Charles, launched the first hydrogen filled balloon from the ground which came down 20 miles away near Le Bourget. Blanchard, a year later, launched a balloon complete with basket and ailerons... in which he landed on the far side of Paris at Billancourt.

The Festival of Federation. – It was decided to commemorate the 14 July 1790, the first anniversary of the taking of the Bastille, by a Festival of Federation on the Champ-de-Mars. Stands were erected; mass was celebrated by Talleyrand, Bishop of Autun, assisted by 300 priests at the national altar in the centre of the ground. La Fayette, at the altar, swore an oath of loyalty to the nation and the constitution which was repeated by the listening crowd of 300 000 and finally by Louis XVI, in the midst of the general enthusiasm.

Festival of the Supreme Being. – In 1794, Robespierre had the Convention decree a state religion recognising the existence of a Supreme Being and the immortality of the soul. These hypotheses were solemnly affirmed on 8 June at a mammoth festival presided over by Robespierre, the Incorruptible, as he was known. The procession began in the Tuileries and ended on the Champ-de-Mars.

The capital's fairground. – From time to time the ground has been given over to exhibitions; on 22 September 1798 the Directory commemorated the anniversary of the Republic with an Industrial Exhibition destined to replace the old Saint-Germain and Saint-Laurent Fairs – an innovation was the payment of exhibitors.

World exhibitions were held in 1867, 1878, 1889, 1900 and 1937 – the Eiffel Tower remains as a souvenir of the Exhibition of 1889. In the same year, the army exchanged the ground with the City of Paris for a terrain at Issy-les-Moulineaux. The latter has now become Paris' heliport.

The gardens. – The present gardens, laid out by J. C. Formigé, were begun in 1908 and completed in 1928. Part is landscaped with grottoes, arbors, cascades and a small pool at the foot of the tower and part is formal. Wide strips on either side along the Suffren and La Bourdonnais Avenues were sold for building and are now lined by large private houses and blocks of luxury flats.

Some decorative features and structures adorning the Paris streets are typically French and very popular with tourists:

Morris pillars introduced in 1869 when advertising posters came into use (some 300 original ones remain standing)

Wallace drinking fountains donated to the city of Paris in 1872 by Sir Richard Wallace (some 70 can still be seen throughout the city)

gas street lamps wrought iron grilles of métro stations etc.

■ THE EIFFEL TOWER ★★★ ⬚⬚ - fold 28: J 7, J 8

The tower is the capital's look out and Paris' best known monument. When it was erected it was the tallest construction the world had ever known but since then its 300 m – 984 ft have been topped by skyscrapers and telecommunication towers elsewhere. The additions made for television transmission have increased its height by another 20.75 m – 67 ft to 320.75 m – 1 051 ft.

Historical notes. – The idea of a tower came to Eiffel as a natural consequence of his study of the use of high metal piles for viaducts. The first project dates from 1884; between 1887 and 1889 three hundred skyjacks put the tower together with the aid of two and a half million rivets.

Eiffel, in his enthusiasm, cried "France will be the only country in the world with a 300 m flagpole".

Artists and writers, however were appalled; among the 300 who signed a protest were Charles Garnier of the Opera, the composer, Gounod, and the poets and writers François Coppée, Leconte de Lisle, Dumas the Younger, Maupassant... Equally the tower's very boldness and incredible novelty brought it great acclaim and by the beginning of the century it had become a subject of celebration by other poets and dramatists, Apollinaire, Cocteau... and painters such as Pissarro, Dufy, Utrillo, Seurat, Marquet... Since then its form, appearing as millions of souvenirs, has become familiar everywhere.

In 1909, when the concession expired, the tower was nearly pulled down – it was saved through the importance of its huge antennae to French radio telegraphy; from 1910 it also became part of the International Time Service.

In 1916 it was made the terminal for the first radio telephone service across the Atlantic. French radio has used it as a transmitter since 1918 and television since 1957. The top platform serves as the base for a revolving light beacon (replaced in 1975 by a fixed red light) and as an aircraft meteorological and navigation station.

Nobody now questions the tower's aesthetic appeal or its utility – it has taken its place on the capital's skyline and beckons a welcome to all who come to Paris. It is often the venue for artistic and publicity events.

The tensile masterpiece. – The tower's weight is 7 000 tons; the deadweight of 4 kg per cm^2 – 57 lbs per sq inch – is about that of a man sitting in a chair. A scale model made of pig iron 30 cm high – 11.8 inches – would weigh 7 grams or 1/4 oz; 52 tons of paint are used every seven years when it is repainted.

The sway at the top in the highest winds has never been more than 12 cm – 4 1/2 inches – but the height can vary by as much as 15 cm – 6 inches – depending on the temperature.

The visitor, standing between the tower's feet and looking upwards through the interesting latticework of pig iron, gets an incredible feeling of the stupendous: there are three platforms: the 1st is at 57 m – 187 ft; the 2nd at 115 m – 377 ft; the 3rd at 274 m – 899 ft. The bold will climb the 1 652 steps to the top; others will take the lifts which have had to have special brake attachments fitted because of the variation in the angle of ascent.

Ascent. – *10am (9.30am on weekends) to 11pm. Fare by lift including the museum: stage 1 – 10F, 2 – 24F, 3 – 40F; by the steps: stages 1 and 2 – 7F.*

The **view ★★★** for the visitor to the 3rd platform may extend 67 km – 42 miles if the atmosphere is really clear – but that is rare. Paris and its suburbs appear as on a giant map – the best light is usually one hour before sunset. From the open terrace (3rd floor), through a window Eiffel's sitting room can be seen.

(Photo J. Bottin)

Eiffel Tower.

On the first floor there is an audio-visual museum which presents the tower's history.

Beneath the tower, by the north pillar, is a bust by Bourdelle of the engineer, Eiffel, who presented the country with one of the most frequented French monuments: over 4 million visitors in 1984.

■ THE ÉCOLE MILITAIRE★★ ⬜ - fold 29: K 9

The École Militaire, the French Military Academy, and one of the finest examples of French 18C architecture, was perfectly sited by its architect at the end of what is the Champ-de-Mars.

Construction. – Thanks to Mme de Pompadour, Louis XV's favourite, the financier and supplier to the army, Pâris-Duverney, obtained, in 1751, permission to found and personally to supervise the building of a Royal Military Academy where young gentlemen without means would be trained to become accomplished officers. The parade ground was given the name Champ-de-Mars.

Jacques-Ange Gabriel, architect of the Petit Trianon at Versailles and of the Place de la Concorde, produced sumptuous plans which the financier duly modified. The final construction nevertheless remains incredibly magnificent when one remembers that it was designed as a barracks. The king took no interest in the future school and, in fact, money to pay for the building was raised from a tax imposed on playing cards and a lottery.

The academy numbered 500 students; the course lasted three years. In 1769 Louis XV agreed to lay the foundation stone for the chapel; by 1772 the buildings were complete.

Bonaparte the Military Cadet. – In 1777 the Royal Academy became the Higher Officers' School. In 1784 Bonaparte, who had been to the lesser military academy at Brienne and was then 15, was admitted on the recommendation that he would "make an excellent sailor". He passed out as a lieutenant in the artillery with the mention that he would "go far in favourable circumstances".

The Military Tradition. – The institution was suppressed by the Revolution, but the buildings, which had been enlarged in the 18C, have retained their military tradition both as quarters and instruction centre. The Swiss Guards of the Ancien Régime, the National Guard of 1848, have been replaced by French and foreign officers attending the School of Advanced War Studies, and the Higher School of National Defence.

THE EXTERIOR

The impressive **central pavilion** which you see as you approach up the Champ-de-Mars, is ornamented with eight superb Corinthian columns each two storeys high; completing the decoration are a carved pediment, trophies, allegorical figures and a crowning quadrangular dome. Low lying wings frame the main building. The barracks on either side are 19C. Facing the central pavilion, is the equestrian statue of Marshal Joffre by Real del Sarte (1939).

Leave the **Village Suisse** (antique and second-hand dealers' shops – *open 11am, to 7pm, closed Tuesdays and Wednesdays)* on your right, to circle the academy by way of Suffren and Lowendal Avenues to the Place Fontenoy. (Lowendal commanded part of the French army which defeated the British and Dutch at Fontenoy in 1745).

From the semicircular square, you look across the sportsground to the **main court-yard★★**, lined on either side by beautiful porticoes with paired columns. At the back is the central pavilion, flanked by colonnaded buildings ending in advanced wings.

Inside, the chapel, the main staircase, the Marshals' Saloon and the Guardroom on the first floor are remarkably decorated *(guided tours for military bodies in principle on written application to the Général Commandant Militaire, École Militaire, 13 Place Joffre. The Chapel is open to the public on Saturdays at 6pm and Sundays, 11am; closed in August).*

Fontenoy Square has entirely lost its 18C character. The huge blocks on its east side include the Ministries of Health, Merchant Navy and Post Office, on its south side lies UNESCO.

■ UNESCO HOUSE★ ⬜ - fold 41: K 9

Displays, debates, film shows for groups on application: ☏ 45.68.10.00.

The home of UNESCO (United Nations Educational, Scientific and Cultural Organization) was opened in 1958 and is the most truly international undertaking in Paris, the membership is 158 states and construction jointly of the buildings by Breuer, Nervi and Zehrfuss, American, Italian and French architects respectively, demonstrating unique cooperation.

The buildings. – The main building, in the form of a Y supported on piles, houses the secretariat (sales counters in the entrance hall with souvenirs, newspapers, periodicals and stamps). A second building with fluted concrete walls and an accordion pleat designed roof contains the conference halls and committee rooms. The small cubic construction four storeys high beside the Japanese garden, is a secretariat annexe. Additional accommodation was provided in 1965, by means of two floors being constructed underground and lit naturally by six low level patios, and in 1970, at No. 1 Rue Miollis.

Decoration. – The decoration is also the result of international artistic cooperation. There are frescoes by the Spaniard, Picasso, and the Mexican, Tamayo, a monumental statue by the Englishman, Henry Moore *(Figure in Repose),* a black steel mobile by the American, Calder, *Sun and Moon,* walls by the Spanish ceramic artists, Miro and Artigas, mosaics by the French, Bazaine and Herzell, a relief by Jean Arp, tapestries by Lurçat, and the French-Swiss, Le Corbusier, and a Japanese garden by Noguchi. In and around the later annexes are works by the Italian, Giacometti, the Spanish, Chillida, the Venezuelan, Soto and the American, Kelly.

The overall impression is a remarkable synthesis of mid 20C art.

Michelin plan Paris **⬚⬚** - folds 31 and 32: from J 14 to K 16.

Start from the Cité métro station. See also plan p 63

The Ile de la Cité is the heart of Paris and together with the neighbouring Ile St-Louis, forms an area remarkable for its beauty, its architecture and its history.

Lutetia. – Between 250 and 200 BC Gaulish fishermen and boatmen of the Parisii tribe discovered and set up their huts on the largest island in the Seine – Lutetia was born. The township, whose Celtic name meant "habitation surrounded by water", was conquered by Labienus' Roman legions in 52 BC. The Gallo-Roman town prospered on river transport, so that the vessel which was later incorporated in the capital's coat of arms *(p 17)* is a reminder both of the shape of the island and of the way of life of its earliest inhabitants. The boatmen's existence has been confirmed by the discovery of one of their pagan altars beneath Notre-Dame *(p 118)*.

In the 4C the name Lutetia was changed to that of its inhabitants and thus became Paris.

(Photo Christiane Olivier, Nice)
Illuminated façade of Notre-Dame.

St. Genevieve. – In 451 Attila crossed the Rhine at the head of 700 000 men; the Parisians began to flee at his approach until Genevieve, a young girl from Nanterre who had consecrated her life to God, calmed them assuring them that the town would be saved by heavenly intervention. The Huns arrived, hesitated, and turned, to advance on Orleans. Parisians adopted the girl as their protector and patron.

Ten years later the island was besieged by the Franks and suffered famine; Genevieve escaped the enemy watch, loaded boats with victuals in Champagne and returned, again miraculously avoiding detection. She died in 512 and was buried at King Clovis' side *(p 114)*.

The Count of Paris becomes King. – In 885, for the fifth time in forty years, the Northmen sailed up the Seine. The Cité – the island took the name in 506 when Clovis made it his capital – was confronted by 700 ships and 30 000 warriors bent on advancing into Burgundy. Assault and siege proving unsuccessful, the Northmen took their boats out of the water, mounted them on logs and rolled them on land round Paris. Eudes, Count of Paris and the leader of the resistance, was thereupon elected king.

Cathedral and Parliament. – During the Middle Ages the population spread from the island along both banks of the river. But while the episcopal see remained under Sens (Paris did not have its own archbishop until 1622), schools were established within the cathedral's shadow which were to become famous throughout Europe. Among the teachers were Alexander of Paris, inventor of the poetic alexandrine line and, at the beginning of the 12C, the philosopher Abelard, whose moving romance with Heloise began in the cloister of Notre-Dame. Chapels and convents multiplied on the island: St-Denis-du-Pas (where St. Denis' martyrdom is said to have begun), St-Pierre-aux-Bœufs (the porch is now the St-Séverin porch), St-Aignan *(p 63)*, St-Jean-le-Rond (where unwanted children were abandoned), were but a few of the belfried edifices which by the end of the 13C numbered at least twenty-three.

The Cité, the seat of parliament, the highest judiciary in the kingdom was, inevitably, involved in revolutions and uprisings such as that attempted by Étienne Marcel in the 14C and the Fronde in the 17C. During the Terror of 1793-94 the Conciergerie prisons were crowded, while next door, the Revolutionary Tribunal continued to sit in the Law Courts, endlessly pronouncing merciless sentences.

Transformation. – Under Louis-Philippe and to an even greater extent, under Napoleon III, the entire centre of the island was demolished: 25 000 people were evacuated. Enormous administrative buildings were erected: the Hôtel-Dieu, a barracks (now the police prefecture), the commercial courts. The Law Courts were doubled in size; the Place du Parvis before the cathedral was quadrupled; the Boulevard du Palais was built ten times wider than before.

In August 1944 the Paris police barricaded themselves in the prefecture and hoisted the tricolour. For three days they held the Germans at bay until relieved by the arrival of the French Army Division under General Leclerc.

The construction of Notre-Dame, which began after that of St-Denis and Sens in about 1140, heralded the age of great Gothic cathedrals in France: Strasbourg (c 1176), Bourges (c 1185), Chartres (c 1194), Rouen (1200), Reims (1211), Amiens (1220), Beauvais (1247).

■ NOTRE-DAME CATHEDRAL ★★★ 🔲 - fold 32: K 15

The cathedral of Paris, which can be seen in all its radiant glory from the parvis or Viviani Square, stands in an admirable setting. Notre-Dame has a perfection all its own, with balanced proportions and a façade in which solid and void, horizontal and vertical, combine in total harmony. It is a beautiful religious edifice and one of the supreme masterpieces of French art.

Construction. – For 2 000 years prayers have been offered from this spot: a Gallo-Roman temple, a Christian basilica, a Romanesque church preceded the present sanctuary founded by Bishop Maurice of Sully. A man of humble origin, he had become a canon at the cathedral and supervisor of the diocese by 1159 and, shortly afterwards, undertook to provide the capital with a worthy cathedral to rival the basilica built at St-Denis by Abbot Suger *(p 183)*.

Construction began in 1163, during the reign of Louis VII. To the resources of the church and royal gifts, were added the toil and skill of the common people: stone masons, carpenters, iron workers, sculptors, glassworkers, moved with religious fervour, worked with ardour under Jean of Chelles and Pierre of Montreuil, architect of the Sainte-Chapelle. By about 1345 the building was complete – the original plans had not been modified in any way.

Ceremonial Occasions. – Long before it was completed, Notre-Dame had become the setting for major religious and political occasions: St. Louis placed the Crown of Thorns in the cathedral in 1239 until the Sainte-Chapelle was ready to receive it; in 1302 Philip the Fair went to the cathedral solemnly to open the first States General; ceremonies, acts of grace, state funerals, the Te Deum, processions, have followed down the centuries; the young Henry VI of England was crowned there in 1430; Mary Stuart was crowned there on becoming Queen of France by her marriage to François II; and Marguerite of Valois stood alone in the chancel while the Huguenot, Henri of Navarre, waited at the door as their marriage ceremony was performed in 1572 – although he came later to agree that "Paris is well worth a mass" and attended subsequent ceremonies inside the cathedral!

With the Revolution, the Church of Our Lady was dedicated to the cult of Reason and then of the Supreme Being. All but the great bell were melted down and the church interior was used to store forage and food. On 2 December 1804 the church was decked with hangings and ornaments to receive Pope Pius VII for the coronation of the Emperor (see the picture by David in the Louvre: *p 37*). After the anointing, however, Napoleon seized the crown from the pontiff and crowned first himself and then Josephine.

Restoration. – Gradually the building began to fall into disrepair, until in 1841, in accordance with popular feeling roused by the Romantic Movement and Victor Hugo's novel *The Hunchback of Notre-Dame*, the July Monarchy ordered that the cathedral be restored. A team of men under Viollet-le-Duc worked for twenty-three years on the statuary and glass, on removing additions, repairing the roof and upper parts, re-ordering the doors and chancel and erecting the spire and the sacristy. Notre-Dame emerged virtually unscathed from the Commune of 1871 and the Liberation of 1944 and remains the focal point for great occasions in Paris' history: the magnificent Te Deum of 26 August 1944, the Requiem Masses for General de Gaulle on 12 November 1970 and President Pompidou on 6 April 1974 and the Magnificat of 31 May 1980, followed by Mass on the parvis celebrated by Pope John Paul II.

PLACE DU PARVIS

The square, the zero point from which all road distances are measured, is dominated by the grandiose façade of Notre-Dame, somewhat diminished by the parvis having been quadrupled in size and the surroundings opened out by Haussmann in the 19C.

In the Middle Ages, when mysteries were played before churches and cathedrals, the porch represented paradise from which the word parvis evolved.

The Hôtel-Dieu. – The Hôtel-Dieu hospice, founded in the 7C had, by the 17C, been enlarged to two buildings linked by the Pont au Double *(p 65)*. In about 1880 these buildings were replaced on the island by the present Hôtel-Dieu and a square laid on the old site with, at the centre, a statue of Charlemagne.

The Archaeological Crypt★. – *Open 10am to 6pm (5.30pm 1 October to 31 March); closed holidays; 20F; 9F in winter.*

Excavations beneath the parvis – the layout is marked on the parvis pavement – have uncovered 3 to 19C vestiges. Included are two Gallo-Roman rooms heated by hypocaust *(to the left on entering),* fragments of the Late Roman Empire rampart, mediaeval cellars and foundations of a children's home and of a church.

THE NOTRE-DAME FAÇADE

The façade's overall design is majestic and perfectly balanced. The central portal is taller and wider than the others; that on the left is surmounted by a gable. It was a mediaeval practice to avoid monotony by dissymmetry.

The West Face Portals. – In the Middle Ages the portals looked completely different: the multicoloured statues stood out against a gilt background affording a bible in stone from which those who could not read could learn the scriptures and the legends of the saints. The six panels of the portals are adorned with splendid wrought iron strap hinges. According to legend the side portals were carved by the devil himself to whom the ironsmith, Biscornet, had forfeited his soul, but it proved impossible for him to decorate the central one through which the Host was carried in procession. Its hinges are 19C replicas.

Portal to the Virgin   Portal of the Last Judgment   Portal to St. Anne

The three portals remain worthy of examination in detail:

Portal to the Virgin. – The beautiful tympanum (1), a model to sculptors throughout the Middle Ages, shows below, the Ark of the Covenant, prophets and kings, above, a moving Dormition of the Virgin in the presence of Christ and the Apostles, and at the apex, the Coronation of the Virgin: in an attitude full of nobility, Christ gives a sceptre to his mother who is crowned by an angel.

The arching (2) is delicately beaded, leaves, flowers and fruit framing angels, patriarchs, kings and prophets of the celestial court. The Virgin and Child at the pier (3) are modern. The small low-reliefs on the side walls and arch shafts (4) show the labours of the months and the signs of the Zodiac.

The statues in the embrasures (5) were added by Viollet-le-Duc and include St. Denis framed by two angels, St. John the Baptist and St. Stephen.

Portal of the Last Judgment. – The tympanum (6) was breached by Soufflot in 1771 to allow the processional dais through. Viollet-le-Duc restored the two lower lintels. Below is illustrated the Resurrection and, above, the Weighing of the Souls, the good being led to heaven by angels, the damned to hell by demons. At the apex, Christ sits in Majesty with the Virgin and St. John interceding for the sinners.

The six archivolts (7) show the celestial court. Below, heaven and hell are symbolised by Abraham receiving the souls (left) and grimacing demons (right). The statue of Christ at the pier (8) is 19C; the Wise and Foolish Virgins, beneath open (left) and shut (right) doors to Paradise on the archway shafts (9) are modern. In the embrasures (10), the Apostles by Viollet-le-Duc rise above medallions depicting the Vices (lower tier) and the Virtues (upper tier).

Portal to St. Anne. – The cathedral's oldest statues, carved in about 1170 some sixty years before the portal was erected, and intended for a narrower door, fill the two upper levels of the tympanum (11). At the apex is a Virgin in Majesty with the Christ Child in the Romanesque tradition; she is surrounded by two angels with Bishop Maurice of Sully (standing, left) and Louis VII (kneeling, right) consecrating the cathedral. The 12C central lintel shows the Life of the Virgin, the lower, that of St. Anne and St. Joachim (13C).

Framing the tympanum, the four archivolts (12) illustrate a celestial court of angels, kings and patriarchs; the pier (13) supports a long and slender statue of St. Marcel, Bishop of Paris in the 5C when he is said to have delivered the capital from a dragon – he is sticking his crozier down the monster's throat. It is very similar to the Romanesque statue-columns. The original statue is in the north tower chapel. In the embrasures (14) on either side of the portal are statues of kings, queens and saints.

The buttresses between the portals are adorned with modern statues (15) of St. Stephen, the Church, the Synagogue (with a blindfold) and St. Denis.

The Kings' Gallery. – *Above the portals.* The 28 statues are of the Kings of Judea and Israel, Christ's forebears. In 1793 the Commune took them for the Kings of France and shattered them on the parvis *(see p 118, The Baths);* Viollet-le-Duc restored them.

The Rose Window Level. – The design of the great rose window, nearly 10 m – 30 ft across, is so perfect that it has never shifted in over 700 years and was used as a model by all master-builders. It forms a halo to the statue of the Virgin and Child, supported by two angels, before it. In the lateral bays, surmounted by relief arches, are statues of Adam (left) and Eve (right). The ensemble portrays the Redemption after the Banishment (restored by Viollet-le-Duc).

The Great Gallery. – The gallery is a superb line of ornately carved arches linking the towers. At the balustrade's buttress corners Viollet-le-Duc placed fantastic birds, monsters and demons which although large, are scarcely visible from below as they are partly obscured by the projecting balustrade.

Towers. – The majestic and graceful twin towers, 69 m – 226 ft high, are pierced by slender lancets more than 16 m – 50 ft in height. Emmanuel, the great bell in the south tower, tolled only on solemn occasions, weighs 13 tons and its clapper nearly 500 kg – 9 3/4 cwts. It is said that when it was recast in the 17C, women threw gold and silver jewellery into the heated bronze, which is why the tone is so pure.

Ascent. – *Open 10am to 5.30pm; closed 1 January, 1 and 8 May, 1 and 11 November, 25 December. Access at the foot of the north tower; 20F April to September; 9F the rest of the year; children 3F.*

Steep steps lead to the south tower platform from which you get a splendid view of the spire and flying buttresses, the Cité and Paris generally. In the south tower upper chapel, a video-museum traces the highlights of Notre-Dame.

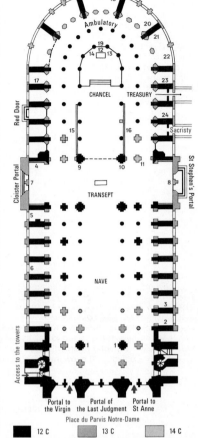

THE CATHEDRAL INTERIOR

Notre-Dame impresses immediately by its size, its lighting, the noble uplift of its lines. A congregation of 9 000 can be accommodated within its 130 m length, 48 m width and 35 m height – 427 × 158 × 115 ft.

The plan is the prototype of all large Gothic cathedrals. In the 13C the upper windows and galleries were enlarged and lowered respectively to increase the light reaching the chapels off the outer aisles. Flying buttresses were then added to support the roofing. Part of the 12C architecture can still be seen at the transept crossing in the small rose and tall windows. The redoubtable pillars (1) supporting the towers measure 5 m – 16 ft across.

The stained glass of the Middle Ages was succeeded by clear glass with *fleur-de-lys* design in the 18C and grisaille glass in the 19C; the modern glass by Le Chevalier, installed in 1965, returned to mediaeval manufacturing processes and colours. The organ which was remodelled in 1868, has 110 stops, *concerts: (Sundays at 5.45pm)*.

Chapels. – Notre-Dame is entirely surrounded by chapels. They were built between the buttresses in response to the great number of foundations made by guilds and the rich in the 13 and 14C. This called for a lengthening of the transepts, which would have otherwise lost their profile.

In accordance with a tradition renewed in 1949, the goldsmiths of Paris offer a work of art to the cathedral every year in May – the most beautiful are by Le Brun (2, 3) and Le Sueur (4). On the left are the tombstones of a 15C canon (5), and of Cardinal Amette (6).

Transept. – The diameter – 13 m – 42 1/2 ft and lightness of the rose **windows** are brilliant evidence of the advances made in architecture in the Gothic period. The north rose (7) which has remained practically intact since the 13C, shows Old Testament figures around the Virgin; in the restored south rose (8) Christ sits surrounded by saints and angels.

The statue of St. Denis (9) by Nicolas Coustou makes a pair, against the transept pillars at the entrance to the chancel, with the beautiful 14C **Virgin and Child** (10) – Our Lady of Paris, previously in St-Aignan *(p 63)*. A pavement inscription recalls the conversion of the 20C poet Paul Claudel (11).

Chancel. – Louis XIII, childless after twenty-three years of marriage, consecrated France in 1638 to the Virgin – a vow materialised in the redecoration of the chancel by Robert de Cotte. Of this there remain the stalls, and a *pietà* by Coysevox (12), flanked by statues of Louis XIII (13) by Guillaume Coustou and Louis XIV (14) by Coysevox.

It was at this time that the stone chancel screen was cut back leaving, of the remarkable 14C **low reliefs**, only scenes from the Life of Christ (15) and His Apparitions (16) which were restored by Viollet-le-Duc.

Mausoleums of bishops of Paris, buried in the crypt, line the ambulatory (17-24).

Treasury. – *Open 10am (2pm Sundays and holidays) to 6pm; 15F.*

The former sacristy built by Viollet-le-Duc contains 19C manuscripts, ornaments and church plate. The Crown of Thorns, the Holy Nail and a fragment of the True Cross are displayed on Good Friday in the main area of the cathedral.

EXTERIOR

Notre-Dame's lovely exterior presents an excellent summary of 13C architecture. There are fine vistas of the soaring towers silhouetted against the sky.

North Face. – A canons' cloister, now destroyed, gave its name to the street and north transept face.

The magnificent **Cloister Portal** erected in about 1250 by Jean of Chelles, on the experience acquired at the Sainte-Chapelle which was completed in 1248, served as a model throughout the Gothic period. The great and finely worked transept rose rests on a clerestory with which it forms an unprecedented and delicate opening 18 m – 58 ft high. It is slightly bigger – 13 m – 43 ft in diameter – but as perfectly designed as the west façade rose on which it is modelled. Below the rose is the many gabled carved doorway, richly decorated by comparison with the thirty years older doors of the main west face. On the lower level of the tympanum are events from the Life of the Virgin and above, scenes from a mystery play which was performed on the parvis.

The portal's jewel is the figure at the pier, a superb **Virgin** (the Child was lost during the Revolution) with a gentle smile and the infinite nobility of a 13C masterpiece. It is more expressive than the Romanesque Virgin of the St. Anne's portal and has a nobler mien than the 14C transept statue.

Opposite, at No. **10**, is the **Cathedral Museum** *(open Wednesdays, Saturdays, Sundays and 1 September to 31 July, 2.30 to 6pm; 10F; ☎ 43.25.42.92)* which evokes the cathedral's major historical moments since the 17C.

Further along, the **Red Door**, built by Pierre of Montreuil and used only by members of the cathedral chapter, has, on the tympanum, the Virgin being coronated by her Son between St. Louis and Margaret of Provence, and on the archivolts, scenes from the Life of St. Marcel.

Seven 14C **low-reliefs** inlaid into the chancel chapels' foundations depict the Death and Assumption of the Virgin.

John XXIII Square. – Until the beginning of the 19C, the area between Notre-Dame and the tip of the island was crowded with houses, chapels and also the Archbishop's Palace built in the reign of Louis XIII between the chevet and the Seine. On 2 November 1789, the clergy's possessions were nationalised and in 1831 the buildings were severely damaged in a riot and later razed to the ground. The square opened as a formal garden with a Neo-Gothic fountain in 1844.

From this spot there is an outstanding view of the **east end** of the cathedral with its intricate decoration of balustrades, gables, pinnacles, gargoyles and the 14C flying buttresses rising 15 m – 50 ft into the air to form the boldest mediaeval crown of all.

If you take a few steps back you can see the 13C roof which retains the original timberwork. Viollet-le-Duc reconstructed the **spire,** destroyed during the Revolution, above the transept crossing using at least 500 tons of oak and 250 tons of lead, so that it could rise once more to 90 m – 295 ft. He included himself among the decorative copper figures of Evangelists and Apostles!

Beyond the 19C sacristy is the magnificent **St. Stephen's portal,** a pair with the cloister door but even richer in sculpture. A railing prevents close approach. Begun in 1258 by Jean of Chelles and completed by Pierre of Montreuil, it has a remarkable tympanum comprising three tiers and illustrating the life and stoning of St. Stephen to whom the church preceding the cathedral had been dedicated. The statue of St. Stephen at the pier and that of St. Marcel on the gable and most of the coving carvings were executed in the 19C. At the base of the buttresses, eight small 13C low-reliefs depict street and university scenes.

Splendid vistas of Notre Dame and the Seine can be enjoyed from the small, verdant, southfacing John XXIII Square which is always very crowded.

■ **THE LAW COURTS ★★★** (PALAIS DE JUSTICE) ▯▯ - fold 31: J 14

See also local map p 63.

On the Ile de la Cité stands not only the Gothic splendour of Notre-Dame but the seat of the civil and judicial system – the Law Courts. It forms with the Sainte-Chapelle and the Conciergerie an architectural ensemble of great historical interest.

The King's Palace. – The Roman governors, the Merovingian kings, the early Capetian kings, lived in turn on the Cité, establishing administrative quarters, building a dwelling of the finest stone for royal use, inaugurating a mint and, lastly, constructing a chapel and keep.

In the 13C St. Louis lived in the Upper Chamber (today the First Civil Court), dispensed justice in the courtyard and built the Sainte-Chapelle; Philip the Fair constructed the Conciergerie, a sumptuous palace "more beautiful than anyone in France had ever seen". The Hall of the Men-at-Arms was the largest ever built in Europe. The former St-Michel Chapel which gave its name to the bridge and boulevard on the left bank, was razed to the ground in the 18C.

On 22 February 1358, the mob under Étienne Marcel *(p 67)* entered the apartments of the Dauphin, the future Charles V, whose father John the Good had been taken prisoner by the Black Prince at Poitiers and held in England, and slew his counsellors before his eyes. On regaining control, Charles V left the palace, preferring to live at the Louvre or outside Paris – an example followed by Charles VII, Henri IV and Louis XIV who all subdued Paris; Louis XVI, Charles X and Louis-Philippe, who refused to abandon the palace, all lost their thrones.

Parliament's Palace. – Parliament, installed in the former royal residence, was the kingdom's supreme court of justice. Originally its members were nominated by the king, but in 1522 François I sold the rights which thus became hereditary. The highest dignitaries in the land were members by right or privilege. Conflicts between the officers of state and the king were settled by courts presided over by the monarch, and offenders were sometimes sentenced to exile or imprisonment.

Judges, barristers, clerks and others thronged the lesser courts in the palace. Fires were frequent: the Great Hall was badly damaged in 1618, the Sainte-Chapelle spire in 1630, the Debtors' Court in 1737, the Marchande Gallery in 1776. In 1788 Parliament demanded the convocation of the States General – not a good idea – the General Assembly announced its suppression and the Convention sent the members to the guillotine.

Palace of Justice. – The Revolution overturned the judicial system. New courts were installed in the old building which took the name of Palace of Justice. Restoration began in 1840 and continued until 1914, interrupted only by the Commune fire, after which the building was given the façade which now overlooks the Place Dauphine and the wing on the Orfèvres Quay.

TOUR

The palace is open from 9am to 6pm except on Saturdays and Sundays and all the courts, galleries and halls may be entered with the exception of the Busts Gallery, and the Juvenile Court (Galerie des Bustes, Tribunal pour Enfants).

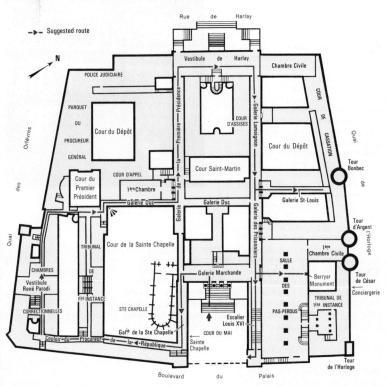

The May Courtyard (Cour du Mai). – The courtyard, which overlooks the Boulevard du Palais is separated from it by a fine Louis XVI wrought iron gateway. The name of this forecourt was due to a very old custom by which the clerks of the court – an important corporation – planted a tree on the 1 May in this courtyard. The tree used in these celebrations, which were similar to the traditional English festivities, came from one of the Royal Forests.

A small yard to the right abuts on the old Conciergerie wicket gate *(guichet-plan p 61)* through which the victims of the Terror passed on their way to the tumbrils beneath the watchful eyes of the curious and the *tricoteuses* – the women knitting – perched upon the steps.

From the Marchande Gallery to the Harlay Vestibule. – Turn left in the Marchande Gallery (Galerie Marchande) formerly the most animated part of the building, bustling with plaintiffs, lawyers, clerks, court officials and hangers-on, then left again to walk down the Sainte-Chapelle Gallery. Turn right, up the Procureur de la République's Corridor and right again up a passageway which skirts the lively petty court area (Chambres Correc-tionnelles). Turn right at the end into the Duc Gallery, getting an open **view**★ of the Sainte-Chapelle from the corner.

Turn left beyond the ornate Chamber of the Civil Court of Appeal, into the Première Présidence Gallery and leave on the left the **C.I.D.** (Police Judiciaire) known to all admirers of Inspector Maigret. From the vast and empty Harlay Vestibule steps lead to the Assize Court *(open only when in session)* on the right. At the end is the Chamber of the Court of Cassation *(frescoes and tapestries – but not often open).*

From the Harlay Vestibule to the May Courtyard. – Walk down to the right the Lamoignon Gallery (glance at the St. Louis Gallery in passing, on your left) and the following Prisoners' Gallery.

Enter the **Lobby** (Salle des Pas-Perdus), formerly the Gothic Great Hall of Philip the Fair, twice destroyed and reconstructed most recently after the Commune of 1871. The two Classical aisles, crowded with plaintiffs, barristers in their gowns but without the English distinctive wig, clerks and officials, are now the busiest place in the building – Balzac called it "the cathedral of chicanery".

Notice the tortoise – a malicious dig at the delays in the law – in the monument, on the right, of the 19C barrister, Berryer. At the end on the left is the former apartment of St. Louis, later the Parliamentary Grand Chamber, when Louis XII had it decorated with a fine ceiling, then the Revolutionary Tribunal under Fouquier-Tinville (1793-93 – *p 61*) and now the **First Civil Court.**

Walk down the grand Louis XVI staircase built by the architect Antoine, noting the old shop names.

■ THE SAINTE-CHAPELLE★★★ ▯▯ - fold 31: J 14

The chapel is a Gothic marvel – the deep glow of its windows one of the great joys of a visit to Paris.

Baudouin, a French nobleman and Emperor of Constantinople, when in need of money, pledged the Crown of Thorns. St. Louis redeemed the Crown from the Venetians in 1239. For additional relics and the shrine made to contain them, he paid two and a half times the amount spent subsequently on the Sainte-Chapelle building, which was erected to shelter them.

Pierre of Montreuil (known also as Pierre of Montereau) was probably the architect of the building which was completed in record time – less than thirty-three months – and consecrated in 1248.

Originally the chapel stood in the centre of the court, linked at the upper level of the porch to St. Louis' apartments by a small gallery.

(Photo Musées Nationaux)
Window of the Ste-Chapelle.

When the palace was remodelled in the 18C, parliament, unfortunately, built a wing of the May Courtyard abutting on the chapel.

Services, when the chapel was in use, were elaborate; in the 17C the organ was played by the Couperins – the instrument is now at St-Germain-l'Auxerrois.

During the Revolution, although some of the relics were saved and are now in Notre-Dame *(p 57)*, the reliquary shrine was melted down. From 1802 to 1837 the building became the judiciary archive; restoration, when it came, took from 1841 to 1867.

Exterior. – The Sainte-Chapelle made a great impression when it was built: for the first time a building was seen to possess practically no walls – its roof being supported on slender pillars and buttresses between which were windows 15 m high – 50 ft. It was a feat of balance – balance so perfect that no crack has appeared in seven centuries.

The spire rises 75 m – 246 ft – into the sky. Its lead covered wooden frame has three times been destroyed by fire and rebuilt, the last time in 1854. The lead angel above the apse used to turn so as to show the Cross in his hands to all points of the compass.

The small adjunct to the fourth bay was constructed by Louis XI and comprises a chapel at ground level with an oratory above.

Interior. – *Open 10am to 5.30pm, closed 1 January, 1 and 8 May, 1 and 11 November, 25 December; 20F April to September; 9F the rest of the year; children 3F.*

You enter through the **lower chapel** which was intended for the palace servants. The chamber is 17 m wide and only 7 m high – 56 × 23 ft. Columns, garishly decorated in the 19C, uphold the central vault, and are supported, in their turn, by elegantly pierced flying buttresses. The pavement is made up of the tombstones of canons buried beneath it.

A spiral staircase to the left leads to the **upper chapel,** a wondrous jewel, which attracts even the faintest ray of sunlight. The **stained glass windows** are the oldest in Paris and amongst the finest to be produced in the 13C in their vividness of colour and the vitality of the thousands of small characters they portray; the 1 134 scenes on glass spread over an area of 618 m^2 – 6 672 sq ft – form a veritable illustrated bible. The mid-19C restorations are hard to detect.

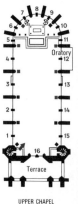

UPPER CHAPEL

The windows which illustrate scenes from the Old and New Testaments, should each be read from bottom to top and left to right. Nos. **6, 7, 9** and **11** must be read lancet by lancet.

1) Genesis - Adam and Eve - Noah - Jacob.
2) Exodus - Moses on Mount Sinai. – 3) Exodus - The Law of Moses.
4) Deuteronomy - Joshua - Ruth and Boaz.
5) Judges - Gideon - Samson. – 6) Isaiah - The Tree of Jesse.
7) St. John the Evangelist - Life of the Virgin - The Childhood of Christ.
8) Christ's Passion. – 9) John the Baptist - Daniel. – 10) Ezekiel.
11) Jeremiah - Tobias. – 12) Judith - Job. – 13) Esther.
14) Kings: Samuel, David, Solomon.
15) St. Helena and the True Cross - St. Louis and the relics of the Passion.
16) 15C Flamboyant rose window: the Apocalypse.

The vessel is encircled by blind arcades with capitals delicately carved with leaf motifs; against each pillar stands a statue of an apostle holding one of the Church's twelve crosses of consecration – six of the figures are old *(red on the plan)* and in spite of their modern colouring, are very lifelike (others are in the Cluny Museum: *p 118*).

Two small niches in the third bay were reserved for the king. In the next bay, on the right, is the door to the oratory built by Louis XI: a grille enabled him to follow the service.

The reliquary shrine stood at the centre of the apse in a gallery *(no access)* covered by a wooden baldachin and reached by twin circular staircases enclosed in openwork turrets. The original staircase on the left was often mounted by St. Louis who then, himself, opened the door to the shrine, inlaid with sparkling jewels.

The porch onto the terrace is a reconstruction with a 19C tympanum and pier.

■ THE CONCIERGERIE ★★ ▨ – fold 31: J 14 — *See also local map p 63.*

The Conciergerie includes three superb Gothic halls built by Philip the Fair in the 14C, revolutionary prisons and mementoes of its tragic history.

A noble keeper. – The name Conciergerie was given in the old palace to the part controlled by a person of high degree: the *concierge* or keeper of the king's mansion – a remunerative office involving the licensing of the many shops within the palace walls. Among pre-Revolutionary prisoners were several who had made successful or unsuccessful attempts on successive kings' lives: Montgomery on Henri II; Ravaillac on Henri IV...

The guillotine's antechamber. – At the Revolution as many as 1 200 men and women were held at one time in the Conciergerie; during the Terror the building became the antechamber to the Tribunal, which in nine cases out of ten meant the guillotine.

Among those locked in the cells were: Queen Marie-Antoinette; Madame Elisabeth, sister to Louis XVI; Charlotte Corday who stabbed Marat; Mme du Barry, the favourite of Louis XV; the poet André Chénier; Philippe-Égalité; the chemist, Lavoisier; the twenty-two Girondins condemned by Danton who, with fifteen of his companions, was in turn condemned by Robespierre, who himself condemned with twenty of his followers by the Thermidor Convention, and finally the public prosecutor Fouquier-Tinville, and the judges of the Revolutionary Tribunal. In all nearly 2 600 prisoners left the Conciergerie between January 1793 and July 1794 for the guillotine.

The Exterior. – The best view is from the Mégisserie Quay on the right bank from where you can also see the four towers reflected in the Seine which originally flowed right up to their base. It is the oldest part of the palace built by the Capetian kings. The ground level was raised appreciably at the end of the 16C when the Quai de l'Horloge was built.

The crenellated Bonbec Tower (Tour Bonbec), on the right, which is the oldest, got its name babbler, because it was used as a torture chamber.

The twin towers in the centre of the 19C Neo-Gothic façade commanded the palace entrance and the bridge of Charles the Bald. The Argent Tower (Tour d'Argent) on the right contained the royal treasure. In the César Tower (Tour César), to the left, were the apartments of the Public Prosecutor, Fouquier-Tinville, during the Terror.

The 14C Horloge Tower (Tour de l'Horloge) has since 1370 housed the first public clock installed in Paris. The carvings on the face are by Germain Pilon (16C – restored). The silver bell, having chimed the hours for the monarchy, was melted down in 1793.

The Interior. – *No 1 Quai de l'Horloge. Go through the porch, cross the courtyard and go down on the right to the Guardroom. Guided tours: 10am to 5pm (last tour); 9F.*

Guardroom (Salle des Gardes). – Stout pillars with interesting capitals support the Gothic vaulting in this dark room which now lies some 7 m – 23 ft below the level of the 16C quay.

The Hall of the Men-at-Arms (Salle des Gens d'Armes). – This magnificent four aisled Gothic hall has an area of 1 800 m² – 19 375 sq ft, unfortunately obscured by the 18C building erected in the May courtyard. Exactly above was the palace's Great Hall and the royal apartments. Additional supporting vaulting pillars were added in the 19C by Viollet-le-Duc.

Kitchens (Cuisines). – The four huge chimneys and fires in the kitchens were each intended for a separate purpose – spit roasting, boiling cauldrons, etc. – and between them, could serve the royal family and 2 000 to 3 000 others. The canopies are supported by unusual buttresses.

The "Rue de Paris". – The Rue de Paris was the name given to the last bay, closed by a grille from the Hall of the Men-at-Arms, as it led to the quarters of the executioner, known traditionally as Monsieur de Paris. During the Terror, penniless prisoners slept in it on the ground while the rich paid for their own cell and better food.

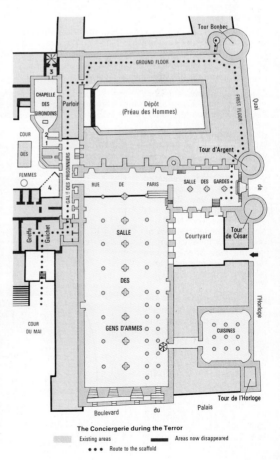

The Conciergerie during the Terror

▨ Existing areas   Areas now disappeared

••• Route to the scaffold

Prisoners' Gallery (Galerie des Prisonniers). – The gallery was the busiest part of the building, with prisoners arriving and departing, lawyers, police and gaolers.

From the 1st floor, the police escorted the prisoner down the spiral staircase, situated in one of the turrets of the Bonbec Tower, and into the gallery (through a door on the right which has since been walled up). This room gave onto the council room which on one side served as antechamber *(parloir)* to the men's prison yard *(Préau des Hommes)* and on the other side it opened onto a staircase (**3**), which led to the Tribunal. The prisoners were most likely herded into the room, which is now used as the kitchens for the Law Courts restaurant and from there, one by one, they were taken to a neighbouring room where they were sat on a stool and their last toilet was performed.

Then they walked through the wicket gate *(guichet)* to the clerk of the court (register office – *greffe*) – abutting on the May Courtyard – and out to the tumbrils.

Marie Antoinette's Prison. – The cell (**1**) where the queen lived from 2 August 1793 to 16 October 1793 included the area now a chapel. A screen separated the queen from the day and night watch. The cell now communicates with the next one (**2**) in which first Danton and then Robespierre are said to have been held.

The Girondins' Chapel (Chapelle des Girondins). – The chapel was transformed into a collective prison where prisoners heard mass through the grille on the upper storey. Twenty-two Girondins were held there together in 1793.

The museum contains Marie-Antoinette's crucifix and other mementoes, contemporary documents, a cell door, a guillotine blade, etc.

The Women's Courtyard (Cour des Femmes). – In the centre, as always, is a pathetic patch of grass and a tree. During the day the prisoners were allowed out into the courtyard.

Only the first floor of the buildings is old; the rest was added in the 19C.

In the corner is the Place of the Twelve (**4**) where men and women prisoners could talk and where the twelve selected daily for the guillotine said their farewells.

■ ADDITIONAL SIGHTS OF THE ILE DE LA CITÉ★

Distance: 3.5 km – 2 miles – Time: one day. Start from the Cité métro station.

For a long time the Cité ended in the west in a sort of river level archipelago, separated from the main island by the arms of the Seine. It was on one of the islets that Philip the Fair had the stake erected in 1314 for the Grand Master of the Order of Templars, Jacques de Molay, watching him burn from his palace window. The King's Garden (Jardin du Roi), extended from the islands to the Conciergerie.

It was only at the end of the 16C that Henri III decided to re-order the Cité point: the mud-filled ditches were drained, the islets joined (the Vert-Galant Square is at the old ground level), the central earth terrace of the future Pont Neuf built up and the south bank raised by some 6 m – 20 ft. By about 1580 the new terrain was ready for the builders.

Vert-Galant Square★. – Walk down the steps behind the Henri IV statue. The Vert-Galant Square – the nickname given to Henri IV, meaning gay old spark – at the extreme tip of the island, is a peaceful spot from which to enjoy a **view★★** of the Pont-Neuf, the Louvre and the Mint.

Pont-Neuf★. – *Description p. 70.*

Place Dauphine. – In 1607 Henri IV ceded the land between the palace and the Pont-Neuf for the development of a triangular square to be surrounded by a series of houses constructed of brick, white stone and slate to a uniform design. The square was named in honour of the Dauphin, the future Louis XIII. In the 18C the square was the scene, each spring, of the Exhibition of Youth, when young painters presented their works in the open air.

Only a few façades, such as the two houses opposite the Pont-Neuf and No. 14 in the square, look as they did originally. Further on, the side of the square facing the palace was razed in 1874 to make way for a monumental staircase.

Quai des Orfèvres. – The Quai des Orfèvres – literally the gold and silversmiths' quay – was the jewellers' centre of 17 and 18C Paris: Strass, inventor of the synthetic diamond, Boehmer and Bassenge who fashioned Marie-Antoinette's celebrated necklace, had their shops in the Place Dauphine and on the quay. No. **36** is today well known as the headquarters of the C.I.D. (Police Judiciaire).

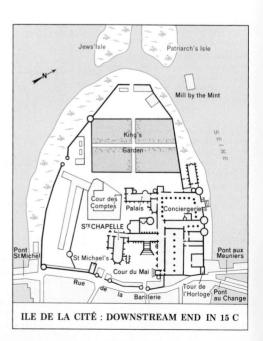

ILE DE LA CITÉ : DOWNSTREAM END IN 15 C

Boulevard du Palais. – On the Quai du Marché-Neuf nearby lived **Théophraste Renaudot,** physician to Louis XIII, Huguenot, founder of the first periodical, the *Gazette de France.*

On the Palais de Justice's wall a tablet marks the site of the former St-Michel chapel, the palatine chapel until the reign of St. Louis (13C).

Opposite the May Courtyard, the construction of the Boulevard du Palais by Haussmann did away with the gallows area.

The Commercial Law Courts (Tribunal du Commerce) stand on the site of the former St. Bartholomew's, the royal parish church from the 9C to the Revolution. Cross the vestibule to look at the dome which rises majestically to a height of 42 m – 141 ft.

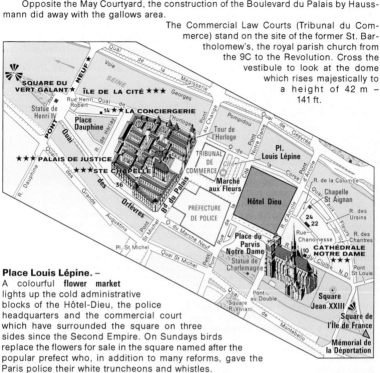

Place Louis Lépine. – A colourful **flower market** lights up the cold administrative blocks of the Hôtel-Dieu, the police headquarters and the commercial court which have surrounded the square on three sides since the Second Empire. On Sundays birds replace the flowers for sale in the square named after the popular prefect who, in addition to many reforms, gave the Paris police their white truncheons and whistles.

The Ancien Cloître Quarter★. – By the Quai aux Fleurs, from the Rue d'Arcole.

The area between the north face of Notre-Dame and the Seine was the property of the cathedral chapter. Students boarded with the canons. Although considerably restored, the quarter is the only reminder of what the Cité looked like in the 11 and 12C when students such as Abelard, St. Bonaventure and St. Dominic built up the reputation of the cathedral school which was later to merge with the Sorbonne.

In the middle of the Quai aux Fleurs, which affords a vast panorama of St-Gervais and of the tip of the Ile St-Louis, is the picturesque corner of the Rue des Ursins and Rue des Chantres on which stands a mediaeval mansion. Go down some steps to admire the Notre-Dame spire in the perspective along the Rue des Chantres.

Go down to the Rue des Ursins which is level with the old banks of the Seine, the site until the 12C, of Paris' first quay, the Port St-Landry, before the facilities on the Hôtel de Ville foreshore were established. At the end of the narrow street stand the remains of the Cité's last mediaeval chapel, St-Aignan, where priests celebrated mass secretly during the Revolution.

Turn left into the Rue de la Colombe where there is a curious tavern at the top of some steps and traces of the Lutetian Gallo-Roman wall in the pavement. Take on the left the Rue Chanoinesse, the main thoroughfare of the former cloister, now blighted by an annexe of the police headquarters. Nos **24** and **22** are the last two mediaeval canons' houses; note the 16C doorways and stone posts in the courtyard.

Ile-de-France Square. – This ancient upstream point of the island now bears, at its tip, the **Deportation Memorial**: sculpture by Desserprit, funeral urns and the tomb of the Unknown Deportee. The **view** of the cathedral from the square includes the majestic east end.

(Photo J. Bottin)

East end of Notre-Dame.

THE ILE ST-LOUIS ★★ ▥ - fold 32: K 15, K 16

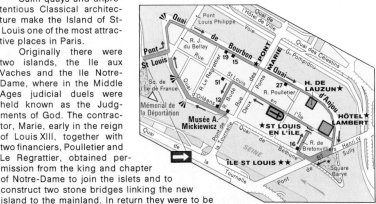

Calm quays and unpretentious Classical architecture make the Island of St-Louis one of the most attractive places in Paris.

Originally there were two islands, the Ile aux Vaches and the Ile Notre-Dame, where in the Middle Ages judicial duels were held known as the Judgments of God. The contractor, Marie, early in the reign of Louis XIII, together with two financiers, Poulletier and Le Regrattier, obtained permission from the king and chapter of Notre-Dame to join the islets and to construct two stone bridges linking the new island to the mainland. In return they were to be allowed to sell the land for building. The work began in 1627 and was completed by 1664. The Ile St-Louis, therefore, like the nearby Marais *(p 83)*, is Classical in style. But what makes the island unique is its atmosphere of old world charm and provincial calm. Writers, artists and those who love Old Paris have taken up their abode in its peaceful setting.

On the island you see a 17C house at almost every step: nobly proportioned façades, most bearing historical or anecdotal tablets, wrought iron balconies and tall brick chimneys. Behind massive panelled doors, studded with bosses and great nails, are inner courts where the stone sets and mounting blocks have not changed since the days of horse-drawn carriages.

Quais de Bourbon and Anjou. – At the end of the new St-Louis Bridge turn left and follow the Bourbon Quay round the picturesque tip of the island where chain linked stone posts, canted 18C medallions, anglers and the view of St-Gervais Church combine to make an altogether delightful **scene**★. A little further on are two magnificent mansions (Nos. **19** and **15**) which once belonged to parliamentarians – steep mansard roofs, mascaroons, spacious stairwells encircled by wrought iron balusters, indicate their former splendour.

The Anjou Quay, beyond the **Marie Bridge**★ (Pont Marie), is lined by some of the island's finest mansions. The Marquise de Lambert, hostess of a famous literary *salon*, lived at No. **27** *(Hôtel de Nevers, p 95)*.

Hôtel de Lauzun★. – *Enter through No. 17. Apply to: Chef du Protocole, Hôtel de Ville,* ☎ *42.76.54.04.*

The mansion, erected in 1657 by Le Vau for the caterer to the army, Gruyn, who was imprisoned shortly afterwards for corruption, belonged for only three years to the Duke of Lauzun, Saint-Simon's brother-in-law, who nevertheless left it his name. The poet, Théophile Gautier, lived there in the 1840's, also Baudelaire, Rilke, Sickert and Wagner. The house now belongs to the City of Paris.

In spite of the plain façade and modest size of many of the rooms, the **interior decoration**★★ which is splendid with gilded panelling, painted ceilings, tapestries, Italian style false perspective, and woodwork, makes it one of the richest private mansions of the 17C.

Hôtel Lambert or **Le Vau**★. – *No. 2 Rue St-Louis-en-l'Ile; not open.* The mansion of President Lambert de Thorigny, known as Lambert the Rich, was built in 1640 by Le Vau and decorated by Le Sueur (whose designs may be seen at the Louvre) and Le Brun.

From the Hôtel Lambert to St-Louis-en-l'Ile. – The Square Barye has been laid out at the tip of the island – last trace of the terraced gardens of the financier, Bretonvilliers.

No. **16** Quai de Béthune, previously known as the Quai des Balcons from the number of overhanging balconies, was the house of the Duke of Richelieu (great nephew of the cardinal). Turn right into the Rue de Bretonvilliers which ends beneath an arcade, part of the former mansion of the same name, then left into the Rue St-Louis-en-l'Ile, the island's main street.

St-Louis-en-l'Ile Church★. – *Open 9.30am to noon and 3 to 7pm; closed Mondays and Sunday afternoons.* The church is marked outside (No. 21) by an unusual iron clock and an original pierced spire. Building began in 1664 to plans by Le Vau, who lived on the island, but was only completed in 1726. The interior, in the Jesuit style, is ornately decorated, with woodwork, gilding and marble of the *Grand Siècle* (17C), statuettes and enamels. A plaque presented in 1926 in the north aisle bears the inscription: "In grateful memory of St. Louis in whose honor the City of Saint Louis, Missouri, USA is named".

From the Church to the St-Louis Bridge. – Continue along the Rue St-Louis-en-l'Ile to No. **51** which, in the middle of the 19C, was the archbishopric and where there is a very fine doorway surmounted by a faun mask, also a majestic balcony.

The Rue Budé, on the left, comes out onto the Orléans Quay which you follow to the right, leaving on your left the Polish Library and the small **Adam-Mickiewicz Museum** (No. 6). *Guided tours Thursdays 3 to 6pm;* ☎ *43.54.35.61.*

From the Orléans Quay there is a splendid **view**★★ of the east end of Notre-Dame and the Left Bank.

Distance: 5 km – 3 miles – Time: 3 hours. Start from the St-Michel métro station.

(Photo A. Nadeau/Explorer)

Booksellers' stalls.

As you circle the Cité and Ile St-Louis along the quays and bridges over the Seine, you will get the most magnificent **views**★★★ that Paris has to offer.

Trees shade the banks of the river which remains, even today, Paris' greatest thoroughfare; fourteen bridges span its course of a little over a mile through the capital; **booksellers' stalls** garnish the parapets and offer early editions and etchings, but bargains are rare.

Quai St-Michel. – Bookshops line the quay, broken only by two old and narrow streets, the Rues Xavier Privas and du Chat-qui-Pêche.

The **Petit Pont** (1853) stands on the site of the oldest river crossing in Paris – the Romans built a wooden bridge there as a terminal to their Orleans Road (now the Rue St-Jacques). It was first built in stone in 1185 by Bishop Maurice of Sully, architect of Notre-Dame, and was the only bridge which minstrels were allowed to cross toll free. It has been destroyed eleven times by floods and fire.

Quai de Montebello. – In the Middle Ages, wood for building and heating was floated on rafts down to Paris and was stored at the Port-aux-Bûches between the Petit Pont and the Pont au Double.

In the 17C the two hospital buildings, the Hôtel-Dieu, on the river bank and the Cité respectively, were linked by a bridge, the **Pont au Double**, so named because the toll levied by the hospital was a *double tournois* or a doubloon struck in Tours (coin minted in Tours – until the 13C – had only 75 % of the value of Parisian coin). The present bridge was built in 1885.

René-Viviani Square. – The small church close was enlarged in 1928 to its present size, care being taken to preserve the Robinia or false acacia planted in 1680, one of the two oldest acacias in Paris, and now supported with a prop. (The species was introduced from the United States by the botanist, Robin, and called after him.)

The **view**★★★ is remarkable: St-Julien itself stands out clear and white behind a curtain of trees; the street St-Julien-le-Pauvre bustles with life beneath the picturesque jumble of roofs; the Ile de la Cité; and finally, and above all, Notre-Dame seen from a three quarters angle in all its mass, its delicacy and its grandeur.

Quai de la Tournelle. – Among the old houses lining the Tournelle Quay which lies just before the Archevêché Bridge (1828) is No. 47, the Hôtel Martin (1630) and variously a private house, a community of young girls, a bayonet forge – during the Revolution – a hospital pharmacy – during the Empire – and now a **Social Service Museum** (Musée de l'Assistance Publique). *Open 10am to 5pm; closed Mondays, Tuesdays, in August and holidays; 10F; ☎ 46.33.01.43.* The museum traces the history of the hospital system from the earliest religious institutions and almshouses.

No. 15, opposite the Tournelle Bridge, is the very old Tour d'Argent restaurant where Henri IV is said to have discovered the use of a fork *(a small museum is open to restaurant patrons).*

The Tournelle Bridge was first built in wood in 1370 and has been reconstructed several times since. A statue of St. Genevieve by Landowski marks it out from its neighbours. It was at this point in the Middle Ages that a chain curtain, to stop attacks from the river, was suspended from a tower in the now vanished 14C **Tournelle Castle**, across the Seine to the Barbeau Tower *(p 91)* on the Right Bank. Splendid **view**★★★ of Notre-Dame from the bridge.

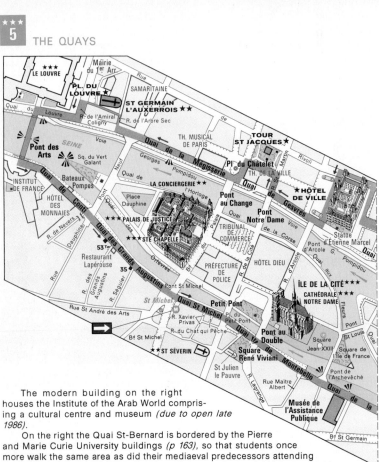

The modern building on the right houses the Institute of the Arab World comprising a cultural centre and museum *(due to open late 1986).*

On the right the Quai St-Bernard is bordered by the Pierre and Marie Curie University buildings *(p 163),* so that students once more walk the same area as did their mediaeval predecessors attending St. Victor's Abbey. The Tino Rossi gardens are the setting for an **open-air sculpture museum** (*Chronos 10* by Schöffer, *Belt II* by Kiyomizu, and *Development of Form* by Zadkine). In the 17C, before the quay was built, noblemen and even Henri IV, accompanied often by the Dauphin, used to come to the river foreshore to bathe.

Sully Bridge (Pont de Sully). – This bridge, which dates from 1876, rests on the tip of the Ile St-Louis. From the first section there is a good **view★** of Notre-Dame, the Cité and the Ile St-Louis. At the centre of the bridge, on the Ile St-Louis, is a formal garden, all that remains of the Bretonvilliers Mansion terraced gardens *(p 64).* The **view** from the bridge's second section is delightfully unspectacular – the Anjou Quay and Lambert Mansion, Célestins' Quay, Marie Bridge and St-Gervais belfry.

Henri-Galli Square. – The square at the end of Sully Bridge contains stones from the Bastille. In the Middle Ages the area between the Hôtel Fieubet *(p 90)* and the Arsenal Library was occupied by the Celestine Monastery *(p 154);* while on your right, that between the Boulevard Morland and the river bank was **Louviers Island.** It was joined to the mainland in 1843.

The Quais des Célestins and de l'Hôtel de Ville. – Walk left, along the Quai des Célestins from where there is an attractive **view★** of part of the Ile St-Louis and the Marie bridge. When level with the Square de l'Ave Maria on the right you can catch a glimpse of the Hôtel de Sens.

The **Marie Bridge★**, named after one of those who sold off land on the Ile St-Louis, marks the start of the Quai de l'Hôtel de Ville. The **International City of the Arts** (1965), to the right, provides studios and living accommodation for a year for both French and foreign artists, musicians, architects and sculptors.

In line with the Louis-Philippe Bridge on your left, which replaced a suspension bridge during the reign of Louis-Philippe, are the Pantheon and St-Etienne-du-Mont.

Take the Rue des Barres for a clear view of the east end of St-Gervais church and its original buttresses. At No. 15 is the fine balcony of a former charnel-house.

Walk down the Rue François-Miron on the left. In the **St-Gervais precincts,** note the uniform façades of the 18C houses adorned with wrought-iron balconies featuring an elm.

Church of St-Gervais-St-Protais★. – *Closed on Mondays.* The church stands on a low mound emphasized by steps leading up to the façade and from the Rue François-Miron. A basilica dedicated to the saints, Gervase and Protase, Roman officers martyred by Nero, has stood on the site since the 6C. The main part of the present building, in Flamboyant Gothic, was completed in 1657.

Exterior. – The imposing façade (1616-1621) with superimposed Doric, Ionic and Corinthian orders was the first to be built in the Classical style in Paris and is attributed to Métezeau or Salomon de Brosse. The elm in the square was, according to mediaeval custom, a place where justice was dispensed as well as a place for transactions.

Interior. – There remain the Flamboyant vaulting, 16C windows and 16C and 17C stalls. The organ built in 1601 and enlarged in the 18C is the oldest in Paris. Eight members of the Couperin family held the position of organist from 1656 to 1826.

In the north aisle, near the font, is a model of the church façade carved by du Hancy who executed the large panels in the main door. The altar front in the third chapel is a 13C low relief of the Death of the Virgin. To the left of the arm of the transept is a beautiful 16C Flemish painting of the Passion on wood and, left of the crossing, against a pillar, a Gothic stone statue of the Virgin and Child. A wooden Christ by Préault (1840) and a fine 17C wrought iron grille adorn the sacristy exterior. In the Lady Chapel there is a remarkable Flamboyant keystone, hanging 1.5 m – 5 ft below the vault and forming a circlet 2.5 m – 8 ft in diameter.

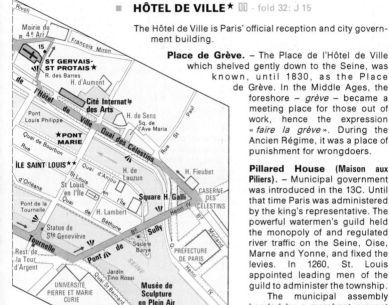

■ **HÔTEL DE VILLE ★** ⬜⬜ - fold 32: J 15

The Hôtel de Ville is Paris' official reception and city government building.

Place de Grève. – The Place de l'Hôtel de Ville which shelved gently down to the Seine, was known, until 1830, as the Place de Grève. In the Middle Ages, the foreshore – *grève* – became a meeting place for those out of work, hence the expression « *faire la grève* ». During the Ancien Régime, it was a place of punishment for wrongdoers.

Pillared House (Maison aux Piliers). – Municipal government was introduced in the 13C. Until that time Paris was administered by the king's representative. The powerful watermen's guild held the monopoly of and regulated river traffic on the Seine, Oise, Marne and Yonne, and fixed the levies. In 1260, St. Louis appointed leading men of the guild to administer the township.

The municipal assembly headed by a merchant provost and four aldermen elected by the notables, who nominated the town councillors, moved from the Place du Châtelet to the Pillared House on the Place de Grève in 1357, at the instigation of Etienne Marcel.

Etienne Marcel. – This rich draper who was a merchant provost, became leader of the States General in 1357 and came out in open revolt against royal power *(p 58)*. He held Paris, attempted to make the whole of France rise up in arms, made an alliance with the peasants in revolt, let the English into the city. But Charles V who had taken refuge in the Hôtel St-Paul *(p 83)* was victorious and Marcel died miserably at the hands of the Parisians in 1358 as he opened the gates of the city to Charles the Bad.

The Hôtel de Ville. – Under François I, the Pillared House fell into ruin. The king, intent on building a large town hall, had plans drawn up by Il Boccadoro, and the first stone was laid in 1533. The building was completed, however, early in the 17C. The middle part of the present façade is a copy of the original.

Until the Revolution the municipal authority was weak, the king making his own appointments, although those selected had to be citizens of Paris.

July 1789. – After the fall of the Bastille, the rioters took over the town hall. On 17 July 1789 Louis XVI appeared in the hall to kiss the newly adopted tricolour cockade. Red and blue had been the city colours since the provostship of Etienne Marcel in the 14C. La Fayette introduced the royal white.

The Commune. – Throughout the Revolution the hall was in the hands of the Commune. The popular insurrection of 10 August 1792 directed by Danton, Robespierre and Marat forced the king to flee the Tuileries Palace and take refuge with the Legislative Assembly. The Montagnard faction, or deputies of the extreme left, was an offshoot of the Commune and dominated the National Convention (1793-4).

The 9 Thermidor (27 July 1794) the National Convention tired of Robespierre's tyrannical behaviour, had him taken to the Luxembourg prison. Released by the Commune he was given refuge in the town hall where he was injured in the jaw by a pistol shot. Robespierre was guillotined the next day (10 Thermidor).

In 1848 when Louis-Philippe was dismissed, it was in the Hôtel de Ville that the provisional government was set up and from there that the Second Republic was proclaimed on 24 February 1848.

The Second Empire and Commune of 1871. – Napoleon proclaimed himself emperor in 1851 and it was at this time that Baron Haussmann, as Prefect of the Seine, undertook the work of replanning the area around the Hôtel de Ville. He razed the adjoining streets, enlarged the square and built the two barracks in Rue de Lobau.

On 4 September 1870, after the defeat of Sedan, Gambetta, Jules Favre and Jules Ferry proclaimed the Third Republic from the Hôtel de Ville and instituted a National Defence Government. The capitulation of Paris on 28 January 1871, however, roused the citizens and in their anger they removed the government, installing in its place the Paris Commune of 1871. In May during its final overthrow, the Hôtel de Ville, the Tuileries and several other buildings were set on fire by the Federalists.

TOUR

Guided tours of the State Rooms, Mondays 10.30am. Visitors should go to the Bureau d'Accueil, 29 rue de Rivoli (☎ 42.76.40.40.) where temporary exhibitions are held.

The Hôtel de Ville was entirely rebuilt between 1874 and 1882 in the Neo-Renaissance style by Ballu and Deperthes, complete with 146 statues of the illustrious and of French towns to adorn the building's facades.

Inside, the sumptuous main staircase by Ballu and Deperthes, leads to a state hall and reception rooms. Ornate **decoration**★, part Renaissance, part *Belle Époque,* reveals the official style in the early years of the Third Republic. Amid the caryatids and rostra, coffered ceilings and chandeliers are panels by Laurens and mural paintings by Puvis de Chavannes. Note the unusual architecture of the triple chambers of the Arcade Room (Salon des Arcades).

The Place de l'Hôtel de Ville adorned with a fountain on either side, is paved in granite with the boat motif, the coat of arms of the 13C watermen's guild *(p 17),* at the centre.

Quai de Gesvres. – As you walk along this quay which begins at the Arcole Bridge (rebuilt 1888) with its bird and grain merchants, you can gaze at Haussmann's monumental creations – the Hôtel-Dieu, Police headquarters, commercial courts, and Law Courts. In line with the Rue St-Martin on the right, the St-Jacques Tower rises majestically.

The **Notre-Dame Bridge** (Pont Notre-Dame – 1913) was the Great Bridge in Roman times, as opposed to the Small Bridge (Petit Pont) on the far side of the island. Burnt down by the Normans and rebuilt on piles in 1413, it was the first to be given an official name, and the houses built on it were the first to be numbered in Paris. It fell down in Louis XII's reign, but was rebuilt and lined with identical houses with richly decorated façades, since it was on the royal route of solemn entries into Paris. One of the houses belonged to the art collector Gersaint who befriended Watteau. The gallery figures in Watteau's famous picture *L'Enseigne de Gersaint* which now hangs in the Charlottenburg Museum in Berlin.

St-Jacques Tower★ (Tour St-Jacques). – The tower is the former belfry of the church of St-Jacques-la-Boucherie, built in the 16C and one of the starting points for pilgrims making the journey to Santiago de Compostela in Spain. The church was pulled down in 1802. A weather point has been installed at the top of the 52 m – 171 ft tower. When the Rue de Rivoli was constructed the tower had to be consolidated as the mound on which it stood previously was razed.

The statue of the physicist and philosopher, Pascal, recalls his experiments into the weight of air carried out on this spot in 1648.

Place du Châtelet. – The square gets its name from the Grand Châtelet or Great Barbican which commanded the Pont au Change. It was lined with the halls of powerful guilds. The Châtelet or Palm Fountain (1808) commemorates Napoleon's victories; the base was decorated with sphinxes in 1858. The two theatres on either side were built by Davioud in 1862. The Châtelet, after extensive renovation, is now the Théâtre Musical de Paris and has the largest auditorium in Paris after the Palais des Congrès *(p 165).* Opposite, the Théâtre de la Ville, formerly the Sarah Bernhardt Theatre, is a centre of popular culture.

The Quai de la Mégisserie. – The **Pont au Change** or Money Changers' Bridge in front of the Châtelet Square, established in the 9C by Charles the Bald, was closely occupied all through the Middle Ages by jewellers and money-changers. It was to this bridge that all foreigners and visitors to Paris had to come to change their money. The present bridge dates from the Second Empire.

Walk along the Mégisserie Quay, so called because until the Revolution, the quayside was the public slaughterhouse (*mégisserie:* tawing). Now there are pet shops and seed merchants. An attractive **view**★★ extends over the Law Courts, Conciergerie, and the old houses along the Horloge Quay and Pont-Neuf.

At the end of the Pont-Neuf stands the Samaritaine department store – from the terrace of Samaritaine shop no. 2 there is an excellent **view**★★ over the whole of Paris.

■ ST-GERMAIN-L'AUXERROIS★★ ▦ - fold 31: H 14

The present church, on the site of an 8C sanctuary demolished by the Northmen and a later one built by Robert the Pious, combines five centuries of architectural design with a Romanesque belfry, radiant Gothic chancel, Flamboyant porch and nave and Renaissance doorway. The tympanum and pier and the magnificent roodscreen by Lescot and Jean Goujon were removed in the 18C to allow the passage of processions.

When the Valois moved into the Louvre in the 14C, St-Germain became the royal parish church and the receptacle for gifts and decoration.

It was from this tower that the bells rang on the night of 24 August 1572 giving the signal for the Massacre of St. Bartholomew when thousands of Huguenots, invited to celebrate the marriage of Henri of Navarre to his cousin, Marguerite of Valois, were slaughtered in accordance with a plan laid by the Cardinal Duke of Guise, Catherine dei Medici, Charles IX and the future Henri III.

During the Revolution, it became a barn; in 1831 it was further desecrated. Finally, however, it was restored (1838-1855) by Baltard and Lassus, which explains its composite style.

Many poets: Jodelle, Malherbe; painters: Coypel, Boucher, Nattier, Chardin, Van Loo; sculptors: Coysevox, the two Coustous; architects: Le Vau, Robert de Cotte, Gabriel the Elder, Soufflot and others associated with the court, are buried in the church.

Since 1926, because of a wish by the painter and drawer Adolphe Willette (1857-1926) artists come to St. Germain on the first Sunday in Lent to receive ashes and to pray for those artists who will die in the year.

Exterior. – From the Samaritaine pavement you will get a good view of the east end and Romanesque belfry which abuts on the transept.

The chancel aisles are covered by a series of small attic-like structures in which the bones taken from tombs in the cloisters, which at one time surrounded the church, were heaped. The apsidal chapel given by the Tronson family is decorated with a frieze of carp.

The Porch. – The porch, which is the building's most original feature, was built between 1435 and 1439. The statues at the pillars are modern. The outer bays which are also the lowest, are surmounted by small chambers, covered with slate, in which the chapter placed the church archives and treasure.

The three central bays have multi-ribbed Flamboyant vaulting, while the other two are plain Gothic. The centre doorway, the most interesting, is 13C. The figure in the right embrasure is St. Genevieve with a candle which a small devil is trying to snuff out and an angel *(next niche)* stands ready to relight.

Interior. – The nave is flanked by double aisles which continue round the chancel to the flat apse. The restored 17C organ (1) comes from the Sainte-Chapelle *(p 60)*. The **churchwarden's pew** (2), dating from 1684, is thought to have been used by successive kings and their families. At its back is a 15C polychrome carved wood triptych (3 *– light switch*) and, in the chapel opposite, a fine early 16C, Flemish **altarpiece** (4 *– light switch*).

The **stained glass** in the transept, and the two rose windows are late 15C. The much comparti-mented vaulting above the transept is a good example of the Flamboyant style.

The chancel is surrounded by an 18C grille before which stand 15C polychrome statues of St. Germanus (5) and St. Vincent (6). In the 18C, when the roodscreen was removed (the low reliefs are in the Louvre), the columns were fluted and their Gothic capitals transformed into gar-landed torri.

The Chapel of the Holy Sacrament contains a 14C polychrome stone statue of the Virgin (7); a 14C Crucifixion (8); one of the original statues from the main doorway, St. Mary the Egyptian (9); a Last Supper (10) by Theo Van Elsen (1954) and a 13C statue of St Germanus (11).

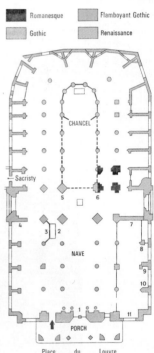

Romanesque / Flamboyant Gothic / Gothic / Renaissance

CHANCEL

Sacristy

NAVE

PORCH

Place du Louvre

Place du Louvre★. – The square was the site on which the Roman, Labienus, pitched his camp when he crushed the Parisii in 52 BC, and the Northmen when they besieged Paris in 855 *(p 54)*. Until the Second Empire, between the Louvre and St. Germain-l'Auxerrois church stood fine mansions including the Petit Bourbon (demol-ished 1660) where the States General met in 1614, Molière performed his plays in 1658 and the young Louis XIV danced before the court.

In 1854 Haussmann transformed the narrow Rue des Poulies into the wide Rue du Louvre (this part is now Rue de l'Amiral-de-Coligny), demolishing in the process the last of the 17C houses. These were replaced by a Neo-Renaissance building by Hittorff and a Neo-Gothic belfry by Ballu with a 38 bell carillon *(Wednesdays, 5 to 5.30pm, April to September; 1 to 1.30pm, October to March)*

The Pont des Arts. – The "academic" bridge faces the Institut de France *(p 140)*. In 1803 the bridge was novel on two counts: it was the first to be built of iron and it was for pedestrians only – there were chairs to sit on and glasshouses with rare plants to shelter in, in case of rain. It was a toll bridge and on the day it was opened 65 000 Parisians paid to walk upon it.

The **view★★★** is outstanding encompassing the Pont-Neuf and the Vert Galant Square *(p 62)*. Behind the Square are the Law Courts, the Sainte-Chapelle spire and the towers of Notre-Dame; visible beyond are the top of the St-Jacques Tower, the Hôtel de Ville and the St-Gervais belfry; downstream the Louvre, the Grand Palais and the Carrousel Bridge.

Quai de Conti. – The quay is overlooked by the impressive buildings of the Institute of France *(p 140)* and The Mint *(p 139)*. In 1906, the scientist Pierre Curie, was run over by a horse-drawn carriage and killed near the Pont-Neuf.

Avoid visiting a church during a service.

Pont-Neuf★. – The Pont-Neuf is the oldest of the Paris bridges. The two halves begun in 1578 to the designs of Androuet Du Cerceau and completed in 1604 are not strictly in line. The twelve rounded arches are decorated with humourous grotesques, the half circles resting on each pile with carvings of open-air shops, tooth drawers at work, comic characters such as Tabarin and the Italian Pantaloon and a host of gapers and pickpockets. The Pont-Neuf's other attributes included the view down river – the first unencumbered by houses and other buildings – and the first pavements in Paris to be properly separated from the hurtling traffic in the roadway. A pump beneath an arch, which drew water from the river to supply the Louvre until 1813 and was decorated with a figure of the woman of Samaria giving Jesus water at the well, became known as the Samaritain – a name later adopted by a department store nearby *(p 68)*.

Suddenly it was decided to place the first statue to be erected on a public highway in France on the bridge. The figure chosen was an equestrian bronze of Henri IV. This was melted down by the Revolution in 1792 but replaced at the Restoration by the present figure, cast in bronze from the Vendôme Column's first statue and another from the Place des Victoires, by a Bonapartist who is said to have included in the monument a copy of Voltaire's epic poem *La Henriade* (on the League and Henri IV), a statuette of Napoleon and various written articles glorifying the Emperor!

The bridge has been restored many times but the basic construction remains unchanged. Its most recent transformation was in the autumn of 1985 when Christo wrapped the bridge.

Quai des Grands-Augustins. – This quay is the oldest in Paris. It was built in 1313 by Philip the Fair and in 1670 was named after the Great Augustine Monastery *(p 139)* which stood on the site extending from the Rue Dauphine to the Rue des Grands-Augustins. Its fine Gothic chapel was razed to make way for a game and poultry market. In 1869 the premises were then taken over by the Omnibus Company to serve as a depot with its headquarters at No 53 bis. The building is now the head office of the Paris Transport Authority which has a tourist office at No 53 ter.

Further on are two 17C mansions: No. 51 at the corner of the Rue des Grands-Augustins, now the famous Lapérouse Restaurant, and No. 35 at the corner of Rue Séguier.

The Place St-Michel, which dates from the reign of Napoleon III, was the scene of student fighting against the Germans in August 1944. The fountain is by Davioud. The Pont St-Michel built in the 14C was remodelled at the same period as the square.

(Photo Christiane Olivier, Nice)

The quays and the Pont-Neuf.

THE INVALIDES

Michelin plan 🔢 - fold 29: from H 10 to K 10.

Distance 2.5 km – 2 miles – Time: 4 to 5 hours (including visits to the museums). Start from the Invalides métro station.

This is the most outstanding single monumental group in Paris which attracts large numbers of visitors.

The adjacent Army Museum, is rich and spectacular.

Barracks for 4 000 men. – Before Louis XIV's reign, old soldiers, invalided out of the service, were, in theory, looked after in convent hospitals. In fact most were reduced to beggary.

In 1670 the Sun King founded the Invalides on the edge of what was then the Grenelle Plain. Funds were raised in part by a levy on acting soldiers' pay over a period of five years. Construction of the vast edifice capable of providing quarters for 4 000 men began in 1671 to plans by Libéral Bruand and was completed only five years later. A dome, added to the original undertaking by Jules Hardouin-Mansart, lifted the project out of the utilitarian into the monumentally inspired.

Pillage. – On the morning of 14 July 1789 rebels advanced on the Invalides in search of arms. They crossed the moat, disarmed the sentries and entered the underground rifle stores. As further crowds blocked the stairs fierce fighting broke out in the half darkness. The mob finally made off with 28 000 rifles towards the Bastille.

Napoleon's return. – The major event in the history of the Invalides was the return of Napoleon's body in 1840. After seven years of negotiation with the British Government, the French King, Louis-Philippe, was able to dispatch his son, the Prince of Joinville, to St. Helena in the frigate, *The Belle Poule (model in the Maritime Museum; p 50)* to collect the Emperor's remains. On the prince's arrival on 8 October, the coffin was exhumed and opened for two minutes during which it was seen that the body of the Emperor who had been dead nineteen years, had remained in a state of perfect preservation; those present, including the generals Gourgaud and Bertrand, the 19C historian Las Cases and Napoleon's valet, Marchand, viewed the Emperor once more in his guardsman's uniform.

The coffin, after its long sea voyage, was disembarked at Le Havre and brought up the Seine to Paris where it was landed at Courbevoie. The funeral was held on 15 December 1840. A snowstorm enveloped the city as the hearse passed beneath the Arc de Triomphe, down the Champs-Élysées and across the Concorde Square to the Esplanade.

The coffin lay under the cupola and in St. Jerome's Chapel until the tomb, designed by Visconti, was completed. The transferring took place on 3 April 1861.

The institution's revival. – After the two world wars the institution is used as originally intended: to provide shelter and care for the war wounded in modernised hospital facilities. The buildings today are occupied by the military services and the Army Museum.

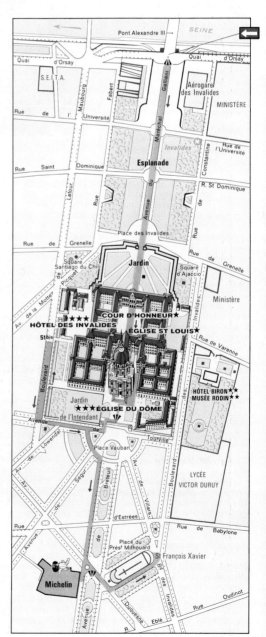

■ **THE INVALIDES**★★★ **(HÔTEL DES INVALIDES)** ▯▯ - fold 29: J 10

From the Alexandre III Bridge, there is a superb **overall view** of Libéral Bruand's Classical style buildings and Mansart's crowning gold dome.

Esplanade. – The Esplanade, designed and constructed between 1704 and 1720 by Robert de Cotte, Mansart's brother-in-law, affords a spectacular vista 500 m long and more than 250 m wide, ending of course in the Classically balanced Invalides buildings.

The wide expanses of green lawns are bordered by avenues of limes. On the left beside the quay is the air terminal, Aérogare de Paris.

Garden. – Preceding the Invalides are a garden, bordered by a wide dry moat, ramparts lined by 17 and 18C bronze cannon and an 18 piece triumphal battery used to fire salutes on such occasions as the 1918 Armistice and 14 July 1919 Victory March.

The battery, removed by the Germans in 1940 and returned in 1946, now stands disposed on either side of the entrance.

Façade★★. – The façade is majestic, in style and line, in proportion and size – it is 196 m long – 645 ft. At the centre is a magnificent doorway, flanked at

The Invalides.

either end by pavilions. Decoration appears in the form of trophies surrounding the dormer windows and in the equestrian statue of Louis XIV supported by Prudence and Justice in the rounded arch above the entrance.

The first statue by Guillaume Coustou (1735), damaged during the Revolution, was replaced by the present figure by Cartelier in 1815.

Restoration work on the **lateral walls**★ has uncovered noble buildings on the right side, along the Boulevard des Invalides and on the left, alongside the Boulevard de Latour-Maubourg, the fine proportions of Robert de Cotte's Order of Liberation Chancellery and the original trench.

Main courtyard★ **(Cour d'honneur).** – Go through the entrance to the main courtyard, lined on all sides by two superimposed arcades.

Four central pavilions with carved pediments break the even architectural lines as do the sculptured horses, trampling the attributes of war, at the corner angles of the roof. The dormer windows are decorated, like those on the façade, with trophies. The fifth window to the right of the east central pavilion *(left on entering)* has a peculiar history: Louvois had been in charge of the construction of the Invalides and a mason thought up the idea of encircling a window with the paws of a wolf, making a play on the intendant's name and surveillance; *loup voit* – the wolf sees all.

The end pavilion, which is the most ornate, serves as the façade to St. Louis' Church. At the centre is the Seurre statue of Napoleon, known as the Little Corporal, which stood for some years at the top of the column in the Place Vendôme.

In the Classical courtyard with its perfect proportions, its steeply pitched slate roofs and cobbled paving, there is an impressive series of cannon lined up along the walls: note the "Catherina" (1487) bearing the name of Sigismund of Austria, the "Württemberg culverin" (16C) with its chiselled breech and its barrel entwined by a snake.

Church of St-Louis-des-Invalides★. – *Closes 5.45pm in summer and 4.45pm in winter.*

The church, also known as the Soldiers' Church, was designed by Libéral Bruand and built by Mansart who later added the dome to the group, and is cold and functional. The only decoration derives from the captured enemy banners overhanging the upper galleries. A window behind the high altar enables one to see through to the baldachin in the Dome Church.

The organ, enclosed in a loft designed by Hardouin-Mansart, is a magnificent 17C instrument on which Berlioz's *Requiem* was played for the first time in 1837.

The banners were more numerous at the end of the Empire but when the Allies entered Paris in March 1814, the Invalides governor burnt 1417 of them in the courtyard; the history of each is commemorated on the church pillars.

In the crypt *(not open)* lie former governors of the Invalides and 19 and 20C marshals and generals of the field, including Joffre, Leclerc, Giraud and Juin.

Conserved in an urn is the heart of Mademoiselle de Sombreuil, daughter of the Governor of 1789. During the massacres of September 1792, her filial love moved the murderers to spare her father.

■ THE ARMY MUSEUM★★★ (MUSÉE DE L'ARMÉE) ▯▯ - fold 29 : J 10

Open 10am to 6pm, 1 April to 30 September (5pm the rest of the year). Closed 1 January, 1 May, 1 November and 25 December. Ground floor, east: films shown on the two World Wars; 16F (ticket also valid, two consecutive days, for the Dome Church and films shown). ☎ 45.55.92.30, extn. 33.936.

The galleries of one of the world's richest army museums lie on either side of the main courtyard.

Ground floor. – The number and diversity of **arms** and **armour** attractively displayed, enable one to follow the evolution of military defence and attack. *West side.* The fine armour for hand-to-hand combat *(Gallery Henri IV)*, the splendid royal chased harnesses *(Gallery Louis XIII)*, the Renaissance swords, daggers and rapiers, two 16C helmets *(Pauilhac Gallery)*. *East side.* Note also the banners dating from 1619 to 1945 including Napoleon's flag of

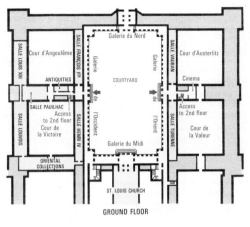

GROUND FLOOR

farewell flown at Fontainebleau as he signed his abdication in 1814 *(Turenne Gallery –* one of the four former refectories decorated with frescoes of 17C battles) are of particular interest.

There are also remarkable collections of arms and armour from China, Japan, India and Turkey (helmets, turbans, daggers).

2nd floor. – *East side.* These rooms are devoted to **military history** from the Ancienne Monarchie (1618-1792) to the 2nd Republic. Among the countless souvenirs of French military history are the cannon-ball which killed Turenne (1675), *(Louis XIV Gallery)*, mementoes of Napoleon: his coat, hat, sword and medals *(Boulogne Gallery)*, charming souvenirs of the King of Rome *(Montmirail Gallery)*. The room in which Napoleon died on St Helena is also movingly reconstructed in the Restauration Gallery.

West Side. In the room devoted to the First World War (1914-1918) the three stages of the war are outlined. Note Marshal Foch's military map and the 1918 Armistice bugle.

In the gallery reserved for the Second World War (1939-1945) are exhibited mementoes, documents and photographs relating to the military aspect (model of the invasion) as well as to civilian life, deportation and resistance.

3rd floor. – *East side.* The Pelissier Gallery is devoted to the early part of the Second Empire (1852-1860): the Imperial Guard, Crimean (photographs) and Italian campaigns.

The Chanzy gallery deals with the end of the Second Empire (overseas expeditions) and the 1870-1871 Franco-Prussian war.

The models displayed in these two galleries help to trace the evolution of regimental uniforms, equipment and arms. The cooks' costumes are unusual.

■ THE DOME CHURCH★★★ (ÉGLISE DU DÔME) ▯▯ - fold 29: J 10

From the front courtyard you have a **general view** of the Dome Church. On the left, behind Mansart's original trench, the Intendant's Garden has been replanted.

It is one of the major masterpieces of the age of Louis XIV. In this building Hardouin-Mansart perfected the French Classical style which had first appeared in the Carmelite Church, St-Joseph des Carmes, and been developed in St-Paul-St-Louis *(p 83)*, the Sorbonne *(p 111)* and the Val-de-Grâce *(p 130)*. To complete the Baroque effect, the original plan envisaged the creation before the south face, of a colonnaded esplanade in the manner of Bernini before St-Peter's. Instead, to afford a good vista, a wide avenue was cut through the then open countryside, the Avenue de Breteuil.

The Dome arose when Louis XIV commissioned Hardouin-Mansart to build a church to complement the Invalides buildings of Libéral Bruand and to epitomise the splendour of his reign. In 1677 therefore, work began on the Dome Church, oriented towards the north and joined to the Soldier's Church by a common sanctuary. It was completed by Robert de Cotte in 1735. The Dome Church stands, finally, as the greatest example of the French 17C or *Grand Siècle* religious architecture, just as Versailles does of the civil architecture of the same period.

In 1793 the Revolution transformed the two churches, which were still united, into a Temple to Mars. It was also decided to transfer to them the captured enemy standards previously hung in Notre-Dame. With Napoleon's interment of Turenne in the church in 1800, it became a military mausoleum, receiving also countless trophies from the imperial campaigns. It was guarded by the old soldiers, known as the *grognards* or grumblers, billeted in the Invalides barracks.

In 1842, two years after the return of Napoleon's body *(p 71)*, Visconti enlarged the central altar, replaced the original baldachin and had the crypt dug to receive the coffin. The big window was constructed only in 1873. These alterations disturbed the inner balance, but the grandeur remains.

Façade. – The façade consists, in the usual Jesuit style, of a projecting central section flanked by outer wings. All are the same height, thus avoiding heavy connecting areas.

Between the Doric columns at ground level are statues of St. Louis by Nicolas Coustou and Charlemagne by Coysevox; above a projecting entablature are Corinthian columns, statues of the four Virtues and a pediment carved by Coysevox.

The dome. – Hardouin-Mansart's masterpiece captures the imagination both by its sweeping lines and its dignity; it has a beauty all its own whether standing out against a clear summer sky or rising, almost invisibly, a deeper shadow, against the darkness of the night. The design was based on a prodigious knowledge of balance and proportion which enabled it to rise in a single thrust without buttressing. Forty columns separate the windows round the drum; the cupola base, pierced by round arched windows, is ornamented with consoles while above, divided into twelve sections, rises the massive gilded dome, decorated with trophies, garlands and other ornament. Windows in the form of helmets provide air and light inside. Crowning all are an elegant lantern and a spire which rises 107 m – 351 ft – into the sky.

The dome's covering of lead sheeting, attached by copper nails to the wood frame was gilded for the first time in 1715 and has been restored several times since.

Interior. – *Same times as for the Army Museum (p 73) but closed at 7pm in June, July and August.* The decoration is sumptuous: painted cupolas, walls adorned with columns and pilasters and low reliefs by the greatest contemporary artists and inlaid marble pavements.

1) Tomb of Joseph Bonaparte, elder brother of Napoleon, King of Spain.
2) Monument to Vauban by Etex. The Emperor himself commanded that the military architect's heart be brought to the Invalides.
3) Foch's tomb by Landowski.
4) Ornate high altar surrounded by twisted columns and covered by a baldachin by Visconti. Vaulting decoration by Coypel.
5) General Duroc's tomb.
6) General Bertrand's tomb.
7) At the back – the heart of La Tour d'Auvergne, first grenadier of the Republic; in the centre, the tomb of Marshal Lyautey.
8) Turenne's tomb by Tuby.
9) St. Jerome's Chapel (carvings by Nicolas Coustou). The tomb at the foot of the wall is Jerome Bonaparte's, younger brother of Napoleon, King of Westphalia.
10) The Emperor's tomb.

CHURCH OF ST. LOUIS DES INVALIDES

Crypt entrance

Crypt

The Cupola. – Painted on the pendentives are the four Evangelists by Charles de la Fosse and then, in ascending order, the Kings of France (in medallions) and the Twelve Apostles by Jouvenet. On the cupola itself a vast composition by La Fosse of St. Louis presenting Christ with the sword with which he conquered the infidels.

Napoleon's tomb★★★. – The majesty of the setting perfectly befits the Emperor's image. Visconti designed a circular crypt in which to stand the red porphyry sarcophagus upon a base of green granite from the Vosges. It was completed in 1861.

The Emperor's body is placed in six coffins, each contained inside the other: the innermost is of tin sheeted iron; the second of mahogany; the third and fourth of lead; the fifth of ebony; the last of oak.

The crypt. – At the base of the stairs, behind the baldachin, two massive bronze statues stand guard at the crypt entrance, one bearing an orb, the other the imperial sceptre and crown. Low reliefs around the gallery depict institutions founded by the Emperor.

The sarcophagus stands at the centre of the inlaid marble pavement, designed as a star while, against the pillars circling the crypt, are twelve colossal statues by Pradier symbolizing Napoleon's campaigns from the Italian victories of 1797 to Waterloo in 1815.

In the *cella*, before a statue of the Emperor in his coronation robes, lies the King of Rome. He died in Vienna in 1832 and remained in the crypt of the Habsburgs before being transferred to Paris on 15 December 1940 exactly one century after his father, and finally entombed in 1969.

■ **MUSEUM OF THE ORDER OF LIBERATION**★★ ▥ - fold 29: J 10

Pavillon Robert-de-Cotte, 51 bis, Boulevard de Latour-Maubourg. Open 2 to 5pm; closed Sundays, in August and holidays; 8F; ☏ 47.05.35.15.

The Order of Liberation, created by General de Gaulle at Brazzaville in 1940, honoured as "companions", those who made an outstanding contribution to the final victory. The list, which was closed in 1946 consists of service personnel and civilians, a few overseas leaders including King George VI, Winston Churchill and General Eisenhower, and several French localities (Paris, Nantes, Grenoble, Vassieux-en-Vercors, Ile de Sein). The memory is also perpetuated of French heroes and major operations of the Resistance (ground floor). On the first floor, there is a section devoted to deportation.

From the Invalides to St. Francis Xavier

Walk from the Place Vauban along the Avenue de Breteuil to No. 46.

The Michelin Tourist Services. – In France in 1900 there were 3 000 vehicles on the road – phenomena which threw country folk into a panic. Car owners bought petrol at the local grocer and it was for these car owners and drivers that André Michelin, brother of Édouard who manufactured tyres, compiled a little red book: the Guide FRANCE. This, with its selection of hotels and restaurants and pages of practical information, has grown in size and fame until it is now known to seasoned travellers the world over complete with its star award system for restaurants.

The young André Michelin next created in Paris, in 1908, a Car Travellers' Information Bureau which provided enquirers with itineraries and road information. He went on to supply the local authorities with name plates for towns and villages, to undertake, in 1910, the mapping of France to a scale of 1 :200 000 – 1 inch: 3 miles – the numbering of all roads (1913) and the production, from locally quarried pumicestone near Clermont-Ferrand, of large square milestones covered in distinctive vitreous enamel. After the 1914-1918 War, guides were published to the Battlefields and in 1926, the Regional Guide Brittany, the first tourist guide in the series now known as the Michelin Green Tourist Guides.

Michelin, formerly located at No. 97 Boulevard Pereire with nearly three quarters of a century of experience, and still at work producing and improving maps and guides for the motorist and the tourist, is to be found at No. 46 Avenue de Breteuil.

The façade of the building is adorned with a series of ceramic panels which evoke the part played by Michelin in the first great cycle and motor races. The large tiled panel to the right *le coup de la semelle,* demonstrates their concern for the quality and performance of the tyres.

Retrace your steps along the Avenue de Breteuil for a good view of the Invalides Dome. St. Francis Xavier Church, on the right is a late 19C Romanesque pastiche.

(Photo J. Feuillie/© C.N.M.H.S./S.P.A.D.E.M. 1983)

Napoleon's Tomb.

Paris was not built in a day...

Unlike Rome and New York but like London, no one knows when Paris was founded. Julius Caesar sighted Lutetia in 53 BC and made the first written reference to the town in his Commentaries.

In 1951 Paris officially celebrated its second millenium.

Michelin plan ⑪ - folds 6, 7 and 19: from C 12 to D14.

Distance: 5 km – 3 miles – Time: 4 hours. Start from the Blanche métro station.

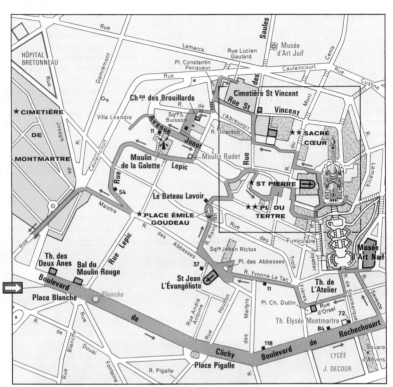

The "Butte", as it is known locally, is the part of Paris most full of contrasts – anonymous boulevards run close to delightful village streets and courts, steep stone steps lead to open terraces, Sacré-Cœur pilgrims tread the streets beside nightclub revellers.

Martyrs' Mound. – Although it is known that the name Montmartre derives from the Mound of Mercury, a local legend dating from the 8C prefers ascription to the local martyrs, St. Denis or Dionysius, first Bishop of Paris, the priest, Rusticus, and the deacon, Eleutherius. These are said, in about 250 AD, to have been first tortured on the grill in the Cité and then decapitated, whereupon Denis picked up his blood covered head and walked north to the place now known as St-Denis *(p 182)*.

A powerful abbey. – The Rue des Abbesses perpetuates the memory of the forty-three mother superiors of the Benedictine convent established on the hill in the 12C and used by the King of Navarre, the future Henri IV as his headquarters four centuries later when he laid siege to Paris in 1589. He failed to take the city before his next campaign, his only conquest it is said, being that of the 17 year old abbess, Claude de Beauvilliers.

In the reign of Louis XIV the ruined "upper" convent and its chapel, St. Peter's, at the top of the hill, were abandoned in favour of the "lower" convent on the hillside below. 1794 saw the name of the hill changed, provisionally, to Mont-Marat, the last abbess guillotined and the convent buildings razed.

Shortly afterwards the gypsum quarries, whose miles of underground galleries threatened to undermine the hill, were abandoned and the thirty old flint and grain mills were also closed.

The early days of the Commune. – In 1871, after the fall of Paris, the people of Montmartre collected 171 cannon on the hill to prevent their capture by the Prussians. Forces sent by the government seized the cannon on 18 March but were unable to remove them, the generals being taken prisoner and shot by the crowd – a bloody episode which was to mark the beginning of the Commune. Montmartre remained under Federal control until 23 May.

Bohemian Life. – Throughout the 19C artists and men of letters were drawn to the free and easy, picturesque way of life as lived on the Butte. Berlioz, the writers and poets, Nerval, Murger and Heine, were the precursors of the great generation of 1871-1914; young painters sought inspiration on the Place Pigalle, artists' models and seamstresses led a free, Bohemian existence. The early poets' circles transformed themselves into café groups from which flowed songs (Aristide Bruant), poems, humour, drawings (Caran d'Ache, André Gill, Toulouse-Lautrec). Everyone went to the newly opened Moulin-Rouge (1889) to applaud the singers, clowns and dancers – Yvette Guilbert, Valentin le Désossé, Jane Avril, La Goulue.

The Butte, thanks to the Lapin Agile café and Bateau-Lavoir studios, remained, until 1914, the capital's literary and artistic centre, then inspiration moved to Montparnasse *(p 127)* and Montmartre abandoned itself to night life.

From the Place Blanche to the Place du Tertre

Boulevard de Clichy. – Walk along the Boulevard de Clichy, laid along the line of the Farmers General wall. Restaurants, cinemas, theatres and nightclubs of every type make the boulevard a centre of the Paris night life. On the left, the **Deux-Anes Theatre** at No. 100 maintains the Parisian cabaret tradition.

Further along, the **Place Blanche**, which owes its name to the quarries beneath the hill, is dominated by the sails of the famous **Moulin Rouge**, the French music-hall, which was the cult of Paris at the time of the *Belle-Époque* and which has been immortalized in the drawings of Toulouse-Lautrec.

The next square, the **Place Pigalle** and the adjoining streets were at the end of the 19C, lined with artists' studios and literary cafés, of which the most famous was the Nouvelle Athènes. Today the quarter is as brilliantly lit and populous as ever.

Boulevard de Rochechouart. – Places of entertainment continue: at No. **118** the former Belle-en-Cuisses cabaret. It was at No. **84**, that Rodolphe Salis opened the Chat-Noir cabaret night-club made famous in a song by Aristide Bruant:

Je cherche fortune   *Au clair de la lune*
Autour du Chat Noir   *A Montmartre le soir.*

Belle Époque façade (No. **72**) on the former Élysée-Montmartre music-hall.

The Abbesses' Quarter. – Walk left up Rue Seveste. The former St-Pierre Hall on the right houses the **Max Fourny Museum of Naive Art** *(open 10am to 6pm; 15F; ☎ 42.58.72.89).*

Turn left into Rue Steinkerque then right into Rue Orsel to reach the quiet little Place Charles-Dullin. On the square is the small **Atelier Theatre** (Théâtre de l'Atelier) which grew to fame between the wars.

Bear left from the Rue des Trois-Frères into the Rue Yvonne-Le-Tac where, at No. **11**, stands a chapel *(open weekends 2.30-5pm)* on the site of a mediaeval sanctuary marking the **Martyrium**, the place where St. Denis and his companions are presumed to have been decapitated. It was in the former crypt that on 15 August 1534 Ignatius Loyola, Francis Xavier and their six companions made apostolic vows in the service of the Church from which was born the Society of Jesus. Six years later the order was recognized by Pope Paul III.

Continue to the Place des Abbesses. On the right is Jehan-Rictus Square, on the site of the former town hall of Montmartre. Opposite is the **Church of St. John the Evangelist** (St-Jean l'Évangéliste) designed by Baudot and the first to be built of reinforced concrete. The building is still interesting in the bold use made of its structural material, the slenderness of its pillars and beams, particularly as it was completed as long ago as 1904. The church's rose facing has earned it the local nickname of the Brick St. John.

To the right of the west face steps lead up to the Rue André Antoine. At the bottom of the steps, at No. **37**, a modest hall, which has been pulled down, saw the amateur beginnings of the Antoine Theatre.

The Bateau-Lavoir. – This world renowned artistic and literary Mecca, which disappeared in a fire in 1970 – preceded, in the evolution of art, the no less outstanding Ruche of Montparnasse *(p 127)*. Now rebuilt as artist studios and apartments and located at No. 13 in the delightful **Place Émile-Goudeau** ★ this small wooden building saw the birth in 1900 of modern painting and modern French poetry. It was here that Picasso, Van Dongen, Braque, and Juan Gris, created cubism – with Picasso's famous *Demoiselles d'Avignon* – and Max Jacob, Apollinaire and Mac Orlan broke away from traditional poetic form and expression.

A few old streets★. – The Rue Ravignan ends at the Place J.-B. Clément (at the end of the street, on the left is a former water tower) which you cross to take the Rue Norvins on the right. The **crossroads**★ formed by the meeting of the Rue Norvins, the Rue des Saules and the Rue St-Rustique will be known to many visitors from Utrillo's paintings. Even today it is typical of the old Montmartre.

The Bonne-Franquette nightclub was very famous around 1890. The narrow and often deserted Rue Ste-Rustique marks the highest point of the Butte and of Paris (129.37 m – 427 ft). Nearby, in the Rue Poulbot on the right, is the **Historial,** or waxworks museum where fourteen dioramas pinpoint the greatest events in Montmartre's history *(guided tours, weekend of Palm Sunday to 31 October, 10.30am to 12 noon and 2.30 to 5.30pm; the rest of the year, Wednesdays, Saturdays, Sundays school and public holidays, same times; 15F; ☎ 46.06.78.92).*

The Place du Calvaire commands an exceptional view of Paris.

(Photo H. Veiller/Explorer)

Rue Foyatier.

Place du Tertre★★. – This longstanding meeting place has an almost village atmosphere at times, particularly in the morning. At other times, however, it is transformed into the tourist centre of Montmartre as crowds wander under the flaring lights, pause before the restaurants, glance at the paintings of unknown artists.

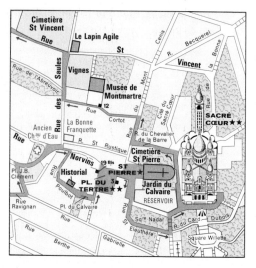

No. 19 bis is the house of the Free Commune founded in 1920 by Jules Dépauit to keep alive the imaginative and humorous traditions of the Butte. No. 3, once the local town hall, is now Poulbot House to commemorate local children, popularized in the artist's delightful line drawings.

■ **ST. PETER'S CHURCH★** 🕮 - fold 7: C 14, D 14

The church, the Église St-Pierre, only remaining building of the great Abbey of Montmartre and, with St-Germain-des-Prés and St-Martin-des-Champs, one of the oldest churches in the capital, was begun on the site of an earlier Merovingian church in 1134 and completed before the end of the century. The nave vaulting was reconstructed in the 15C; the banal west façade in the 18C. The three bronze west doors are the work of the Italian sculptor, Gismondi (1980).

Interior. – Four marble columns with capitals said to have come from a Roman temple which crowned the mound, have been placed in pairs, against the inside of the façade in line with the columns of the nave, and in the chancel, where the oldest ogive arches in Paris (1147), their torri very roughly hewn, meet above the single bay. In the north aisle is the tombstone of Queen Adélaïde of Savoy, wife of Louis VI the Big, who spent her last days in the abbey which she had founded in 1133.

The Romanesque style capitals are worn originals or replacements. The apse and aisles are lit by modern stained glass designed by Max Ingrand (1953). The four sides of the high altar are adorned with enamelled plaques depicting the Butte Montmartre with its vineyard and mills by Froidevaux (1977). The Way of the Cross is also by Gismondi.

Calvary Garden (Jardin du Calvaire). – *Not open.* The garden is on the site of the old Benedictine abbey. In 1794 the Convention used the church apse as a suitable site for the new invention by the engineer, Chappe, of a telegraph station linking Paris and Lille.

St. Peter's Cemetery (Cimetière St-Pierre). – *Open only 1 November.* North of the church lies the very old and minute church cemetery, in which are the tombs of the explorer, Bougainville (only his heart is interred here), the brothers Debray, original owners of the Moulin de la Galette and Montmartre's first Mayor, Félix Desportes. The bronze door by Gismondi features the Resurrection.

Bear left round the vast Montmartre reservoir towards the Sacré-Cœur terrace. This overlooks the Square Willette laid out in 1929 and approached by steps and slopes and also a funicular. The square commands a magnificent **view★★** of Paris *(viewing table).*

Note how the simple grace of St. Peter's belfry contrasts sharply with the rounded mass of the Sacré-Cœur.

■ **THE SACRÉ-CŒUR BASILICA★★** 🕮 - fold 7: C 14, D 14

After the disastrous Franco-Prussian War of 1870, some Catholics vowed to raise money by public subscription to erect a church to the Sacred Heart on Montmartre hill. The proposal was declared a state undertaking by the National Assembly in 1873.

Abadie, who had become known for his restoration of St. Frontius' Church in Périgueux, recalled the old church's design as he drew Romano-Byzantine plans for the new basilica. It was begun in 1876 (Abadie died in 1884 when only the foundations had been laid), completed only in 1910 and consecrated in 1919; it cost 40 million francs. For over a century worship has continued, without interruption, within its walls.

The Edifice. – The tall white outline is very much a part of the Paris skyline. The Basilica's many cupolas are dominated by the dome and 80 m – 262 ft high campanile.

The interior of this pilgrim church is decorated with mosaics. On the chancel vaulting Luc-Olivier Merson has evoked France's devotion to the Sacred Heart. The stained glass windows, shattered during 1944, have now been replaced.

Ascent of the dome *(access through the north aisle, 9am to 6pm 1 April to 30 September; 9.30am to 12.30pm and 1.30 to 5pm the rest of the year, 6F)* affords a bird's-eye view of the interior and, from the gallery outside on a clear day, a **panorama★★★** extending over 50 km – 30 miles.

The crypt *(in season same access and times; 10F)* contains the treasure and presents an audio-visual history of the basilica.

In the belfry hangs the Savoyarde, cast in 1895 at Annecy, given by the Savoy dioceses and, at 19 tons, one of the world's heaviest bells.

From the Sacré-Cœur to Montmartre Cemetery

Walk along the Rue Chevalier-de-la-Barre and turn right into Rue du Mont-Cenis.

Round the vineyard. – No. 12 in the Rue Cortot had as tenants over the years Renoir, Othon Friesz, Utter, Dufy, Suzanne Valadon and her son, Utrillo. It is the entrance to the **Montmartre Museum** (Musée de Montmartre) *(open 2.30 to 5.30pm weekdays; 11am to 5.30pm Sundays; closed 1 January, 1 May and 25 December; 12F; ☎ 46.06.61.11)* which is rich in mementoes of Bohemian life in the quarter with its nightclubs and artists, and of Clemenceau, one time local mayor, and the composer Charpentier. It features interesting temporary exhibitions. The house itself was the country residence of the actor Rosimond (d 1686).

Walk round the famous Montmartre vineyard where at the beginning of October, the grape harvest is always a great festive event.

The **crossroads★** where the Rue des Saules meets the Rue St-Vincent is one of the most delightful corners of the Butte: small steps leading away mysteriously, the road rising steeply beside the cemetery, a leafy vista of the Sacré-Cœur, all add to the rustic charm which is further enhanced by the famous **Lapin Agile,** half-hidden by an acacia. This former Cabaret des Assassins, rechristened when André Gill painted it a new sign, was, between 1900 and 1914, the haunt of writers and artists. Among those who began the tradition of literary evenings continued to this day *(every evening, except Mondays, at 9pm)* were Francis Carco, Roland Dorgelès, Pierre Mac Orlan, Picasso, Vlaminck...

Continue down the Rue St-Vincent on the left, immortalized by Bruant. On the far side of the Place Constantin-Pecqueur you will find the Rue Lucien-Gaulard and on the far right, the modest **St-Vincent cemetery** where the artist Steinlen, the musician Honegger, the painter Utrillo, the writer Marcel Aymé and many others lie buried.

Château des Brouillards. – Walk up the steps from the Place Constantin-Pecqueur. On the left is the Rue de l'Abreuvoir, named after the water trough once used by the cattle which grazed the mound. Turn right into the shaded alley skirting the **Château des Brouillards,** an 18C folly, later a dance hall. Its grounds have become the Square Suzanne-Buisson. The statue of St-Denis stands on the spot where he is said to have washed his decapitated head.

Avenue Junot. – Opened in 1910, this wide peaceful thoroughfare gave onto the Montmartre maquis, an open space of ill repute where mills still turned their sails to the wind. Amidst the artists' studios and private houses are at No. 11 the Hameau des Artistes, and at No. 25 the Villa Léandre. Walk back until level with No. 10. From here there is a view of the windmill.

Moulin de la Galette. – The former dance hall, the Moulin de la Galette, which was the rage at the turn of the century, inspired many painters including Renoir, Van Gogh, Willette... The windmill which has topped the hill for more than six centuries, is the old Blute-fin defended against the Cossacks in 1814 by the heroic mill-owner Debray whose corpse was finally crucified upon the sails. Close by stands the 1736 Paris north bearing *(plan p 132)*. The Radet mill *(p 96)* stands at the corner of Rue Lepic.

Walk down the steeply winding **Rue Lepic,** the old quarry road, and the scene each autumn of a veteran car rally. Van Gogh lived with his brother at No. 54.

Take the Rue Joseph-de-Maistre, then turn right into the Rue Caulaincourt; on the left a steel bridge spans the Montmartre Cemetery (1795).

Montmartre Cemetery★
(Cimetière de Montmartre). – Access by the stairs on the left.

1) Lucien and Sacha Guitry (playwrights and actors).
2) The Cavaignac family (statue by Rude).
3) Emile Zola (novelist).
4) Hector Berlioz (composer).
5) Greuze (painter).
6) Heinrich Heine (poet and writer).
7) Th. Gautier (poet and critic).
8) Alexandre Dumas the Younger (novelist).
9) Ernest Renan and Ary Scheffer (philosopher; painter).
10) Henri Murger (writer – *p 127*).
11) Edgar Degas (Impressionist painter – *p 42*).
12) Leo Delibes (composer).
13) Poulbot (cartoonist).
14) J. Offenbach (composer).
15) Edmond and Jules de Goncourt (novelists).
16) Charcot (explorer).
17) Stendhal (H. Beyle) (novelist).
18) Alfred de Vigny (poet, dramatist).
19) Louis Jouvet (actor).
20) Alphonsine Plessis, the Lady of the Camelias (*p 80*).
21) François Truffaut (film producer).

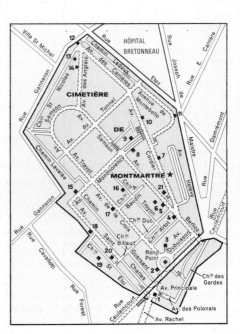

Distance: 2.5 km – 2 miles – Time: 1 1/2 hours. Start from the Madeleine métro station.

The Opera quarter boasts some of the most elegant streets in Paris. In the evening the pavements are thronged with lively crowds attracted by the numerous theatres.

From the Madeleine to the Opera

Boulevard de la Madeleine. – Immediately on your right as you start to walk towards the Opera from the Place de la Madeleine *(p 92)* stands the Trois Quartiers store. No. **11** is where Alphonsine Plessis died. She was celebrated in *The Lady of the Camelias* by Alexandre Dumas the Younger and in Verdi's *Traviata*.

Boulevard des Capucines. – It was named after a Capuchin monastery which stood between the Place Vendôme and the boulevard.

In the Rue des Capucines there is a fine house at No. **19** which is now occupied by a bank. The writer Stendhal collapsed and died on the pavement opposite in 1842.

The boulevard was the scene of the call to arms, barricades and street fighting throughout the night of 23 February 1848 which was followed by the abdication of Louis-Philippe.

On the left, the Olympia music-hall at No. 28 is a popular venue for entertainers and at No. **14** a tablet commemorates the first public showing of 16 m – 52 ft films by the Lumière brothers on 28 December 1895.

Cognacq-Jay Museum★★. – *Open 10am to 5.40pm; closed Mondays and holidays; 9F, free on Sundays.* ☏ *42.61.94.54.*

This collection of 18C European art was donated to the city of Paris. The splendid Louis XV and Louis XVI panelled rooms contain outstanding oils and pastels by Boucher, Fragonard, Latour, Perronneau, Greuze, Tiepolo and Reynolds, drawings (Watteau), furniture signed by the greatest 18C cabinet-makers, porcelain and precious ornaments. The harmony and taste of the collection give a wonderful impression of gallant and sophisticated life in the Age of Enlightenment.

Place de l'Opéra. – Haussmann did not see the Opera Square simply as a setting for the National Music Academy but as a circus from which a number of roads should radiate and constructed his boulevards accordingly. Public opinion, at the time, was divided as to whether the square was not altogether too vast; today it barely copes with the milling traffic.

The square is lined with luxury shops which invite window shoppers to gaze at the elegant displays of leather goods, gifts (Lancel) and jewellery (Clerc) while the Café de la Paix terraces provide an international meeting place. Behind the Opera are the popular Printemps and Galeries Lafayette stores.

■ THE OPERA★★

⊞ - fold 18: F 12

The celebrity of France's first home of opera, the prestige of its opera and ballet companies, the architectural magnificence of the great staircase and foyer, the sumptuous decoration of the auditorium, invite the tourist to treat himself to an enjoyable evening.

Construction. – The site of Garnier's Opera House was determined by Haussmann's town planning project. In 1820 the idea developed of building a new opera house, forty years later a competition was held to find an architect. Charles Garnier, a 35-year old architect, winner of the Rome prize in 1848 but otherwise unknown, was chosen from

(Photo J. Bottin)

The Opera Staircase.

the 171 contestants. Within a year Garnier had solved the problem raised by an underground spring and building started but subsequently the work was interrupted for several years and the opera was opened, at last, in 1875.

Garnier dreamed of creating a Napoleon III style of architecture, but the opera house created no new school, having insufficient originality. It is nevertheless remarkable and, in its way, is the most successful monument of the Second Empire.

It is also the largest theatre in the world with a total area of 11 000 m² – 118 404 sq ft and a vast stage for up to 450 artists. But the offices and exits are so extensive that the auditorium seats only 2 200. The central chandelier weighs over six tonnes.

Tradition and Revival. – Although glittering performances of classical opera and ballet remain the main attraction modern music and dance now figure frequently in the programme of the Opera. The Salle Garnier has undergone extensive technical modernisation. The company performs on other Parisian stages (Palais des Sports, Palais des Congrès) and in the summer season in the Cour Carrée at the Louvre. Its choir enjoys an international reputation. The permanent company numbers about 1 100 members.

Exterior. – The main façade overlooks the Place de l'Opéra. At the top of a flight of steps and preceding the arcades to the theatre are statues by various sculptors, including a Paul Belmondo copy of Carpeaux' **Dance** (the original which was showing signs of wear from the elements is now in the Louvre – *p 35*).

A majestic balcony fronts the foyer. Above are the dome over the auditorium and a triangular pediment marking the stagefront. Go round the building starting from the right. The projecting wing was originally for subscribers who could drive in their carriages into the courtyard lit by lamp-posts decorated with statues of women by Cartier-Belleuse. The so-called Emperor's Pavilion, on the Rue Scribe, had a double ramp to enable the sovereign to ride straight to the royal box in his carriage.

The pavilion is now occupied by the **Opera Library** and **Museum** *(open 10am to 5pm; closed Sundays and holidays and the Easter fortnight; 6F)*. The museum contains busts, reduced scale models of decors and mementoes of famous artists. In the library are all the scores for the works performed by the company since 1669, relevant documents and 80 000 books and etchings.

Interior. – The **Great Staircase** is visible from the main entrance hall *(access by the main door, open 11am to 4.30pm; closed 14 July to 15 August 12F)*. The **main foyer** and the **auditorium** which can be visited when rehearsals are not in progress, are remarkable and at their best on state occasions. Original features are the incorporation by Garnier of marble of every hue – white, blue, rose, red and green – from all the quarries of France, and a false ceiling inspired by opera and ballet, painted by Chagall in 1964.

From the Opera to the Place Vendôme

The **Rue de la Paix,** laid in 1806 over the site of a Capuchin monastery, was originally known as the Rue Napoléon. Napoleon, on his column, can be seen with his back towards it. The beautiful jewellers' shops, Cartier (No. **11**) among others, which line the street have made its name a synonym for elegance and luxury throughout the world.

■ THE PLACE VENDÔME★★ ⊞ - fold 30: G 12

The Place Vendôme is a superb display of the majesty of French 17C architecture.

In about 1680, Louvois, Superintendent of Buildings, conceived the idea of building upon the land to the north of the Rue St-Honoré, a square which would serve as a setting for a monumental statue of Louis XIV and be surrounded by suitable buildings housing academies, the National Library, the Mint and the Residence for Ambassadors Extraordinary. It would be even grander than the Place des Victoires *(p 125)*. In 1685, the Duke of Vendôme's mansion and the neighbouring Capuchin convent were purchased.

Hardouin-Mansart was commissioned to design the square which was originally known as the Place des Conquêtes but soon renamed Place de Vendôme or Louis-le-Grand. In 1699 the equestrian statue of the king by Girardon was unveiled.

But the square was just a beautiful façade for only gradually were the lots at the back taken up. The first building was completed in 1702, the last in 1720. The royal statue was destroyed during the Revolution and the square temporarily renamed Place des Piques. In 1810 Napoleon placed the Austerlitz column at its centre.

The Square. – Arcades at ground level, pilasters rising two floors above and finally steeply pitched roofs with dormer windows, surround the square. The pedimented façades of the principal buildings and of those standing obliquely at each of the square's four corners add variety.

As you walk round the square (224 × 213 m – 245 × 233 yds) by the right, every house evokes a memory or a name: No. **19** is the former Hôtel d'Evreux (1710); No. **15** is now the Ritz Hotel; Nos. 13 and 11, now the Ministry of Justice, were formerly the Royal Chancellery – the official measure for the metre was inlaid in the façade in 1848; No. **9** was the house of the military governor of Paris at the end of the 19C. Chopin died at No. **12** in 1849; No. **16** was the home of the German, Dr. Mesmer, founder of the theory of mesmerism.

The square with its surrounding area is the place for great names among jewellers and bankers: Van Cleef & Arpels, Boucheron, Chaumet, Rothschild...

The Column. – The column's stone core, 44 m – 132 ft high, is entwined in a spiral made from the bronze from 1 200 cannon captured at the Battle of Austerlitz (1805) and decorated with military scenes similar to Trajan's column in Rome.

The first statue to be placed at the top of the column was of Napoleon as Caesar; he was replaced by Henri IV, who was removed for the 100 Days. Louis XVIII hoisted a colossal fleur-de-lys; Louis-Philippe re-established Napoleon, this time in military uniform. Napoleon III substituted a copy of the original statue. The Commune tore down the column in 1871; the Third Republic re-erected it and placed upon it a replica of the original statue.

From the Place Vendôme to the Place de la Concorde

The windows of the Rue St-Honoré between the Rue de Castiglione and the Rue Royale are a window-shopper's paradise. The street's repute goes back many years, even centuries: before the Revolution, the court, the nobility, financiers, all came to shop. At No. **374** Mme Geoffrin established a salon which was frequented by all the great names of Louis XV's reign. In the Rue Cambon, is the house from which Coco Chanel reigned over the fashion world for half a century.

The **Church of Notre-Dame de l'Assomption,** now the Polish Church, was formerly the chapel of the Convent of the Sisters of the Assumption on the Place Maurice-Barrès. This round 17C building is capped by a disproportionately large dome. Inside are respectively at the altar and to its right, an Annunciation by Vien (18C) and an Adoration of the Magi by Van Loo, and on the dome a 17C fresco of the Assumption by Charles de la Fosse. Abutting on the church are the modern buildings of the Cour des Comptes (Auditor General's Office, 1912).

No. **398** is the site of the house in which Robespierre lived until the eve of his execution on 9 Thermidor.

Turn left into the Rue St-Florentin towards the Place de la Concorde *(p 43)*.

(Photo Christiane Olivier, Nice)

Place de la Concorde.

THE MARAIS

Michelin plan □□ - folds 32 and 33: H 16, H 17 — J 16, J 17.

Visitors should tour the area on a weekday when it is possible to gain access to the buildings. Distance 3 km – 2 miles – Time: one day. Start from the St-Paul métro station.

(Photo Y. Arthus-Bertrand/Explorer)

Place des Vosges.

A tour of the Marais quarter which has undergone careful restoration is a very rewarding experience. A Drama and Music Festival is held in June and July every year.

Historical Notes. – It was in the 13C that the swamp lying on either side of the raised Rue St-Antoine, a highway since Roman times, was cleared.

Philippe Auguste's wall and the Charles V wall ending in the powerful Bastille fortress in the east, brought the Marais within the city bounds – an event confirmed by the flight of Charles V and Charles VII from the royal palace to the **Hôtel St-Paul.**

By the beginning of the 17C the then Place Royale, now Place des Vosges, built by Henri IV, had become the focal point of the Marais. The Jesuits had settled along the Rue St-Antoine, the nobility and courtiers had built splendid mansions decorated by the best contemporary artists. It was at this time that the *Hôtel,* a discreet Classical building, standing between entrance court and garden, developed as a distinctive feature in French architecture. Women of the world attracted free-thinkers and philosophers through their *salons* – the brilliant conversational groups who frequented their houses.

Then, gradually the nobility began to move west. After the taking of the Bastille, the quarter was virtually abandoned.

From the Church of St-Paul-St-Louis to the Hôtel Carnavalet

From the 14C the **Rue St-Antoine** was unusually wide and became the local meeting place and the setting for all popular celebrations. It was here that in 1559 **Henri II** received a fatal blow to his eye in a tourney with his Scots captain of the guard, Montgomery. The king died in the Hôtel des Tournelles. Montgomery fled but was executed in 1574.

■ CHURCH OF ST-PAUL-ST-LOUIS ★ □□ - fold 32: J 16

In 1627, on land donated by Louis XIII, the Jesuits adding to the monastery founded in 1580, built a new church (completed in 1641) dedicated to St. Louis. The Jesuits were expelled in 1763 and the monastery reverted to secular use. After the old St-Paul church was razed, the edifice in the Rue St-Antoine became known as the Church of St-Paul-St-Louis (1796).

Façade. – The tall classically ordered façade with superimposed columns hides the dome, the great novelty of the Jesuit style.

Interior. – *Closed 1 and 8 May, Easter and Whit Mondays and 14 July.* It has a single aisle and no inter-communicating chapels, cradle vaulting and a cupola with a lantern above the transept crossing. Tall Corinthian pillars line the walls.

This well-lit, spacious church with its ornate decoration and sculptures, was attended by an elegant congregation drawn by musical excellence and eloquent preaching. The rich furnishings were lost at the Revolution. The twin stoups at the entrance were given by Victor Hugo who lived in Place des Vosges. In the transept three 17C paintings illustrate the life of St. Louis. A fourth has disappeared and has been replaced by a painting of Christ on the Mount of Olives by Delacroix (1826). In the chapel to the left of the high altar there is a Mater Dolorosa in marble by Germain Pilon (1586).

In the courtyard of No. **101** *(left of the church),* the former Jesuit convent and now the Lycée Charlemagne, is a fine **stairwell** crowned by a dome in *trompe-l'œil* depicting the Apotheosis of St. Louis *(apply to the caretaker except on Saturday afternoons, Sundays and holidays).*

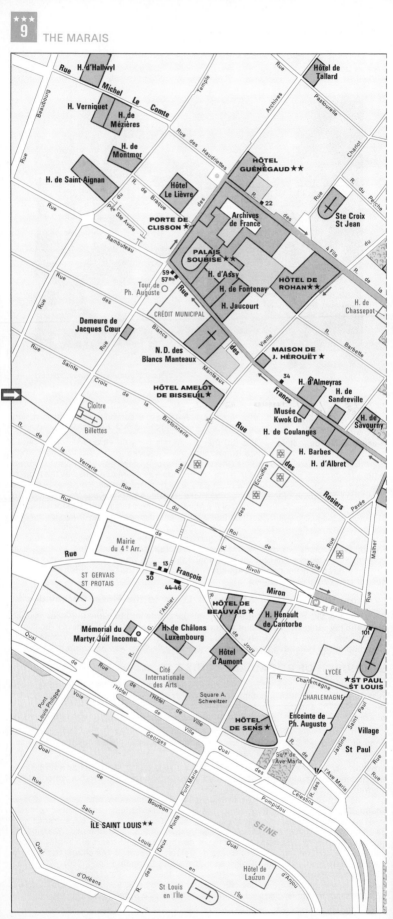

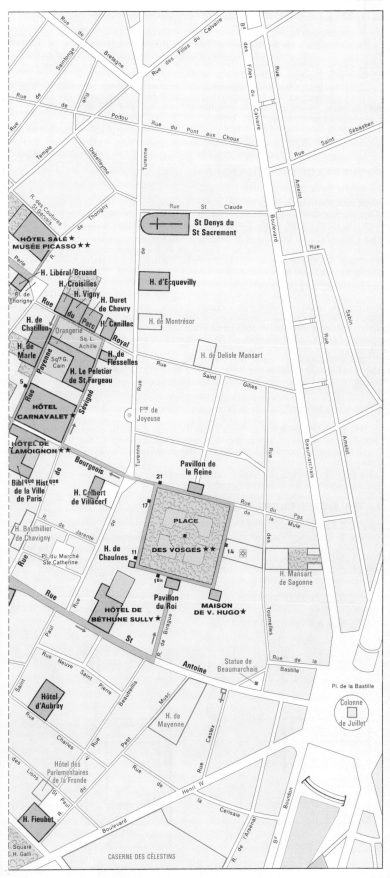

■ **HÔTEL DE BÉTHUNE-SULLY★** *(62, Rue St-Antoine)* 🔲 - fold 33: J 17

The house was built in 1624 by Jean Androuet Du Cerceau and bought ten years later by the ageing Sully, former minister of Henri IV. The Ancient Monuments and Historic Buildings Commission (la Caisse Nationale des Monuments Historiques et des Sites) occupies part of the building *(information centre: open Mondays to Fridays 9am to 12.30pm and 2 to 6pm, 5pm Fridays. ☎ 48.87.24.14).*

The main gate, between massive pavilions, has been restored and opens once more into the inner **courtyard★★**, an outstanding Louis XIII architectural group with an ordered decoration of carved pediments and dormer windows and figures representing the Elements and the Seasons.

Inside *(guided tours Saturdays and Sundays at 3pm; time: 1 1/2 hours: 25F)* are fine 17C painted ceilings and panelling.

Turn left into Rue de Birague (formerly Rue Royale) leading to the Place des Vosges.

■ **THE PLACE DES VOSGES★★** 🔲 - fold 33: J 17

This is Paris' oldest square.

Hôtel des Tournelles. – The house, acquired by the crown in 1407 on the assassination of the Duke of Orléans *(p 89)* was the residence of Charles VII where Louis XII ended his days and Henri II died *(p 83)*. Catherine dei Medici had it pulled down.

Place Royale. – In 1605, Henri IV determined to transform the Marais into a splendid quarter with a vast square at its centre in which all the houses would be "built to a like symmetry". On its completion in 1612, the Royal Square became the centre of elegance, courtly parades and festivities. At the Revolution the square lost its central statue of Louis XIII (replaced in 1818) and was named Place de l'Indivisibilité.

From 1800 it took the name of Place des Vosges after the Vosges department.

The square today. – The 36 houses retain their original symmetrical appearance with arcades, two storeys with alternate stone and brick facings and steeply pitched slate roofs pierced by dormer windows, and with courts and hidden gardens. The soberly decorated **King's Pavilion** (Pavillon du Roi) on the south side and the largest house in the square, is balanced by the Queen's Pavilion (Pavillon de la Reine) to the north.

No. 9, the **Hôtel de Chaulnes** is the Academy of Architecture *(not open)*. The ceilings from the Hôtel de La Rivière (No. **14**) by Lebrun are in the Carnavalet Museum *(p 87)*. Also of interest: No. **1 bis** where Madame de Sevigné was born; No. **17** where Bossuet lived; No. **21** where Richelieu lived (1615-1627) and No. 6 Victor Hugo's residence.

Victor Hugo House★ (**Maison de Victor Hugo**). – *Open 10am to 5.40pm; closed Mondays and holidays; 7F, free on Sundays; ☎ 42.72.16.65.*

The former Hôtel de Rohan-Guéménée (1605) was the home of the poet from 1833 to 1845. On the first floor drawings by Hugo himself recall his many voyages. The second floor and onetime home of the poet contains a collection of family mementoes and documents.

Leave the Place des Vosges by the Rue des Francs-Bourgeois, cross the Rue de Turenne and turn right into the Rue de Sévigné.

■ **THE HÔTEL CARNAVALET★** 🔲 - folds 32 and 33: J 16, J 17
Entrance: 23 Rue de Sevigné.

The Renaissance mansion (1544) was given its present appearance by Mansart in 1655. Marie de Rabutin, the Marquise de Sevigné, who wrote the famous *Letters* which, with a light touch and quick wit give a lucid picture of day to day events, lived in the house from 1677 to 1696. The buildings surrounding the three garden courts are 19C.

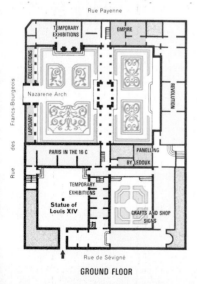

GROUND FLOOR

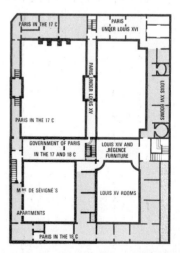

FIRST FLOOR

Stages in construction : ▬▬▬ The Mansion during the Ancien Régime ▬▬▬ Additions

Exterior. – Jean Goujon carved the lions at the main entrance which is 16C, and the keystone cornucopia. The supporting globe was later recarved into a carnival mask in allusion to the mansion's name. The **statue ★** of Louis XIV in the courtyard by Coysevox was originally at the Hôtel de Ville. The building at the end is Gothic; only the four statues of the Seasons are Renaissance. The large figures on the wings are 17C; the cherubs with torches decorating the end of the left wing are again by Jean Goujon. The Nazarene arch in the Rue des Francs-Bourgeois is 16C.

Museum★★. – *Open 10am to 5.40pm; closed Mondays and holidays; 15F, free on Sundays,* ☏ *42.72.21.13. Temporary exhibitions are held several times a year.*

In addition to mementoes of Mme de Sevigné, the museum is devoted to the history of Paris from François I to the *Belle Époque* (early 20C): unique documents, relief maps, views of Paris, souvenirs of the Revolution, shop and inn signs.

Several rooms have been reconstructed with panelling from other mansions and Louis XIV, Regency, Louis XV and Louis XVI furniture. In the main stairwell leading up to the first floor are paintings in *trompe-l'œil* by Brunetti from the Hôtel de Luynes in the Boulevard St. Germain.

From the Hôtel Carnavalet to the Hôtel Salé

Rue de Sevigné. – No. 29 is the **Hôtel Le-Peletier-de-Saint-Fargeau,** now part of the museum, named after its owner who was responsible for Louis XVI's death sentence. No. 52, the much restored **Hôtel de Flesselles,** bears the name of Paris' last provost.

Rue du Parc-Royal. – The 17C mansions lining the street opposite Léopold-Achille Square, form a remarkable architectural group notwithstanding remodelling: **Canillac** (No. 4), **Duret-de-Chevry** (No. 8, extensively restored), **Vigny** (No. 10, a National Documentation Centre) and **Croisilles** (No. 12, *restoration work in progress*) which is to house the library and archives of France's historic buildings commission.

Rue Payenne. – The Square Georges-Cain lined by the orangery and façade of the Hôtel St-Fargeau, is a stone garden. The **Hôtel de Chatillon** (No. 13) has a paved courtyard and an interesting staircase. The neighbouring **Hôtel de Marle** or **de Polastron-Polignac** (No. 11) has a fine mask above the entrance and a keel-shaped roof attributed to Philibert Delorme. The mansion which once belonged to the Countess of Polignac the governess of Marie-Antoinette's children is now a Swedish Cultural Centre. It was at No. **5** that Mansart died. The old gateway has been uncovered during restoration.

Cross the Rue des Francs-Bourgeois.

Hôtel de Lamoignon★★. – The Hôtel d'Angoulême, built around 1585 for Diane, the legitimized daughter of Henri II, was bought in 1658 by Lamoignon, president of the first parliament to sit in Paris. There he entertained Racine, Mme de Sevigné, the Jesuit preacher, Bourdaloue, and the poet and critic, Boileau. Another member of the Lamoignon family who was born here was the jurist and royal administrator, Malesherbes, who conducted Louis XVI's defence before the Convention.

An unusual square turret overlooks the street. On the far side of the courtyard the majestic building is divided by six Corinthian pilasters which rise unbroken to the cornice – the first example in Paris of the Colossal Order. Two rudimentary wings are crowned with curved pediments adorned with attributes of the chase and crescent moons (allusions to the goddess Diana).

Historical Library of the City of Paris (Bibliothèque Historique de la Ville de Paris). – *Open 9.30am to 6pm; closed Sundays, holidays and 1 to 15 August,* ☏ *42.74.44.44.*

Founded in 1763 the library is rich in French Revolution documents and has precious collections of books, journals, manuscripts, maps, posters, photographs and cuttings...

The **reading room** is beautiful with its painted ceiling.

Walk back and turn left in the Rue des Francs-Bourgeois.

Rue des Francs-Bourgeois. – This old street was originally known as Rue des Poulies after the pulleys *(poulies)* on the looms of the local weavers' shops. It took its present name in 1334 when almshouses were built in it for the poor who were known as "the men who pay no tax" or *francs bourgeois.*

Hôtel d'Albret. – Nos. 29 bis and 31. The house built in the 16C for the Duke of Montmorency, Constable of France, was remodelled in the 17C. It was in this house that the widow of the playwright Scarron, the future Marquise de Maintenon, became acquainted with Mme de Montespan. Appointed in 1669 governess to the latter's children by Louis XIV, she later became the king's mistress. The façade was interestingly reordered in the 18C. Following restoration the mansion will house the city's Cultural Affairs Department.

The **Hôtel Barbes** (No. 33, *go into the courtyard*) was built around 1634. The **Hôtel de Coulanges** (Nos. 35-37), now Europe House, is 18C. The **Hôtel de Sandreville** (No. 26) opposite, dates from 1586.

At No. 30, the brick and stone façade of the **Hôtel d'Almeyras** is hidden behind a gateway featuring curious rams' heads. No. 41 houses the **Kwok On Museum** *(p 91).*

No. 34, the former Hôtel Poussepin, now serves as the Swiss Cultural Centre.

On the corner of the Rue Vieille-du-Temple, at No. 54 stands the **House of Jean Hérouët ★**, treasurer to Louis XII. Built around 1510, it still has its mullioned windows and an elegant corbelled turret. Nearby, stood in the 15C the **Hôtel Barbette,** the discreet residence of Queen Isabella of Bavaria who began the fashion for masked balls, while the King, Charles VI, was living at the Hôtel St-Paul.

Opposite the Crédit Municipal Bank, a former pawnbroker's, are the Hôtels **de Jaucourt** (No. 54), **de Fontenay** (No. 56), **d'Assy** (No. 58), annexes to the French Archives.

Behind the gateway of No. **57 bis** rises one of the towers of Philippe Auguste's 800 year-old perimeter wall. At No. **59,** against the wall is a fragment of the façade of a 1638 Hôtel.

■ SOUBISE PALACE★★ (PALAIS SOUBISE) *(60, Rue des Francs-Bourgeois)*
- fold 32: H 16

In about 1375 the Constable of France, Olivier de Clisson, companion in arms of Du Guesclin, began to build a manorhouse on the site of the present buildings. Only the **gateway**★ remains, flanked by a pair of corbelled turrets *(58 Rue des Archives)*.

In 1553 the manor passed to the Guise family who made it their headquarters during the Wars of Religion. The massacre of St. Bartholomew (1572) was planned here.

In 1700 Madame de Soubise, the wife of François de Rohan, Prince of Soubise, acquired the house thanks to generous gifts from Louis XIV. The plans were entrusted to an unknown architect, Delamair, who incorporated the Clisson gateway into the new house. Simultaneously the architect was occupied with building a second house for another member of the Rohan family, the Cardinal Bishop of Strasbourg. The outstanding decoration inside the Soubise Palace is due to Boffrand, a pupil of Mansart.

The Archives. – The National Archives established under the National Assembly in 1789, have been housed in the Soubise Palace since 1808 where the 6 000 million government and legal papers and personal archives occupy nearly 280 km – 175 miles of shelving. The Hôtel de Rohan, converted into the imperial printing house under Napoleon, was taken over as an annexe in 1927. Three adjoining mansions also serve as annexes.

The palace. – The main building, the former Guise mansion, stands behind the façade built by Delamair in 1705. It overlooks an elegantly majestic **courtyard**★★ created on the site of a former riding school, hence its plan. The statues of the Seasons on the façade, the figures of Glory and Magnificence on the pediment, and the groups of children, are all copies of the originals by Robert Le Lorrain.

The most gifted painters (Boucher, Natoire, Van Loo) and sculptors of the period (1735-1740) worked with exquisite fantasy in decorating in the Rococo style the wood-work, panelling and high reliefs of the magnificent **apartments**★★ of the Prince *(ground floor: guided tours)* and Princess *(first floor: Historical Museum, see below)* of Rohan-Soubise.

Historical Museum of France★★. – *Open 2 to 5pm; closed Tuesdays and holidays; 4F. Temporary exhibitions.* ☎ 42.77.11.30 Ext. 2178.

Among the great historical documents dating from the 7 to the 20C on display in the former guardroom are the Edict of Nantes (1598) and its Revocation (1685), Louis XIV and Napoleon's wills, the Declaration of Human Rights. The oval room is decorated with paintings by Natoire of the legend of Psyche.

Turn right into the Rue des Archives.

■ HÔTEL GUÉNÉGAUD★★ *(60, Rue des Archives)* - fold 32: H 16

This mansion, built between 1648 and 1651 by Mansart, was minimally remodelled in the 18C. With its plain harmonious lines, its majestic staircase and its small formal garden, it is one of the finest houses of the Marais.

Museum of the Chase and of Nature★★. – *Open 10am to 5.30pm; closed Tuesdays and holidays; 10F;* ☎ 42.72.86.43.

The collection includes arms from prehistory to the 19C *(first floor)* and trophies and souvenirs from Mr. Sommer's (who restored the Hotel) own big game expeditions *(2nd floor)*. On the stairs and in the red, green and blue salons are pictures by Desportes, Oudry, Chardin and Carle Vernet. There are also tapestries, ceramics and sculptures on the theme of the hunt in the museum.

Walk left in the Rue des Quatre-Fils to see the garden and rear façade of the mansion. At No. **22** Mme du Deffand held a famous salon in the 18C.

■ HÔTEL DE ROHAN★★ *(87, Rue Vieille-du-Temple)* - fold 32: H 16

Open for temporary exhibitions and lecture tours.

The mansion built by Delamair in 1705 bears the official name of Hôtel de Strasbourg.

The courtyard bears no comparison with that of the Soubise Palace as the main façade gives on to the garden which serves both properties.

On the right the former stables are crowned by the wonderful **Horses of Apollo**★★ by Robert Le Lorrain. The quivering horses are depicted at the drinking trough.

A staircase leads to the Cardinals' **apartments**★. A Gobelins tapestry hangs in the entrance hall. The first salons are adorned with Beauvais tapestries after cartoons attributed to Boucher. Also of interest are the Gold Salon and the amusing small Monkey Room with animal decorations by Christophe Huet, and the delicate panelling and wall hangings of the smaller rooms (Fable Room).

Turn right into Rue de la Perle. The Hôtel de Chassepot is at Nos. 3 and 5.

■ HÔTEL LIBERAL BRUAND *(1, Rue de la Perle)* - fold 32: H 16

Built in 1685 by the architect of the Invalides for himself, this elegant mansion has been restored to its original appearance and now houses a **Lock Museum** known also as the **Bricard Museum**★ *(open 10am to noon and 2 to 5pm; closed Sundays, Mondays, holidays and in August; 9F;* ☎ 42.77.79.62).

In five well-lit rooms the art of the lock is traced from the Roman era to the Empire: collections of iron and bronze keys, wrought iron Gothic locks; Venetian door knockers; gilded bronze locks from the Tuileries and Palais-Royal, combination lock, etc., as well as 20C ironwork and pieces from the Bricard workshops.

■ **HÔTEL SALÉ**★ (or Hôtel Aubert-de-Fontenay or Hôtel de Juigné)
(5, Rue de Thorigny) ▦ - fold 33: H 17

The house was built in 1656 for a salt tax collector, hence its name, Hôtel Salé or Salted. In the 18C it passed to the de Juigné family, then became the École Centrale (1829-84) and subsequently the École des Métiers d'Art. Recently restored and refurbished the mansion now houses the Picasso Museum. Inside the main **staircase**★ with its spacious stairwell and splendid wrought ironwork, rises majestically to the first floor and the profusely sculptured ceiling.

Picasso Museum★★. – *Open 9.45am to 5.15pm (10pm Wednesdays). Closed Tuesdays. 20F.* ℡ *42.71.25.21.*

One of the dominant figures of 20C art, Pablo Ruiz Picasso (1881-1973) was born in Malaga. The young Picasso took courses in art at both Barcelona, where his father was a teacher and Madrid. Aged only 23 he left his native country to settle in France, where he pursued his long and active career.

Following his death at Mougins in 1973, Picasso's heirs donated an outstanding collection of the artist's works in lieu of estate duties. The collection comprises over 200 paintings, an excellent group of sculptures, 3-dimensional pictures, more than 1000 prints, 88 ceramics, illustrated books and manuscripts.

To follow the chronological order of the different phases *(explanatory notices)* of Picasso's prodigiously productive and long painting career, start on the first floor with his *Self Portrait* from the Blue Period. All the artist's styles and techniques are represented from his sketches for *Les Demoiselles d'Avignon, Still life with cane chair* and *Pipes of Pan*. Some of Picasso's favourite themes were nudes, travelling acrobats and portraits of couples and the family (portrait of his son *Paul as Harlequin*).

Also included in the holding *(1st and 2nd floors)* is Picasso's private collection known as the Picasso Donation with works by Braque, Cézanne, Rousseau... Part of the 2nd floor is also reserved for temporary exhibitions. Films on the artist, his life and work are shown on the 3rd floor.

The Rue des Coutures St-Gervais skirts the gardens and affords glimpses of the imposing garden front.

■ **ADDITIONAL SIGHTS**

Hôtel Amelot-de-Bisseuil★ (or Hôtel des Ambassadeurs de Hollande). – *47, Rue Vieille-du-Temple.* The present mansion replaced an earlier building in 1655, the mediaeval residence of the Marshals de Rieux, companions in arms of Du Guesclin and Joan of Arc. In 1407, Duke Louis d'Orléans after visiting Queen Isabella at the Hôtel Barbette *(p 87)*, was assassinated nearby by the supporters of John the Fearless. This led to civil war during which Paris was occupied by the English (1420-1435) and besieged by Charles VII and Joan of Arc.

The 17C house, which has been remodelled at various periods, was at one time let to the Dutch ambassador's chaplain, hence its name. By 1776 the house, by now the home of the playwright Beaumarchais who wrote the *Marriage of Figaro* there, had become a depot for arms to be dispatched to the American rebels, and later a poor home.

The **gateway**★, decorated with masks and allegories, is one of the Marais' most outstanding. *(Ring to see the courtyard – the house is not open to the public.)* The house and wings are ornamented with sculptured motifs and four monochrome sundials.

Hôtel d'Aubray (or de la Brinvilliers). – *12, Rue Charles-V.* There is a fine wrought iron banister in the left wing. In the 17C it belonged to the notorious poisoner, the Marquise de Brinvilliers.

Hôtel d'Aumont. – *7, Rue de Jouy.* The house was built in the early 17C by Le Vau; it was later remodelled and enlarged by Mansart and decorated by Le Brun and Simon Vouet. The formal garden is attributed to Le Nôtre. Until 1742 the house was the residence of the Dukes of Aumont who built up several collections and gave lavish parties. The inner court and façades are almost severe in line. A large garden has been created between the house and the river. During the 19C the mansion suffered considerable damage but it has now been restored and serves as the Paris administrative court.

Hôtel de Beauvais★. – *68, Rue François-Miron.* In the 13C the Abbot of Châalis, near Senlis, had his town house on this site. Below were mediaeval **cellars**★ with pointed vaulting *(to visit apply to the Association pour la Sauvegarde et la mise en valeur du Paris historique – address as above,* ℡ *48.87.24.14. The association's office is open daily 2 to 6pm, except Sundays).*

In 1654 Catherine Bellier, known as One-Eyed Kate, first woman of the bedchamber to Anne of Austria, bestowed her favours on the sixteen year old Louis XIV and was rewarded by a fortune. In addition, for her services, her husband, Pierre Beauvais, and she were ennobled and acquired the site of the former town house of the Abbots of Châalis. They commissioned the architect, Lepautre, to build them a splendid mansion. Anne of Austria, the Queen of England, Cardinal Mazarin and dignitaries watched the triumphal entry of Louis XIV and Marie-Thérèse into Paris in 1660 from its balcony.

When Mozart came to Paris at the age of seven in 1763, accompanied by his father and sister, he stayed in this house and gave several concerts.

The façade has lost its exterior decoration. The covered entrance, where stone guards still protect the walls, extends to a vestibule where Doric columns support a cupola. Beyond is a courtyard with a rams' head decoration – Kate's canting arms. The stairway on the left has a carved stone banister, a rare ornament in the Marais.

Hôtel de Châlons-Luxembourg. – *26, Rue Geoffroy-l'Asnier.* Built in 1610 it has a carved main gate and an interesting stone and brick façade.

Hôtel Colbert-de-Villacerf. – *23, Rue de Turenne.* Its fine salon decorated with painted panelling has been reconstructed in the Carnavalet Museum *(p 87).*

Hôtel d'Ecquevilly (or **de Grand Veneur**). – *60, Rue de Turenne.* The house has a fine façade decorated with emblems of the chase and a magnificent **great staircase ★** adorned with hunting trophies *(to visit apply to the caretaker).*

Hôtel Fieubet. – *Square Henri Galli.* The house was built by Jules Hardouin-Mansart in 1680 for Gaspard Fieubet, Marie-Thérèse's chancellor. An ornate decoration was added to the plain façade around 1850 and since 1877 it has been turned into a school.

Hôtel Le Lièvre. – *4 and 6, Rue de Braque.* It was built in 1663 and has interesting twin doorways and balconies. There is a formal grand staircase at No. 4.

Hôtel de Montmor. – *79, Rue du Temple.* The house, erected in the reign of Louis XIII for his treasurer Montmor was remodelled in the 18C. Montmor's son invited the great physicians and doctors of the day to join the Abbot Gassendi who lived there for many years; these meetings heralded the founding of the Academy of Science (1666).

A fine balcony with a carved pediment adorns the façade pierced with tall windows overlooking the first court. The wrought iron ramp of the stairway is outstanding.

Hôtel de Saint-Aignan. – *71, Rue du Temple.* The house built in 1650 by Le Muet, was acquired in 1680 by the Duke of Saint-Aignan, Colbert's son-in-law and joint tutor with Fénelon of Louis XIV's three grandsons. A monumental gateway decorated with fantastic masks precedes the main colossally ordered façade. The left side of the courtyard, in fact, is a facing (windows in *trompe-l'œil*) applied by Le Muet to the Philippe Auguste wall.

The house was greatly disfigured during the Revolution when it became a town hall (1795-1823). The garden is to be recreated. The outbuildings house a section of the Paris Archives' Reading room. The stables (No. 75) have attractive pointed vaulting.

Hôtel de Savo;;rny. – *4, Rue Elzévir.* Picturesque inner courtyard.

Hôtel de Sens ★. – *1, Rue du Figuier.* The Hôtel de Sens, the Hôtel de Cluny and Jacques Cœur's house are the only great mediaeval private residences to remain in Paris.

The mansion was constructed between 1475 and 1507 as a residence for the archbishops of Sens of which Paris was a dependency until 1622. During the period of the Catholic League in the 16C it became a centre of intrigue conducted by the Cardinal of Guise. In 1594 Monsignor de Pellevé died of apoplexy within its walls while a Te Deum was being sung in Notre-Dame to celebrate Henri IV's entry into Paris.

In 1605 Queen Margot, Henri IV's first wife, came to live in the mansion.

In 1760 the house was occupied by the office of the Lyons stage coach which made a journey reputed to be so unsafe that passengers made their wills before setting out.

The mansion. – The old houses which originally surrounded the mansion have been pulled down. Its façade is ornamented with corner turrets and a tall dormer window with a stone finial. A large and a small door each with basket handle arches are surmounted by pointed arches. Walk through the Flamboyant porch into the courtyard where you will see a square tower, cut by a machicolated balcony and enclosing a spiral staircase. Turrets and beautiful dormer windows adorn the façades.

The **Forney Library** *(open 1.30 to 8.30pm; closed Sundays, Mondays and holidays; ☏ 42.78.14.60; temporary exhibitions),* is devoted to decorative and fine arts and industrial techniques. It has a large collection of posters and wall paper.

The garden front and the formal gardens may be admired from the Rue de l'Hôtel de Ville.

Hôtel de Tallard. – *78, Rue des Archives.* After restoration it has regained its classical aspect as given it by Bullet and its medallions on the garden side.

Rue François-Miron. – This road, once a highway through the marshes, still bears the name of a local magistrate of the time of Henri IV. In the Middle Ages it began on the low St-Gervais hill *(p 66)* and was lined with the town houses of several abbots of the Ile-de-France. The half-timbered and much restored Nos. **11** and **13** date back to the reign of Louis XI in the 15C. The beautiful Marie Touchet, mistress of Charles IX, is said to have lived at No. **30**.

The Association pour la Sauvegarde et la mise en valeur du Paris historique *(address p 89)* was created to safeguard the city's historical treasures. It has undertaken the restoration of Nos. **44-46** and uncovered fine Gothic **cellars ★** which once belonged to the Paris house of Ourscamp Abbey on the Oise. *Temporarily closed.*

Hôtel de Beauvais ★. – *See p 89.*

No. **82,** the **Hôtel Hénault-de-Cantorbe** has attractive balconies and a pleasant inner courtyard.

Rue Michel-le-Comte. – In this street are the ruined **Hôtel de Mézières** (No. 19) and the **Hôtel Verniquet** (No. 21) named after the geometrician who at the end of the 18C completed the first detailed maps of Paris *(p 119).*

The **Hôtel d'Hallwyl** (No. 28), where Mme de Staël was born in 1766, was built in the late 17C and remodelled by Ledoux, architect to Louis XVI. The works in progress will restore its gardens and 18C portico.

Rue des Rosiers. – This street, together with the adjoining Rue des Ecouffes which derives its name from a pawnbroker's shop sign, is typical of the **Jewish quarter** which has grown up in Paris' 4th arrondissement.

Church of Notre-Dame-des-Blancs-Manteaux. – *Rue des Blancs-Manteaux. Closed 12.45 to 4pm.* The Crédit Municipal bank stands on the site of a monastery founded by St. Louis for the mendicant order of the Serfs of the Virgin whose members wore white cloaks *(blancs manteaux).* In 1695, the Benedictines of St. William, the

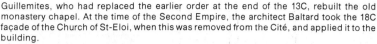

Guillemites, who had replaced the earlier order at the end of the 13C, rebuilt the old monastery chapel. At the time of the Second Empire, the architect Baltard took the 18C façade of the Church of St-Eloi, when this was removed from the Cité, and applied it to the building.

The interior has remarkable woodwork – an inner door, organ loft, communion table- and a magnificent Flemish **pulpit**★ in which marquetry panels are inlaid with ivory and pewter and framed in gilded and fretted woodwork in the Rococo style of 1749. Concerts of organ music are held in the church, especially during the Marais Festival.

Church of St-Denys-du-St-Sacrement. – *Rue de Turenne.*

The church, built in the form of a Roman basilica at the time of the Restoration, contains a remarkable **Deposition**★ by Delacroix (1844) at the back of the chapel to the right of the entrance *(lighting).*

Church of Ste-Croix-St-Jean. – *To visit apply at 6 ter, Rue Charlot.* This much restored church was erected in 1624 as a Capuchin monastery chapel and was attended by Mme de Sevigné. It is now the Armenian church.

The chancel is adorned with 18C gilded panelling from the former Billettes church. To the left stands a remarkable **statue**★ of St. Francis of Assisi by Germain Pilon (16C), and to the right St. Denis by J. Sarazin.

Jacques Cœur's House (Maison de Jacques Cœur). – *40, Rue des Archives.* Resurfacing work on a building in 1971 uncovered a façade decorated with panels in a red and black lattice pattern. This led to the identification of the 15C house of Jacques Cœur, Chancellor of the Exchequer to Charles VII. It is one of the oldest buildings in Paris.

St-Paul Village (Village St-Paul). – The area bordered by the Rues des Jardins-St-Paul, Charlemagne, St-Paul and Ave-Maria has been restored. Houses and antiquarian shops crowd around the inner courts.

A long section of the **Philippe Auguste Wall** (Enceinte de Philippe Auguste) intersected by two towers which once skirted the city can still be seen in the Rue des Jardins St-Paul. It linked the **Barbeau Tower** (Tour Barbeau) at 32 Quai des Célestins to the St-Paul postern and is the largest fragment still in existence.

Rabelais died in this street in 1553.

At the far end there is a view of the east end and dome of the St-Paul-St-Louis Church.

Memorial to the Unknown Jew (Mémorial du Martyr Juif Inconnu). – *17, Rue Geoffroy-l'Asnier. Open 10am to noon and 2 to 5pm; closed Sundays (except afternoons in July and August), Saturdays and Jewish holidays; 12F,* ☎ *42.77.44.72.*

In the crypt burns the eternal flame to the Jewish victims of National Socialism. There is also a museum devoted to the Jewish struggle against Hitlerism.

Kwok-On Museum (Oriental Theatre Museum). – *41, Rue des Francs-Bourgeois. Open noon to 6pm; closed Saturdays, Sundays and holidays; 10F;* ☎ *42.72.99.42.*

This museum named after its patron, is devoted to the oriental theatrical traditions.

Shadow theatre is greatly appreciated in India, Malaysia, Thailand, Cambodia and Indonesia: paper puppets, often painted and fretted, are activated by wands.

There is a large collection of theatrical costumes, musical instruments and glove, string and wand puppets.

The two famous traditions in Japan are the Noh, classical drama with singing and dancing, and Kabuki, a popular entertainment with colourful decors and costumes. There is a good collection of head carvings from the Bunraku puppet theatre.

(J. Feuillie/ ©C.N.M.H.S./S.P.A.D.E.M. 1983)

Hôtel de Rohan-Horses of Apollo

Michelin plan 🔟 - folds 17, 18 and 30:
F 10, F 11 — G 10, G 11

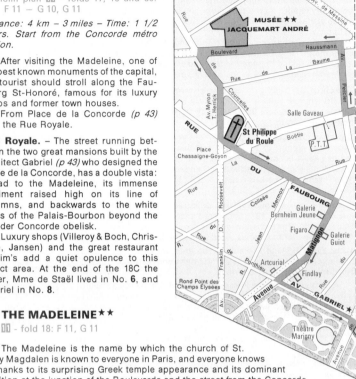

Distance: 4 km – 3 miles – Time: 1 1/2 hours. Start from the Concorde métro station.

After visiting the Madeleine, one of the best known monuments of the capital, the tourist should stroll along the Faubourg St-Honoré, famous for its luxury shops and former town houses.

From Place de la Concorde *(p 43)* take the Rue Royale.

Rue Royale. – The street running between the two great mansions built by the architect Gabriel *(p 43)* who designed the Place de la Concorde, has a double vista: ahead to the Madeleine, its immense pediment raised high on its line of columns, and backwards to the white mass of the Palais-Bourbon beyond the slender Concorde obelisk.

Luxury shops (Villeroy & Boch, Christofle, Jansen) and the great restaurant Maxim's add a quiet opulence to this select area. At the end of the 18C the writer, Mme de Staël lived in No. **6**, and Gabriel in No. **8**.

■ THE MADELEINE★★

🔟 - fold 18: F 11, G 11

The Madeleine is the name by which the church of St. Mary Magdalen is known to everyone in Paris, and everyone knows it, thanks to its surprising Greek temple appearance and its dominant position at the junction of the Boulevards and the street from the Concorde.

Few churches have had such a stormy history. It was begun by one architect in 1764 on plans based on the Invalides church of St-Louis, a second razed what had already been erected to begin on a building modelled on the Pantheon; all work ceased between 1790 and 1806 as various projects were considered. Napoleon announced that on this spot should be erected a temple to the glory of the Great Army and gave the commission to Vignon. Once more the existing structure was razed and building started on the Greek temple; work proceeded slowly. In 1814 Louis XVIII confirmed that the Madeleine should indeed be a church. In the reign of Charles X it was still surrounded by waste land.

In 1837 the building was nearly selected for use as Paris' first railway terminal. The church's vicissitudes ended with its consecration in 1842 although its priest was shot by the Commune in 1871.

Tour. – A majestic colonnade of Corinthian columns – 52 in all, each 20 m – 66 ft tall – frames the church on all sides and supports a sculptured frieze. A monumental flight of steps (28) leads to the imposing peristyle giving on to the Place de la Madeleine and affords a splendid view down the Rue Royale, beyond the obelisk to the Palais-Bourbon and the Invalides dome. The gigantic pediment is adorned with a sculpture by Lemaire of the Last Judgement and the reliefs on the bronze door are inspired from the Ten Commandments.

The single nave church has a vestibule and a semicircular chancel. In the dark vestibule note at the far end on the right a Marriage of the Virgin by Pradier and on the far left a Baptism of Christ by Rude. The nave is crowned by three domes with statues of the Apostles carved by Rude, Foyatier and Pradier on the pendentives. A group featuring St. Magdalen ascending to Heaven dominates the high altar.

Next to the church is a flower market. The Place de la Madeleine is also famous for its superb provision stores.

■ RUE DU FAUBOURG ST-HONORÉ★★

The superstitious Empress Eugénie had No. 13 suppressed which it remains to this day. The street imparts a leisured elegance with its luxury shops, art galleries, antiquarian shops and fashion houses particularly around the Rue Royale and the Rue de l'Élysée.

The Élysée Palace (Palais de l'Élysée). – *Not open to the public.* The mansion was constructed in 1718 for the Count of Evreux. It was acquired for a short time by the Marquise de Pompadour and then by the financier Beaujon who enlarged it, during the Revolution it became a dance hall. Caroline Murat, Napoleon's sister, then the Empress Josephine both lived in and redecorated it. It was in this palace that, after Waterloo, Napoleon signed his second abdication on 22 June 1815 and that the future Napoleon III lived and planned his successful *coup d'état* of 1851.

Since 1873 the Élysée Palace has been the Paris residence of France's presidents. The Council of Ministers meets on Wednesdays in the Murat Salon.

In the Place Beauvau (1836), a fine wrought iron gate marks the entrance to the Ministry of Home Affairs installed since 1861 in the 18C mansion built for the Prince of Beauvau.

Jacquemart-André Museum ★★ (**Musée Jacquemart-André**). – *Open 1.30 to 5.30pm; closed Mondays, Tuesdays, holidays and in August; 10F; ☏ 45.62.39.94.*

This elegant late 19C house contains outstanding European and Italian Renaissance art.

On the ground floor the Louis XV period is vividly recalled with paintings and drawings by Boucher, Greuze, Chardin, Watteau; sculpture by Pigalle and Lemoyne, Beauvais tapestries, furniture and objets d'art. 17 and 18C schools of painting are represented by Rembrandt, Canaletto, Reynolds and frescoes by Tiepolo (ceilings in Rooms 4, 5, 13 and over the stairs). There are also beautiful 16C Limoges enamels and ceramics by Palissy.

In the Italian rooms are displayed a remarkable collection of Tuscan Primitives, works from the Quattrocento (Botticelli paintings, Della Robbia terracottas, Donatello sculptures), the Venetian Renaissance (Mantegna, Tintoretto, Titian). Ucello's famous St. Georges Slaying the Dragon and a fine bronze bust by Bernini are noteworthy.

From the Jacquemart-André Museum to the Place de la Concorde

Take the Rue de Courcelles and the Avenue Myron-T.-Herrick to the Place Chassaigne-Goyon.

Church of St-Philippe-du-Roule. – *Closed 1 to 4pm at weekends.* The church designed by Chalgrin in imitation of a Roman basilica, was erected between 1774 and 1784. The semicircular chancel was added in 1845. A fresco over the chancel of the Descent from the Cross is by Chassériau *(ask at the sacristy for the painting to be lit).*

On leaving the church turn left into the Rue du Faubourg St-Honoré. There are several art galleries, notably Artcurial, in the **Avenue Matignon** to the right.

Avenue Gabriel ★. – It runs between the Rond-Point and the Concorde along the landscaped garden area of the Champs-Élysées *(p 44).* Beside the Marigny Theatre, the Stamp Market is open on Thursdays, Saturdays and Sundays. On the right is a landscaped garden with a statue of President Pompidou by Louis Derbré.

At the corner of the Avenue de Marigny, on the left, the gardens of the Élysée Palace (fine Cock iron grille wrought in 1905) form an enclave. The avenue then runs along the back of the shaded gardens of the mansions on the Faubourg St-Honoré: the British Embassy, the Interallied Union Circle.

The Espace Pierre Cardin, formerly the Théâtre des Ambassadeurs, is the venue for exhibitions, concerts, cinema, theatre and dance shows. Near the Place de la Concorde stands the American Embassy (once the house of the gastronome Grimot de la Reynière, whose culinary judgment was absolute).

Michelin plan 🔟 - folds 19, 30 and 31: G 12, G 13 - H 13.

Distance: 3 km – 2 miles – Time: 3 hours. Start from the Palais-Royal métro station.

In this part of Paris the Palais-Royal, the Bibliothèque Nationale and St-Roch Church remind one vividly of the city's past in contrast to the Avenue de l'Opéra and the Rue de Rivoli which seem to epitomize the present.

To the right of the métro station is the **Louvre des Antiquaires** *(open Tuesdays to Sundays 11am to 7pm)* a building containing 250 art galleries and antique shops.

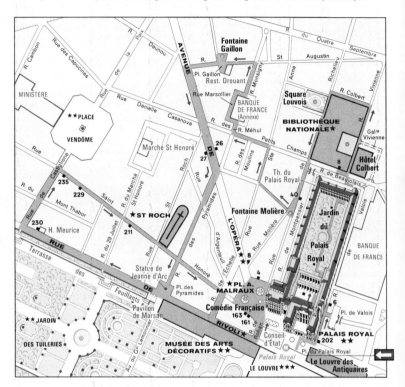

■ **THE PALAIS-ROYAL**★★ 🔟 - fold 31: H 13

The façades of Richelieu's palace, now the office of the Council of State can be seen though not entered. The quiet garden has retained its 18C atmosphere.

The Cardinal's Palace. – In 1624, Richelieu, who was First Minister, acquired a mansion near the Louvre with ground extending to the Charles V perimeter wall. In 1632 he commissioned Le Mercier to build the huge edifice known as the Cardinal's Palace.

The Royal Palace. – The Cardinal on his deathbed in 1642 left his mansion to Louis XIII who soon followed him to the grave. His widow, Anne of Austria, with her son, the young Louis XIV, then quit the Louvre for the smaller and more beautiful mansion which henceforth became known as the Royal Palace. The Fronde in 1648 forced their hasty departure. When Louis XIV returned to Paris he went to live in the Louvre and lodged Queen Henrietta Maria, widow of Charles I of England, and then her daughter, Henrietta in the palace.

The Orleans. – After a lightning illness had carried off Henrietta, the palace was given in apanage to her husband Philippe of Orleans, brother of Louis XIV and subsequently to his son, appointed Regent during the minority of Louis XV. Philippe II of Orleans was highly gifted and also highly dissolute – palace suppers at that period were notorious.

In 1780 the palace passed to Louis-Philippe of Orleans, who being short of money, undertook the construction round three sides of the garden, of apartment houses with ground level shopping arcades and uniform façades. The three new streets skirting the frontages were called after the younger Orleans brothers: Valois, Montpensier and Beaujolais. The palace precinct became the favourite idling place for Parisians. Between 1786 and 1790 the same architect, Louis, was commissioned by Philippe-Égalité to build the Théâtre-Français, now the Comédie-Française *(p 98)* and the Palais-Royal Theatre at the corner of Rues de Montpensier and Beaujolais; it is now a vaudeville theatre.

After the Revolution, the palace became a gambling house until, in 1801, Napoleon converted it into offices, and in 1807, into the Exchange and Commercial Court.

Louis XVIII returned the mansion to the Orleans and it was from there that Louis-Philippe set out for the Hôtel de Ville, in 1830, to be proclaimed king.

The garden formerly. – During the Revolution, the garden became a popular meeting-place. In the 18C it was the setting for cafés which attracted a varied clientele, a circus, a riding school, a dance hall, a theatre until this went up in flames, a wax museum, funfair attractions and gambling houses. The July monarchy closed the gaming houses in 1838 and the popularity of the arcade shops began to decline. The Commune set the buildings on fire but they have been restored (1872-1876).

THE PALACE AND THE GARDEN

The palace. – The façade overlooking the square consists of a central building and two receding wings decorated with 18C carvings of military trophies and allegorical figures by Pajou.

The east wing now stands on the site of the theatre built by Richelieu and in which Molière created his major plays between 1661 and 1673 (when he collapsed on stage while acting out *Le Malade Imaginaire;* he died at No. **40** Rue de Richelieu). It later became an opera house where Lulli's works continued to be performed until it was burnt down in 1763.

At No. **6**, Rue de Valois (beautiful balcony), in 1638 Richelieu conducted the early sessions of his new foundation, the French Academy. Nearby is the quiet Place de Valois which is on the site of the palace's former outbuildings.

Main courtyard ★ . – Enter by the covered passage. Enclosed by projecting wings lined with galleries, it is dominated by an impressive central façade, surmounted by allegorical statues. Overlooking the garden is a double colonnade, built at the time of the Restoration (1814-1830). The Valois side gallery is known as the Prow Gallery because of its nautical decoration (Richelieu was minister for the navy). The sculptures in the fountains are by Pol Bury.

The garden. – It is overlooked by the elegant façades designed by the architect Louis. There are shops in the arcade specialising in the unique, the luxurious: decoration, medals, porcelain, stamp and antique shops. On the grass by the palace, on a pedestal behind a statue, stands a toy cannon, known as the Palais-Royal cannon. From 1786 until 1914 it used to go off at midday provided the sun, when reflected through a magnifying glass, was hot enough to ignite the charge.

Leave the Palais-Royal by the peristyle of the Beaujolais arcade.

From the Palais-Royal to the Bibliothèque Nationale

On your way look through the grille at No. 8, Rue des Petits-Champs, to admire the courtyard and sombre brick and stone façade of the Tubeuf mansion built by Le Muet in 1633. Opposite stands Colbert's mansion (1665) now an annexe of the National Library. At street level the charming Colbert Arcade houses two museums: the **Charles Cros Museum** *(due to open September 1986)* retracing the history of the phonograph and a **Dramatic Arts Museum** *(window displays only)* presenting costumes, sketches of scenery and costumes, posters, photographs... From the Rue Vivienne turn into Rue Colbert which was spanned at the far end by the Hôtel de Nevers, a former literary salon. **Louvois Square** on the left, is adorned with a fountain by Visconti (1844).

■ **THE BIBLIOTHÈQUE NATIONALE ★** ⬚⬚ - fold 31: G 13

In the Middle Ages the kings of France collected manuscripts; Charles V mustered nearly 1 000 volumes in the Louvre Library *(p 24);* Charles VIII and Louis XII had libraries at Blois; François I at Fontainebleau. A copyright act in 1537 ensured that a copy of every book printed enters the royal, now national, library – today extended to include records and photographs.

In the 17C the Tubeuf Mansion was enlarged by Mansart and on coming into Mazarin's possession housed his 500 pictures and personal art objects. By 1666 the Royal Library numbered 200 000 volumes and Colbert decided to move it to his own mansion in the Rue Vivienne; fifty-four years later, it was moved again when it was added to the original Mazarin collection. The Nevers and Chivry mansions were taken over in the 19C.

The Library today: – The Bibliothèque Nationale is divided into departments covering 16 500 m² – 177 600 sq ft with several annexes elsewhere in Paris. It includes among others, the following departments:

Printed Books: About 11 million volumes dating from the 15C and including two Gutenburg Bibles, first editions of Villon, Rabelais, Pascal... The central storeroom comprises 11 levels and 240 km – 149 miles of shelving. The Reading room designed by Labrouste is a masterpiece of architecture (19C).

Manuscripts: papyri, Dead Sea scrolls, illuminated manuscripts including Charlemagne's Gospel, Charles the Bald's Bible and St. Louis' Psalter; parchments, letters, MSS of Hugo, Proust, Pasteur and Marie Curie...

Engravings and Photographs: This is the richest collection in the world: 12 million engravings, 2 million photographs.

Maps and Plans: 13 - 20C.

Medals and Antiques: 400 000 coins, medals, cameos, bronzes and objets d'art. This department is also responsible for research into the treasure troves discovered in France.

Music and Record Library: 360 000 records, 16 000 tapes, 600 talking machines.

Tour. – The east side of the main courtyard is by the 18C architect, Robert de Cotte. The reading room (1868) – *members only* – can be seen through a window. At the end of the hall on the right is the Mansart Gallery *(free access during exhibitions)* and opposite, the State Room with the original plaster bust of Voltaire by Houdon (the marble original is at the Comédie-Française). The philosopher's heart was placed in the statue's pedestal.

The great staircase leads to the **Medals and Antiques Gallery ★** (on the mezzanine): the art objects from royal and confiscated collections on display include ivory chess pieces, Dagobert's legendary throne and coins. *Open 1 to 5pm; 6F.*

On the floor above is the magnificent **Mazarin Gallery ★** by Mansart *(access during temporary exhibitions).*

From the Bibliothèque Nationale to St-Roch Church

On leaving the library, walk left down the Rue de Richelieu to the Rue Molière.

Molière Fountain. – The 19C fountain by Visconti stands not far from what is now No. **40** Rue de Richelieu, the site of Molière's house. It was there that he was taken when he collapsed on stage at the first Palais-Royal Theatre, on 17 February 1673. He was 51.

Make for the Rue des Petits-Champs by way of the Rues Thérèse and Ste-Anne – No. 47 is the house Lulli had built in 1671, borrowing *11 000 livres* from Molière to do so. Musical motifs can be seen upon the façade.

The Rue des Moulins gets its name from the windmills which stood upon a hillock built of public waste like the neighbouring Butte St-Roch. The mound was razed in 1668, but one of the mills, the Radet, was saved and transported to Montmartre *(p 79)*.

The brief Rue Méhul leads to the old Ventadour Theatre where Victor Hugo's melodrama, *Ruy Blas*, was first played in 1838. It is now an annexe of the Bank of France.

Walk to the Rue Monsigny and the Rue St-Augustin on the left. Facing the **Gaillon fountain** (Fontaine Gaillon) erected in 1707 on the square of the same name (remodelled by Visconti in 1827), is the Restaurant Drouant, known in the world of letters as the place from which the names of the Goncourt prizewinners are announced annually in autumn.

On reaching the Avenue de l'Opéra turn left.

Avenue de l'Opéra★★. – This luxurious thoroughfare was begun simultaneously at either end by Haussmann in 1854 and completed in 1878. The most serious obstacle in the road's path was the Butte St-Roch, which covered the area between what are now the Rue Thérèse and the Rue des Pyramides and rose to sufficient height for Joan of Arc to position her large supporting cannon upon it when her troops were preparing to attack the St. Honoré Gate *(p 98)*. The mound had been partly levelled off in 1615 but remained a poor area until the end of the 17C when the slums were demolished and the vast heaps of rubble were utilised to build up the lowlying areas around the Champ-de-Mars.

The Avenue de l'Opéra, still not quite a hundred years old, has become one of Paris' prestige streets where big business and commerce reign. For the tourist the avenue is the place for making purchases: perfume, scarves, gifts and *articles de Paris* (fancy goods). It is also a business district with many large banks, estate agents and international bookshops *(see Useful Addresses p 10)*. More obviously the avenue and the streets off it have become the stronghold of the advertising and travel industries with the Havas Travel Agency at No. **26,** and foreign tourist and air and shipping lines occupying offices all around. No. 29 is the National Centre for the Visual Arts with an entrance in *trompe-l'œil*.

Turn right into the Rue des Pyramides and, after crossing the Rue d'Argenteuil where Corneille died in 1684, continue to the square, **Place des Pyramides,** at the end of which there stands an equestrian statue of Joan of Arc by the 19C sculptor, Frémiet.

Rue de Rivoli★. – The Rue de Rivoli, between the Place des Pyramides and the Rue de Castiglione on the right, crosses the site of the former Tuileries **Riding School.** In 1789 the school was hastily converted into a meeting place for the Constituent Assembly. Sessions were subsequently held there by the Legislative Assembly and the Convention, until on 21 September 1792, the day following the French victory over the Prussians at Valmy (commemorative tablet on a pillar in the Tuileries railings opposite No. **230**), it became the setting for the proclamation of the Republic and the trial of Louis XVI.

It was Napoleon who, in 1811, had this part of the avenue constructed, although it was not to be completed until nearly the middle of the century. The houses facing the Tuileries are of uniform design above arcades lined with both luxury and souvenir shops.

In 1944 the Rue de Rivoli was the scene of a momentous decision in the capital's own history when the German General von Choltitz, Commandant of Paris, who had his head-quarters at the Meurice Hotel at No. 228, refused to obey Hitler's orders to blow up the capital's bridges and principal buildings when the tanks of General Leclerc's division and the Resistance were known to be approaching. He surrendered on 25 August and Paris was liberated intact.

(Photo Halin-Rapho)

Place Vendôme.

Turn right up the Rue de Castiglione, known formerly as the Passage des Feuillants after the Benedictine monastery which it skirted, and right again, into the Rue St-Honoré. The crossroads of the Rue de Castiglione and Rue St-Honoré affords a view of the Place and Colonne Vendôme *(p 81)*.

The Rue St-Honoré at the time of the Revolution. – The **Feuillants Monastery,** which had grounds extending to the Tuileries riding school, augmented its income by building an apartment house which can still be seen between Nos. **229** and **235** in the Rue St-Honoré. It was here that the short-lived Feuillants Club of moderates who, in line with La Fayette, Bailly, Sieyès and Talleyrand, disassociated themselves from the extremist Jacobin group, met in 1791.

No. **211** is the former Noailles Mansion where General La Fayette married one of the daughters of the house in 1774. It is now the St. James and Albany Hotel. On the left there used to be a **Jacobin Monastery** (a Dominican order of St. James). In 1789 a club installed itself in the monastery and took its name, becoming famous during the Revolution under the leadership of Robespierre.

The Rue du Marché St-Honoré now cuts across the site of the monastery church and a market dating back to 1810 occupies the ground on which the monastery once stood.

St-Roch Church, on the left, was the site on 13 Vendémiaire – 5 October 1795 – of bloody fighting. A column of royalists leading an attack on the Convention, then in the Tuileries, aimed to march through the Rue St-Roch. Bonaparte, however, who was in charge of the defence, mowed down with gun fire the men massed on the church steps and perched on its façade. The bullet holes can still be seen.

Some idea of the scale of Haussmann's earth moving undertakings can be gained from the fact that to enter the church nowadays you have to walk up twelve steps, whereas before the construction of the Opera Avenue, you had to go down seven.

■ **CHURCH OF ST-ROCH★** ▯▯ - fold 31: G 13
Closed Sundays, 1 to 4pm.

The foundation stone of the church dedicated to the early 14C saint who tended those suffering from the plague in Italy, was laid by Louis XIV in 1653. The Moulins hillock site compelled the architect, Le Mercier, to reorientate the church so that it faces south to north.

Funds soon ran out but work was able to continue after a lottery had been organized in 1705. Instead of completing the nave, a series of chapels one behind the other were constructed beyond the apse, lengthening the church from the planned 80 to 125 m – 262 to 410 ft (5 m – 16 ft shorter than Notre-Dame) and obliterating all unity of design. In consequence, in line behind the altar are a Lady Chapel by Jules Hardouin-Mansart, with a tall richly decorated dome, a Communion Chapel with a flat dome and finally a Calvary Chapel *(closed for restoration)* rebuilt in the 19C.

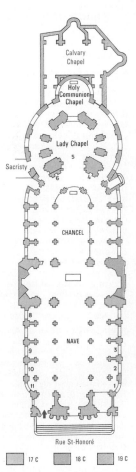

Calvary Chapel

Holy Communion Chapel

Lady Chapel
5

Sacristy

CHANCEL

8

NAVE
9
3

10
2

11

Rue St-Honoré

17 C   18 C   19 C

In 1719 a gift of 100 000 *livres* from John Law *(p 103),* recently converted to Catholicism, enabled the nave to be completed. Robert de Cotte designed the façade in the Jesuit style in 1736.

Among those buried in St-Roch in the Lady Chapel and side chapels are the playwright Corneille, the garden designer Le Nôtre, the Abbot de l'Épée *(p 132),* the philosophers Diderot and d'Holbach and Mme Geoffrin, hostess of a famous 18C *salon*. The 17C mariner, Duguay-Trouin, has been transferred to Saint-Malo.

Works of Art:

1) Tomb of Henri of Lorraine, Count d'Harcourt by Renard (17C) and bust of the 17C Marshal de Créqui by Coysevox (17C).
2) Funeral monument of the astronomer, Maupertuis by d'Huez and statue of Cardinal Dubois by Guillaume Coustou.
3) Tomb of Duke Charles de Créqui.
4) Godefroy de Bouillon Victorious by Claude Vignon (17C). Funerary plaque to Duguay-Trouin.
5) The Triumph of the Virgin, painting by J. B. Pierre on the dome *(illumination: apply to the sacristan).* The **Nativity★** at the altar by the Anguier brothers, was brought from the Val-de-Grâce.
6) Resurrection of the Son of the Widow of Naïm by Le Sueur (17C).
7) Le Nôtre bust by Coysevox and funerary inscription.
8) Monument to the Abbot de l'Épée (19C).
9) Bust of the painter Mignard and statue of his daughter by Lemoyne (18C).
10) Baptism of Christ by Lemoyne. Medallion by Falconet.
11) Baptismal Chapel: frescoes by Chassériau (19C).

Continue left down the Rue St-Honoré to the Rue de l'Échelle, so called after the ladder or flight of steps leading to a scaffold which stood on the site during the Ancien Régime. The ecclesiastical courts then sent polygamists, perjurers and blasphemers to the steps where they were exposed in shame before the public.

On the right is the Marsan Pavilion, which, with the Flore Pavilion (reconstructed), are all that remain of the Tuileries Palace, burnt down in 1871 *(p 25).*

Avoid visiting a church during a service.

Costume and Fashion Museum (Musée des Arts de la Mode). – *Pavillon de Marsan, 109, Rue de Rivoli. Open Wednesdays to Saturdays 12.30 to 6.30pm; Sundays 11am to 5pm; 22F. ℡ 42.60.32.14. Start on the 9th floor and work downwards.*

A series of tableaux (changed regularly) present the elegant and often fantastic fashions of yesteryear (17C to the present). Follow the vagaries of the very Parisian world of fashion with such evocative names as Schiaparelli, Poiret, Vionnet, Chanel and Worth the Englishman who was Paris' first couturier.

■ MUSEUM OF DECORATIVE ARTS★★ (MUSÉE DES ARTS DÉCORATIFS)
▯▯ - fold 31: H 13

107 Rue de Rivoli. Open 12.30 to 6.30pm; 11am to 5pm Sundays; closed Mondays and Tuesdays; 20F. ℡ 42.60.32.14.

The temporary exhibitions organized by the museum are often extremely interesting *(opening times as above; 18F)*.

Art courses (drawing, modelling, metal engraving) are offered. *Information can be obtained at the Secrétariat des Ateliers: ℡ 42.60.32.14 ext 933.*

The numerous exhibits provide a vivid panorama of the evolution in form and taste in sculpture, painting, furniture, tapestry, banqueting settings and all forms of decoration in France.

First floor: 1950 to the present, including a reconstitution of Jeanne Lanvin's flat; Second floor: Middle Ages to the Renaissance; Third and fourth floors: reign of Louis XIV to the Second Empire; Fifth floor: specialist departments (wallpaper, drawings...); Sixth floor: Dubuffet Donation including paintings drawings, watercolours and sculpture by the artist.

On leaving the museum, you pass on your right the latest Louvre façade (remodelled during the Third Republic). The statues in the niches are of the generals of the First Empire.

Turn left into the Rue de Rohan, which leads to the Place André-Malraux. The street runs over the original site of the Quinze-Vingts Hospital for the blind which in the reign of Louis XVI was transferred by Cardinal de Rohan, the institution's administrator, to barracks in the Rue de Charenton where it remains to this day *(p 160)*.

■ PLACE ANDRÉ-MALRAUX★ ▯▯ - fold 31: H 13

From this altogether Parisian crossroads – formerly known as the place du Théâtre-Français – created in the time of Napoleon III and decorated with attractive modern fountains there is a splendid view up the Avenue de l'Opéra.

Comédie-Française. – In 1680 Louis XIV combined the former Molière company with that at the Hôtel de Bourgogne *(p 102)* at the same time granting it the sole right of performance in the capital. The new company took the name Comédie-Française.

The company, however, found itself the butt of hostility simultaneously from the Sorbonne and the orthodox and was compelled to move home frequently – from the Guénégaud *(p 139)* to the Rue de l'Ancienne-Comédie *(p 139)*, the Palais des Tuileries *(p 25)* and the Odéon *(p 121)*.

At the Revolution a dispute broke out in the company between players who supported the Republicans and those favouring the Royalists. In 1792 the former, led by Talma, took over this theatre.

Napoleon showed a great interest in the Comédie-Française, in Talma – and also in the leading lady, Mlle Mars. In 1812 he presented the company with a foundation making it an association of currently acting and apprentice players and players on pension. Today the theatre is still under a director nominated by the state.

On 21 February 1830 the company, playing *Hernani,* was involved in the famous battle – a battle of taste – which marked Victor Hugo's triumphal *début* as a playwright. The repertoire of the Comédie-Française has, by tradition, been classical, with set rules in style of acting and in interpretation – Molière, Corneille, Racine, Marivaux, Musset, Beaumarchais. Recently, however, works by foreign and 20C French authors have been admitted – Pirandello, Claudel, Giraudoux, Anouilh...

In the foyer are Houdon's famous bust of **Voltaire★★** *(p 95)* and the chair in which Molière was sitting when taken fatally ill on stage *(p 96)*.

At No. **161** Rue St-Honoré was the Café de la Régence founded in 1681 in the Place du Palais-Royal and forced to move in 1854 when the square was enlarged.

Memories of Joan of Arc. – Joan came to the gate in the Charles V perimeter wall which stood where No. **163** Rue St-Honoré is now, when leading her attack on the capital in 1429. She had already freed Orleans *(see Michelin Green Guide Châteaux of the Loire)* and accompanied the King to Rheims for his coronation, but her task, as she saw it, was far from complete. Paris was still in the hands of the English under the Regent Bedford who wished not only to retain the city but to make it safe enough to bring over the young Henry VI and crown him in Notre-Dame, King of England and France.

The girl soldier paused to pray at the small St-Denis-de-la-Chapelle (the church, now remodelled, is at No. 16, Rue de la Chapelle, 18ᵉ), before undertaking her attack on the gate fort defended by a moat. Realising this would have to be filled in, she moved to measure the water's depth with her lance when she was wounded in the thigh by an arrow. She was given first aid in what is now No. **4** in the square while her men beat a hasty retreat. Henry VI was crowned in Notre-Dame (1431).

Although this is the only episode linking Joan of Arc with the capital there are, in addition to the medallion by Réal del Sarte on the Café de la Régence façade, four statues of her in the city – in the Place des Pyramides *(p 96)*, Rue de la Chapelle, Place St-Augustin *(p 171)* and at 41 Boulevard St-Marcel.

Michelin plan ▦▦ - folds 31 and 32: H 14, H 15

Distance 4.5 km – 3 miles – Time: 1 day. Start from the Halles métro station, exit Porte Lescot. ▬

The demolition of the central market has made possible the creation of a leisure and commercial centre. Also with the building of the Pompidou Centre and the renovation of the decrepit Beaubourg plateau, the character of this old quarter has radically changed.

■ LES HALLES ▦▦ - fold 31: H 14

The Halles formerly. – Paris' central market was on the Ile de la Cité; the second on the Place de Grève now the Place de l'Hôtel de Ville; the third settled on the present site around 1110. In 1183 under Philippe Auguste it was extended, permanent structures being erected and a surrounding wall built. The king levied site and sales taxes.

Twice a week the City merchants and craftsmen were required to close their shops and conduct their business in the market where each street specialised in a trade.

By the 16C with a population of 300 000 in the capital the food market assumed a paramount importance, eventually replacing all other types of trade in the market. On the orders of Napoleon, the wine and leather markets were transferred to the Left Bank. Until the Revolution, close to the nearby St-Eustache crossroads was the market **pillory** where dishonest traders, thieves and prostitutes were publicly exposed.

The Halles yesterday. – By the 19C the great market was in urgent need of reconstruction. As Rambuteau and Haussmann thrust wide avenues through the quarter (Rues de Rivoli, du Pont-Neuf, du Louvre, des Halles, Etienne Marcel), a stone pavilion was built by the architect **Baltard** commissioned by Louis Philippe, and being unsuitable, razed. He then designed plans of a hall of iron girders and skylight roofs, reminiscent of the Gare de l'Est, which were accepted by Napoleon III.

Ten halls in all were constructed between 1854 and 1866 and the buildings became the model for covered markets throughout France and abroad. Two further halls were opened in 1936. The animated market scene and the rich variety of colour and smell are vividly described by the writer Emile Zola as "the stomach of Paris" in his novel *Savage Paris (Le Ventre de Paris)*. The old tradition still exists of eating onion soup, snails and pig's trotters at 5am in simple but excellent restaurants with colourful names.

The Halles today. – An underground pedestrian concourse, **The Forum,** on four levels extends to the east of the Commercial Exchange. The glazed galleries overlook the Place Basse; in the centre rises a pink marble sculpture by the Argentine Julio Silva, of **Pyegmalion:** next to a unicorn, the Buddha-like figure of the Dream-Keeper presenting her twin lunar and solar faces watches over the young girl asleep created by Pygmalion. The latter is depicted stilled for eternity in his fruitless quest while his desire is exemplified by a pig-headed man devouring the snake of temptation. On level -4, on the Porte Lescot side, the theme of a **bronze low-relief** by Trémois representing a golden wall with amazing reliefs, is light travelling through the ages. On level -3 by Rue de l'Arc-en-Ciel, imaginary porticoes opening on to infinity painted by Attila, form a rainbow-coloured dome. **Moretti's fresco** (same level, by Rue des Piliers) in vivid colours evokes the evolution of man from prehistoric times (bronze human mask from Tautavel) to the age of writing including giant portraits of Victor Hugo and Louis Armstrong.

New Grévin Museum ★ . – *Level -1. Guided tours 10.30am to 6.45pm weekdays, 1 to 7.15pm Sundays and holidays; 32F;* ☏ *42.61.28.50.*

The display, in this annexe of the waxworks museum on Boulevard Montmartre, portrays the Paris of the *Belle Époque* (1885-1900) by means of twenty scenes with animation and sound effects on the highlights of the capital.

(Photo G. Boutin/Explorer)

Forum des Halles.

Holography Museum. – *Level -1. Open 10.30am to 7pm (1 to 7pm Sundays, Mondays and holidays); 22F; ☎ 42.96.96.83.*

Holography is a process which with the aid of coherent light or laser beams, creates three-dimensional images known as holograms. Invented in 1947 by Dennis Gabor it experienced a rapid expansion with the invention of the laser beam. Among the many interesting exhibits are a series of disconcertingly lifelike portraits.

Arranged around the Forum at street level palm-shaped glass and metal pavilions house cultural facilities for art, poetry and music. The upper terrace, bordering the inside of these pavilions, provides a good view of the rest of the site, now landscaped as a **garden.** New facilities underground, include a tropical glasshouse. Admire the luxuriance from the observation points.

Rue St-Honoré. – This street, as of the 12C, was one of the quarter's major arteries.

Further along, on the left, is an edifice built by Soufflot. The sculptor Boizot reproduced a nymph by Jean Goujon on the façade and erected by the side of the building on the Rue de l'Arbre Sec, a fountain adorned with a bronze mascaron surmounted by a marble plaque bearing France's coat of arms. This monument replaced the Croix-du-Trahoir fountain (Fontaine de la Croix-du-Tra-hoir) erected by François I but in no way resembles it. The original stood in the middle of the road, raised on a flight of steps on which vegetables were spread for sale. To one side stood the gallows from which the street on the left took its name of the Arbre Sec or withered tree. It is said also that in 613 at these crossroads, on the orders of her enemy, Frédégonde, the old Queen Brune-haut of Austrasia was tied by her hair to a wild horse's tail and broken. More than a thousand years later, on 26 August 1648, the arrest of the parliamentarian, Broussel, by Anne of Austria's forces in the same spot began a street row which, by the following morning, had developed into civil conflict: the Fronde had begun.

Opposite, is the Rue Sauval, formerly known as the Rue des Étuves after the public baths once situated in it which had become haunts of debauchery in the Middle Ages and were finally closed in the 17C. The site of No. 96 on the corner is where the poet and comedy writer Regnard was born in 1655 and where some historians allege Molière was born in 1662. Wagner lived there in 1839.

The Oratory Church (Oratoire). – This was the site of Gabrielle d'Estrées' house in the 16C. In 1616 the Carmelite Oratorian Congregation, later to rival the Jesuits, had a church built by Le Mercier which became the royal chapel in the reigns of Louis XIII, Louis XIV and Louis XV. Preachers such as Bossuet, Malebranche, Bourdaloue and Massillon attracted the royal family and court. The funerals of Louis XIII and his Queen, Anne of Austria, were held in the church. The Oratorians were suppressed at the Revolution; the chapel became an arms depot and in 1811, a Protestant church. The façade is 18C.

From the arches of the Rue de Rivoli there is a view of the church's east end which is well preserved, and of the statue of Admiral de Coligny placed there last century. He was assassinated on the night of the St. Bartholomew's massacre (24 August 1572).

Take the Rue Jean-Jacques Rousseau on the right where the philosopher lived at the end of his life (No 52). On the left is the former red light street, the Rue du Pélican, and beyond the **Vero-Dodat arcade** (Galerie Vero-Dodat), created in 1822 by two pork butchers who installed gas lighting along it and let the shops for fabulous rents.

The Place des Deux-Écus is still overlooked by some old houses but several were razed at the time of the construction of the Rue du Louvre at the end of the 19C.

The Commercial Exchange (Bourse du Commerce). – This circular building is hemmed in to the west by a semicircle of tall porticoed mansions and to the east by gardens and the Forum. It stands on a site where for the past 800 years French history has been made.

Blanche de Castille, mother of St. Louis, died in the first building (Hôtel de Nesle) in 1252 on a bed of straw as a sign of humility. It then became the Hôtel de Bohème, then Hôtel d'Orléans. Louis XII lost the mansion at cribbage to his chamberlain who converted it into a convent for repentant sinners. These were dislodged in 1572 when Catherine dei Medici left the Tuileries *(p 24)* and had a mansion, the Hôtel de la Reine, constructed by Delorme and Bullant. The building subsequently became the Hôtel de Soissons where in 1663 was born Prince Eugene of Savoy who served the Austrian empire and fought the infidels. Under the Regency it was turned into a gambling hall, then razed in 1748.

A wheat market built in Louis XVI's reign was replaced in 1889 by the present rotunda. Abutting the market side wall to the south of the building, is a fluted column, 30 m – 98 ft high, the only remaining feature of the mansion built by Bullant.

Inside, the vast circular hall lit by a glass dome is reserved for accredited brokers.

Take the Rue Coquillère to St-Eustache Church.

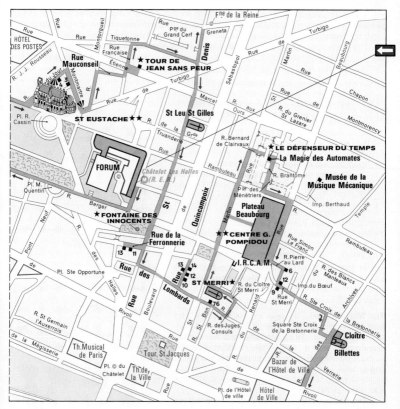

■ ST-EUSTACHE CHURCH★★ 📖 - fold 31: H 14

St-Eustache, Gothic in plan and outline, Renaissance in decoration, is one of Paris' most beautiful churches. It has a long tradition of organ and choral music. Last century it was the setting for first performances of works by both Berlioz and Liszt.

Construction. – In 1214 a small chapel, dedicated to St. Agnes was built on this spot. A few years later, the chapel was rededicated to St. Eustache, a Roman general converted, like St. Hubert, by the vision of a cross between a stag's antlers.

But the Halles parish, which had become the biggest in Paris, dreamed of a church worthy of its new status. Grandiose plans were made with Notre-Dame as the model.

The foundation stone was laid in 1532. Construction was slow, however, in spite of liberal gifts and the church was only consecrated a century later, in 1637. The original plan had been adhered to, although the west front had never been completed, when in 1754 it was decided to replace this Renaissance front by a Classical one with columns.

During the Revolution the church was renamed the Temple of Agriculture; in 1844 it was badly damaged by fire and subsequently reconstructed by Baltard.

St-Eustache, so close to the Louvre and the Palais-Royal, at the centre of everything going on in the capital and also the parish church of the Halles corporations, became a focal point of public ceremony – the baptisms of Armand du Plessis, the future Richelieu, of Jean-Baptiste Poquelin (Molière), the future Marquise de Pompadour, Louis XIV's first communion, the funerals of La Fontaine, Molière and the Revolutionary orator, Mirabeau.

The church was at one time paved with tombstones including those of Louis XIV's statesman, Colbert, Admiral de Tourville who beat the Anglo-Dutch fleets off Beachy Head in 1690 and was defeated, in turn, off La Hogue in 1692, and the composer Rameau.

Exterior. – Take the narrow Rue du Jour. Opposite No. **4** there is a good view★ of the buttresses and upper part of the church. No. **4**, once the Paris seat of Royaumont Abbey, passed to Montmorency-Bouteville, who was executed by Richelieu for contravening his edicts on duelling; it then became the property of his son, Marshal of Luxembourg.

From No. **3**, Rue Montmartre a blind alley ends at the beautiful north transept door.

Transept façade★. – This fine Renaissance composition is flanked by twin staircase turrets ending in pinnacles. Beneath the gable point is a stag's head with a Cross between the antlers recalling St. Eustace's conversion. The statues on the door shafts are modern. The pilasters, niches, mouldings and grotesques are delicately fashioned.

Chevet. – From the corner where the Rues Montorgueil and Montmartre meet you can see the church chevet and the final circular Lady Chapel.

Interior. – St-Eustache measures 100 m long, 44 m wide and 34 m high – 328 × 144 × 112 ft. The church's majesty and rich decoration are striking.

The plan is that of Notre-Dame with nave and chancel encircled by double aisles and flat transepts. The vaulting above the nave, transept and chancel is Flamboyant, adorned with numerous ribs and richly carved hanging keystones.

The elevation, however, is entirely different to the cathedral's. The aisles, devoid of galleries, rise very high, the arches being so tall that between them and the clerestory windows there is only space for a small Renaissance style gallery.

The stained glass windows in the chancel are after cartoons by Philippe de Champaigne (1631) and recall the mediaeval skill in this craft. St. Eustace appears at the centre, surrounded by the Fathers of the Church and the Apostles.

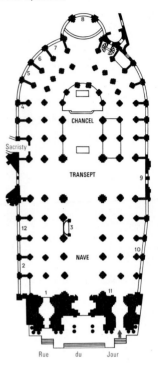

1) On the door tympanum: the *Martyrdom of St. Eustace* by Simon Vouet (17C).
2) *Adoration of the Magi*, a copy of a painting by Rubens.
3) Churchwarden's pew presented by the Regent, Philippe of Orleans in 1720.
4) *Tobias and the Angel*, by Santi di Tito (16C).
5) *The Ecstasy of Mary Magdalene*, painting by Manetti (17C).
6) *The Pilgrims at Emmaüs*, an early Rubens.
7) Colbert's tomb designed by Le Brun, Coysevox carved the statues of the minister and of Abundance; Tuby that of Fidelity.
8) Statue of the Virgin by Pigalle. Chapel frescoes by Thomas Couture (19C).
9) 16C statue of St. John the Evangelist.
10) Bust of the composer Jean-Philippe Rameau who died in 1764.
11) Epitaph to 17C Lieutenant-General Chevert.

In the St-Joseph chapel, a colourful naive sculpture (12) by Raymond Mason commemorates the fruit and vegetable market's move out of Paris on 28 February 1969.

Rue Mauconseil. – In 1548 a theatre was built on land belonging to the Hôtel de Bourgogne to the left of the street. The company had no women players until 1634 and all female roles were played by masked men. Racine first presented *Mithridate* and *Iphigénie* in this theatre. In 1680 the company, by royal command, merged with that of the Rue Mazarine *(p 141).*

The Italians took over the theatre. Among the comedians was a clown, Scaramouche, who could still knock off his partner's hat with a high kick at the age of 83. The company was disbanded in 1697 after an attack on Mme de Maintenon. The last troupe to play the theatre before it disappeared was the Comic Opera (1716-1782).

John the Fearless' Tower★ (Tour de Jean sans Peur). – Follow the Rue Française on the left. At No. 20 in the Rue Étienne-Marcel, in a schoolyard, is a square machicolated tower *(not open)* built by John the Fearless for his own protection in 1408 following the assassination, on his orders, of the Duke of Orleans. The tower formed part of the **Hôtel de Bourgogne,** the former Artois mansion abutting on the Philippe Auguste perimeter wall.

Continue along the Rue Française, then take the Rue Tiquetonne (old houses with fine restored façades) on the right to the Rue St-Denis.

Rue St-Denis. – The street, opened in the 7C, soon became the busiest and most prosperous in Paris. Kings rode along it when making solemn entries to the capital and visiting Notre-Dame; royal funerals followed it on their way to St-Denis Abbey.

The new king was greeted with triumphal arches, porticoes and even fountains – the last much preferred as they played free wine or milk! One, much restored, remains from the time of Louis XI, the Queen's Fountain at No. 142 (corner of the Rue Greneta).

At No. 145, the Grand-Cerf Passageway was built in 1825 on the site of the inn of the same name, a staging point until the Revolution.

Church of St-Leu-St-Gilles. – Two 6C saints, Lupus (Leu in French), Bishop of Sens, and the Provençal hermit, Giles, are patrons of this church, built in 1320 and remodelled several times. A new east end and the north tower belfry were constructed in 1858 when the Sébastopol Boulevard was laid. Inside *(open daily from 1pm),* the nave's Gothic bays contrast with the taller Classical chancel. The keystones are interesting, also a 16C marble group by Jean Bullant of St. Anne and the Virgin, 15C alabaster low reliefs fragments of an altarpiece from the former Innocents' Cemetery *(at the sacristy entrance)* and a Christ Entombed *(in the crypt).*

Walk left down the Rue St-Denis, past the Rue de la Grande-Truanderie – Vagabonds' Row, contemporary with the mediaeval Court of Miracles *(p 126).*

Fountain of the Innocents★ (Fontaine des Innocents). – The 19C square stands on the site of the Cemetery and Church of the Holy Innocents which dated back to the 12C.

The cemetery with its communal graves was encircled by a charnel house about which horrific tales were told of events during the siege of Paris in 1590 by Henri of Navarre; at other times, however, in spite of a famous illustration of the Dance of Death, the area was a popular place for a stroll. In 1786 the cemetery became a market after some two million skeletons had been transferred to a quarry, renamed the Catacombs.

A Renaissance masterpiece, this fountain by Pierre Lescot, carved by Jean Goujon, stood in 1550, at the corner of Rue St-Denis. Backed against a wall, it had only three sides; when removed to its present site in the 18C, a fourth side was added; a new base was substituted in 1865 – the original low reliefs are in the Louvre.

Rue de la Ferronnerie. – It was while riding in this street in his carriage that Henri IV was assassinated on 14 May 1610 in front of No. **11**. The sign at No. **13** was a crowned heart pierced by an arrow – the witnesses to the murder felt this to be an omen. His assailant, Ravaillac, was later quartered on the Place de Grève.

Rue des Lombards. – Its name is a reminder of the mediaeval Lombard moneylenders. The right hand corner has remained empty since 1569.

Rue Quincampoix. – This street was the scene of the Scots financier, **John Law's** "South Sea Bubble". Law founded a bank there in 1719. Soon speculation began to run rife: the houses all around, the street itself were crowded with those making fortunes overnight – a hunchback was said to have gained 150 000 livres for the use of his back as a desk. The frenzy lasted until 1720 when the bank crashed and the speculators fled.

There are several old houses at Nos **10, 12, 13, 14** with unusual paved courtyards, mascarons, intricate wrought iron balconies and nailed or craved doors.

Continue to the Rue St-Martin, one of the oldest streets in Paris, now tree-lined, which affords a fine view.

From St. Merry to the Georges Pompidou Centre

The St. Merry presbytery *(76 Rue de la Verrerie)* with its fine 18C porch gives access to the church.

St. Merry Church★ (Église St-Merri). – St. Merry or Medericus who died on this spot in the 7C used to be invoked for the release of captives. The building although begun in 1520 and completed in 1612, is curiously, in the 15C Flamboyant Gothic style. It was formerly the rich parish church of the Lombard moneylenders (who gave their name to the nearby street – *see above*). The outside with the west face stands directly on the narrow Rue St-Martin, and small houses and shops crowd the south wall and chancel.

The Flamboyant interior was remodelled under Louis XV by the architect Boffrand and the Slodtz brothers. There remain, nevertheless, good 16C stained glass windows, in the first three bays of the chancel and transept, and fine ribbed vaulting at the transept crossing.

In addition to the majestic 17C organ loft – the organ *(concerts: Saturdays 9pm and Sundays 4pm except in August)* itself was at one time played by Camille Saint-Saëns – and the beautiful woodwork by the Slodtz brothers in the pulpit, sacristy and the glory at the back of the choir, the church possesses a series of interesting pictures.

One bell dating from 1331, probably the oldest in Paris, remains from the mediaeval chapel which stood on the site of the present church.

Leave St. Merry's to the left by the Rue de la Verrerie; go round the church by way of the Rue des Juges-Consuls (officers created by Charles IX to settle differences between merchants). At the corner of the Rue du Cloître-St-Merri stands an 18C house.

In the square, the Stravinsky fountain with black and coloured mobile sculptures by Tinguely and Niki de Saint-Phalle respectively illustrating the works of the great composer (the Rites of Spring, Firebird...) is of interest.

Return to the Rue St-Martin on the right.

The St. Merry Quarter. – The quarter round the church has always been crowded with craftsmen. In the Middle Ages there were linen drapers, rivalling those of Flanders, haberdashers and hairdressers – Paris' taste and fashions had begun their influence throughout Europe.

At every political insurrection the barricades went up. In June 1832, a young boy and an old man, flourishing a tricolour, were killed near the Rue du Cloître-St-Merri – an event on which Victor Hugo based his description of the death of Gavroche in his novel *Les Misérables*. Today the quarter is adjusting to its new role as the cultural centre of contemporary art.

■ THE GEORGES POMPIDOU CENTRE★★ ▢▢ - fold 32: H 15

Open noon to 10pm (10am to 10pm Saturdays and Sundays). Closed Tuesdays, 1 May and 25 December. 15F National Museum of Modern Art only; 30F for a pass valid all day. ☎ 42.77.12.33.
Beaubourg is the name of an old village that was included within the Philippe Auguste perimeter wall at the end of the 12C. Situated in the heart of a very old quarter; cleaned up in 1936 of its decaying houses; included in 1968 in the redevelopment plan for the site of the former Halles market *(p 99)*, the plateau was to have been the site of a public library. However, in 1969, on the initiative of Georges Pompidou (1911-1974), the then President of France, a vast programme, which would change the whole aspect of the quarter, was envisioned – it was decided to create a multi-purpose cultural centre.

Architecture. – The architects Richard Rogers (British) and Renzo Piano (Italian) have achieved a building (1972-1977) totally futuristic in conception.

A gigantic parallelepiped unfolds its steel frame, glass walls and bright colours 166 m long, 60 m wide and 42 m high (545 × 197 × 138 ft). Devoid of any decoration, it stands a pile of steelwork, a surrealistic sculpture confronting its onlooker. The façade is a tangle of pipes and tubes latticed along its glass skin, giving an effect of a solid yet pliant superstructure. On the façade the caterpillar-like clear tube envelopes the escalators.

The skeletal construction of the centre sheathed with tubes and funnels recalls a ship or factory – the past conception of a traditional museum is rejected in its entirety.

The elimination of all possible clutter brought on by the utilities – stairs, lifts, escalators, corridors, ventilation shafts, water and gas conduits – liberates 7 500 m² – 80722 square feet of free space on each floor for research, animation and information.

A slightly inclined Piazza in front of the centre – the museum's outside reception area – is the playground of artists revealing their talents: whether it be the troubadour, fire-eater, poet, mime or juggler. On the right the Children's Workshop can be seen through the window.

On the ground floor, a large open area, the Forum, made up of several levels, contains temporary exhibits, a poster shop and book store. On the left is a large hexagonal portrait of *Georges Pompidou* by Vasarély.

Activities. – The Centre seeks to demonstrate that there is a close correlation between art and daily activities. For both the specialists – artists, researchers – and the general public, this multi-purpose cultural centre offers an astonishing variety of activities and modern communication techniques encouraging curiosity and participation.

The Centre includes the following:

The **Public Information Library** (BPI) – entrance on 2nd floor – offers to the public a wide variety of French and foreign books, slides, films, periodicals...

The **Industrial Design Centre** (CCI) on the ground floor and mezzanine, demonstrates the relationship between individuals and spaces, objects and signs through: architecture, urbanism, industrial design, visual communication and community services.

The **Institute for Acoustic and Musical Research** (IRCAM) *(located underground, between the Centre and St. Merry Church)* unites musicians, composers and scientists for the purpose of creating music with what modern technology has to offer *(apply in advance to visit Thursdays at 5pm and 6.30pm)*.

The **National Museum of Modern Art** (MNAM) – entrance on the third floor – presents collections of paintings, sculptures and drawings from 1905 to the present time. Special exhibitions are held on the fifth floor.

The **Children's Workshop.**

Facilities for theatre, dance, video and film shows, discussion groups etc.

The **Film Library** (5th floor) – an annexe of the Chaillot Palace Cinema Library – holds 20 film shows every week. *Programme advertised on the premises and in the press; 13F; ☏ 42.78.35.57.*

NATIONAL MUSEUM OF MODERN ART★★★

One of the largest contemporary art museums in the world; this museum has gathered under one roof an exceptional quality and variety of painting and sculpture, permitting the visitor to follow the evolution of international art beginning with Fauvism and Cubism and continuing through the entire contemporary art scene.

The majority of the works were formerly in the Museum of Modern Art in the Tokyo Palace *(p 135)* complemented more recently by acquisitions and gifts.

(Photo A. Roux/Explorer)

The Pompidou Centre.

Ground floor. – *Access from the Piazza; open noon to 6pm.*

The reconstructed studio reveals where Constantin Brancusi (1876-1957), the pioneer of modern abstract sculpture, created.

4th Floor. – From 1905 to 1965.

To the right on entering is the Graphic Arts Room with its changing displays of photographs, collages and airbrush works.

Terraces. – Displayed among other sculptures are *Le Capricorne* by Ernst, *Une machine* by Tinguely, a Calder stabile and works by Miró and Laurens.

Galleries. — St. Merri side. – Early 20C to post World War I: Fauvism and Cubism.

Fauvism, a reactionary art movement, is characterised by thick colourful brushstrokes. The following works are of interest: *Rue de Marly-le-Roi* by Vlaminck; *Affiches à Trouville* by Dufy and *Les Deux Péniches* by Derain.

The *Violonniste à la fenêtre* and the cut out watercolour *Nu-bleu* are good examples of Matisse's works. In the early **Cubist** period (1907) the painters translated their pictorial vision by more or less geometrical forms depicting the volume or make-up of objects. Follow the evolution of Picasso (*Joueur de guitare*, 1910) and Braque (*Guéridon*, 1911; *Homme à la guitare*, 1914). Others who belonged to the movement were Duchamp-Villon (*Le Grand cheval majeur*, 1914), Juan Gris *(Le petit déjeuner)* and Fernand Léger (*La Noce* and his vast canvas *Composition avec deux perroquets*).

Galleries. — Rue Rambuteau side. — Post World War I to the 1960's: Abstract Expressionism, Surrealism, New Figurative Art of the 1950-60's, Pop-Art and New Realism.

The Abstract Expressionism to be found in Piet Mondrian's *Composition* is also revealed in works by Kandinsky, the movement's founder and theoretician.

The works of the **Surrealists** give glimpses of a dream world: Miró, Magritte and Dali *(Vache Spectrale).*

In the 1950-60's the artists Bazaine, Soulages, Hartung, De Staël and Pollock used glowing blocks of colour, brooding black forms, slashing streaks and energetic lines to record their feelings.

As a reaction to Abstract Expressionism **Pop Artists** were inspired by their everyday environment (Rauschenberg), while **New Realists** exploited even further the everyday object thus creating works of art (Martial Raysse, Christo of the Pont Neuf fame and Arman known for his accumulations).

3rd Floor. — Contemporary art from 1965 to the present.

This section is liable to regular re-arrangement and is the place to see the works of contemporary and new generation artists.

Le Magasin de Ben, a store which had evolved into a centre of creativity, shows great originality and Dubuffet's *Jardin d'hiver* (must take off your shoes) communicates a feeling of pleasure.

After visiting the museum, go up to the fifth floor.

From the top of the escalators a beautiful **view** of the rooftops of Paris can be seen – from right to left: hill of Montmartre and the Sacré-Cœur, St-Eustache, the Eiffel Tower, Maine-Montparnasse Tower, St. Merry and Notre-Dame.

■ THE HORLOGE QUARTER

To the north of the Georges Pompidou Centre, between the Rue Beaubourg and the Rue St-Martin, lies this recently renovated pedestrian quarter (colourful shops).

The Clock★. — *Rue Bernard-de-Clairvaux.* This unusual brass and steel clock is by Jacques Monestier. Electronically operated the clock has a lifesize Jack known as the Defender of Time (Le Défenseur du Temps). With his double-edged sword he gives battle on the hour with one of the three animals, symbolising the elements: a dragon (earth) a bird (air) and a crab (water). At noon, 6 and 10 pm all three attack together.

The Magic World of Automata. — *8, Rue Bernard-de-Clairvaux. Open 11am (2pm Tuesdays) to 6pm; time: 50 min; 30F, children 20F. ℡ 42.71.28.28.*

Merlin the Magician invites you to visit this wonderland of animated tableaux (Ali Baba's Cave, the circus...).

At the corner of Rues Brantôme and Rambuteau stands Zadkine's Prometheus *(see museum p 176)* represented stealing fire from heaven.

Opposite the Passage des Ménétriers and at the far end of the Impasse Berthaud is another museum.

Musical Instruments Museum. — *Guided tours weekends and holidays from 2-7pm; 20F, children 10F; time: 1 1/4 hours; ℡ 42.71.99.54.*

The collection includes over 100 mechanical reproducers of music (late 19C-early 20C) all in good playing order.

From the Georges Pompidou Centre to the Hôtel de Ville

To the right, the Rue Beaubourg runs along the façade of the Centre, which holds all the conduits used for the functionning of the building; colours designate these functions: white conduits: ventilation system; blue conduits: air conditioning system; green conduits: fire prevention system; yellow conduits: electrical system; red conduits: transportation system.

Turn left into the narrow Pierre au Lard Alley. On the corner of Rue St-Merri there are two fine 17C houses (Nos. **12** and 9), and a little along on the left is the sordid Cul-de-Sac du Bœuf, one of the oldest blind alleys in Paris. The Rue St-Merri continues as the Rue Ste-Croix-de-la-Bretonnerie.

Take the road to the right called Square Ste-Croix-de-la-Bretonnerie, which opens into Rue des Archives, opposite the Billettes Church.

The Billettes Church (Église des Billettes). — It is here, according to legend, that the miracle of the "boiled God" occured in 1290: a usurer, Jonathan, cut a host and threw the pieces into a cooking pot; the water turned to blood and ran into the street attracting attention to the moneylender who was burned alive. In the 14C a monastery was erected on the site by the Brothers of Charity known as the Billettes on account of the heraldic billet on their habits. They were succeeded by Carmelites who in 1756 built the present sanctuary which became a Lutheran church in 1812.

The Billettes Cloister (Cloître des Billettes). — *1st door to the left after the Church.* The only remaining mediaeval cloister in Paris gives onto a small courtyard. Note the simplicity of its architectural elements.

Michelin plan **⑪** - folds 30, 31: J 12, J 13 - K 13.

Distance: 2 km – 2 miles – Time: 1 1/2 hours. Start from St-Germain-des-Prés métro.

This old quarter on the Left Bank is known for its beautiful church as well as for its narrow streets, antique shops, restaurants, cafés and cellars.

■ **ST-GERMAIN-DES-PRÉS CHURCH**★★ **⑪** - fold 31: J 13

In 542 King Childebert, son of Clovis, on his return from Spain with a piece of the True Cross and St. Vincent's tunic, had a monastery built in the open fields *(prés)* to shelter the relics. He was buried in the church as were subsequent members of his line until King Dagobert (639) who is buried in St-Denis Cathedral. Also interred here is St. Germanus, Bishop of Paris, after whom the church had taken its name of St-Germain-des-Prés or St. Germanus in the Fields.

A powerful abbey. – St-Germain-des-Prés was from the 8C, a link in the prodigious chain across Europe of 17 000 Benedictine abbeys and priories and in its own right, sovereign ruler of a domain of some 17 000 ha – 42 000 acres. Spiritually it acknowledged only the pope.

The monastery was sacked four times in forty years by the Northmen and the present church is, therefore, a rebuilding dating in its earliest parts from 990 to 1021.

There followed enlargement of the chancel in 1163 – an addition consecrated in person by Pope Alexander III at a service from which the bishop of Paris was excluded, as a mark of the order's independence – the building of Gothic cloisters and refectory, and a Lady Chapel in the 13C by Pierre of Montreuil, making the monastery a most beautiful mediaeval group. The church, the oldest in Paris, and the abbatial palace are all that remain of the famous Benedictine abbey.

In the 14C while Paris was being given its third defence perimeter by Charles V *(p 16),* the abbey surrounded itself with a crenelated wall intersected by towers and preceded by a moat connected with the Seine. These fortifications remained until the end of the 17C when they were replaced by houses, so creating the district of St-Germain *(p 133)* which extends to the west.

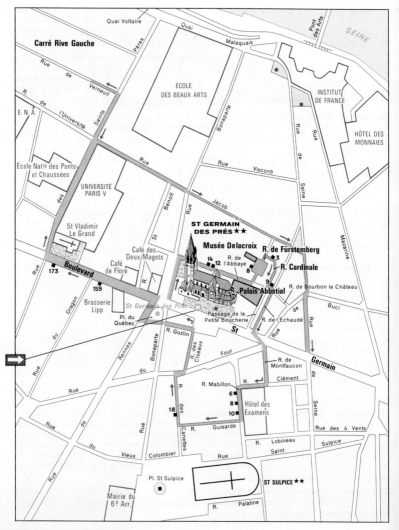

A centre of learning. – The Cluniac rule was followed in the abbey from the 11 to the 16C when it became debased; it was reformed in 1515 and in 1631 and then attached itself to the austere Congregation of St. Maur which earned the community a reputation for holiness and learning.

The monks devoted themselves to the study of inscriptions (epigraphy), ancient writing (paleography), the Church Fathers, archaeology, archives and mediaeval documents.

Decadence. – The abbey was suppressed at the Revolution: the rich library was confiscated, the church, from which the royal tombs disappeared, turned into a saltpetre works and the greater number of its buildings sold, knocked down or burnt. In spite of everything, however, the nave was saved although the twin transept towers disappeared. The vessel received a decoration of somewhat stiff frescoes between 1841 and 1863 by the painter, Flandrin.

Exterior. – With all that has happened to it, inevitably the 11C Romanesque church has altered considerably in appearance. Of the three original towers there remains only the massive one above the façade, one of the oldest in France. The top arcaded storey, rebuilt in the 12C was restored in the 19C and, in the same century, crowned with the present steeple. The original porch is hidden by an outer door added in 1607; on the right, the presbytery is an 18C addition.

The twin square towers at the end of the chancel were truncated instead of being repaired in 1822.

The chancel itself, rebuilt in the middle of the 12C when its buttresses were strengthened by a series of flying buttresses, is contemporary with Notre-Dame.

The small square to the south is on the site of the monks' cemetery and in September 1792 was the setting for the massacre of the 318 priests and monks who had been locked up in the adjoining Abbey Prison.

The glazed limestone portico placed against the far wall was executed by the Sèvres factory for its pavilion at the 1900 Universal Exhibition.

Interior. – St-Germain, built as a monastery chapel, is not large – it measures 65 × 21 × 19 m high – 213 × 69 × 62 ft. Proportions and carving are diminished by the irritating 19C multicolour restoration.

To the right of the cradle vaulted porch is the St. Symphorian Chapel *(not open)* where St. Germanus was buried in Merovingian times. Excavations in the chapel have uncovered several decorated stone and plaster sarcophagi and also a fragment thought to be part of the 11C church or of the Merovingian edifice.

The Gothic vaulting above the nave and transept, similar to that in the chancel, replaced an earlier wooden roof in 1646; the capitals are copies of the 11C originals now in the Cluny Museum *(p 118)*.

The frescoes above the arches are by Flandrin, a student of Ingres, and depict scenes from the life of Christ together with the parallel episodes from the Old Testament, e.g. The Resurrection and Jonah and the whale.

The chancel and ambulatory remain 12C. Originally the arches, some of which are still semicircular, supported galleries but in 1646 these were converted into a purely ornamental triforium; the 6C marble shafts in the slender columns are from the original Childebert church and along with the remains found in St. Symphorian Chapel and Notre-Dame are the only traces of Merovingian buildings in Paris.

The chancel capitals are Romanesque and depict traditional themes: foliage, birds, monsters.

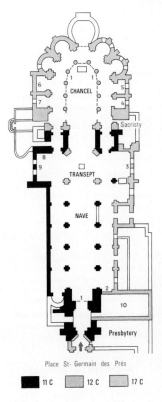

Place St- Germain des Prés

■ 11 C   ▨ 12 C   ▢ 17 C

1) Modern wrought iron grille by Raymond Subes.
2) Our Lady of Consolation (1340).
3) Tomb by Girardon (17C).
4) Mausoleum of James Douglas, a 17C Scottish nobleman attached to the court of Louis XIII.
5) Descartes' and the learned Benedictines, Mabillon and Montfaucon's, tombstones.
6) Boileau, the poet and critic's, tombstone.
7) Tomb of William Douglas, a Scottish nobleman attached to the court of Henri IV.
8) Statue of St. Francis Xavier by N. Coustou.
9) Tomb of John Casimir, King of Poland, who died in 1672, Abbot of St-Germain-des-Prés.
10) St. Symphorian Chapel *(closed)*.

A Picasso sculpture, *Homage to Apollinaire,* has been placed in a small square on the corner of the Place St-Germain-des-Prés and the Rue de l'Abbaye amidst fragments of the Lady Chapel built by Pierre of Montreuil and removed from the church in 1802 (the portal is in the Cluny Museum, *p 118*).

Walk along the quiet Rue de l'Abbaye.

The refectory designed in 1239 by Pierre of Montreuil and burnt down in 1794 stood at Nos. **14-12** and the chapter-house at No. 11.

Abbatial Palace. – The former abbatial palace (Nos. 5 to 1) is an impressive brick and stone edifice which was constructed in 1586 by the Cardinal-Abbot Charles of Bourbon, proclaimed King of France in 1589 during the League. His reign, as Charles X, however, was shortlived since he died the following year, a prisoner of his nephew Henri IV.

The palace was remodelled in 1699 by the Cardinal de Fürstemberg and sold in 1797. The angle pavilion and the Renaissance façade have been restored to their original aspect.

The severity of the façade is tempered by the twin-casement windows and, above, the alternate round and triangular pediments.

■ THE ST-GERMAIN QUARTER

The Old Streets ★. – Turn left into the **Rue de Fürstemberg**, an old fashioned street with a charming square shaded by paulownia and white-globed lamp-posts. The street was built in 1699 by the cardinal of the same name, through the acquisition of the monastery stableyard. The Nos. 6 and **8** are the remains of the outbuildings.

Delacroix, leader of the Romantic painters set up his studio in No. 6 which is now the **Eugène Delacroix Museum** *(open 9.45am to 5.15pm; closed Tuesdays and on some holidays; 8F; ☎ 43.54.04.87).* He died there in 1863.

Bear right into the curious winding **Rue Cardinale**, again opened (1700) by Fürstemberg, this time overlooking the monastery tennis court and still partially lined by old houses (Nos. **3** to **9**). From the Rue Cardinale you can enjoy an overall view of the Abbatial Palace and of the picturesque crossroads of Rue de l'Échaudé (1388) and Rue Bourbon-le-Château. Continue past the Petite Boucherie passage to the Rue de l'Abbaye on the left and subsequently turn right into the Rue de l'Échaudé (1388).

The construction of the Boulevard St-Germain brought about the disappearance, in about 1870, of the meeting point of several small roads which had served as the abbey's place of public chastisement. Justice was meted out on thieves, counterfeiters, pimps, who were punished by gibet and pillory – a penalty suppressed by Louis XIII in 1636.

The old St-Germain Fair. – Cross the boulevard into the Rue de Montfaucon which at one time led to the St-Germain fairground. Then take the Rue Clément to the right. Gangways leading up to the road from Nos. **8** and **10** in Rue Mabillon show that the ground level has been raised.

The fair, founded in 1482 by Louis XI for the benefit of the abbey, lasted until the Revolution (1790), its annual celebration an important event in the Paris economy. In 1818 the site was made over to the local market. A part was taken in 1900 to build university examination halls with premises for the market's stall holders on the ground floor. A cultural centre is planned for the remaining section.

Take the Rue Guisarde on the right. Built in the 17C, it derives its name from the secret meetings of the League formed by the Duke of Guise's supporters.

Return in the direction of St-Germain-des-Prés by way of the Rue des Canettes, so named after the low-relief depicting ducklings at No. **18**, and the Rue des Ciseaux where there are still some old houses.

Turn left into Rue Gozlin, cross Place du Québec with its fountain and then left again along the Boulevard St-Germain.

Boulevard St-Germain. – Near the Place St-Germain-des-Prés you will see on the right the famous Café des Deux-Magots and the Café de Flore where intellectuals and artists meet. Opposite is No. 151, the Brasserie Lipp, a popular venue with politicians, writers and celebrities. Further on some 18C mansions remain standing (Nos. **159** and **173**).

The antiquarian quarter. – The numerous art galleries and antiquarian shops in the streets between the boulevard and the river will delight art lovers and collectors. The area known as the **Carré Rive Gauche** organises a five day antiques fair in May to present a selection of objects outstanding for their rarity, craftsmanship or beauty.

Turn right into the Rue des Saints-Pères.

On the right stands the former St-Pierre Chapel (17C) which was part of the Charity Hospital; its name was distorted to Saints-Pères. It is now the Ukrainian church of St. Vladimir the Great. The Engineering School is housed in the 18C mansion at No. 28.

Opposite, the great buildings erected on the site of the Charity hospital are the premises of the Paris V University. Note the fine bronze doorway by Paul Landowski. Beyond at No. 13 is the National Administration School (E.N.A.).

Continue along the pretty Rue de Verneuil with its old houses and 18C mansions.

Return to the Rue Jacob and walk along the left hand side of the road (publishing houses, antiquarian shops). Then turn right into the old Rue de Seine, built in the 13C, which leads back to the Boulevard St-Germain.

MICHELIN publications for your stay in Paris

PARIS and environs Hotels and Restaurants
(red annual booklet – extract from the Guide FRANCE)

Plan de PARIS 🔟 *scale 1:10 000*

PARIS Atlas 🔟 *practical information, useful addresses, street index, public transport (métro, bus, car)*

Map 🔟🔟 *Outskirts of PARIS*
to cross Paris rapidly, to find your way in the suburbs, to avoid Sunday evening bottle-necks

MONTAGNE STE-GENEVIÈVE ___ 

Michelin plan ⑩ - folds 43 and 44: K 14, K 15 - L 14, L 15.

Distance 3.5 km – 2 miles – Time: 2 1/2 hours (tour of the Police Museum not included).
Start from the Maubert-Mutualité métro.

This is an unusual walk among university faculty buildings and famous schools with the Sorbonne, the Pantheon and St-Étienne-du-Mont Church as the principal landmarks.

Gallo-Roman Lutetia. – In the 3C Lutetia was a small town of some six thousand inhabitants: Gauls occupied the Ile de la Cité, Romans the summit and some slopes of what was later known as Mount St. Genevieve. All the usual public monuments associated with any city colonized by the Romans are to be found: an aqueduct, in this case 15km – 9 miles – long from the Rungis plain, to bring water to the public baths, a network of paved roads to serve the first Latin quarter, a temple to Mercury crowning Montmartre Hill. Lutetia itself was crossed by the great Soissons – Orleans road, so congested with traffic that it was made oneway.

The preaching of St. Denis on the Ile de la Cité would lead one to presuppose the existence of a Christian church of some kind from the year 250 AD, although no trace of such a building has been discovered. Shortly afterwards the Barbarian invasions ravaged the entire Left Bank with fire (276-280).

The mediaeval Alma Mater. – In the 12C teachers, clerks and students threw off the tutelage of the bishops of the Ile de la Cité *(p 63)* and moved to the area

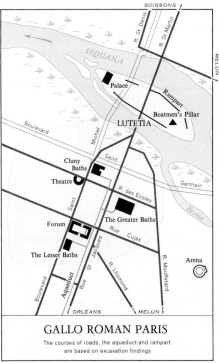

GALLO ROMAN PARIS

The courses of roads, the aqueduct and rampart are based on excavation findings

around the St. Genevieve and St. Victor Monasteries on the Left Bank. In 1215 Pope Innocent III authorised the group's incorporation so founding the University of Paris, the first in France.

Students came from provincial France and abroad, registering under disciplines – theology, medicine, the liberal arts, canon law – or by "nationality", in the colleges founded upon the hill: Sorbon College, 1253; Harcourt College, 1280 on the ruins of the Lutetia Theatre and now St Louis Lycée; Coqueret College *(p 110);* Scottish College *(p 114);* Clermont College, founded by the Jesuits in 1550 and now Louis-le-Grand Lycée; St. Barbara's, Navarre and many others.

The youthful student crowd, turbulent and a terror to the local populace, did not even hold the king in respect. The University had its own jurisdiction of which it was extremely jealous, in 1407 even compelling the royal marshal, who had hanged several students, to come personally and cut down the corpses from the gibet before seeking the Sorbonne's pardon.

The Franciscans (St. Bonaventura), Dominicans (St. Albert the Great, St. Thomas Aquinas) and later the Oratorians (Malebranche, Massillon) and the Jesuits also drew thousands of students and although the University tried, on several occasions, to prevent their following courses, it failed.

From tutelage to autonomy. – In 1793, the Convention disbanded all universities; Latin ceased to be the official language of scholarship.

In 1806 Napoleon founded the Imperial University of France, with a series of academies as the actual bodies of instruction. But university tradition and the enormous influx of students made the system unwelcome and finally unworkable...

New buildings were erected in the Rue des Saints-Pères, Halle aux Vins, Censier and elsewhere and lately in the suburbs, Orsay, Nanterre, Châtenay-Malabry... but still did not prevent the student uprising of May 1968.

October 1970 saw the disappearance of the University of Paris as such and the creation, in its place, for a present student population of 292 000, of thirteen autonomous universities in the Paris region, each with a full range of disciplines, its own curricula and examinations.

The Latin Quarter. – The quarter remains the home of students and younger people of all nationalities, of Bohemianism and fantasy. The Boulevard St-Michel, or Boul'Mich, as it is known, is the heart of the area with its café terraces, publishing houses and bookshops, particularly around the Librairie Gibert, selling new and secondhand books, textbooks, French and foreign language editions, luxury volumes and paperbacks.

In the surrounding streets "cellars", night-clubs, exotic restaurants, experimental cinemas provide night long entertainment.

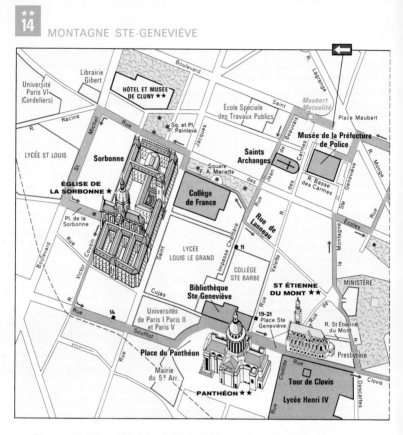

From the Place Maubert to the Place de la Sorbonne

Leave the Place Maubert by the Rue Jean-de-Beauvais where, in the 14C, the **Beauvais College Chapel** was erected. Since 1882 the much restored chapel has been the seat of the Romanian Orthodox Church in Paris *(No. 9 bis; open Fridays and Saturdays 6 to 7pm, Sundays and holidays 10am to 12.30pm;* ☎ *43.54.67.47).*

The street crosses the Rues des Écoles which, when it was laid in 1651, caused the 150 year old print shop of the erudite publishing house of Estienne to be pulled down.

Coqueret College, where in the 16C under the Hellenist master, Dorat, the students included the poets Ronsard, Antoine de Baïf and, later, Rémy Belleau, Jodelle, Pontus de Tyard and du Bellay, who together formed the Pléïade literary group, stood at No. 11 in the Impasse Chartière, left of the Collège de France. Coqueret itself has been incorporated in St. Barbara's.

The **Rue de Lanneau,** by the entrance to the Chartière blind alley, is picturesque with 16C houses. Turn left for the Collège de France.

■ THE COLLÈGE DE FRANCE ▯▯ - fold 43: K 14

The Collège de France has a great past and an equal reputation in present times. The building stands on the site of large Gallo-Roman baths discovered in 1846 *(map p 109)* of which nothing remains.

Three Language College. – The mediaeval university spoke only Low Latin; the Classical authors were proscribed; Virgil was unknown. In 1530, at the suggestion of the great humanist, Guillaume Budé, François I created a new centre of learning with twelve "king's readers" freed from the constraints of Sorbonne intolerance, scholasticism and disdain of pagan literature. The teachers received payment from the king and so could give instruction free.

In the "three language college" students learned to read the greatest Latin, Greek and Hebrew authors. Henri II installed the staff and students in two colleges, Cambrai and Tréguier which were replaced on the same site in the 17C by Louis XIII with the Royal College of France. New subjects of study were added: mathematics, medicine, surgery, philosophy, Arabic, Syriac, botany, astronomy, canon law and, in the reign of Louis XV, French literature.

The college today. – In 1778 the building was reconstructed by Chalgrin and, at the Revolution, took its modern name of Collège de France. 19C reconstructions have been replaced in the 20C by vast additions. The poor labs, at the corner of Rue des Écoles and Rue St-Jacques in which Claude Bernard worked on the function of the pancreas from 1847 to 1878 have disappeared in favour of new halls and laboratories and equipment such as the cyclotron on which Frédéric Joliot-Curie produced fission in a uranium particle. Other outstanding members of the College have been Cuvier (zoologist), Ampère (physicist), Michelet (historian), Champollion (Egyptologist), Renan and Bergson (philosophers), Marcelin Berthelot (chemist), Paul Valéry (poet) and more recently François Jacob (physician). The college retains total scholastic independence although dependent financially, since 1852, on the state.

■ THE SORBONNE ⬚ - fold 43: K 14

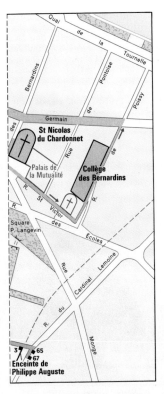

Foundation. – In 1253 a college for sixteen poor students who wished to study theology was founded by a Paris canon, Robert of Sorbon – named, in accordance with mediaeval custom, after his native village of Sorbon in the Ardennes – and the King, Saint Louis, to whom the priest was confessor. From such a simple beginning was to develop the Sorbonne, the centre of theological study in pre-Revolutionary France and the seat of the University of Paris.

It was in the same buildings that three printers summoned from Mainz by Louis XI established the first printing house in France in 1469.

Political and religious struggles. – The theological faculty at Philip the Fair's request condemned the Templars which resulted in their dissolution; in the Hundred Years War, the Sorbonne sided with the Burgundians and the English, recognising Henry V of England as King of France and seconding one of their greatest advocates, Bishop Pierre Cauchon as prosecutor in the trial of Joan of Arc. The Sorbonne steadfastly opposed all Protestants and, in the 18C, the philosophers.

From Richelieu to the present day. – Richelieu, on his election as Chancellor of the Sorbonne, put in hand reconstruction of the buildings and church (1624-1642). In 1792 the Sorbonne and University were suppressed; in 1806 they were re-established by Napoleon. Between 1885 and 1901 large scale rebuilding and expansion prepared the way for the Sorbonne to become the principal centre of higher learning in France.

THE PRESENT BUILDING *Entrance: 47 Rue des Écoles*

The building is a remarkable feat of design when one realises that it includes twenty-two lecture halls, two museums, sixteen examination halls, twenty-two lecture rooms, thirty-seven rooms for the teaching staff, two hundred and forty laboratories, a library, a physics tower, an astronomy tower, offices, the chancellor's lodge, etc.

The most interesting areas are the entrance hall, the main staircase and great lecture theatre *(to visit apply in writing to the Rectorat de Paris)* with Puvis de Chavannes' famous painting the **Sacred Wood**★. The lecture rooms, galleries and halls are decorated with historical and allegorical paintings.

The main courtyard, lined on the left by the library wing, is dominated by the chapel's Classical pediment and cupola. Decorative panels by Weerts beneath the arches illustrate the traditional Lendit Fair held at St-Denis and formerly a great university occasion (11 June).

The Sorbonne Church★ (Église de la Sorbonne). – *Open only when there are temporary exhibitions or cultural events.*

The church was erected by Le Mercier between 1635 and 1642 in the Jesuit style. The façade, unlike St-Paul-St-Louis *(p 83)*, is not so proportioned as to overwhelm the rest of the building and its design of two (instead of three) superimposed orders became the style model.

The **face**★ overlooking the main courtyard of the Sorbonne is completely different: above the ten Corinthian columns marking the doorway, rise, first the transept, then the cupola. The effect is outstanding and worth walking into the courtyard to see.

Inside, in the chancel is the **tomb**★ of Cardinal Richelieu, the white marble magnificently carved by Girardon in 1694 to drawings by Le Brun. The tomb was violated in 1794 when the church became the Temple of Reason.

The cupola pendentives were painted by Philippe de Champaigne.

The Duke of Richelieu, minister to Louis XVIII, is also buried in the church. In the crypt are the tombs of faculty members who died for their country.

From the Place de la Sorbonne to the Place du Panthéon

On leaving the church take the Rue Victor-Cousin on the left and then Rue Soufflot. The **Jacobin Monastery** Church, founded by the first brothers of St. Dominique, who arrived in Paris in 1217, on the site of a former Chapel to St. James, stood at No. **14**. Jacques Clément who assassinated Henri III in 1589 was a brother in the monastery, also Humbert II, last of the line of Dauphiné princes who, by taking holy orders, brought his province under the French crown.

The Rue Soufflot and the semicircular square are lined by the symmetrical buildings of the former Law Faculty (by Soufflot, 1772) now the offices of Paris I, Paris II and Paris V Universities, and buildings by Hittorff, 1844.

If you are only staying a few days in Paris,
the map on p 12 shows you how to see the capital's unique sights in four days.

On the left is the **St Genevieve Library** (Bibliothèque Ste-Geneviève) which replaced the Montaigu College in the 19C. The college was known for its teaching, its austere discipline and its squalor – its scholars were said to sleep on the ground amidst lice, fleas and bugs. Manuscripts, incunabula and 16-18C works from St. Geneviève Abbey were transferred to the new building designed by Labrouste, a master of steel architecture, in 1850 to form the nucleus of the new library (some 2 700 000 volumes). *Reader's ticket holders and students only.* Behind the library is St. Barbara's College, founded in 1460 and the last of the Latin Quarter Colleges to survive.

A hexagonal tower dating from 1560 and known as Calvin's Tower, stands in the courtyard at No **21** Rue Valette. It is all that remains of Fortet College where, in 1585, the Duke of Guise founded the Catholic League which was to expel Henri III from Paris.

■ THE PANTHEON ★★ ▥ - fold 43: L 14

The Pantheon's renown makes it one of the capital's most popular sights.

A royal vow. – Louis XV, when he fell ill at Metz in 1744, vowed that if he recovered he would replace St. Gene-vieve Abbey's half ruined church by a magnificent edifice. He entrusted the fulfilment of his vow to the Marquis of Marigny, brother to the Marquise de Pompa-dour.

Soufflot, Marigny's *protégé,* was charged with the plans. In his effort to combine the nobility and purity of Antiquity and the sweeping lines of the Mid-dle Ages, he designed a vast church 110 m long by 84 m wide by 83 m high – 361 × 276 × 272 ft – in the form of a Greek cross with a vast crypt. At the centre of the chancel he placed a huge dome beneath which would lie the saint's shrine. The foundations were laid in 1758 but financial difficul-ties intervened and it was only completed after Souf-flot's death by his pupil, Rondelet, in 1789.

(Photo J. Bottin)

The Pantheon.

The Temple of Fame. – In 1791 the Constituent Assembly decided that the now closed church should henceforth "receive the bodies of great men who died in the period of French liberty" – the church thus became the national Pantheon. Mirabeau, Voltaire, Rousseau were buried there, and for a short time, Marat also.

Successively the Pantheon has been a church under the Empire, a necropolis in the reign of Louis-Philippe, a church again under Napoleon III, headquarters of the Com-mune and finally a lay temple (Victor Hugo was buried within it in 1885).

Exterior. – The Constituent Assembly ordered the blocking of Soufflot's forty-two win-dows which has deadened the design in spite of the frieze and garland which encircle the building. Two storeys were also removed from the towers flanking the apse.

The **dome ★★** with its iron framework, can only be appreciated from a distance.

The peristyle is composed of fluted columns supporting a triangular pediment, the first of its kind in Paris. In 1831 David d'Angers carved a representation upon it of the Nation distributing palms presented by Liberty to great men. The central doorway is framed by marble groups depicting Clovis' Baptism, St. Genevieve and Attila.

Interior. – *Restoration work in progress – only the crypt is open to the public.*

Flattened domes and, to divide the nave from the aisles, a line of columns support-ing a frieze, cornice and balustrade, were used by Soufflot instead of more orthodox elements. The great central dome was also intended to be supported on columns but Rondelet substituted heavy masonry, so spoiling the effect. The upper cupola has a fresco commissioned by Napoleon in 1811 from the artist, Gros, of *St. Geneviève's Apotheosis.* In 1849 Foucault took advantage of the dome's height to conduct an experiment proving the rotation of the earth *(see Conservatoire des Arts et Métiers, p 158).* The walls are decorated with **paintings ★** dating from 1877 onward; *Scenes from St. Geneviève's Life* (right wall), the *Saint watching over Paris and Bringing Food to the City* – left wall beyond the dome *(p 54)* are by Puvis de Chavannes.

Crypt. – *Guided tours from 10. 30am to 5.30pm; closed on certain holidays; time: 1/2 hour; 10F 1 April to 30 September; 6F the rest of the year.* The crypt extends under the whole building and contains an urn with the heart of Gambetta and the tombs of great men in all walks of life throughout France's history: La Tour d'Auvergne, Voltaire, Rousseau, Victor Hugo, Émile Zola, Marcelin Berthelot, Louis Braille (inventor of a system of writing for the blind), Jean Jaurès, the explorer Bougainville *(see p 78).*

■ ST-ÉTIENNE-DU-MONT CHURCH★★ ▣▣ - fold 44: L 15

Closed on Mondays.

It is in this church that St. Genevieve is venerated particularly. Both outside and inside, the church building is unique.

Until 1220 the servants of the Abbey of St. Genevieve attended services in the church crypt then, their number becoming too great, a parish church, dedicated to St. Stephen, was built adjoining the abbey church. By the end of the 15C St. Stephen's had become too small. Rebuilding began in 1492 with the belfry tower and apse; in 1610 the foundation stone for the new façade was laid by Queen Margot, first wife of Henri IV, and in 1626 the new church was consecrated.

The façade★★ is highly original. Three superimposed pediments stand at the centre, their lines emphasized by the upward sweep of the belfry. The south aisle rises to a considerable height above the chapels. The chancel, the first part to be built, has Flamboyant style broken arch bays, the nave, the later, rounded windows of the Renaissance.

The interior of the church is Gothic although it is 16C. The height of the arches over the nave and chancel, however, prevented the usual triforium being constructed and instead there is a line of windows. The walls along the aisles are also tall enabling wide, luminous bays to be hollowed out. An elegant balustrade course cuts the height of the tall pillars.

The Flamboyant vaulting above the transept catches the eye with its multiple ribbing and 5.50 m – 18 ft intricately carved hanging keystone.

The 17C organ loft is highly ornate. Recitals are given regularly on the organ (90 stops).

The stained glass, which for the most part dates from the 16 and 17C is worth looking at in detail, particularly in the ambulatory and chancel.

The roodscreen★★ is the only one in existence in Paris. In the 15 and 16C all the major churches possessed roodscreens from which the Epistles, the Gospels and sermons were delivered. The screens' disadvantage, however, was that they hid all liturgical ceremony performed in the chancel from the faithful in the nave and in Paris they were, therefore, all removed apart from this one in which the wide arch gave a clear view.

The centre is decorated in the Renaissance style; the twin side doors are Classical. Two lovely open spiral staircases lead to the rood loft and the course along the chancel pillars. Delightful feminine figures adorn the arch at either end.

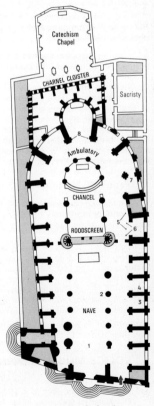

Place Ste Geneviève

1) Marble slab marking the spot where an archbishop of Paris was stabbed to death by an unfrocked priest (3 January 1857).

2) 1650 pulpit★ supported by a figure of Samson.

3) Stained glass window★ of 1586 illustrating the parable of those invited to the feast.

4) 16C Entombment.

5) Over the arch, two ex-votos offered by the City of Paris: on the right, the City giving thanks to St. Genevieve, painted by de Troy in 1726; on the left, an earlier painting by Largillière (1696).

6) The epitaphs of Racine (by Boileau) and Pascal.

7) St. Genevieve's shrine. – St. Genevieve's relics, originally buried in the crypt of the neighbouring abbey *(p 114)*, were exhumed and burnt upon the Place de Grève in 1793. When the abbey church was pulled down in 1802, the saint's sarcophagus stone was found and is now encased by the modern gilded copper shrine containing a few small relics.

8) Pascal (1623-1662) and Racine (1639-1699) lie buried near the pillars to the Lady Chapel. Racine was originally interred at Port-Royal-des-Champs and translated in 1711.

The Cloister. – It is sometimes called the Charnel House Cloister. At one time the church was bordered to the north and east by two small burial grounds in which lay the remains, notably, of Mirabeau and Marat after they had been removed from the Pantheon. The right side of the ambulatory opens onto the cloister which surrounded the burial ground at the church's east end and which, it is thought, may at one time have been used as a charnel house. The cloister's main gallery at the end and on the left was glazed early in the 17C with stained glass★ beautiful in vitality and colour. The small Catechism Chapel was added by Baltard in 1859.

In general buses run from 7am to 8.30pm. To find out about:

the routes operated by city lines

the fare stages

the services extended to midnight

night buses or Sunday and holiday services...

Consult the **Michelin Paris Atlas No ▣▣.**

From the Place du Panthéon to St-Nicolas-du-Chardonnet

Henri-IV Lycée (Lycée Henri-IV). – It was on this site that Clovis, following his victory over the Visigoths at Vouillé near Poitiers, had a rich basilica erected in 510 in which he and his wife Clotilda were both buried and also St. Genevieve. The widespread devotion to the saint soon called for the foundation of an abbey which came under the rule of Augustine canons and rivalled the Abbey of St-Germain-des-Prés in spiritual, juridical and territorial power. Medieval piety was expressed on all occasions by fasting and vast processions walking behind the saint's shrine through the decorated streets of Paris to the sound of ringing church bells.

The Revolution suppressed such festivities and even the abbey so that there remain only the refectory (along the Rue Clotilde), Gothic cellars and the church belfry, known as **Clovis' Tower** (Tour de Clovis). Since 1796 the buildings have been occupied by the Henri-IV Lycée.

On the corner of the Rue Descartes is St-Etienne's presbytery erected by the Duke of Orleans when he retired to the St. Genevieve Abbey where he died in 1752.

Further along, a large section of the **Philippe Auguste perimeter wall** (Enceinte Philippe-Auguste – *p 16*) can be seen at No. **3**, Rue Clovis. It originally stood 10 m – 33 ft high and here lacks only its crenelations. Opposite, at No. **65,** Rue du Cardinal-Lemoine is the **Scottish College,** a building with a noble façade which has belonged to the Roman Catholic Church of Scotland since the 14C. Inside, a magnificent staircase leads to the Classical style chapel where a royal relic was deposited in 1701 on James II's death in exile *(p 131).* The building is now a girls' hostel, the Foyer Ste-Geneviève. *Apply at the porter's lodge a few days in advance (☎ 43.54.11.41) to visit the chapel.* The philosopher Pascal died in 1662 at No. **67.**

Return to the Rue Descartes and turn right to skirt the former Ecole Polytechnique (recently moved to the outskirts of Paris) which replaced the earlier Navarre College, founded in 1304 by Jeanne of Navarre, wife of Philip the Fair; and is now the Institut Auguste-Comte. The institution, originally intended for seventy poor scholars later numbered among its students Henri III, Henri IV, Richelieu and Bossuet. The École Polytechnique, founded by the Convention in 1794, moved to this site in 1805. Two years of military discipline and scholarship "for country, science and glory" ensure a high standard of technical knowledge among the few selected. The "X", as they are known, have included such diverse personages as Foch, the positivist philosopher Auguste Comte, Borotra, André Citroën and the French Presidents, Albert Lebrun and Valéry Giscard d'Estaing. Women were admitted for the first time in 1972.

Return to the Rue de la Montagne Ste-Geneviève, then take the Rue des Ecoles on the right and the Rue des Bernardins on the left to the Church of St-Nicolas-du-Chardonnet.

St-Nicolas-du-Chardonnet Church. – A chapel was constructed on this site in a field planted whith thistles *(chardons)* in the 13C. In 1656 it was replaced by the present north to south oriented building; the façade was completed only in 1934. It is dedicated to St. Nicholas, the patron saint of boatmen.

The side door★ (Rue des Bernardins), with remarkable wood carving after designs by Le Brun, a parishioner, is the best exterior feature.

The Jesuit style interior is liberally decorated with paintings including works by Restout, Coypel, Claude, Corot and Le Brun (his funeral monument, by Coysevox, stands in an ambulatory chapel on the left near Le Brun's own monument to his mother). There is an interesting monument by Girardon to the right of the chancel. The 18C organ loft is from the former Church of the Innocents *(p 102).*

From St-Nicolas-du-Chardonnet Church to the Place Maubert

On leaving the church, walk left along the Rue St-Victor. In the Middle Ages, **St-Victor Abbey** with its monastery buildings, gardens and church where Bishop Maurice of Sully was buried, extended from this area as far as the Seine. Walk past the Palais de la Mutualité.

Turn left into Rue de Poissy constructed in 1772 on the site of the **Bernardins College** gardens. Founded in 1244 it was a school for monks and was taken over by the Cistercians in the 14C. After it was closed down at the Revolution, the building was used as a staging-point for prisoners condemned to the galleys. Since 1845 it has been a fire-station (18-24 Rue de Poissy). From the road, one can catch a glimpse of the upper part of the refectory with its three ogive-vaulted aisles divided into twenty bays. It is one of the finest Gothic halls in Paris. *Not open to the public.*

Continue to the Boulevard St-Germain and walk left to the Place Maubert. Then take the Rue des Carmes to visit the Police Museum.

■ **POLICE MUSEUM (MUSÉE DE LA PRÉFECTURE DE POLICE)** ▢▢ - fold 44: K 15

1 bis Rue des Carmes. Open Mondays to Thursdays 9am to 5pm, Fridays, which do not fall on holidays, 9am to 4.45pm. ☎ 43.29.21.57. extn 336.

The **Historical Collections of the Police Museum** display the evolution of the Paris police and firemen from the early Middle Ages to 1870. There are also legal documents such as *lettres de cachet* or royal warrants, prison registers, criminals weapons and souvenirs of famous conspirators.

Taxi telephone numbers and addresses
of car hire firms are to be found
in the **Michelin publication No ▢▢** *Paris Atlas.*

Distance: 2 1/2 km – 2 miles – Time: 2 1/2 hours. Start from the St-Michel métro station.

This is one of Paris' mediaeval quarters with narrow, winding streets, old and modern schools, university buildings, churches and the treasure filled Hôtel de Cluny.

Start from the Place St-Michel and take the Rues de la Huchette, de la Harpe and St-Séverin to reach the Church of St-Séverin.

■ CHURCH OF ST-SÉVERIN ★★ 🗺 - fold 31: K 14

In the 6C there lived in this area, which was then open country, a hermit by the name of Séverin who persuaded Clodoald, grandson of King Clovis and future saint (St. Cloud in France), to take holy orders.

An oratory, in due course, was raised to his memory but was burned down by the Northmen. It was replaced first by a chapel and later by a church dedicated not to the original Séverin but to a Swiss namesake, St. Severinus.

By the end of the 11C, St-Séverin was serving as the parish church for the Left Bank; the following century Foulques de Neuilly was preaching from its pulpit the 4th Crusade, which was to found the Latin Empire of Constantinople (1204).

Building of the present church began in the first half of the 13C when a master builder, maintaining the Romanesque façade, began to reconstruct the first three bays of the nave in the Gothic style. This substitution of Romanesque by Flamboyant Gothic continued until 1530. In 1681 the capricious Grande Mademoiselle, cousin to Louis XIV, who had broken with her own parish church of St-Sulpice, adopted St-Séverin and, pouring moneys from her vast fortune, had the chancel modernized by the architect, Le Brun. Under his supervision pillars were faced with marble and wood; pointed Gothic arches were transformed into rounded arcades.

Exterior. – Chapel and aisle bays are covered by ridge roofs, each gable being ornamented with mouldings and monster gargoyles.

The west door, which is 13C, comes from the Church of St-Pierre-aux-Bœufs which stood on the Ile de la Cité and was demolished in 1839. Above, windows, balustrades, the rose window, are all 15C Flamboyant Gothic.

The original porch can be seen on the north side of the tower (the tympanum has been recarved). Still on the north side, in the corner formed by the chapels, is a niche containing a statue of St. Severinus. The tower superstructure and spire are both 15C.

Ground plan. – *Open Mondays to Fridays 11am to 1pm and 3.30 to 7.30pm.* The width of the building compared to its length, strikes you immediately on entry. This extra breadth occured in the 14 and 15C when the church's enlargement was being mooted but land was only available on either side. The original building with single side aisles was, therefore, flanked by outer aisles and a series of chapels. There is no transept. The Communion chapel, on the north side, is a 17C addition.

The actual dimensions are: length 50 m width 34 m and height 17 m – 164 × 112 × 56 ft *(cf. the proportions of Notre-Dame, p 57).*

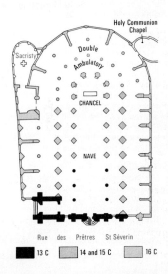

Rue des Prêtres St Séverin

13 C | **14 and 15 C** | **16 C**

Nave. – The first three bays of the nave are far superior to the rest. Their short columns are ornamented with capitals while above the broken arch arcades rises the triforium, a narrow gallery replacing an earlier wide tribune similar to those of Notre-Dame. The bays of the triforium are filled, like those of the windows above, with a regular tracery of trefoils and roses.

In the following Flamboyant style bays, the columns lack capitals; the tracery in the arcades is angular and complicated.

The sides towards the nave of the capitals along the aisles are carved with the figures of angels, prophets and urchins. The organ is as outstanding as the Louis XV organ loft. The two apostle paintings in the north aisle are 17C.

Chancel. – The chancel's five apsidal arches stand higher than those lining the chancel; the Flamboyant vaulting follows a single, much compartmented, design.

The church's wonder is the double **ambulatory ★★**, circling the chancel. As you walk, the fall of the rib tracery onto the column stems recalls strolling through a grove of palm trees. On the central pillar the ribs continue in further ornament as spirals down the shaft.

In the chapel adjoining the sacristy is a late 15C mural, the Last Judgment.

Windows ★. – The beautiful stained glass in the upper windows is late 15C; the bay in the west end illustrating a Tree of Jesse behind the organ is 16C; the modern glass in the east end chapels is by Bazaine.

Charnel House. – *Not open to the public.* A small garden exists, where there was formerly a burial ground surrounded by a charnel house. Part of the galleries although restored, look much as they did in mediaeval times. They are the only ones still extant in Paris today. (The practice was to remove the bones of the dead from their graves and put them in cavities in the charnel house walls as the burial ground became overcrowded).

It was in this burial ground that in 1474 the first operation was made for gall stones. An archer, condemned to death, was a sufferer and was offered his freedom by Louis XI should he survive an experimental operation that a surgeon of the time wished to try out. The operation was successful; the archer was cured and freed.

Walk left round the church by way of the Rue des Prêtres-St-Séverin and the Rue de la Parcheminerie or Parchment Street, so called after public letter writers and copyists who lived there. Once past the east end of the church in the Rue St-Jacques, bear right into the Rue Galande for St-Julien-le-Pauvre and the René-Viviani Square (p 65).

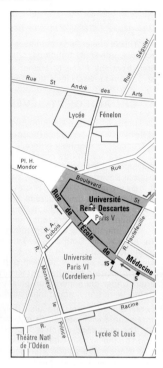

■ ST-JULIEN-LE-PAUVRE CHURCH★

⬚⬚ - fold 31: K 14

This corner of Paris has an appeal all its own with its small local church in a picturesque setting and an unforgettable view of Notre-Dame.

Several of the chapels which have stood successively on this site since the 6C have been named St. Julian – after the 3C Martyr, Bishop of Brioude; after the Confessor, the mediaeval Bishop of Le Mans, who was also known as the Poor because he gave so much away that his purse was always empty; and finally after the ferryman and Hospitaller. In the end it was the name of the mediaeval bishop which prevailed: St. Julian the Poor.

The present building was constructed by the monks of Longpont, a monastery a few miles outside Paris, between 1165 and 1220 (when Notre-Dame was being built).

From the 13 to the 16C the University held its assemblies, including the election of chancellor, in the church, but in 1524 the students made such a rumpus and damaged the interior so gravely that university proceedings were barred henceforth. In 1655 the priory was suppressed and the church attached as a chapel to the Hôtel-Dieu Hospital. Since 1889 it has been a Melchite Chapel.

The square. – The square, on the site of a couple of the church's bays, is more a close than a square. It is bordered to its right by a night-club in the cellars of an old house. The **view**★★ across the opening of the Rue Galande to St-Séverin is one of the best known of old Paris and is still being faithfully reproduced by painters. An iron wellhead, originally over a well inside the church, now stands against the doorway near two paving stones from the old Orleans – Lutetia Roman road (Lutetia was the Roman name for Paris).

No. 14 in the Rue St-Julien-le-Pauvre dates from the 17C and was at one time the house of the governor of the Petit Châtelet or lesser Barbican.

The Church. – The portal onto the square was constructed only in 1651 when two bays of the nave and the south aisle were removed. The north face and chancel, flanked by twin apsidal chapels, overlook the Square René-Viviani.

Inside, although the nave, which lacks a transept, was recovered with cradle vaulting in 1651, the Gothic vaulting over the aisles was left. The chancel, the most beautiful part of the building, is closed by a wooden iconostasis on which hang icons or holy pictures. The two chancel pillars have **capitals**★ remarkably carved with acanthus leaves and harpies. There is also an unusual 15C tombstone in the south aisle.

From the church, take the Rue Galande on the left.

Maubert Quarter. – This old quarter with its small winding streets, the haunt of students, has been restored. The **Rue Galande** where cellars and pointed mediaeval arches have been unearthed at Nos. **46** and **54** and a carved stone above the door of No. **42** shows St. Julian the Hospitaller in his boat, was the Lyons-Paris Roman road. The Rue du Fouarre on the left was one of the places where university lectures were given in the open air in the Middle Ages and it got its name from the bundles of straw (fouarre) on which students sat. Dante is said to have attended lectures in this street in 1304.

Follow the Rue Galande (15C gable at No. **31**) to the Rue Lagrange. Cross the Rue Lagrange and take Rue de l'Hôtel-Colbert.

At the corner of the Rue de la Bûcherie is situated the Paris Administration School on the premises of the first Medical School founded in the 15C. The rotunda dates from the 17C.

Turn right into the Rue de la Bûcherie.

By the corner of the Rue Frédéric-Sauton, take a few steps to the right into the Impasse Maubert where the first Greek College was founded in 1206, and also the laboratory where the infamous Marquise de Brinvilliers concocted her poisons.

Follow the Rue des Grands Degrès to the Quai de Montebello, an embankment which protected the low-lying areas from high tides. You can enjoy lovely vistas of Notre-Dame to the left.

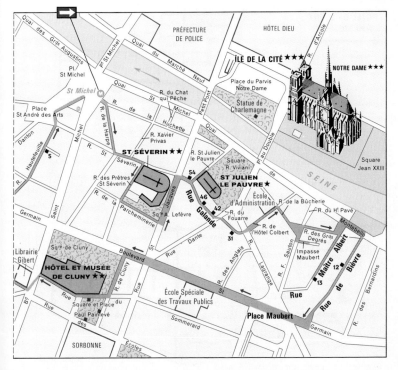

On the right is the small **Rue Maître-Albert** named after the Dominican Albert the Great who taught in the square in the 13C (Maubert is probably a contraction of his name). Its old houses rise above an underground network which led to the banks of the Seine and to the adjoining alleyways where rogues and conspirators found shelter. Mme du Barry's negro attendant, Zamor, who denounced her and caused her to be sent to the guillotine, died in 1820 at No. **13**. Continue along the quay and turn right into the **Rue du Bièvre** named after a tributary of the Seine. This quarter was frequented by boatmen and tawers. The entrance of the former St-Michel College at No. **12** is surmounted by a statue of St. Michael slaying the dragon.

Since the early Middle Ages, the **Place Maubert** has been a traditional meeting-place where barricades have gone up in times of popular uprising.

The Rue des Anglais, off the Boulevard St-Germain, was named after the English students who lived there in the Middle Ages.

The Rue de Cluny leads to the Place Paul-Painlevé and the Hôtel de Cluny.

■ THE HÔTEL DE CLUNY AND ITS MUSEUM★★   ▯▯ - fold 31: K 14

The old residence of the Abbots of Cluny, the ruins of the Roman baths and the wonderful museum, make a supremely interesting group.

The Roman baths. – The present ruins cover about one third of the site which must have been occupied at the beginning of the 3C by a vast Gallo-Roman public bath house, constructed by the powerful guild of Paris boatmen. By the end of the 3C it had been sacked and burnt to the ground by the Barbarians.

The residence of the Abbots of Cluny. – About 1330, Pierre of Châlus, Abbot of Cluny-en-Bourgogne bought the ruins and the surrounding land on behalf of the influential Burgundian Abbey to build a residence for abbots visiting the college founded by the abbey near the Sorbonne. Jacques of Amboise, Bishop of Clermont and Abbot of Jumièges in Normandy, rebuilt the residence to its present design between 1485 and 1500.

The house received many guests including Mary Tudor, eldest daughter of Henry VII who at 16 had been married to Louis XII of France, a man in his fifties who only survived three months. The queen passed her period of mourning in the residence strictly watched by Louis' cousin and successor, François I, lest she should bear a child which might cost him his throne. In fact when Mary was discovered one night in the company of the young Duke of Suffolk the king compelled her to marry the Englishman there and then in the chapel and then despatched her straightaway to England.

In the 17C the house served as residence for the papal nuncios, the most illustrious being Mazarin.

Abandonment. – At the Revolution the residence was sold for the benefit of the state. It had a variety of owners – a surgeon who used the chapel as a dissecting room, a cooper, a printer. The navy installed an observatory in the tower and discovered 21 planets. The baths were covered with six feet of soil and vegetables and an orchard planted.

The founding of the museum. – In 1833 a collector by the name of Alexandre Du Sommerard came to live in the house. On his death in 1842 the mansion and its contents were purchased by the state and opened as a museum in 1844.

HOTEL DE CLUNY AND MUSEUM

0 — 20 m
— Baths

FIRST FLOOR

XX — Chapel
XIV
XIX
XV
XIII — XVI — XVIII XXI XXII XXIII
XII — XVII
Access to ground floor
XI
The Lady and the Unicorn Tapestries
Access to ground floor

GROUND FLOOR

Boulevard Saint Michel
Gymnasium — Gymnasium
Pool
Cluny
TEPIDARIUM (Warm water bath)
FRIGIDARIUM (Cold water bath) X
Notre-Dame de Paris Gallery
Access to first floor
VI
V
VII
IV III II I XXIV
Ticket Office
CALDARIUM (Steam room)
Access to first floor
VIII
X
IX
Arcades
COURTYARD
Well
Painlevé
Rue Du Sommerard — Place Paul
Rue de
GROUND FLOOR

THE HOUSE★★

The Hôtel de Cluny with that of Sens and Jacques Cœur's house, is one of the three large private houses dating back to the 15C to remain in Paris. The mediaeval tradition can be seen in several features such as the crenelations and turrets although these have only a decorative function. Comfort and delicate ornament are important elements in the mansion's design.

Enter the main courtyard where there is a beautiful 15C well curb. The left wing is decorated with arches; the central building has mullioned windows while above, a frieze and Flamboyant balustrade, from which gargoyles spurt, line the base of the roof which in its turn is ornamented with picturesque dormer windows swagged with coats of arms. A pentagonal tower juts out from the central building to contain a wide spiral staircase.

THE MUSEUM★★

Open 9.45am to 12.30pm and 2 to 5.15pm; closed Tuesdays and holidays; 15F (8F on Sundays). ☎ 43.25.62.00.

The museum's twenty-four galleries are entirely devoted to the Middle Ages; the collection as a whole, gives an outstanding picture of the period.

The Baths★ (Thermes). – Excavations have determined the plan of these public baths dating from 200 AD. The best preserved area, the frigidarium **(room X)** which measures 21 × 11 m – 69 × 36 ft, was 14.5 m – 47 1/2 ft high and had walls 2 m – 6 1/2 ft thick was built of small quarry stones divided by red brick courses. The ribbed vaulting rests on consoles carved as ships' prows – an unusual motif which has inspired the idea that the building was constructed by the Paris boatmen. This same guild, in the reign of Tiberius, (14–37 AD), dedicated a pillar to Jupiter which was discovered beneath the chancel of Notre-Dame *(map p 109)* and is now on view in the court; known as the **Boatmen's Pillar** (1) it is Paris' oldest sculpture.

The Notre-Dame de Paris Gallery contains fragments of sculpture from Notre-Dame. Among the exposed pieces are **21 heads** from the King's Gallery. Discovered in April 1977 during the restoration of Hôtel Moreau in the 9th *arrondissement,* these works date from the mid-12C to the mid-13C. In spite of their condition, the heads evoke an unexpected freshness and a surprising intensity. The doorway belonged to the Lady Chapel of St-Germain-des-Prés Church.

The tapestries. – Several rich series of tapestries, woven in the south of the Netherlands in the 15 and early 16C, are of the "thousand flower" type, which is typified by harmony and freshness of colour, love of nature, and the grace of the people and animals portrayed by the artists.

The most perfect example is **The Lady and the Unicorn★★★** series (room **XI** rotunda, 1st floor). In the six hangings the lion (chivalric nobility) and the unicorn (bourgeois nobility), standing on either side of a richly clad lady, probably symbolize the armorial bearings of different members of the Le Viste family from Lyons. Five of the hangings are believed to depict allegories of the senses but the sixth remains unexplained. Note the blue-green grass and uniform red backgrounds, the lack of decoration, the richness of the animal and plant life.

The decorative arts in the Middle Ages. – In addition to the tools and utensils of everyday life, the museum possesses pieces of sculpture (original statues from Notre-Dame and the Sainte-Chapelle, rooms **IX, X**), jewellery, gold and silverwork, furniture, illuminated manuscripts, arms and armour, ironwork, liturgical vestments, stained glass, etc. Some of the finest masterpieces (paintings, tapestries and sculpture) of the late Middle Ages are grouped in **room XII**.

The chapel★ (room **XX**). – The chapel, on the first floor, was formely the abbots' oratory. It has elegant Flamboyant vaulting which falls upon a central pillar and twelve niches, each with its console and carved canopy and formerly containing the statue of a member of the Amboise family. Below there now hang fine tapestries from Auxerre Cathedral illustrating the life of St. Stephen. A stone staircase with an open well leads down to the garden.

On leaving the Hôtel de Cluny, continue along the Rue Du Sommerard and across the Boulevard St-Michel to the Rue de l'École-de-Médecine, another old Gallo-Roman road.

Rue de l'École-de-Médecine. – At No. **5** the long gowned Brotherhood of Surgeons, founded by St. Louis in the 13C, performed anatomical operations of every kind until the 17C. Barbers or short gowned surgeons were only allowed to undertake bleeding and confinements. The 1695 lecture theatre has been incorporated in the Paris III University.

At No. **15** stood a Franciscan monastery of high repute in the Middle Ages for its teaching. In Louis XVI's reign, the geometrician **Verniquet** worked there on the first trigonometrical plan of Paris. Shortly afterwards, in 1791, the revolutionary group formed by Danton, Marat, Camille Desmoulins and Hébert took over both the monastery and its name, the Cordeliers. Marat lived opposite and it was there that he was stabbed in his bath by Charlotte Corday on 13 July 1793.

The present buildings, now a university centre (Paris VI), were built between 1877 and 1900 to house the School of Practical Medicine. Of the vast conventual buildings, only the monks' Flamboyant Gothic refectory-dormitory *(not open)* remains in the courtyard.

The central part of the former Medical School (No. 12), now known as the **René Descartes University** (Paris V), dates back to 1775. An Ionic colonnade precedes a large courtyard at the centre of which stands a statue of the 18C French anatomist, *Bichat,* by David d'Angers. In pre-Revolutionary times students of medicine and surgery were taught separately; they were united in 1808. All students now complete their practical studies in the eleven university medical centres of the Paris region.

Continue round the school and along the Boulevard St-Germain to the Rue Hautefeuille, on the left. The old street, in which No. **5,** with an attractive 16C turret, was once a residence of the abbots of Fécamp, ends in the Place St-André-des-Arts, a square with picturesque houses on the site of a church of the same name.

(Photo Musées Nationaux)

The Lady and the Unicorn-detail.

Michelin plan ⅓⅓ - folds 31, 43: K 13, L 13.

Distance: 3 km – 2 miles – Time: 2 hours (tour of the Luxembourg Palace not included).
Start from the Odeon métro station.

This pleasant walk takes in one of the city's finest gardens.

From the Carrefour de l'Odéon to the Luxembourg

Take the Rue de Condé. It was in this street, lined with old houses, that Beaumarchais wrote the _Barber of Seville_ in 1773 (No. **26**). Continue along the Rue Crébillon to the Place de l'Odéon.

Place de l'Odéon. – This semicircular square was created in 1779 in the former Condé house grounds and has always been a place of repute. The houses surrounding it have plain façades; the roads leading to it were named after famous writers: Corneille, Racine, Voltaire (now renamed Casimir-Delavigne), Molière (Rotrou), Crébillon, Regnard. No. **1**, the Café Voltaire, was frequented by the Encyclopaedists and, at the turn of the 20C, by Barrès, Bourget, Mallarmé and Verlaine.

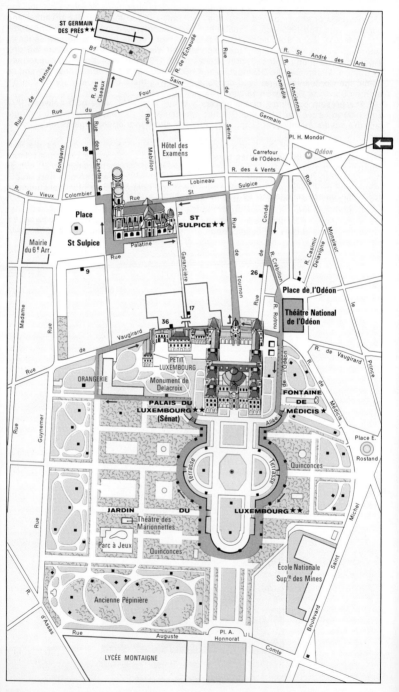

Théâtre National de l'Odéon. – In 1782 a theatre was built in the gardens of the former Condé mansion to accommodate the French Comedians who for the past twelve years had been installed in the Tuileries Palace Theatre. The new theatre, built in the antique style of the day, was given the name Théâtre Français.

Came the Revolution; the company divided and in 1792 those for the Republic left under Talma for the theatre in the Rue Richelieu, the present Comédie-Française *(p 98)*. The Royalists who remained were soon removed to prison.

In 1797 a new company took over the theatre, renamed it the Odeon and failed. In 1807 the building was burned down but was reconstructed and the company started up again. In spite of the success of the play by Alphonse Daudet, the *Arlésienne* (1872) to music by Bizet, the theatre never became popular until 1946 when it began to specialize in 20C plays. It changed its name to Théâtre de France and for several years, with a company headed until 1968 by Jean-Louis Barrault and Madeleine Renaud, became the best filled theatre in Paris. Inside is a modern ceiling designed in 1963 by André Masson.

Walk down the Rue Rotrou and turn right for the Luxembourg Palace.

■ THE LUXEMBOURG PALACE AND GARDENS★★ ▢▢ - fold 43: K 13

The site, after the abandonment of the encampment and villas of Gallo-Roman times, became a desert and later the haunt of a ghostly highwayman named Vauvert, after his lair in an old ruin. Terror spread far and wide until in 1257 the Carthusians, installed by St. Louis at Gentilly, suggested to the king that they rid the neighbourhood of the outlaw. They succeeded and built a vast monastery in the area.

Marie dei Medici's Palace. – After the death of Henri IV, his Queen, Marie dei Medici decided to build a palace which would recall the house of her youth in Tuscany. In 1612 she bought the mansion of Duke François of Luxembourg and a considerable adjoining area; in 1615 her architect, Salomon de Brosse, began to construct a palace inspired by the Pitti Palace of Florence. The building was much admired and in 1621 Rubens was commissioned to paint a series of 24 large pictures retracing allegorically the queen's life – the pictures now hang in the Medici Gallery in the Louvre *(pp 28, 38)*.

The day of deceit. – In 1625 the queen installed herself in the palace but her joy was short-lived for she had entered into opposition with Richelieu. She extracted a promise from her son, Louis XIII, on 10 November 1630 to dismiss the Cardinal but it was revoked twenty-four hours later and she was banished to Cologne where she died penniless in 1642. The palace reverted to its original Luxembourg title and, although abandoned, remained crown property until the Revolution.

The palace as parliament. – In 1790 when the monastery was suppressed, the gardens were enlarged and the palace vista extended the full length of the Avenue de l'Observatoire. Under the Terror the palace became a prison. The building next became a parliamentary assembly for the Directory, the Consulate, the Senate and its successor the Peers' Chamber. Chalgrin, architect of the Arc de Triomphe and the Odéon, completely transformed the interior, while from 1836 to 1841 Alphonse de Gisors enlarged it on the garden side by the addition of a new front to the main building and two projecting wing pavilions. At various dates Marshal Ney, the conspirator Louis-Napoleon Bonaparte (the future Napoleon III) and members of the Commune who turned against it, were all tried in the palace. In the Second World War the building was occupied by the Germans. On 25 August 1944 it was freed by Leclerc's Division and the French Resistance.

It is now the seat of the **Senate** (Sénat), the French Upper House. The Senate is composed of 283 members chosen by an electoral college consisting of deputies, departmental and municipal councillors. Should the Presidency of the Republic fall vacant, the Senate President will exercise the functions of Head of State in the interim.

THE PALACE

Guided tours, daily, from 1 January to 31 March and 1 July to 30 September when the senators are not in session. During session times (20 October to 23 December and 1 April to 30 June): tours only at weekends providing there are no exceptional sittings. Closed holidays; time: 1 hour; by appointment. ☏ 42.34.20.60.

To give a Florentine air to his design for the palace, Salomon de Brosse employed bosses, ringed columns and Tuscan capitals but he kept the French style ground plan of a courtyard surrounded by a central building, two wings at right angles and closed by twin arcaded galleries meeting in a central gateway surmounted by a cupola. The fine balustraded terrace has been recently reconstituted according to Brosse's original plan.

Interior. – The library is decorated with **paintings**★ by Delacroix *(Dante and Virgil walking in Limbo, Alexander placing Homer's poems in Darius' gold casket)*. The ceiling of the library annexe is decorated with a painting of the *Signs of the Zodiac* by Jordaens.

In the Golden Book Room are the 17C panelling and paintings which once adorned Marie dei Medici's apartments. The Senate council chamber, the state gallery and most of the saloons were furnished during the reign of Louis-Philippe. The main staircase by Chalgrin leads to the gallery in which the Rubens paintings were hung at one time.

Exterior. – Two inner courts, below the level of the Allée de l'Odéon, are decorated in the French garden style. The Petit Luxembourg, now the residence of the president of the Senate, comprises the original Hôtel de Luxembourg presented to Richelieu by Marie dei Medici and also the cloister and chapel of a convent founded by the queen.

The Senate has extended its premises to a series of buildings across Rue de Vaugirard. In the ground floor galleries, can be seen exhibitions of Coins and Medals and Sèvres Porcelain. Incorporated in the new building are, No. **36**, the doorway of a mansion built by Boffrand in 1716 and round the corner at No. **17** Rue Garancière, the façade of another mansion adorned with mascaroons representing the Seasons.

THE GARDENS

The gardens, which in themselves are most attractive, provide the most extensive green open space with harmonious lines and vistas on the Left Bank.

Basically the design is formal, the only free, more English style garden being along the Rue Guynemer and the Rue Auguste-Comte.

The **Medici Fountain** ★ (Fontaine de Médicis) (1624) which stands in a green setting at the very end of a long pool shaded by plane trees, shows obvious Italian influence in its embossed decoration and overall design. In a niche the jealous cyclops, Polyphemus, waits to crush Acis and Galatea (by Ottin, 1863) while on the Rue de Médicis side is a low relief of Leda and the Swan (1807).

Statues began to invade the lawns under Louis-Philippe and today have reached such numbers that they seem to confront one at every step. The best, among this not artistically impressive crowd of figures, is the Delacroix group by Dalou. Queens and illustrious women of France line the terrace.

From the Luxembourg Palace to St-Germain-des-Prés

Walk to the Place St-Sulpice by way of the Rue de Vaugirard and the Rue de Tournon and, on the left, the Rue St-Sulpice.

Place St-Sulpice. – Started in 1754, it was originally intended that the square should be semicircular with uniform façades modelled on that at No. **6** (at the corner of the Rue des Canettes), designed by Servandoni, the 18C Italian architect and painter who worked principally in France *(see below)*. The project for the uniform square fell through.

At the centre of the square stands a fountain erected by Visconti in 1844. It is so fashioned that it includes at the cardinal points of the compass, the portrait busts of four great men of the church: Bossuet, Fénelon, Massillon and Fléchier. None were ever made cardinals and in a play upon words – *point* in French means: both point and never – the fountain is known as *The Fontaine des Quatre Points Cardinaux* – the Fountain of the Cardinal Points or the Four Cardinals who never were.

No. 9 was the site of a former seminary.

■ CHURCH OF ST-SULPICE ★★   ▢▢ - fold 31: K 13

The church, dedicated to the 6C Archbishop of Bourges, St. Sulpicius, was founded by the Abbey of St-Germain-des-Prés as a parish church for the peasants living in its domain. It has been rebuilt several times and was enlarged in the 16 and 17C, reconstruction beginning in 1646 with the chancel. Six architects were in charge successively over a period of one hundred and thirty-four years.

By 1732 work was due to begin on the façade but it was felt that a different style was required from the Graeco-Roman which had been adopted up till then. A competition was organized which was won by the Florentine, Servandoni, who proposed a fine Antique style façade in contrast to the rest of the edifice. Servandoni's project was adopted but modified first by Maclaurin and then by Chalgrin. Delacroix' genius dominated the twenty artists who worked on the interior mural decorations.

Exterior. – The final façade differs considerably from Servandoni's original concept. The colossal pediment has been abandoned; the belfries are crowned not by Renaissance pinnacles but by balustrades; the towers are dissimilar, the one on the left being taller and more ornate than the one on the right which was never completed.

Walk back along the south side of the church, down the Rue Palatine. The transept façade is in the Jesuit style with two superimposed orders and heavy ornaments.

Seen from the corner of the Rue Palatine and the Rue Garancière, St-Sulpice is a building of some size, shouldered by massive buttresses designed as inverted consoles and ending in the dome and corbelled apse of the Lady Chapel.

Interior. – The interior, which measures 113 m long by 58 m wide by 34 m high – 371 × 190 × 112 ft – is extremely impressive.

In the transept, a copper band oriented from north to south and inlaid in the pavement, crosses from a plaque in the south arm to an obelisk in the north arm. During the winter solstice a ray of sunshine, passing through a small hole in the upper window in the south transept, strikes marked points on the obelisk in the far transept at midday exactly. At the spring and autumn equinox the ray falls on the copper plaque. This 1744 meridian *(p 132)* thus serves daily as a midday timepiece. The Christ against the Pillar, the Mater Dolorosa and the Apostles beside the chancel columns are by Bouchardon.

The decoration of the **Lady Chapel** ★ at the centre of the east end of the church, was supervised personally by Servandoni. In the altar niche is a Virgin and Child by Pigalle; on the walls hang paintings by Van Loo and on the dome is a fresco by Lemoyne.

The **organ loft** ★ was designed by Chalgrin in 1776. The organ itself was rebuilt in 1862 and is considered one of the finest in France. The church has a long and august musical tradition.

Mural paintings ★ full of Romantic ardour were carried out by Delacroix between 1849 and 1861 on the walls of the first chapel on the right. On the vaulting is St. Michael killing the dragon; on the right wall Heliodorus is being driven from the Temple (the story is that Heliodorus, a minister of the King of Syria, coveted the treasures of the Temple and was struck down by three avenging angels); on the left wall Jacob struggles with the Angel.

Two stoups against the second pillars of the nave have been made from giant shells given to François I by the Venetian Republic and then Louis XV to St-Sulpice Church in 1745. Their rock supports were carved by Pigalle.

Return to St-Germain-des-Prés by the Rue des Canettes, Duckling Street, which takes its name from the low relief at No. **18** – and the Rue des Ciseaux with its many old houses.

THE GRANDS BOULEVARDS
AND THE SENTIER QUARTER

★★ 17

Michelin plan ⅏ - folds 19, 20 and 31: from F 13 to F 15 - from G 13 to G 17.

The following two walks will allow the tourist to see the varying aspects of this quarter, one of the liveliest in Paris.

① THE GRANDS BOULEVARDS ⅏ - folds 19 and 20: from F 13 to G 17

Distance: 3 km – 2 miles – Time: 1 1/2 hours (not including the visit to the Grévin Museum). Start from the Opera métro station.

Well known buildings; long tree lined vistas; a tide of pedestrians moving earnestly on business or idling slowly; busy roads; wide café terraces with tables overflowing onto the pavement; cinemas, theatres, thousands of shops, a plethora of lights and advertisements; in short the Boulevards – their prestige as high, their fame as great, as ever.

The ramparts transformed. – By 1660 Louis XIV had established himself firmly on the throne and the fortified perimeter walls around Paris had become obsolete and fallen into disrepair. The part of the Charles V wall between the Bastille and the St. Denis Gate, and the ramparts erected under Charles IX and Louis XIII *(p 16),* were therefore knocked down, the moats filled in and a raised terrace thoroughfare constructed in their place. This fareway, sufficiently wide to allow four carriages to ride abreast, was bordered by side roads lined by a double avenue of trees. Triumphal arches replaced the fortified gates.

The project, when it was finally completed in 1705, was known as the Boulevard.

The place to take the air. –
In about 1750 the Boulevard became fashionable: seated in the shade on straw-bottomed chairs Parisians watched horse carriages and riders pass by.

Gradually the west end became the area where the nobility and the rich built their private mansions; the east end, the Boulevard du Temple, almost a fairground, with crowds drawn to the theatres and dance halls, circuses, waxworks, puppets, dancers, acrobats, mechanical figures, cafés, restaurants, booths and barrows. For a hundred years

(Archives R.A.T.P.)

Madeleine-Bastille Omnibus.

the crowd rejoiced; by 1830 the local theatres had played violent melodrama for so long that the area was nicknamed the Criminal Boulevard.

The Boulevard des Italiens, opened under the Directory, acquired an elegance which spread to the Boulevard Montmartre and persisted until the middle of the 19C.

The roads were first paved in 1778 and about the same time street lights, burning animal fat, appeared and were declared altogether blinding; gas lamps were installed in the Passage des Panoramas *(p 125)* in 1817, and on the Boulevard in 1826. The first bus appeared on 30 January 1828 when it travelled from the Madeleine to the Bastille. Footpaths were surfaced.

The modern boulevard. – The creation by Haussmann of the Opera and Republic Squares and the wide highways leading to them, began the transformation which still goes on as crowds replace the fashionable; lights become more glaring; advertising depersonalizes; famous cafés disappear – and the only constant is the Parisian himself.

From the Opera to Richelieu-Drouot

Walk from the Opera Square *(p 80)* along the east end of the Boulevard des Capucines *(p 80)* to the Boulevard des Italiens.

The old Boulevard des Italiens. – The street's history is linked with fads and fashions. *Muscadins* and *Merveilleuses* haunted it at the time of the Directory; *Gandins* during the Restoration, were succeeded by Dandies who also followed English fashion and, in 1835, were the first to smoke in public. Waxed moustaches, imperials and crinolines appeared during the Second Empire.

The boulevard today. – The uninspired Palais Berlitz, at the corner of the Rue Louis-le-Grand, has replaced the Pavillon de Hanovre, the favourite ice-cream restaurant of the *Merveilleuses;* No. **22** is where the Café Tortoni stood; No. **20**, the famous **Maison Dorée** restaurant (built 1839-1841) was once the meeting place for fashionable Paris; elegantly decorated façades line the boulevard and Rue Lafitte; No. **16** is where the Café Riche received its patrons from 1791 until early this century.

The Opéra-Comique. – The present building stands on the site of the theatre constructed by the Duke of Choiseul in 1782 in his own grounds for the Comic Opera company *(p 102),* commonly called "the Italians". The boulevard took its name from the company.

The company gradually changed its repertoire from French to Italian light opera and ultimately, with Offenbach and Johann Strauss, included operettas.

Today the Opéra-Comique, or Salle Favart is the second auditorium of the Paris Opera Company where French works are sung by an exclusively French company.

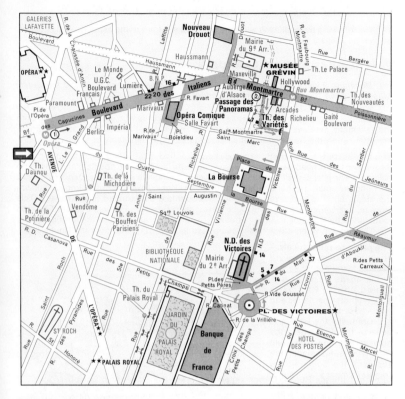

Richelieu-Drouot Crossroads. – The Auberge d'Alsace, stands on the site of what was known, in the 17C, as the "modest and secluded" house of the poet, Regnard. Opposite, in 1796, was the famous Café Frascati which closed down when gambling was banned by Louis-Philippe.

To the left of the road junction at No. 9 Rue Drouot is the new building, **Nouveau Drouot**, (☎ 42.46.17.11; closed in August, for 10 days at Christmas, 5 days at Easter) of the Paris art auctioneer company. Reopened on 13 May 1980 the 16 auction rooms, with daily auctions at 2pm, provide a lively and interesting spectacle.

From Richelieu-Drouot to the Place de la République

Boulevard Montmartre. – On the right at No. 11 is the **Passage des Panoramas** (p 125). At No. 7 stands the **Théâtre des Variétés** built in 1807, the home of light comedy and operetta presenting the wit and gaiety of Meilhac and Halévy, Offenbach, Flers and Caillavet, Tristan Bernard and Sacha Guitry.

Grévin Museum ★ (Musée Grévin). – 10 Boulevard Montmartre (see also p 99). Open 1pm (10am during school holidays) to 7pm (last admission 6pm); 34F; children 22F. ☎ 47.70.85.05.

Grévin, a caricaturist, founded the museum in 1882. (The first waxworks were introduced to Paris in the 18C). It contains historical scenes, distorting mirrors, conjuring sessions – amusement for one and all.

Continue along the Boulevards Poissonnière and Bonne-Nouvelle. The **Rue de la Lune**, to the right, forms a sharp angle with the Rue de Cléry, typical of old Paris.
Further on, these boulevards become the St-Denis and St-Martin Boulevards, each marked at its start by a monumental gate.

Porte St-Denis ★. – The gate was erected by the City in 1672 in celebration of Louis XIV's victories on the Rhine – 40 strongholds captured in less than two months. On either side are carvings of the pyramids superimposed with trophies and on the boulevard side, allegorical figures representing Holland (left) and the Rhine (right); above the arch can be seen the crossing of the Rhine; and on the faubourg side, the Fall of Maëstricht.

Porte St-Martin ★. – The gate which is only 17 m high – 56 ft was erected by the dean and aldermen in 1674 to commemorate the capture of Besançon and defeat of the German, Spanish and Dutch armies. The carvings illustrate not only the taking of Besançon but also the breaking of the Triple Alliance, the capture of Limburg and the defeat of the Germans.

Boulevard St-Martin. – Built in an undulating area, the boulevard runs below the pavement in order to avoid steep inclines. Two adjoining theatres stand near the gate: the Renaissance (1872) and the Porte St-Martin. The latter was built in 1781 to house the company from the Palais-Royal opera house which had been destroyed by fire. The first masked Opera balls were held there. It became a dramatic theatre after 1814. Burned down during the Commune uprising, it was rebuilt in 1873.

Continue down the Boulevard to the Place de la République (p 171).

② **THE STOCK EXCHANGE AND SENTIER QUARTERS**

▢▢ - folds 19, 31, 32 and 20: F 14, G 14, G 15

Distance: 3 km – 2 miles – Time: 2 hours (not including the visit to the Stock Exchange).
Start from the Rue Montmartre métro station. Try to do this visit on a weekday.

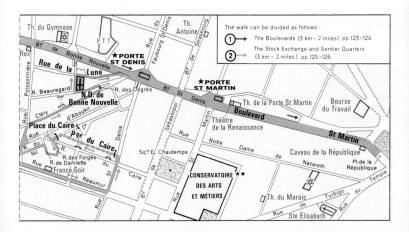

No. 11 Boulevard Montmartre is the **Passage des Panoramas** which was opened in 1799. The name comes from the two vast panoramas of capital cities and historic scenes painted and displayed in rotundas by the American, Henry Fulton, who also invented submarines and perfected steam ships. No. **47**, an engraver's shop, has kept its old aspect.

Turn right into the Rue N.-D. des Victoires to reach the Place de la Bourse.

The Stock Exchange (Palais de la Bourse). – The building stands on the site of a Dominican convent which was secularized in 1795 and became the seat of the royalist faction responsible for the insurrection of 13 Vendémiaire – 5 October 1795 – *(p 97)*.

Paris' first exchange was John Law's bank *(p 103)*. As a result of this bankruptcy, the public learned so much about shares and holdings that a public exchange was founded (1724). It was situated in the Mazarin Mansion *(p 95)*, then in the church of Notre-Dame des Victoires and in the Palais-Royal. The present building was begun by Brongniart in 1808, completed in 1826 and enlarged in 1902 and 1907.

Inside the public may visit a gallery *(guided tours every 30 min. from 11am to 1pm, except Saturdays, Sundays and holidays; 1 July to 15 September, one tour daily at noon; time: 1 1/2 hours; 8F; for further information ☎ 42.33.99.83).* From another gallery one can see the actual exchange.

Continue along the Rue Notre-Dame-des-Victoires (note the 18C mansion at No. **14**) to the Place des Petits-Pères, which has been built on the site of the Monastery of the Barefoot Augustins.

Basilica of Notre-Dame-des-Victoires. – The basilica (built 1629-1740) served as the monastery chapel and later, was occupied by the Exchange from 1795-1809. Inside are 17C panelling in the chancel, seven paintings by Van Loo *(Louis XIII dedicating the church to the Virgin*, scenes from the *Life of St. Augustine)*, a fine 18C organ loft and a monument to the 17C composer, Lulli *(2nd chapel on the left)*. The church is famous for its annual pilgrimage to the Virgin which goes back to 1836; some 30 000 ex-votos cover the walls.

From the church, walk along the short Rue Vide-Gousset (Pickpocket Street) to the Place des Victoires.

■ **PLACE DES VICTOIRES**★ ▢▢ - fold 31: G 14

In 1685 Marshal de la Feuillade, to curry favour with Louis XIV, commissioned a statue of the king from the sculptor, Desjardins. The statue, unveiled in 1686, showed the king, crowned with the laurels of victory, standing on a pedestal adorned with six low reliefs and four captives representing the vanquished Spain, Holland, Prussia and Austria. Mansart designed the façades overlooking the square where the statue was erected.

The statue was melted down in 1792; a new figure by Desaix replaced it in 1806 only to be melted down in turn in 1815 (and reappear as Henri IV on the Pont Neuf!). The present equestrian statue of the Sun King was sculpted by Bosio in 1822.

The side of the square with even numbers is the least damaged and gives some idea of the intended 17C elegance although its harmony was impaired by the construction of Rue Etienne Marcel in 1883.

One of the façades of the **Bank of France** can be seen on looking along the Rue Catinat, from the entrance of Rue d'Aboukir. The Bank on the Rue de la Vrillière was founded at the instigation of Napoleon in January 1800. First housed at No. 4 Rue d'Aboukir, it moved in 1812, to the mansion *(not open)* built in 1635 by François Mansart and remodelled by Robert de Cotte. The present building dates mostly from the 19C.

From the Place des Victoires to the Boulevard Bonne-Nouvelle

Walk out of the Place des Victoires along the Rue Vide-Gousset and turn into the Rue du Mail.

At Nos. **5** and **7** (both 17C) belonging to Colbert, are, on the upper capitals, a faun's mask and cornucopias and interlaced snakes (the snake – *coluber* in Latin – Colbert's emblem), respectively. At No. **14**, an 18C hôtel, lived Madame Récamier. The newspaper *Le Figaro* is printed in the building located at No. **37** Rue du Mail.

The Sentier. – The Sentier quarter begins on the other side of the Rue Montmartre. It is the centre of the wholesale trade for materials, trimmings, hosiery and ready-made clothes.

After the Rue de Cléry, turn right into the Rue Réaumur (where *France-Soir* is printed) which you follow to the Rue St-Denis, where you turn left to reach the Passage du Caire.

Caire Passage and Square. – Napoleon's victorious campaign in Egypt in 1798 aroused great enthusiasm in Paris – architecture and fashion were greatly influenced and streets and squares in this area were given names in memory of his successes.

Walk under the covered arcades of the strange Passage du Caire to the square (the heart of the old Court of Miracles) where the outlet is overlooked by a house with a façade decorated with Egyptian motifs.

The Court of Miracles. – A Court of Miracles was a place where, in the Middle Ages, miscreants lived out of the reach of the authorities. Blind alleys and passageways, easily defended, opened off the muddy courtyard and the police did not often venture inside the area. It was the refuge of well organised bands of rogues led by their own elected king.

During daylight, the lame, the blind and the maimed went out to beg in town; at night they returned, shed their wooden legs and other props and indulged in the orgies described vividly by Victor Hugo in the *Hunchback of Notre-Dame*. It was this nightly miraculous cure from infirmity that gave the court its name.

Turn left onto the Rue des Forges which runs into the Rue de Damiette and the Rue du Nil. The crowded Rue des Petits-Carreaux leads to the Rue de Cléry.

Mount Orgueil. – The Rue de Cléry is the old counterscarp of the Charles V perimeter wall; turn left into the Rue des Degrés which now crosses the houses by means of steps which once crossed the ramparts. The whole quarter stands on Mount Orgueil, a natural mound used as a redoubt and which, in the 16C, afforded a good viewpoint over the capital – hence the name of the street, Beauregard, which you follow to Notre-Dame de Bonne-Nouvelle.

Notre-Dame-de-Bonne-Nouvelle. – The classical belfry is all that remains of the church restored by Anne of Austria – the remainder of the building dates from 1823-1829. Inside numerous paintings decorate the walls. Note the one by Mignard at the end of the south aisle showing Henrietta of England and her three children before St. Francis of Sales, an Annunciation by Lanfranco *(centre of the chancel, light-switch on the right)*, and a painting by Philippe de Champaigne *(to the right)*.

By taking the Rue de la Lune *(p 124)* on the right one arrives at the Boulevard Bonne-Nouvelle.

(Photo F. Têtefolle/Explorer)

Place des Victoires.

MONTPARNASSE

Michelin plan ▢▢ - folds 41 and 42: L 11, L 12 - M 11, M 12.

Distance: 4 km – 3 miles – Time: 4 hours. Start from the Montparnasse-Bienvenüe métro.

This crowded quarter, which traditionally belonged to artists and the working class is today the scene of one of the major urban renewal projects to be undertaken within the heart of Paris.

Mount Parnassus. – The debris from age-old quarries formed a heathlike grass covered mound. For students, chased away from the Pré-aux-Clercs by Queen Margot *(p 133)*, it became a favourite haunt to declaim poems away from the confines of the city – they nicknamed it Mount Parnassus after the mountain of Apollo and the muses.

In the 18C the mound was razed but the boulevard laid across its site, a fragment of the Farmers General perimeter wall, complete with toll-gates, kept the name alive.

A pleasure ground. – The Revolution saw the springing up of cafés and cabarets on the city outskirts and revellers enjoying the Montagnes-Suisses and Élysée-Montparnasse gardens and the dancing at the Arc-en-Ciel and Grande Chaumière. The polka and the can-can were first seen here before they became the rage of Paris. At the Observatory crossroads, where Marshal Ney was executed *(p 132)* were, first, the Bullier Hall, then, a few years later, the Closerie des Lilas café. Crowds gathered at the Constant Dance Hall and in the inns of

(Bibliothèque Forney)
Poster by A. Choubrac (1896)

the village of Plaisance to dance the mazurka between sips of tart Suresnes wine.

As the quarter began to spread out, Haussmann intervened, he planned to create an entirely built up area which included the old villages of Plaisance, Vaugirard and Montrouge. He then proceeded to divide it up with the Rue de Rennes, the Boulevard Arago and the Boulevard d'Enfer (now Boulevard Raspail).

Bohemian Montparnasse. – At the turn of the century avant-garde artists, poets and writers, moved to the Left Bank of the Seine, particularly Montparnasse. The atmosphere had already been described by Henri Murger many years earlier in his *Scenes of Bohemian Life* on which Puccini had based his opera *La Bohème*.

The 1900 Exhibition Wine Pavilion was reconstructed at No. 52 Rue de Dantzig, renamed the **Ruche** or Beehive, and replaced the Bateau-Lavoir of Montmartre *(p 77)*, providing lodging and studios for Modigliani, Soutine, Chagall, Zadkine and Léger. Talk went on for hours in the café-restaurants (le Dôme, la Rotonde, le Sélect and La Coupole) among the Russian political exiles – Lenin, Trotsky – musicians – Stravinsky, Satie and "the Six" – poets – Cocteau – and foreigners – Hemingway, Foujita, Picasso, Eisenstein, Blasco Ibanez… It was the golden age of the **Paris School** and it lasted into the mid-thirties, ending only with the outbreak of war in Spain and Western Europe.

Montparnasse today. – This former international Bohemian quarter is entirely Parisian. Anonymous crowds of revellers and artists attracted by the cafés, cinemas and night-clubs rub shoulders with the local population of workers, shopkeepers and artisans.

Since redevelopment the Maine-Montparnasse complex has become the nucleus of a business area while the Vandamme-Nord section has a mixture of offices, housing, sporting facilities and hotel accommodation. Beyond the old village of Plaisance, part of Paris for less than a century, is transformed by the presence of modern high-rise blocks.

■ **THE MAINE-MONTPARNASSE COMPLEX**★ ▢▢ - fold 42: L 11 - M 11

Dating from 1934 the original plan for this area was revised in 1958 when it became a major urban renewal project with the aim of creating a high density business area on the Left Bank. Work began in 1961 and the tower was completed in 1973.

Place du 18-Juin-1940. – Until 1967 this site, lined by cafés, was occupied by the old 19C station, the Gare Montparnasse which will be remembered as the headquarters of General Leclerc at the time of the liberation of Paris and the place where, on 25 August 1944, the German military governor signed his garrison's surrender. A mural plaque at the entrance to the commercial centre *(left side)* commemorates this event.

At the corner of Boulevard du Montparnasse and Rue de l'Arrivée, stands the cube shaped building of the **International Textile Centre** (CIT), which houses over 200 firms.

The Commercial Centre. – The podium extending from the Place du 18-Juin-1940 to the foot of the tower consists of 8 levels, 6 of which are underground. On the upper three floors are department stores, 60 or so luxury shops presenting the latest fashions, cafés and restaurants. The remaining floors are occupied by parking space, the technical installations and a sports centre *(entrance Rue du Départ)* with swimming pool. A sunken plaza on the Rue du Départ side gives direct access to the métro.

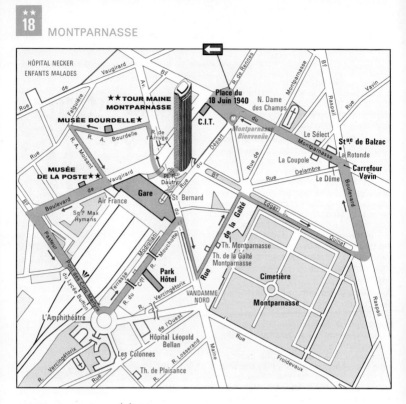

Montparnasse Tower ★★ **(Tour Montparnasse).** – This 209 m – 688 ft high tower, dominating the whole quarter – adds a new landmark to the Paris skyline and is the most spectacular and controversial feature of the project. The strictly geometrical lines of the façades are softened by the harmonious curved form.

This tower, the tallest office building in Europe is the design of a group of French architects. The building, with 52 floors given over to office space, has a working population of 7 000. The technical installations – heating, lighting, etc. – and security systems are controlled by a computer. The foundations go down 70 m – 230 ft – to support the 120 000 tons of masonry and shafts. The weight load of the building is distributed between two different structures: a central reinforced concrete core, of the same shape as the building, and the outer "walls" of closely spaced vertical columns. These are linked by horizontal beams. The curtain walls are covered with bronze tinted glass.

The building is separated from the new railway station, by a parvis paved with pink Sardinian granite under which passes the Avenue du Maine.

Ascent. – *Open 1 April to 30 September 9.30am to 11.30pm; 1 October to 31 March 10am to 10pm; 22.50 F (to the 56th floor); 28 F (to the top, 59th floor).*

The 56th floor observatory affords a magnificent **panorama** ★★★ of Paris and its suburbs. A luminous frieze running round the top of the wall helps you to pick out the main landmarks: the Eiffel Tower with the skyscrapers of the new Défense quarter in the distance, the Louvre, the Sacré-Cœur, Notre-Dame, the Bois de Vincennes, Orly Airport and the Bois de Boulogne. By night Paris becomes a fairytale wonderland. There is also a bar and panoramic restaurant at this level. From the open-air terrace on the 59th floor, the view on a clear day can extend as far as 40 km – 25 miles.

The Station (Gare). – Trains from western France now run into a U shaped terminus surrounded on three sides by immense 18 storey glass, steel and concrete blocks. The station proper, on five levels, occupies the central area – a vast concourse connects with the métro and supplies every amenity, even a small chapel to St. Bernard *(entrance at No. 34)* – the lectern was carved from a railway sleeper.

The longer sides of the U, extending nearly 275 yds back along the track, are occupied by 1 000 flats and a major postal sorting office on the left and, on the right, the Air France and other offices, overlooking the Square Max-Hymans and Boulevard de Vaugirard.

From Maine-Montparnasse to the Montparnasse Cemetery

Walk left along the Avenue du Maine, then turn left into the Rue Antoine-Bourdelle.

Bourdelle Museum ★ **(Musée Bourdelle).** – *No. 16. Open 10am to 5.40pm; closed Mondays and holidays; 9 F – free on Sundays. The museum also has temporary exhibitions; 12 F. ☏ 45.48.67.27.*

Bourdelle's (1861-1929) house, garden and studio have been converted to display several hundred of the artist's sculptures, paintings and drawings. In the great hall are the original plaster casts of his great sculptures – many of which may also be seen at the Champs-Élysées Theatre and in the Alma Quarter *(pp 138, 137)*. The most outstanding items among his immense output are the huge bronzes, now in the garden, his portrait busts of his contemporaries, including his master, Rodin, the writer Anatole France and the spectacular series of **portraits of Beethoven** ★ of whom he made 21 different studies.

Continue along the Rue Antoine-Bourdelle and turn left into Rue Armand-Moisant which leads back to the Boulevard de Vaugirard.

At No. 34 Boulevard de Vaugirard stands the **National Postal and Philatelic Centre.** The unusual façade has five decorative panels of light reflecting prisms to break the monotony of the windowless walls of the 5 exhibition floors.

Postal Museum ★★ **(Musée de la Poste).** – *Open 10am to 5pm; closed Sundays and holidays; 8.50 F. Library, photographic library, stamp collector's workshop, lecture theatres, temporary exhibition galleries and a stamp counter.* ☏ *43.20.15.30*

The museum presents an attractive account of the postal services through the ages. Start on the 5th floor. In Gallery 2 note the parchment scroll, used by religious orders in the Middle Ages as a means of communication between abbeys and the balloon used during the 1870-71 siege of Paris. Gallery 3 shows the development of the postal network in France, from the early relay posts for mounted carriers to the 18 000 post offices of today. The next two galleries display models of different means of postal transport.

Galleries 10-12 are of special interest to the philatelist. Note the model of a present day stamp printing machine. Next comes a complete collection of French stamps since that first issue in 1849 and finally other national collections, usually displayed in rotation. The final two galleries show the present methods and machines for the sorting and franking of mail.

From the Cinq-Martyrs-du-Lycée-Buffon Bridge, there is an impressive **view** ★ of the new quarter. In the opposite direction is the Plaisance quarter at present undergoing redevelopment. In the mid-19C Plaisance was one of the villages surrounding Paris. Note on the right the two strikingly modern buildings by Ricardo Bofill.

After the bridge turn left into the Rue du Commandant-René-Mouchotte, which passes one of the main postal sorting offices and on the right the elegant white building of the Montparnasse Park Hotel, which contrasts with the surrounding buildings. The architect Pierre Dufau was also responsible for two of the towers at La Défense (the Septentrion and Assur towers). The hotel with its 1 000 rooms and conference hall is part of a larger complex comprising office and housing space, a commercial centre and skating rink with ice rinks (one for curling). Two overhead passageways link the Vandamme-Nord centre to the Modigliani Terrace.

Turn right into Avenue du Maine then left into Rue de la Gaîté.

Rue de la Gaîté. – This old country road has, since the 18C, been lined throughout by cabarets, dance halls, restaurants and other pleasure spots – hence its name. The street's tradition which began with the Mère Cadet, the Veau qui Tète and the Gigoteurs Dance Hall, is maintained today by the Gaîté-Montparnasse (No. 26), the Bobino Music-Hall (No. 20, *reconstruction in progress*) and the Montparnasse Theatre (No. 31). The theatre's reputation for popular drama was revived in the 1930's.

Turn right into the Boulevard Edgar-Quinet for the cemetery's main entrance.

Montparnasse Cemetery
(Cimetière Montparnasse):

1) J.-P. Sartre, philosopher.
2) Soutine *(p 127)*, painter.
3) Baudelaire, poet.
4) Laurens, sculptor.
5) Bourdelle (no inscription), sculptor.
6) Dumont d'Urville, admiral.
7) Tristan Tzara, Romanian Dadaist poet.
8) Zadkine, sculptor.
9) Mounet-Sully, actor.
10) Houdon, sculptor.
11) Jussieu *(p 156)*, botanist.
12) Rude *(p 47)*, sculptor.
13) Le Verrier *(p 132)*, astronomer.
14) Baudelaire's Cenotaph.
15) Henri Poincaré, mathematician.
16) Cesar Franck, composer.
17) Guy de Maupassant, writer.
18) Bartholdi, sculptor.
19) Kessel, writer.
20) Andre Citroën, engineer and industrialist.
21) Pigeon, sculptor.
22) The Kiss by Brancusi, Romanian sculptor.
23) Sainte-Beuve, writer-critic.
24) Saint-Saëns, composer.
25) Vincent d'Indy, composer.
26) Leon-Paul Fargue, poet.
27) Boucicaut, businessman.

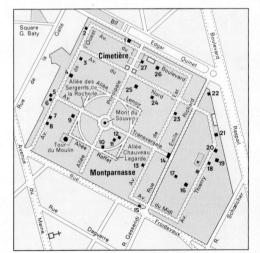

From the Montparnasse Cemetery to the Place du 18-Juin-1940

Make for the Boulevard Raspail and turn left towards the **Vavin Crossroads** (Place Pablo Picasso). This crossroads, originally the summit of the Parnassus Mound, bustles with life and is now the heart of the old quarter. In 1939 the famous statue of **Balzac** by Rodin was placed on an island site in the Boulevard Raspail. Walk up the Boulevard Montparnasse which is lined with big café-restaurants and cinemas. Pass the Church of Notre-Dame-des-Champs (Our Lady of the Fields) whose name recalls a much older country church before reaching the Place du 18-Juin-1940.

Michelin plan **🔟** - fold 43: L 13, L 14 – M 13, M 14.

Distance: 3.5 km – 2 miles – Time : 2 1/2 hours. Start from Port-Royal métro station.

This former "Valley of Grace" is now devoted to medical care and higher education. The first half of the 17C saw the establishment of religious communities: in 1605, the **Carmelites** (No. **284** Rue St-Jacques), Louise de la Vallière retreated to the convent when no longer favoured by Louis XIV; in 1612, the **Ursulines;** in 1622, the **Feuillantines** founded by Anne of Austria; in 1626, the **Visitandines.** The same year, Mother Angélique Arnaud ordered the construction of **Port-Royal,** the dependency of the Jansenist Port-Royal-des-Champs. Her tomb lies in the chancel of the church at No. 123 Boulevard de Port-Royal.

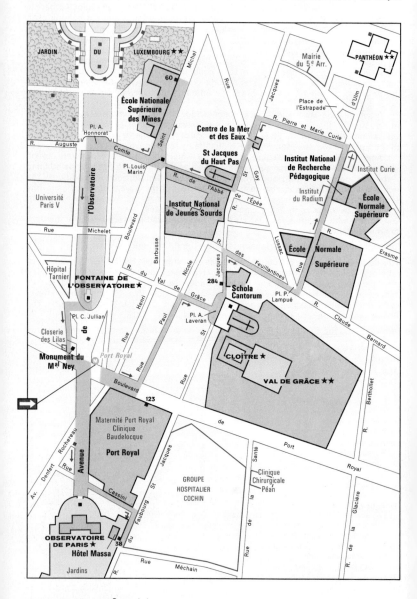

■ VAL-DE-GRÂCE★★ 🔟 - fold 43: M 14

All the 17C buildings of the former abbey remain. A few years after the foundation of the new Oratory congregation *(p 100)* in the Rue St-Jacques in 1611, Anne of Austria bought the mansion to establish in it a Benedictine community which took the same name as its provincial convent, Val-de-Grâce. Anne visited the community frequently to pray and discreetly to intrigue against Richelieu. At 37, Anne, who had been married twenty-three years, was still without a child. She promised the gift of a magnificent church if her prayers were answered and kept her vow on the birth of Louis XIV in 1638. The plans for the Val-de-Grâce Church were drawn by François Mansart.

The foundation stone was laid by the young king himself in 1645. Anne of Austria, finding Mansart too slow, replaced him by Le Mercier, who, until his death, executed his predecessor's plans. The building was at last completed in 1667 and consecrated in 1710 (Louis XIV was 72). Val-de-Grâce became a military hospital in 1793 and a medical school in 1850. The new buildings house a military hospital once again.

Church★★. – The church, probably the most Roman in appearance in France, was erected in the Jesuit style after the Sorbonne and before the Invalides. Above the two tier façade with a double triangular pediment is a dome, less tall but more ornate than its Paris rivals and obviously inspired by St. Peter's.

Inside, the Baroque influence appears in the sculptured vaulting over the nave, the monumental baldachin with six twisted columns framing the altar and the magnificent **cupola★★** decorated with a fresco by Mignard in which there are 200 figures each three times lifesize. The outstanding carvings are by Michel Anguier and Philippe Buyster.

The St. Louis Chapel *(right)* was originally the Benedictine chancel. From 1662 the hearts of members of the royal and Orleans families were deposited in the St. Anne Chapel, on the left. When the caskets were desecrated at the Revolution there were 45, including those of Queen Marie-Thérèse, "Monsieur" (Philippe, Duke of Orleans), the Regent, Philippe of Orleans and Marie Leczinska. Most have disappeared.

Former Convent. – Go through the porch to the right of the church. The **cloister★**, which opens off the end of the court, is Classical in style with two superimposed galleries and a Mansard roof. The gardens, through the court's second arch, give a good view of the convent's majestic rear façade, the pavilion in which Anne of Austria stayed, distinguished by a porch with ringed columns, and the rear of the church dome.

Museum. – *Open 10am to noon and 2 to 5pm (4pm Fridays). Closed Saturdays, Sundays and holidays.* ℡ *43.29.12.31 extn 4052. Access beneath the first porch on the right, at the end of the arcade.*

Displays include documents and mementoes of the great military physicians (Parmentier, premier pharmacist during the Empire; Villemin, Roussin, Broussais, Vincent, Laveran, Nobel prizewinner, 1907) and the French Health Service. Models and equipment indicate treatment meted out to the wounded during the Empire and the First World War.

From the Val-de-Grâce to the Observatory

Schola Cantorum. – *269 Rue St-Jacques.* The conservatory was founded privately in 1896 by Ch. Bordes, Guilmant and the composer Vincent d'Indy, to restore church music. The buildings formerly belonged to a community of English Benedictines who sought refuge in Paris after the Anglican Schism of 1531; the body of James II, who died in exile at St-Germain-en-Laye in 1701, rested in the chapel (now secularised) until the Revolution when the building was desecrated. It is now a music, dance and drama school.

Bear right in the Rue des Feuillantines then left into the Rue d'Ulm.

École Normale Supérieure. – *45 Rue d'Ulm.* The school of higher studies for those entering the teaching profession was created by the Convention in 1794. It transferred to these buildings in 1847. For many university and other learned men and politicians, the "Normale" has proved to be the springboard to a brilliant career.

The **French Office for Modern Methods of Teaching** is at No. 29 Rue d'Ulm. It houses temporary exhibitions on education *(open 9am to 6pm; closed weekends and holidays).*

Turn left into the Rue Pierre-et-Marie-Curie and left again into the Rue St-Jacques.

(Photo C. Michel/Explorer)

The Observatory Fountain.

Sea and Water Centre (Centre de la Mer et des Eaux). – *195, Rue St-Jacques. Open 10am to 12.30pm and 1 to 5.30pm; 10am to 5.30pm at weekends; closed Mondays, 1 January, 1 May, 14 July and 25 December and in August; 12F. Film shows on Wednesdays, Saturdays and Sundays, 3 and 4pm.* ☏ *46.33.08.61.*

The centre which is part of the Oceanographic Institute founded at the beginning of the 20C by Albert I of Monaco, is devoted to the study of the ocean, its role and ressources, and holds exhibitions and audio-visual presentations. Aquariums.

Church of St. James of the High Pass (St-Jacques-du-Haut-Pas). – *Closed 12.30 to 4pm and Monday mornings; during the summer holidays closed 12.30 to 5pm and all day Monday.* The church, built in the Classical style between 1630 and 1685, became a Jansenist centre. The astronomer, Cassini *(see below),* is buried inside.

National Institute for the Deaf (Jeunes Sourds). – A hospital was established on this site to succour pilgrims on their way to Compostela in Spain in the 14C by monks from Altopascio (High Pass) near Lucca in Italy. In 1790, one year after the death of the Abbot de l'Épée who had worked on the education of deaf mutes, the hospital took up his work.

The Rue de l'Abbé-de-l'Épée leads to the Boulevard St-Michel.

School of Advanced Mining Engineering (École Supérieure des Mines). – *Enter through No. 60.* The school was founded in 1783 and moved to the present buildings, the former Hôtel de Vendôme, in 1815. The **mineralogical collection**★★ is among the world's richest. *Open Wednesdays to Fridays 2 to 5pm; Tuesdays and Saturdays 10am to 12.30pm and 2 to 5pm; closed Sundays, Mondays, 14 July, 15 August and 25 December;* ☏ *43.29.21.05 extn 539.*

Avenue de l'Observatoire. – The wide avenue with its central flower borders is lined by the buildings of Paris V University. The **Observatory Fountain**★ (1873) by Davioud is known for its decoration of the four quarters of the globe by Carpeaux (Oceania was omitted for reasons of symmetry!). The view towards Montmartre is attractive.

Before the Closerie des Lilas café, so famous in the 1920's, stands the vigorous François Rude's **statue of Marshal Ney** (1853) – executed nearby in 1815 for his support of Napoleon – greatly admired by Rodin.

■ THE OBSERVATORY★ ▥ - fold 43: N 13

The Observatory's construction, on orders from Colbert and to plans by Claude Perrault, was begun on 21 June 1667, the summer solstice, and was completed in 1672. The Cassinis a family of four astronomers of Italian origin, continued in succession as directors until the Revolution. The dome and wings were added under Louis-Philippe.

The research conducted at the Observatory has included the calculation of the true dimensions of the solar system (1672), of the meridians of longitude, until then more than a little exaggerated – Louis XIV commented that the Academicians' calculations had considerably reduced the extent of his kingdom! – the speed of light, the production of a large map of the moon (1679), the discovery by mathematical deduction of the planet Neptune (Le Verrier, 1846), the invention of new instruments...

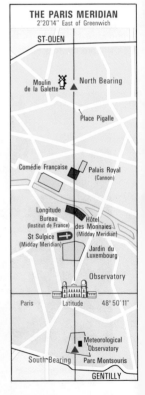

THE PARIS MERIDIAN
2°20'14" East of Greenwich

ST-OUEN

Moulin de la Galette — North Bearing

Place Pigalle

Comédie Française — Palais Royal (Cannon)

Longitude Bureau (Institut de France) — Hôtel des Monnaies (Midday Meridian)

St Sulpice (Midday Meridian)

Jardin du Luxembourg

Observatory

Paris — Latitude — 48° 50'11"

Meteorological Observatory

South Bearing — Parc Montsouris

GENTILLY

The building. – The building's four walls are oriented to the cardinal points of the compass, the south face also determining the capital's latitude. The meridian of longitude, calculated in 1667, which passes through the building was known as the Paris Meridian, until 1884 when the Greenwich mean was adopted generally with the exception of France and Ireland, which only followed suit in 1911. Midday bearings are to be found elsewhere in Paris besides on the actual meridian *(see diagram).*

The Observatory has been the seat of the International Time Bureau which since its inauguration (1919) sets Coordinated Universal Time (UTC) and is itself based on International Atomic Time (IAT). The speaking clock (☏ 36.99) gives Coordinated Universal Time accurate to one millionth of a second.

Guided tours: first Saturday in the month at 2.30pm on written application to the Secrétariat, 61 Avenue de l'Observatoire 75014 Paris, enclosing S.A.E.; ☏ *43.20.12.10:* small museum of old instruments, modern equipment in the park and dome of the upper terrace.

From the Observatory, walk up the Rue du Faubourg St-Jacques to No. **38** the **Hôtel Massa** (*p 44* – the Men of Letters Society).

THE FAUBOURG ST-GERMAIN

Michelin plan ⏚⏚ - folds 29 and 30: from H 10 to J 12.

Distance: 4 km – 2 miles – Time: 3 1/2 hours.
Start from the Chambre-des-Députés métro station.

The "noble faubourg" which lies off the far bank of the Seine from the Tuileries and east of the Invalides, includes many fine old 18C town houses and monuments. The stately private residences have been converted to government offices and embassies and it remains as difficult as ever to see the houses behind the monumental gateways; only through a half-open door will you glimpse the beautiful façades erected by Delisle-Mansart, Boffrand or other 18C architects. The faubourg St-Germain was originally, as its name implies, the suburb *(faubourg)* of the town which developed round the Abbey of St-Germain-des-Prés *(p 106)*. Until the end of the 16C the surrounding countryside was used for farming and hunting, except for a strip of meadow at the river's edge finally won from the abbey by the University and named the Clerks' Meadow.

At the beginning of the 17C Marguerite of Valois, first wife of Henri IV, took the east end of the meadow from the University as part of the grounds in which to build a vast mansion with a garden running down to the Seine. The acquisition was made so casually that the embankment came to be called the Malacquis (distorted to Malaquais) or Misappropriated Quay. On the death of Queen Marguerite in 1615 the University tried to reclaim the land but, after twenty years of legal proceedings, succeeded only in having the main street of the new quarter named the Rue de l'Université.

The district was at its most fashionable in the 18C. Noble lords and rich financiers built houses which gave the streets an individual character: one monumental entrance followed another, each opening on a courtyard closed at the far end by the façade of an elegant mansion behind which lay a large garden.

The Revolution closed these sumptuous town houses and although they reopened their doors at the Restoration, the quarter never fully regained its status, as the fashionable, at the time of Louis-Philippe and Napoleon III, migrated to the Champs-Élysées. Several mansions were pulled down when Boulevard St-Germain and Boulevard Raspail were opened. The finest houses remaining now belong to the state or serve as ambassadorial residences. Something of the quarter's great days can, however, still be recalled in the Rues de Lille, Grenelle and Varenne.

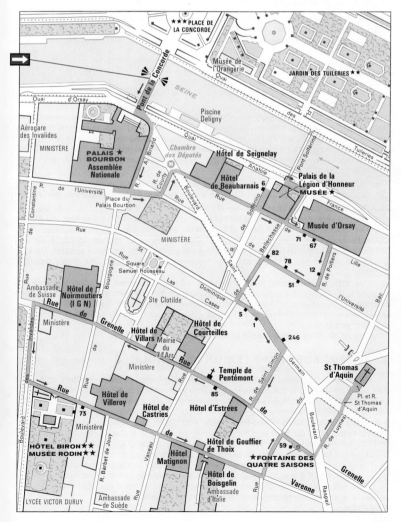

From the Concorde Bridge to the Legion of Honour Palace

The Pont de la Concorde. – The bridge was designed by the civil engineer, Perronet, in 1787 when he was 79. It was completed by 1791, the stones from the Bastille having been used in its construction so that, it was said, "the people could for ever trample the ruins of the old fortress". During Louis-Philippe's reign the bridge was decorated with 12 colossal statues of famous men but the ornament was not liked and the figures were dispatched first to Versailles and subsequently dispersed to provincial towns!

Walk to the centre of the bridge, which was doubled in width in 1932, for remarkable views★★ along the Seine and across the Place de la Concorde to the Madeleine.

■ THE PALAIS-BOURBON★ ▥ - fold 30: H 11

In 1722 the Duchess of Bourbon, daughter of Louis XIV and Mme de Montespan, acquired land on which to build a house fronting on the Rue de l'Université. By 1728 the palace and terraced gardens running down to the Seine were complete.

Twenty-eight years later Louis XV bought the property so that it could be altered to form part of the general scheme of the Concorde Square; in 1784, however, Louis XVI sold it to the Prince of Condé who enlarged and embellished it. Finally, the adjoining **Hôtel de Lassay** was added and renamed the Petit or Little Bourbon.

Work was almost finished when the Revolution broke out. The palace was confiscated to serve as a chamber for the Council of the Five Hundred. Next it was used to house archives and Lassay House and its outbuildings as accommodation for the École Polytechnique. In 1807 Napoleon commissioned Poyet to design the present façade overlooking the Place de la Concorde in harmony with the Greek plan of the Madeleine. At the Restoration the palace was returned to the Condés only to be bought back in 1827 and converted for use by the Legislative Assembly.

Exterior. – The Antique style façade with a portico is decorated with an allegorical pediment by Cortot (1842), statues, on high, of Minerva by Houdon and Themis by Roland, and below, among other figures, those of Henri IV and Louis XIV's ministers, Sully and Colbert. The allegorical low reliefs on the wings are by Rude *(right)* and Pradier *(left)*.

Take the Rue Aristide-Briand, on the left, to the Place du Palais-Bourbon from which you will get a good view of the 18C palace.

Interior. – *To visit apply in writing to the Administrative Office, 126 Rue de l'Université, 75355 Paris;* ℡ *42.97.64.08. Entrance: Quai d'Orsay.*

Among the most impressive of the many rooms decorated with paintings and sculpture, are the lobby, with its ceiling by Horace Vernet, the Council Chamber and the **Library★★**. This is a fine room in itself and, in addition, magnificently decorated with a *History of Civilisation*, painted by Delacroix between 1838 and 1845. Houdon's portrait busts of Voltaire and Diderot are also in the library.

Apply in writing to 33, Quai d'Orsay when the Assembly is in session, to attend a debate in the National Assembly.

Council Chamber. – Proceedings are conducted by the President of the **National Assembly** from the bureau formerly used for the Council of the Five Hundred *(see above)*. He faces the deputies – 577 when all are present – seated on benches arranged in a semicircle. Government members occupy the front bench below the speaker's stand (N. B. the political right and left are as viewed by the president and therefore the reverse as seen from the gallery).

Walk out of the Place du Palais-Bourbon, along the Rue de l'Université, down the Rue de Courty and across the Boulevard St-Germain to the Rue de Lille where you turn right.

This street, named after the town of Lille is typical of the old "noble faubourg".

Nos. 80 and 78 were designed by the architect, Boffrand in 1714. The first, the **Hôtel de Seignelay**, occupied by the Ministry of Commerce and Tourism, was owned originally by Colbert's grandson, then by the Duke of Charost, tutor to the young Louis XV and aristocrat philanthropist who was saved from the guillotine by his own peasants. By 1839 it had passed to Marshal Lauriston, a descendant of John Law, the Scots financier *(p 103)*.

The **Hôtel de Beauharnais**, next door, received its name when Napoleon's son-in-law bought it in 1803 and redecorated it sumptuously for his own and his sister, Queen Hortense's, use. Since 1818 the house has been the seat of first the Prussian and, later, the German diplomatic missions to France. Now restored, it is the residence of the West German ambassador.

The writer Jules Romain lived at No. **6** Rue Solférino from 1947 to his death (1972).

■ THE PALACE OF THE LEGION OF HONOUR ▥ - fold 30: H 11

The **Hôtel de Salm** was built in 1786 for the German Prince of Salm who, finding himself penniless after living in the house for only one year, sold it to his architect and rented it back. In 1795 the property was made the prize in a lottery. It was won by one, Lieuthrand, a former wigmaker who amassed a fortune as supplier to the army and pronounced himself a marquis. He was condemned for forgery, and put in prison where, not long after, he disappeared. Mme de Staël and her husband, the Swedish ambassador, the next owners in 1799, were succeeded by Napoleon who, two years after creating the order, made the mansion the Palace of the Legion of Honour. It was burnt down during the Commune of 1871 and rebuilt, in 1878, by the members of the Legion to the original plans. The only parts remaining of the early building are the low reliefs on the outside walls.

Turn left down to the Quai Anatole-France to look at the back of the palace where there is a delightful semicircular pavilion in complete contrast to the severe lines elsewhere.

The Legion of Honour Museum★. – *2 Rue de Bellechasse. Open 2 to 5pm; closed Mondays, 1 January, Easter and Whit Tuesdays, 15 August, 1 November, 25 December; 10F, free on Sundays. ☏45.55.95.16.*

The museum presents original documents, decorations, pictures, uniforms and arms, the orders of chivalry and nobility of Pre-Revolutionary France (Malta, the Star, St. Michael, the Holy Spirit, St. Louis), and the creation of the Legion of Honour by Napoleon on 19 May 1802, its rapid expansion during the Empire (personal decorations of Bonaparte and his brothers), educational establishments and its subsequent history.

Further galleries show other French civil and military decorations (academic awards, the Military Medal, Military Cross, the Cross of the Liberation, Order of Merit) and foreign orders.

From the Legion of Honour Palace to the Hôtel Biron

Across the Rue de Bellechasse, the former Orsay Station (Gare Paris Quai d'Orsay) illustrates the popular steel architectural style of the late 19C. Built between 1898 and 1900 by Laloux, it was saved from demolition in 1973. It was until 1980 the temporary home of the Renaud-Barrault Theatre Company and the Auction Rooms, while awaiting the reconstruction of their premises, Nouveau Drouot *(p 124)*. In 1977 on Presidential initiative, it was decided by an interministerial committee to house a 19C art museum, **Orsay Museum**, in these premises, thus bridging the gap between the Louvre and the Georges Pompidou Centre. Renovation work is in progress and 1986 is the scheduled opening date. Space will be allocated for temporary exhibitions.

Continue down the Rue de Lille where No. **71**, **Hôtel de Mouchy** dates from 1775 and No. **67**, **President Duret's house**, from 1706. Turn right down the Rue de Poitiers where at No. **12**, the **Hôtel de Poulpry** (1700), the monarchist group known as the Poitiers Street Committee used to meet in 1850.

Turn right in the Rue de l'Université, at one time the quarter's main street and still lined with interesting houses: No. **51**, the **Hôtel de Soyécourt** was built in 1707; No. **78** in 1687; No. **82** is where the poet Lamartine lived from 1837 to 1853 (inscription).

Turn left in the Rue de Bellechasse.

As you emerge on the Boulevard St-Germain, look right to see the more modern – 1877 – part of the Ministry of Defence. The old part overlooking the Rue St-Dominique includes the **Hôtel de Brienne** which consists of two houses and a former monastery. Cross the boulevard and continue down the Rue de Bellechasse before turning left in the Rue St-Dominique.

This street, which got its name from a former monastery for Dominican novices, was amongst the quarter's most interesting before a large part of it was swept away to make way for the Boulevard St-Germain. No. **5**, the **Hôtel de Tavannes**, has a fine round arched doorway surmounted by a scallop and crowned by a triangular pediment. The artist, Gustave Doré, died in the house in 1883. Inside *(open 20 August to 30 September, 9.30am to noon and 2.30 to 6pm)* there is a fine stairwell with a wrought-iron balustrade. No. **1**, the **Hôtel de Gournay**, was erected in 1695.

The Rue St-Dominique ends on the Boulevard St-Germain on which you turn right. No. **246**, now with No. 244 the offices of the Secretary of State for Transport, was formerly the **Hôtel de Roquelaure** (fine courtyard), the residence of the statesman Cambacérès (1753-1824) and later the seat of the Council of State.

Take the Rue St-Simon opposite then turn right into the Rue de Grenelle.

Rue de Grenelle. – At No. **79** stands the great **Hôtel d'Estrées** (1713); No. **85** is the **Hôtel d'Avaray** (1728), the Royal Netherlands Embassy. **Pentémont Temple** with its Ionic cupola of 1750 was at one time a convent chapel; then the nuns were replaced by the Imperial Guard and these, in turn, by the civil servants of the Ministry of War Veterans. No. **110**, the **Hôtel de Courteilles** (1778), dominating the street with its massive façade, is now the Ministry of Education; No. **116** was built in 1709 for Marshal de Villars and considerably remodelled. No. **118**, is the much smaller, **Hôtel de Villars**, built in 1712 and extremely elegant with twin garlanded, oval windows. Continue to Nos. **138-140**, the **Hôtel de Noirmoutiers** (1722), at one time the army staff headquarters and the house in which Marshal Foch died on 20 March 1929. Today it is the office of the IGN – the National Geographical Institute.

Turn left into the Boulevard des Invalides and walk to the Hôtel Biron on the corner of the Rue de Varenne.

■ **HÔTEL BIRON★★** ▯▯ - fold 29: J 11

The house and garden enable one to see Rodin's sculptures in a perfect residential setting.

In 1728, one Abraham Peyrenc, a wigmaker who had accrued a fortune and agrandised his name to Peyrenc de Moras, commissioned Gabriel the Elder to build him a house in the Rue de Varenne. In time the beautiful building came into the hands of the Duchess of Maine, grand-daughter of the great Condé and wife of the son of Louis XIV and Madame de Montespan, and then of Marshal Biron, a general in the Revolutionary government who died, decapitated, in 1793.

In 1797 the house was turned into a dance hall. Under the Empire it reverted to its role of residence, first of the papal legate then of the ambassador of the Tsar. In 1820 it was taken over by the Convent of the Sacred Heart as an educational establishment. Madame Sophie Barat, the mother superior (canonised: 1925), had the Neo-Gothic chapel constructed (1871) and the greater part of the residence's panelling ripped out, seeing in the wood carving a symbol of the vanities of the age – a few ornamented rooms, nevertheless, do still remain.

After the Congregation Law of 1904, under which many convents were dispersed, the educational part of the building and the gardens were converted into the Lycée Victor-Duruy and the house was made available to artists. Thus Auguste Rodin came to live in and enjoy the house until his death in 1917, presenting his work by way of rent. The house has since been converted into a museum and the gardens restored.

Rodin Museum★★ (Musée Rodin). – *Open 10am to 5.45pm (5pm 1 October to 31 March); closed Tuesdays, 1 May and 25 December ; 15F – Sundays 7.50F;* ℡ *47.05.01.34. Turn left out of the hall.*

Rodin's sculpture, primarily in bronze and white marble, is immensely striking, vital, life-like. Creation in the guise of figures emerging from the living rock was a favourite theme **(The Hand of God)** although he excelled in studies of the nude **(St. John the Baptist).**

On the ground floor are some of the most expressive works: **The Cathedral, The Kiss, The Walking Man** and **The Man with a Broken Nose.**

(Musée Rodin, Paris/photo B. Jarret)

The Cathedral by A. Rodin.

At either end of the gallery, in corresponding rotundas which have kept their fine panelling, are **Eve** and the **Age of Bronze.** One room is devoted to drawings by the artist which are exhibited in rotation.

At the top of the beautiful 18C staircase, on the first floor, are the smaller works, the plasters for the large groups and for the statues of **Balzac** *(p 129)* and **Victor Hugo** *(p 166).*

Finally, in the garden, can be seen the sculptures which made Rodin's reputation during his lifetime, **The Thinker** (on the right), **The Burghers of Calais** and **The Gates of Hell** (on the left) and the **Ugolin group** (in the centre of the pool).

The personal collections of the artist (furniture, pictures, antique) are displayed in the house and in the former chapel *(temporary exhibitions).*

From the Hôtel Biron to St. Thomas Aquinas Church

Rue de Varenne. – The street was laid along a rabbit warren – *garenne* which evolved, in time, to Varenne – belonging to the Abbey of St-Germain-des-Prés. There are attractive old houses in this street also: No. **73** the great **Hôtel de Broglie** (1735); Nos. 80-78, the **Hôtel de Villeroy** (1724), now the Ministry of Agriculture; No. 72, the large **Hôtel de Castries** (1700).

The most famous, of course, is the **Hôtel Matignon** at No. 57. The house was built by Courtonne in 1721 and has since been considerably remodelled. Talleyrand, diplomat and statesman to successive regimes, owned it from 1808 to 1811, then Madame Adelaïde, sister to Louis-Philippe. Between 1884 and 1914 it housed the Austro-Hungarian Embassy and in 1935 it became the office of the President of the Council of State and in 1958 the Paris residence of the prime minister.

No. 56, the **Hôtel de Gouffier de Thoix,** has a magnificent doorway ornamented with a shell carving

No. 47, the **Hôtel de Boisgelin** is now the Italian Embassy.

Turn left into the Rue du Bac, then right into the Rue de Grenelle.

The Hôtel Bouchardon, at No. **59,** decorated with the Fountain of the Four Seasons *(see below),* will house a Dina Vierny Museum *(due to open late 1986).*

The Romantic poet, Musset, lived there from 1824 to 1839, when he wrote most of his poetic dramas.

Fountain of the Four Seasons★ (Fontaine des Quatre-Saisons). – The beautiful Four Seasons' Fountain, carved by Bouchardon between 1739 and 1745, was commissioned by Turgot, the dean of the local merchants' guild and father of Louis XVI's minister. The commission was undertaken in answer to complaints that the stately quarter was almost totally without water!

A seated figure of Paris looking down on reclining personifications of the Seine and the Marne adorns the ornate Ionic pillared fountain front. The sides are decorated with figures of the Seasons and delightful low reliefs showing cherubs performing the seasons' labours.

Cross the Boulevard Raspail and take the Rue de Luynes before crossing the Boulevard St-Germain to the Place St-Thomas d'Aquin.

St. Thomas Aquinas Church (Église St-Thomas d'Aquin). – The church, formerly the chapel of the Dominican novitiate monastery, was begun in 1682 in the Jesuit style to plans by Pierre Bullet. The façade was only completed in 1769. Inside are 17 and 18C paintings and a ceiling (apsidal chapel) painted by Lemoyne in 1723 of the Transfiguration. The sacristy has Louis XV panelling.

THE CHAILLOT QUARTER AND AVENUE MONTAIGNE

Michelin plan □□ - folds 16, 17, 28 and 29: G 8, G 9.

Distance: 3 km – 2 miles – Time: 4 hours. Start from the Alma-Marceau métro station.

This walk travels through one of the most luxurious quarters of Paris where the wealthy residential section mingles with the elegance of the couturiers and perfumers.

The Alma Square and Bridge. – The square and bridge created in the time of Napoleon III, are named after the first Franco-British victory in the Crimean War (1854).

The original bridge, slowly undermined by the Seine, was replaced in 1972 by an asymmetrical steel structure with a 110 m – 361 ft span.

Only the **Zouave** (upstream by the single pile) remains of the four Second Empire soldier statues which decorated the old bridge; he serves as a high water marker and is very popular with Parisians – once in January 1910, the water came up to his chin.

■ PALAIS DE TOKYO★ □□ - fold 28: G 8 - H 8

The Palais was built for the 1937 World Exhibition, replacing the Savonnerie Carpet Workshop *(p 162)*. The two wings linked by a portico, look down over a series of terraces, which are adorned by low reliefs and statues by Bourdelle, including his **France**★ *(in the centre)*.

Museum of Modern Art of the City of Paris (Musée d'Art Moderne de la Ville de Paris). – *Enter on Alma side. Open 10am to 5.30pm (8.30pm on Wednesdays); closed Mondays and holidays; 12F; museum and A.R.C. 30F.* ☏ *47.23.61.27. Library.*

This collection of 20C art works includes the Cubist school with Picasso and Braque, Fauvism represented by Matisse and Derain and the Paris school with works by Modigliani, Soutine, Pascin, Gromaire and Dufy. It is dominated by the biggest picture in the world 600 m – 6 095 sq ft: Dufy's *The Good Fairy Electricity,* representing the scientists and thinkers, who mastered this form of energy. Other large-scale canvasses are *La Danse* by Matisse and decorations by Delaunay.

The museum displays works illustrating the trends and techniques of contemporary art. The experimental centre (A.R.C.) presents innovations in the fields of plastic art, music and poetry. Exhibitions are held in the Children's Museum.

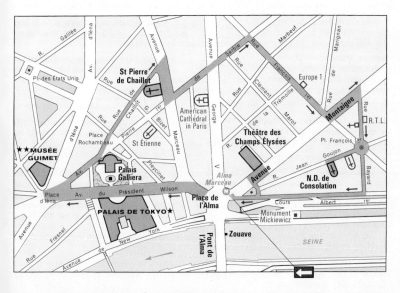

Palais de Tokyo Museums★. – *Entrance: Avenue du Président-Wilson, Trocadéro side. Open 9.45am to 5.15pm; closed Tuesdays and holidays; 12F; Sundays 6F.* ☏ *47.23.36.53.*

Preview of the Orsay Museum. – While awaiting the completion of the Orsay Museum which will cover the 19C, certain works are on display here.

This exhibition of works by Post-Impressionists born before 1870, is organized around the Pointillism of Seurat, the Pont-Aven School, Gauguin one of its leaders, the Nabis movement (1890-1900), the Symbolists and the decorative arts of the *Belle Époque.*

The Pointillists, who believed that the juxtaposition or superimposition of primary colours in dots conveyed the fugitive shimmering of light, are represented here by Signac *(l'Entrée du Port de La Rochelle),* Seurat *(Port-en-Bessin, Le Cirque* – his last work), and Cross *(l'Après-midi à Pardigon).* Maillol's works *(la Femme à l'Ombrelle)* show his talents as an artist as well as a sculptor. Vuillard *(Les Jardins publics),* Vallotton (interiors), and their leader Bonnard with his colourful landscapes belonged to the Nabis movement born of a common admiration for Gauguin *(le Paysage de Bretagne, la Belle Angèle).* Note also *Madeleine au Bois d'Amour,* by Émile Bernard.

Museum of Experimental Art. – A variety of exhibitions (renewed in rotation) are organized around a style, school, particular artist or technique.

In addition there are photographic exhibitions.

■ **GUIMET MUSEUM**★★ **(MUSÉE GUIMET)** ▯▯ - fold 28: G 7

Open 9.45am to noon and 1.30 to 5.15pm. Closed Tuesdays; 9F (4.50F Sundays).
℡ *47.23.61.65.*

The museum, founded by Émile Guimet, a 19C collector from Lyons contains Oriental works of art.

The ground floor is reserved for Far Eastern art: Khmer art (Cambodia), is well represented by intricately carved temple pediments and a series of **heads of Buddha** in the typical pose with eyes half-closed and a meditative smile. The seated Shiva with ten arms is an example of central Vietnamese art.

The Lamaist section includes a remarkable collection of Tibetan and Nepalese banners *(thanka)* as well as ceremonial objects and gilded bronzes; of the latter the most noteworthy is the graceful **dancing Dakini.**

The first floor shows the evolution of Indian art from the 3C BC to the 19C. There are the carved low reliefs from Northern India and the Hindu sculpture and bronzes originating from the southeast. Outstanding among the sculpture is the beautiful **Cosmic Dance by Shiva.** The art of both Pakistan (represented here by the famous Bodhisattva from Shabaz-Garhi) and Afghanistan (the Begrâm treasure: sculptured ivories of Indian origin and Hellenistic plasters) are of special interest. The Chinese collection includes ceremonial bronze objects, jade and laquer ware, Buddhist sculpture and funerary statuettes.

On the second floor are the exceptional displays of **Chinese ceramics** from the Calmann and Grandidier collections (18C *"famille rose"* set) and the series of Buddhist banners which was discovered in a cave of Touen-Houang. The jewels from Korea include a funerary crown.

From Japan can be seen dance masks *(gigaku)* and the "Portuguese Screen" (16C) depicting the arrival in Japanese waters of a Portuguese ship.

From the Place d'Iéna to the Place de l'Alma

On leaving the Guimet Museum, on the Place d'Iéna, note the concrete Economic and Social Council building (Palais du Conseil Économique et Social) designed by Auguste Perret (1937).

In this residential quarter of private mansions *(hôtels)* and luxurious apartment houses live many foreigners.

Palais Galliera. – *10 Avenue Pierre-Ier-de-Serbie.* The Duchess of Galliera, wife of the Italian financier and philanthropist, had this building built (1878-1888) in the Italian Renaissance style. The mansion houses a Costume Museum.

Costume Museum. – *Open 10am to 5.40pm; closed Mondays, holidays and between exhibitions; for further information* ℡ *47.20.85.46; 15F.* Revolving exhibitions (twice yearly) present men, women and children's fashion and dress from 1735 to the present. This vast collection comprises almost 5 000 complete outfits and an additional 30 000 articles.

Follow – on the left – the Rue de Chaillot, the main street of the old village of Chaillot.

Church of St. Peter of Chaillot. – The church was rebuilt in the neo-Romanesque style in 1937. Overlooking its flat façade, on which the life of St. Peter has been carved by Bouchard *(p 157),* is a 65 m high – 213 ft – belfry.

Cross Avenue Marceau.

Take Avenue Pierre-Ier-de-Serbie leading to a bustling quarter dotted with banks, art galleries, luxury boutiques, couturiers and perfumers. After crossing the Avenue Georges-V turn right into the Rue François-Ier (further left the Europe No. 1 broadcasting station) to reach the elegant **Avenue Montaigne.** Until 1870 crowds flocked to the Mabille dance hall in this former gallant Widows' Alley. Nowadays it is lined with great buildings and famous couturier shops.

At No. 22, Rue Bayard is the Radio-Télé-Luxembourg station. Note the façade of the building which was decorated by Vaṣarely.

Church of Notre-Dame de Consolation. – *23 Rue Jean-Goujon.* A fire at a charity bazaar in 1897 killed 117 people on the site on which this memorial chapel, designed by Guilbert, was erected (1901).

The decoration is Neo-Baroque: note the handsome marble columns at the entrance to the side chapels and supporting the entablatures. Niches contain urns and cenotaphs. It is the Italian church in Paris.

Return to the Place François-I and take the Rue Bayard on the right to the Cours Albert-I.

The statue on the left is of the Polish poet and patriot, Mickiewicz (1795-1855) by Bourdelle *(p 64).*

Champs-Élysées Theatre. – *13 Avenue Montaigne.* The theatre, the work of the Perret brothers was in 1912 one of the first large reinforced concrete buildings to be erected in Paris. The high reliefs on the façade are by Bourdelle; the decoration on the ceiling is by Maurice Denis. At times, Diaghilev and his Russian ballet company, the Marquis de Cuevas and his dancers, and the actor Louis Jouvet all starred at the theatre.

Join us in our never ending task of keeping up to date.

Send us your comments and suggestions, please.

Michelin Tyre Public Limited Company
Tourism Department
Lyon Road – HARROW – Middlesex HA1 2DQ.

Michelin plan **11** - fold 31: J 13, J 14 - K 13, K 14.

Distance: 3 km – 2 miles – Time: 2 1/2 hours. Start from the Odéon métro station.

On this walk the Institute, Beaux Arts and Mint are the main monuments. The quays, lined with bookstalls, provide the best vantage points.

From the Carrefour de l'Odéon to the École des Beaux-Arts

Cross the Boulevard St-Germain and opposite Danton's statue, by No. **130**, cut into the Commerce-St-André Court, opened in 1776 on the site of a tennis court.

It was in this passage that a Dr. Guillotin perfected, on some sheep in 1790, his "philanthropic decapitating machine" and at a small printers, No. **8**, that Marat produced his paper, *The People's Friend*. Take the first alleyway (grilles) to the right. From a workshop on the corner, can be seen one of the towers of the Philippe Auguste wall.

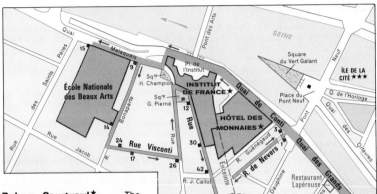

Rohan Courtyard★. – The Rohan Courtyard – a series of three courts was once part of the 15C mansion of the Archbishops of Rouen (Rohan is a deformation of Rouen). These typically provincial style courtyards are very picturesque. The middle courtyard is overlooked by a fine Renaissance façade, which was once part of Diane de Poitiers' mansion.

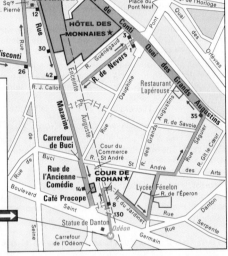

Continue along the peaceful Rue du Jardinet, built on the site of former gardens, into the Rue de l'Éperon where the Lycée Fénelon stands, the first girls' school to be opened in Paris, (1893). Bear right *(Rue St-André-des-Arts)* then left into the Rue Séguier, dating back, to 1179 and lined still by old houses.

Quai des Grands Augustins. – Built in 1313, it is the oldest in Paris. It got its name from the Great Augustine Monastery established by St. Louis in the 13C on the site which extended along the waterfront to the Rue Dauphine. Note, as you pass, two 17C mansions No. **35** and No. 51 now the famous Lapérouse Restaurant.

Quai de Conti. – It begins at the Rue Dauphine. Running off just beyond, between Nos **1** and **3**, is the curious **Rue de Nevers**, a blind alleyway hollowed out in the 13C and remaining mediaeval in character which ends abruptly at the Philippe Auguste wall.

■ THE MINT★ (HÔTEL DES MONNAIES) **11** - fold 31: J 13

A succession of buildings have stood between the Rue Dauphine and the Philippe Auguste wall since the Nesle Mansion was first erected on the site in the 13C. The house was rebuilt by Luigi di Gonzaga, Prince of Nevers, in 1572, remodelled in 1641 and renamed by the Princess de Conti when she came to live there in 1670.

In the 18C Louis XV transferred the Mint to the mansion, selecting a hitherto unknown architect, **Antoine**, to design the workshops. The simplicity of line, sober bossage and decoration pleased the public after the surfeit of Classical orders and colonnades. The architect himself lived in the building until he died in 1801.

Tour. – A staircase rising from the beautiful coffered entrance, circles twice before reaching the suite of panelled rooms overlooking the quay and housing the Coin Museum *(displays on view: 11am to 5pm; closed Saturdays and Sundays; ☎ 43.29.12.48 extn 525)*. Temporary exhibitions are also held *(open Saturdays also)*.

Medals and coins are on sale at No. 2 Rue Guénégaud *(9am to 5.45pm, 11.45am on Saturdays; closed Sundays and holidays)*.

The pressing of blanks into French and other coins, and the production of collectors pieces and dies for the Assay and Weights and Measures offices now take place in Pessac (Gironde). The Mint also produces medals and decorations *(guided tours, Mondays and Wednesdays, 2.15 to 3.15pm, closed during the summer holidays)*.

A pyramid in the second court on the left is a former meridian bearing *(map p 132)*.

■ **THE INSTITUTE OF FRANCE ★** (INSTITUT DE FRANCE) ▢▢ - fold 31: J 13

The Academy dome marks the building from afar.

Long before the present building, the site formed part of the Philippe Auguste perimeter which at its end on the Seine was defended by the **Nesle Tower**, standing where the left wing of the Institute has since been erected (the Mint side). The tower's history became widely known when Alexandre Dumas dramatized it in a play.

In 1661, three days before he died, Cardinal Mazarin, when making final bequests from his immense wealth, left 2 million *livres* for the foundation of a college of sixty scholars from the provinces acquired by France under his ministry. The College of Four Nations – Piedmont, Alsace, Artois and Roussillon – was opened in 1688 and closed in 1790 when the building was successively used for various ends.

The building next became the home of the Institute, a body founded by the Convention and transferred from the Louvre by Napoleon in 1806. It incorporates the French Academy, founded by Richelieu in 1635 and the Academies of Inscriptions and Belles Lettres (1663), Science (1666), Fine Arts (1803) and Moral and Political Sciences (1832).

The French Academy (l'Académie Française). – Membership of the French Academy is limited to forty and since 1980 is no longer exclusively masculine. The admission ceremony, following election and approval by the head of state, the Academy's patron, is made a great Paris occasion. Members are commonly known as "immortals" although the wearing of a green robe at solemn meetings and collaboration in the production of the Dictionary of the French Language have not saved the majority from total obscurity – whereas those refused admission include: Descartes, Pascal, Molière, La Rochefoucauld, Rousseau, Vauvenargues, Diderot, Beaumarchais, Balzac, Maupassant, Proust, Zola...

The majority of present academicians are writers – Julien Green, Ionesco and Marguerite Yourcenar the first woman to be admitted – but also represented are the Church, the army, diplomacy, medicine and technology.

Exterior. – The rounded wings ending in square pavilions and framing the Jesuit style chapel at the centre, were designed by Le Vau to harmonize with the Louvre, of which he was also an architect, on the far bank of the Seine. The cupola drum is adorned with Mazarin's coat of arms.

The courtyard through the gate to the left of the cupola, is lined on either side by twin porticoes which precede respectively, left, the Mazarin Library, originally the cardinal's own collection and, right, the ceremonial hall. A second courtyard, is surrounded by the buildings where the scholars used to live. The third smaller courtyard was the old kitchen yard. The well is still visible. At the far end is the Bureau des Longitudes which houses: laboratories and offices for a group of research workers specialising in astronomy.

Interior. – A tour of the interior *(reserved to cultural associations)* includes the academy council chambers and the former Mazarin Chapel beneath the dome which, since 1806, has been the ceremonial hall. Outstanding among the statuary, pictures and tapestries is Mazarin's tomb by Coysevox.

From the École des Beaux-Arts to the Carrefour de l'Odéon.

Beyond the Place de l'Institut, at the corner of the Rue Bonaparte and the Quai Malaquais stands a 17C stone and brick house (No. **9**). Further along is the École Nationale des Beaux-Arts. The writer Anatole France was born at No. **19** (plaque on No. **15**).

Take the Rue Bonaparte which follows the course of the canal which fed water from the Seine to the moat surrounding St-Germain-des-Prés Abbey *(p 106)*.

■ **THE ÉCOLE NATIONALE DES BEAUX-ARTS** ▢▢ - fold 31: J 13

A monastery dedicated to the Patriarch Jacob was founded in 1608 by Marguerite of Valois, Henri IV's first wife, when she regained her freedom, and was occupied by the Augustine order.

The monastery was closed down in 1791 and the building was used to store works of art from other monuments which had been destroyed or were no longer in use. The archaeologist **Lenoir** founded the Museum of the French Monuments where 1 200 small busts, statues etc. were displayed. Some of the treasures from St-Denis, the Louvre, Versailles and from many churches were thus saved.

The museum was closed in 1816 and replaced by the School of Fine Arts. The church and cloister are all that remain of the monastery. In 1860, the school annexed the **Hôtel de Conti** (11 Quai Malaquais) and in 1885, the Hôtel de Chimay (Nos 15 and 17).

Tour. – The courtyard and some monuments are open at No. **14**, Rue Bonaparte. These include the doorway from the Château d'Anet, the retreat of Diane de Poitiers, fragments from the Hôtel Legendre, demolished in 1841 and low reliefs from the Louvre's south wing.

Temporary exhibitions of the best works produced by the professors and students and part of the collections of drawings and paintings are held in the chapel, the lecture halls and rooms overlooking the Quai Malaquais.

Turn left into the narrow **Rue Visconti**, known in the 16C as "Little Geneva" where many Protestants including the artist Bernard Palissy, lived. Racine died at No. **24** in 1699. Balzac founded a printing-house at No. **17** in 1826. Delacroix had a studio there from 1836 to 1844.

Before you turn left into the Rue de Seine which is lined with art galleries, look on the right at the sign of a famous 17C nightclub, Le Petit-Maure, at No. **26**.

Rue Mazarine. – **Molière's** first appearance as an actor was made in 1643 at the theatre which stood at No. **12**. He had joined the company which lodged next door, at No. 10, and included the Béjart family of two brothers and two sisters, on inheriting some money from his mother. He was 21, had always been stagestruck and gladly abandoned the legal career chosen for him by his father. Symbolically he changed his name from Poquelin to Molière.

The company leased the Real Tennis court at No. 12 and built a theatre inside it which Molière and his companions, with youthful audacity, named the Illustrious Theatre. But the venture failed and a year later, the company moved to Quai des Célestins.

The first Paris **fire station**, home of the capital's first fire brigade which was created in 1722, was at No. **30**. It was mustered by François Dumouriez du Perrier, onetime valet to Molière, and later member of the Comédie-Française.

No. **42**, again an indoor Real Tennis court converted into the **Guénégaud theatre**, was where in 1671, opera was presented for the first time in France. The work, *Pomone* by Perrin and Cambert, played for eight months before the rival composer, Lulli, jealous of its success, had the theatre closed. After Molière's death in 1673, his company, evicted from the Palais-Royal by Lulli again, made the theatre their home until 1689 *(see below)*.

Carrefour de Buci. – By the 18C the Buci crossroads had become the focal point of the Left Bank with bustling pedestrians, wheeled traffic and a sedan chair rank, a guard post, a gibet and a pillar to which miscreants were attached by an iron collar.

There were several **Real Tennis courts** in the area, including three in the Rue de Buci. It was a very popular game. Until the 15C the ball was thrown by hand, then a glove was used and finally the racket was introduced. In 1687, the best players received a fee for appearing in public.

Rue de l'Ancienne-Comédie. – The street got its present name in 1770, the date the Comédie-Française left.

When the Four Nations College opened in 1688, the austere Sorbonne teachers at its head disapproved of the proximity of the Comédie-Française and forced the company to leave the Rue Mazarine *(see above)*. The players amongst whom was Molière's widow, Armande Béjart sought another tennis court and finally found one at No. **14** – the façade between the 2nd and 3rd floors is adorned with a reclining figure of *Minerva* by Le Hongre. The painters David, Gros and Horace Vernet had studios overlooking the court. The theatre opened in 1689 with *Phèdre* by Racine and Molière's *Le Médecin Malgré Lui*. Eighty-one years later, in 1770, the company, by this time once more in low financial waters, left for the Tuileries Palace Theatre before finally moving to the Odéon.

The old **Café Procope**, at No. 13 goes back to 1686 when it was founded by a Sicilian of that name. The establishment's popularity knew no bounds: throughout the centuries, it has been a meeting-place for writers, poets, revolutionaries, philosophers etc.

MICHELIN Paris Atlas No 🔳🔳

This MICHELIN publication contains a wealth of pratical information

A street index

A plan of the capital showing:
   one way streets
   arrondissements boundaries
   public buildings, museums, theatres, post offices...
   car parks
   métro stations and taxi-ranks.

Useful addresses including:
   government and municipal offices
   embassies and other foreign representatives
   churches, post offices, railway stations, department stores, etc.
   museums, sports facilities, cinemas, theatres, etc.

Emergency telephone numbers.

A public transport section: bus, métro and car.

Michelin plan ⚏: detailed map.

This vast park of nearly 900 ha - 2 224 acres is cut by wide shaded roads *(speed limit)*, rides and cycle tracks *(bicycles for hire opposite the Jardin d'Acclimatation's main entrance at the Carrefour des Sablons and near the Royal Pavilion at the Carrefour du bout des Lacs, daily 1 May to 30 September; Saturdays and Sundays, the rest of the year)*. Many roads are now reserved for pedestrians; boating is allowed on the Lower Lake. There are lakes, waterfalls, gardens, lawns and woodland, two racecourses, cafés and restaurants for the enjoyment of the public. Race meetings at Longchamp and Auteuil attract large numbers of racegoers and roads tend to be busy.

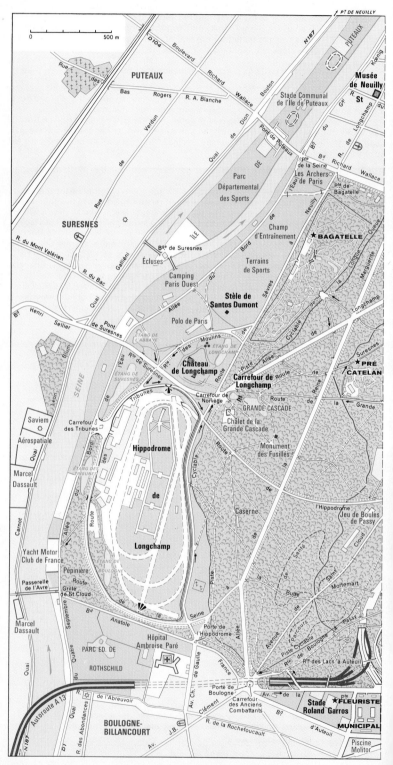

The best time for a pleasant stroll is on weekdays, in the morning.

There are two waymarked paths: the round tour (red and yellow) and the short one (yellow and blue).

A royal forest. – In Merovingian times the forest was hunted for bear, deer, wolves and wild boar; in 1308 local woodmen went in pilgrimage to Our Lady of Boulogne and, on their return, built a church with funds provided by Philip the Fair, which they called Our Lady of Boulogne the Lesser.

As the forest had become a refuge for bandits, in 1556 Henri II enclosed it with a wall pierced by eight gates; the most important are the Porte Maillot and Porte de la Muette.

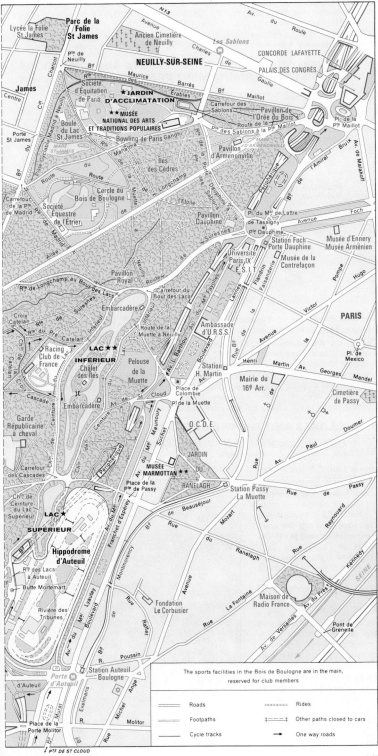

The sports facilities in the Bois de Boulogne are in the main, reserved for club members

Roads		Rides
Footpaths		Other paths closed to cars
Cycle tracks		One way roads

In the 17C Colbert converted it into a Royal Hunt with straight rides marked at their meeting points by crosses, as at the Croix Catelan. Louis XV opened the wood to the public but it was not until the Regency that it became highly fashionable and great houses were built: Neuilly, La Muette, Bagatelle, St-James' Folly and Ranelagh.

Decline. – During the Revolution the forest became the refuge of the pursued, the destitute and poachers. In 1815, the English and Russian armies bivouacked in the forest and because of the resulting devastation, new plantings were carried out.

The wood today. – When Napoleon III gave the forest to the capital in 1852, Haussmann demolished the surrounding wall, landscaped the area after Hyde Park creating winding paths, ornamental lakes and ponds, and built the Longchamp racecourse, restaurants, kiosks and pavilions. 1854 saw the opening of the Avenue de l'Impératrice (now the Avenue Foch); the wood became the fashionable place to take the air. The Auteuil racecourse, famous for its jumps, was built after 1870. The construction of the ring road round Paris and of the **Parc des Princes** stadium, and other planning decisions have caused some disruption but the wood is once again the capital's main recreation area.

■ NATIONAL MUSEUM OF POPULAR ARTS AND TRADITIONS AND CHILDREN'S AMUSEMENT PARK *Métro station: Les Sablons*

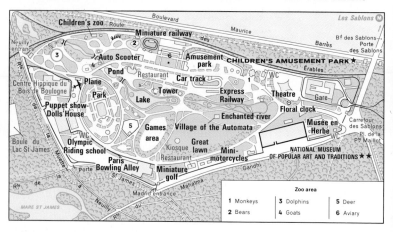

National Museum of Popular Arts and Traditions★★ (Musée National des Arts et Traditions Populaires). – *Description p 171.*

Children's Amusement Park★ (Jardin d'Acclimatation). – *Entrance: Carrefour des Sablons. Open 10am to 6pm; 5.40F. Special attractions on Wednesdays, Saturdays, Sundays and school holidays from 1.30pm.* This park, primarily arranged as a children's amusement park, includes a small zoo (with a typical Norman farm). The **Musée en Herbe** (11F, ℡ 47.47.47.66) is an art museum cum workshop designed for youngsters. The giant **Doll's House** (4F) will delight amateurs of old toys. The **Village of the Automata** (7F). A miniature railway runs from the entrance to the Maillot Gate.

■ THE LAKES AND THE PRÉ CATELAN

Bus: No. 32 (Porte de Passy); No. 63 (Porte de la Muette); PC (Circle Line - get off at Porte de la Muette or Porte de Passy).

Lower Lake★★ (Lac Inférieur). – This lake has a landing stage for the motor boat to the islands *(café-restaurant)* and boats for hire *(24 to 27F an hour).*

Upper Lake★ (Lac Supérieur).
A pleasant recreation area.

From the Carrefour des Cascades walk up the road skirting the Lower Lake to the Route de la Grande Cascade. Bear right immediately after into the Chemin de la Croix-Catelan past the Racing-Club and continue to the Croix-Catelan.

Pré Catelan★. – This attractive well-kept park is named after a court minstrel from Provence murdered there in the reign of Philip IV the Fair. It included a luxurious café-restaurant, lawns and shaded areas and a copper beech nearly two hundred years old with the most widespread branches in Paris – its shade extends nearly 500 m² – 600 sq yds.

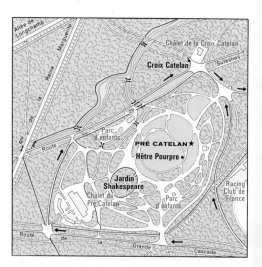

A **Shakespeare garden** *(guided tour 3 to 3.30pm and 4.30 to 5pm; an extra tour on Sundays 11 to 11.30am; 2.60F)* is planted with flowers, herbs and trees mentioned in his plays. There is also an open air theatre.

■ MUNICIPAL FLORAL GARDEN AND AUTEUIL RACECOURSE

Métro station: Porte d'Auteuil.

Municipal Floral Garden★ (Fleuriste Municipal). – *3 Avenue de la Porte d'Auteuil. Open 10am to 6pm (5pm 1 October to 31 March); 2.60F; 4.50F for exhibitions.*

The plants and flowers on display are grown for Paris' municipal parks and for official occasions. There are a palm house and a hothouse with tropical and exotic plants. The azalea *(latter half of April)* and chrysanthemum *(latter half of October)* shows draw large crowds.

Beyond the Floral Garden is the **Roland-Garros stadium** where the French Open Tennis championships are held every year *(late May-early June)*.

Auteuil Racecourse (Hippodrome d'Auteuil). – The racecourse is famous for its jumps including a 8 m – 28 ft water jump. The main events are listed in the Calendar of Events *(p 12)*.

■ BAGATELLE

Bus: No. 43 (stop: Place de Bagatelle).

Bagatelle★. – *Route de Sèvres-à-Neuilly. Admission: 2.60F; 4.50F for exhibitions.*

The first house to be built on the site was in 1720; it fell into ruin and in 1775 the Count of Artois, the future Charles X, bought it, betting his sister-in-law, Marie-Antoinette, and winning, that he would have a house designed and built within three months, complete with its landscaped garden.

By the 19C it had come to be owned by the Hertfords of whom the third and fourth marquesses and the latter's son, Sir Richard Wallace, formed a large collection of 17 and 18C French paintings, furniture and art objects. The City of Paris bought the house from the family in 1905. The art collection had already been transferred to London where, since 1897, it has been on view as the Wallace Collection, Hertford House.

Bagatelle is well known for its beautiful garden, particularly its walled iris garden *(May)*, roses *(June to early July)* and water lilies

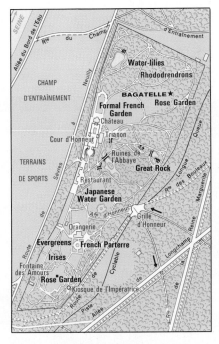

(August). Exhibitions of paintings and sculpture are held *(May to October)* in the Trianon and Orangery.

■ LONGCHAMP

The former abbey. – In 1225 St. Isabel, sister to St. Louis, founded an abbey, Our Lady of Humility, on the site between the Longchamp Pool and the Carrefour des Tribunes. This, in time, became known as Longchamp.

By the 18C, austerity had disappeared from the nunnery. Services at the end of Holy Week were crowded by the fashionable and what came to be known as the Longchamp Procession took place regularly until the last days of the Second Empire – even though the abbey had been suppressed in 1789.

The buildings were razed in 1795. The **mill** at the far end of the racecourse has been rebuilt. A tower, one of the few remains of the abbey, can be seen from the Rue des Moulins.

Longchamp Château. – The château was given to Haussmann by Napoleon III and has since 1949 housed the International Children's Centre. This was the site of the former Longchamp Abbey.

Santos-Dumont Stele. – *Access from the Rue des Moulins, by the Paris Polo Club*. The stele marks one of the early aviation world records established by the Brazilian flier Santos-Dumont on 12 November 1906.

Longchamp crossroads (Carrefour de Longchamp). – Note the manmade but nevertheless picturesque Grande Cascade.

Racecourse (Hippodrome). – Longchamp Racecourse, opened by Napoleon III in 1857, is the setting for famous racing events *(p 12)*. The panoramic restaurant *(open on race days only)* offers a good view of the course.

Michelin plan ⬛⬛: detailed map, and map ⬛⬛⬛ - folds 17, 26 and 27.

Vincennes – a fortress, the focal point of many events in French history, picturesque lake-scattered wood, the largest zoo in France, a delightful floral garden – takes a day to discover and enjoy fully, whether by car or on foot.

■ **THE CHÂTEAU★★** map ⬛⬛⬛ - folds 17, 27

This "mediaeval Versailles " has two distinct aspects within its walls where a tall forbidding keep stands close to a majestic group of 17C buildings.

The manorhouse. – In the 11C the crown acquired Vincennes Forest from St. Maur Abbey; in the 12C Philippe Auguste built a manorhouse within its confines to which St. Louis added a Holy Chapel. This king also forbade anyone to hunt the animals of the forest while, seated at the foot of an oak, he received his subjects without let or hindrance of ushers.

The castle. – The castle was constructed by the Valois: Philippe VI, John the Good and finally Charles V who completed it in 1370. Charles further invited the members of his court to build themselves houses within the walls to create a royal city, but it was not until the reign of Louis XIV that the nobility sought to live in the king's shadow.

The classical château. – Mazarin, appointed governor of Vincennes in 1652, had symmetrical royal pavilions designed by Le Vau and built to frame the main courtyard which faced south overlooking the forest. In 1660, one year after the pavilions' completion, the young Louis XIV spent his honeymoon in the King's Pavilion but subsequently preferred other royal domains.

The prison. – From the beginning of the 16C to 1784, the keep, no longer in favour as a royal residence, was used as a state prison. Supporters of the League, of Jansenism, of the Fronde, libertines, lords and philosophers were held; the disgrace of detention in Vincennes was far less than at the Bastille and, among the many held, the famous included the Great Condé, the Prince de Conti, Cardinal de Retz, Fouquet (guarded by d'Artagnan), the Duke of Lauzun *(p 64)*, Diderot, Mirabeau...

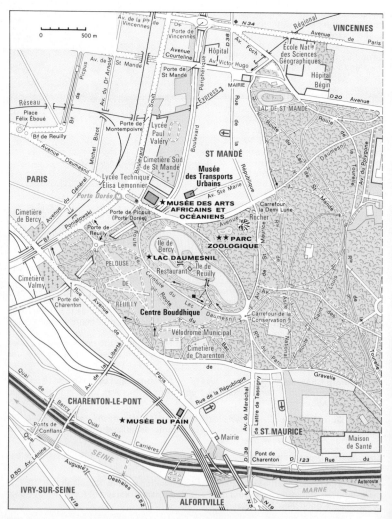

The porcelain factory. – In 1738, quite by chance, the château became a porcelain factory when two craftsmen, dismissed from Chantilly, sought refuge at Vincennes and began to practise their skill.

A company was formed which produced painted objects in soft paste, including sprigged flowers in natural colours. Porcelain bouquets and even "gardens" became highly fashionable before the factory was transferred to Sèvres in 1756 *(p 187)*.

The arsenal. – Under Napoleon the château was converted into a formidable arsenal. The towers were lopped to the height of the perimeter wall and mounted with cannon, the rampart crenelations removed, and the keep once more converted to a prison.

Daumesnil's Refusals. – In 1814 when the Allies called for the surrender of Vincennes, the governor, General Daumesnil, known as Peg Leg since the loss of his leg at the Battle of Wagram, retorted "Give me back my leg and I'll give you Vincennes".

At the end of the Hundred Days, the castle was again invested and there came a second refusal to surrender. Five months later, however, the doors were opened to Louis XVIII.

1830 found Daumesnil still governor and insurgents attempting to attack Charles X's ministers detained in the keep. The governor refused them entry, announcing that before giving in he would blow himself and the castle sky high.

The military establishment. – Under Louis-Philippe, Vincennes was incorporated in the Paris defence system; a fort was built beside it, outer openings were blocked up, the ramparts reinforced with massive casemates and the complex virtually interred by glacis.

On 24 August 1944 the Germans, before their departure from the castle, shot 26 resistance fighters, exploded three mines, breaching the ramparts in two places and damaging the King's Pavilion, and set fire to the Queen's Pavilion.

Restoration. – The restoration of Vincennes was begun by Napoleon III who commanded Viollet-le-Duc to begin the work which lasted a century, and is now completed.

The main courtyard looks again much as it did in the 17C since the moat round the keep has been redug, the 19C casemates removed and the pavilions restored. The château, in fact, is being revealed, once more, as one of the great historic royal houses of France.

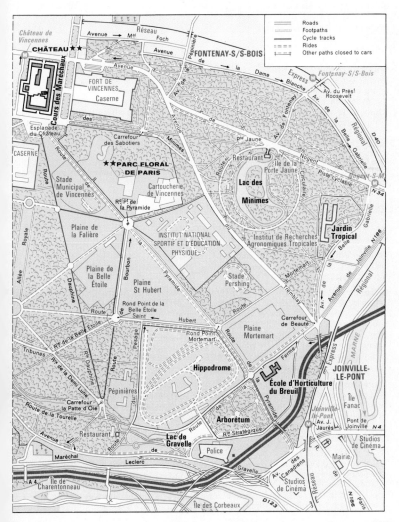

TOUR OF THE EXTERIOR *(plan p 147)*

We suggest you begin by walking right round the outside of the château, following the embankment round the moat.

The Keep★★ (Donjon – exterior). – This magnificent construction epitomizes the greatness of 14C military architecture. The 52 m tall – 170 ft – tower, quartered by turrets, with a spur to the north for outhouses, attiring room and a small oratory, was encircled by a sentry path protected by now vanished battlements and machicolations.

The keep proper was surrounded by a fortified wall and a separate moat. The base of the wall was protected against sappers by massive stonework, corner turrets and a covered watch path, complete with battlements, machicolations and gun embrasures.

The Tour du Bois and the Colonne du Duc d'Enghien. – The arcades of the Classical Vincennes portico overlooking the forest and closing the perimeter wall on the south side, come into view as you arrive on the Château Esplanade. The

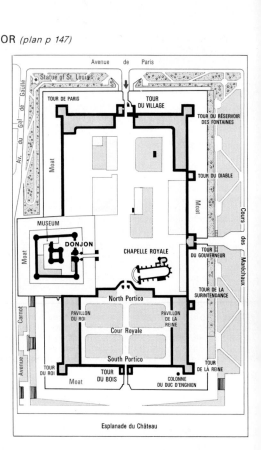

Bois Tower at the centre was reduced by Le Vau in the 17C when he transformed the gate into a state entrance (it appears as a triumphal arch from inside).

From the bridge over the moat can be seen, at the foot of the Tour de la Reine (Queen's Tower) on the right, the column marking the spot where the **Duke of Enghien,** Prince of Condé, accused of plotting against Napoleon, was executed by firing squad on 20 March 1804. (His body was exhumed on the orders of Louis XVIII and reinterred in the Royal Chapel).

The Cours des Maréchaux. – It was in the penultimate of the five truncated towers of the east wall, the Devil's Tower (Tour du Diable), that the porcelain factory was established. The avenue is modern.

TOUR OF THE CHÂTEAU

Guided tours of the keep and chapel: in summer, 10am to 6pm; in winter 10am to 5pm; 15F.

Tour du Village★. – This massive tower 42 m high – 138 ft – the only one beside the keep not to have been lopped in the 19C, served as the governor's residence in the Middle Ages.

Chapelle Royale★. – The Royal Chapel, modelled on the Sainte-Chapelle *(p 60)* and begun by Charles V in the 14C in place of the one built by St. Louis, was only completed in the 16C in the reign of Henri II. The building, apart from the windows and some decoration, is pure Gothic; the façade with its beautiful stone rose windows is Flamboyant. The interior consists of a single elegant aisle with highly decorative consoles and a frieze running beneath the windows which, in the chancel, are filled with unusually coloured mid-16C **stained glass★** featuring Scenes from the Apocalypse. The Duke of Enghien's tomb is in the north chapel.

The Keep★★. – The fortified wall, after the removal of the additional works, is protected by a barbican which guarded the drawbridge. The keep is in the centre of a courtyard. There is a small **museum** *(audio-visual presentation)* retracing the history of the keep and its inmates. Each of the keep's floors, except for the topmost one, is the same with a main chamber with vaulting resting on a central pillar and four small dependent rooms in the turrets serving as waiting room, oratory, attiring room and treasury. These were later converted into prison cells (graffiti on the walls).

First floor. – A gangway provided direct access from the barbican to the first floor which was originally a royal reception room hung with tapestries to brighten the stone walls. Charles V received the Holy Roman Emperor here with great ceremony. Fouquet was imprisoned in this room while Mirabeau was held prisoner for three years in one of the towers where he wrote a scathing condemnation of royal warrants.

Second floor. – A wide spiral staircase leads to what was once the royal bedchamber. Henry V of England, Charles VI's son-in-law, died of dysentry in this room in 1422 and in 1574, Charles IX also died here at the age of twenty-four.

Ground floor. – This was the kitchen. In the great south hall there is a well 17 m – 56 ft deep and a gate which was that of the Temple Tower brought here after the demolition of the prison in which Louis XVI and his family were held *(p 175)*.

Classical Vincennes★. – The main courtyard (Cour Royale) is once more closed to the north by a portico, as Le Vau intended, and is framed by the two royal pavilions. Anne of Austria and Louis XIV's brother lived in the **Queen's Pavilion** (Pavillon de la Reine). The governor, Daumesnil, died there in 1832; and the last royal occupant was the Duke of Montpensier, Louis Philippe's youngest son. Mazarin died in the **King's Pavilion** (Pavillon du Roi) in 1661 while awaiting the completion of his apartment in the Queen's Pavilion. The two pavilions house the historical services of the armed forces.

At the far end of the court, the triumphal arch built onto the Tour du Bois by Le Vau and the colonnades on either side have restored this part of the chateau to its former glory.

■ THE BOIS★★ 🔢 - detailed map

The Bois de Vincennes with its natural attractions, its famous zoo and beautiful flower garden, is a popular recreation area. In addition to facilities for sport there are two waymarked paths: red for the complete tour and yellow and blue for the shorter one.

The Royal Forest. – Philippe Auguste enclosed the wood as a royal hunt with a wall 12 km – 7 miles long and stocked it with game. Charles V built the small Beauté Château within it on a low hill overlooking the Marne.

In the 17C it became a fashionable place to take the air. Strollers gained access to the wood through six gates pierced in the wall. The Pyramid monument commemorates the new plantations which were carried out in Louis XV's reign.

The military firing range which opened in 1798 was the first of a series of enclaves to be created in the forest, a practice which is still current to this day for military and sporting purposes.

The Bois in Modern Times. – Napoleon III ceded Vincennes in 1860 – except the château and military installations – to the City of Paris to be made into an English style park. Haussmann created the Gravelle Lake which was filled with water diverted from the Marne and in turn it fed the lakes and rivers flowing through the woods. A trotting track was also built.

The National Sports Institute dominated by a modern covered stadium offers training facilities for athletics and swimming.

The hundred-year old **Throne** (or Gingerbread) **Fair** is held each spring *(Palm Sunday to end of May)* on the Reuilly Lawn near Lake Daumesnil. This colourful event is the capital's main fair attraction *(p 167)*.

WEST SIDE

Zoological Garden★★. – *Métro Station: Porte Dorée. Entrance: Avenue Daumesnil. Open 9am to 6pm (5.30pm, 15 October to 28 February); 25F.* ☎ *43.43.84.95.*

550 mammals and 700 birds of some 200 different species live in natural surroundings close to their familiar habitat. At the centre is an artificial rock 72 m – 236 ft high inhabited by wild mountain sheep.

Lake Daumesnil★. – *Métro station: Porte Dorée.* A great many people flock to the lake shore and its two islands *(bridge across – café on Reuilly Island). For hire: bicycles – 16F an hour; boats – 26 to 29F.*

African and Oceanian Art Museum★ (Musée des Arts africains et océaniens). – *Métro station: Porte Dorée. 293 Avenue Daumesnil. Open 9.45am to noon and 1.30 to 5.15pm; Closed Tuesdays and 1 May. 12F.*

The façade of the building, erected for a Colonial Exhibition in 1931, is decorated with a great sculptured frieze illustrating the contributions made by the overseas territories to France.

The ground floor and the right side of the main hall are devoted to Oceanian art: large collection of painted bark (Australia), masks (New Guinea), strange funerary figures and root sculptures.

On the left side of the hall are exhibited examples of African art; its themes are life and death: masks, wood and copper figures (Gabon). On the first floor are dance masks, ceremonial masks (Mali, Ivory Coast), gold pendant masks (Ivory Coast, Ghana), and magical statues (Congo).

On the second floor, the North African countries are represented by fine **jewellery★**, ceramics, embroidery from Fez, Algerian headdress, Tunisian pottery, furniture (carved or inlaid with mother of pearl and ivory), and large wool carpets.

In the basement there are a tropical fish **aquarium★** and two terrariums complete with crocodiles and tortoises.

Buddhist Centre (Centre bouddhique du Bois de Vincennes). – *Opening times unspecified at time of going to press.*

South of Lake Daumesnil is the Buddhist Temple of Paris housed in one of the 1931 Colonial Exhibition buildings. The new roof with 180 000 tiles carved out of a chestnut tree with an axe is noteworthy. Inside is a monumental statue of Buddha (9 m – 30 ft) in gold leaf.

EAST SIDE

Paris Floral Garden★★ (Parc Floral de Paris). – *Métro station: Château de Vincennes. Route de la Pyramide. Open 9.30am to 6pm (8pm 1 April to 30 September; 5pm 1 November to 28 February). 3.80F, 7.10F on weekends and holidays from 1 May to 30 September.*

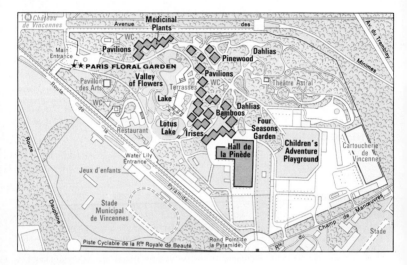

The garden which extends over 35 ha-87 acres includes hundreds of species. The Pavilions dotted in a setting of pine trees and round the lake in Flower Valley and the Hall de la Pinède house exhibitions and shows (photographs, dance, posters and horticulture). Alleys lined with modern sculpture lead to the children's adventure playground. The Dahlia garden from Sceaux, south of Paris, has been recreated near the Pyramid *(in flower September-October)*. The water garden with its water-lilies and lotus is at its best in August to October. There are also a Four Seasons Garden, and gardens growing medicinal plants *(best seen from May to October)*, irises and bamboo. Flower shows are held throughout the year: Orchids *(early March)*, tulips *(from April)* and rhododendrons and azalea *(from May)*.

Minimes Lake. – *Station: Fontenay-sous-Bois (R.E.R.).* The lake, named after a monastery on the same site which formed an enclave in the royal forest, includes three islands, of which one, the Porte Jaune, is accessible across a bridge *(café-restaurant, boats)*.

Tropical Garden (Jardin tropical). – *Station: Nogent-sur-Marne (R.E.R.).* The garden, in which stand the Institute of Tropical Agronomic Research and the Tropical Forestry Centre *(No. 45 bis, Avenue de la Belle-Gabrielle)*, has a Chinese gate by the main entrance and, on the far side of the garden, a Temple (destroyed by fire in 1984) to the Memory of the Indochinese killed in the 1914-1918 War. The nearby alley is inspired by the famous avenue at Angkor Watt.

Breuil School of Horticulture (École de Breuil). – *Station: Joinville-le-Pont (R.E.R.).* Horticulture and landscape design. Beautiful gardens. The arboretum *(entrance: Route de la Pyramide; open Mondays, Wednesdays and Fridays, 1 to 4.30pm)* extends over 12 ha – 30 acres and includes 2 000 trees of 80 different species.

Hippodrome. – *Station: Joinville-le-Pont (R.E.R.).* The main racing events are listed in the Calendar of Events *(p 12)*. Evening race meetings are also held.
On the other side of the Route de la Ferme is **Gravelle Lake** dotted with waterlilies.

IF YOU LIKE...	VISIT...
mediaeval art	*the Cluny Museum.*
monumental art	*the Museum of French Monuments.*
period furnishings	*the Museum of Decorative Arts.*
18C art	*the Carnavalet, Cognacq-Jay, Jacquemart-André, Nissim-de-Camondo Museums; the Soubise Palace.*
19C painting and the Impressionist School	*the Jeu-de-Paume, Marmottan, Beaux-Arts (Petit Palais) Museums.*
Contemporary art	*the G. Pompidou Centre, the National Museum of Modern Art, the Museum of Modern Art of the City of Paris, the Palais de Tokyo Museums.*

LA DÉFENSE

Michelin map **11**: detailed map.

Distance: 3.5 km – 2 miles from Porte Maillot. Central Parking area: Access road Défense 4 from the ring road. Access also by the R.E.R. or bus No. 73.

The quarter gets its name from a monument commemorating the defence of Paris of 1871. The bronze statue by Barrias has been returned to its original site beside the Agam pool.

An impressive achievement. – The urbanisation of the area west of Paris and the creation of a new business and residential centre are the most ambitious town planning projects ever undertaken in the Paris region. The coordinating body EPAD (Établissement Public pour l'Aménagement de la Défense) set up in 1958, is responsible for the management of the project which covers an area of 800 ha – 1 976 acres divided into two zones.

The business sector. – This zone of 130 ha – 321 acres comprising parts of the **Puteaux** and **Courbevoie** districts and the continuation of the Champs-Élysées-Pont de Neuilly axis, has as its centrepiece, a vast concrete **podium** rising in steps from the Seine and forming a central mall with patios and squares on different levels. Construction is nearing completion.

The originality of the plan lies underneath the podium where a complex network of communications exists: local access and link roads, national roads, a ring road, the R.E.R. express metro, suburban line and bus stations, parking areas, basement floors of the towers, air ducts, stairs and lifts, and galleries (15 km – 9 miles) used for cables and pipes.

Architects and town planners from all corners of the world come to visit this underground area which represents a new building concept.

The skyline all around the podium is broken by towers, with the tallest rising 45 storeys high. Since 1964 when the Esso building first opened, thirty towers have been completed and provide office space for over 200 companies, including some of France's most important ones. The towers are equipped with air conditioning, automated mail sorting, close circuit television and open plan offices. In 1985 over 60 000 people worked at La Défense.

Most of the smaller tower blocks are residential: Eve, Défense 2000 and Gambetta. At the foot of the business and residential towers are the commercial, leisure and sports complexes. The shopping centre covering 120 000 m² is the largest in Europe.

The Poissons Tower dominates the Charras development in the Courbevoie district. Its giant clock-barometer gives a weather reading for the Paris region (blue – variable, green – fine, red – rainy) and a flashing light marks the hours.

The park area. – The 90 ha – 222 acre area further to the west in the **Nanterre** plain includes housing, sports facilities and a park.

The Hauts-de-Seine **Police Headquarters** (Préfecture) and the **School of Architecture** were both completed in 1972.

At the heart of this new urban development is a 24 ha – 59 acre **park** which includes a botanical garden office which is overlooked by office buildings, flats and a theatre with a capacity of 900. Note the unusual curved walls pierced by odd-shaped windows set in an irregular pattern. The Opera Ballet School is to have premises here.

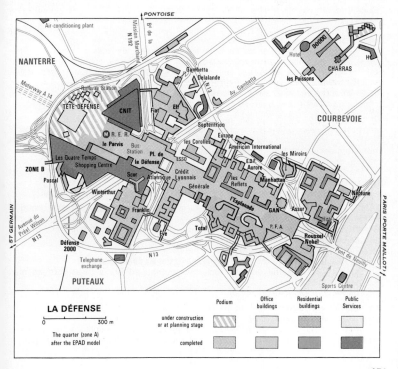

TOUR

La Défense with its curious huddle of offices and building sites is in sharp contrast with the traditional business sector in the centre of Paris.

The official authority, EPAD attempts to tone down the starkness of the development by means of harmony of colour, form and movement.

Parvis. – From the podium there is a fine **vista**★ down the opening between the towers in the direction of the Étoile.

The vast arch, at the western end, known as **Tête-Défense**, comprises two office buildings with oblique walls. They were designed by the Danish architect, Otto von Sprechelson, and will house two ministries (Urbanism, Housing and Transport and the Environment) and a new International Communications Centre.

Palais de la Défense (CNIT). – The National Centre for Industry and Technology, the earliest (1958) and one of the most famous edifices of the complex, is remarkable for its dimensions and the boldness of its architecture. Its concrete vaulting in the form of an inverted shell has only three points of support, each poised on the apex of a triangle. The building is the venue for great commercial exhibitions: the International Boat Show *(January)*, the World Tourism and Travel Show *(March)*, International Sight and Sound Festival *(March)*, the SICOB (Data Processing) *(March and September)*, the DIY Show.

Opposite the CNIT, the **Centre commercial des Quatre Temps** comprises two department stores and over 200 shops, restaurants and cinemas on two different underground levels. The building above, **Élysées-la Défense**, has an interior garden.

In front of the centre is a monumental sculpture of two figures by Mirò (1978).

Opposite, the Place de la Défense is dominated by Calder's last work, the red stabile.

Fiat Tower. – Designed by a team of French and American architects, this is the tallest building, along with the Elf Tower, with its 45 storeys rising 178 m – 584 ft above the podium. Its massive but harmonious lines are particularly attractive at night with its polished granite and black tinted façade looking like a giant chess-board. Contrary to the other towers built with curtain walls, the Fiat tower has load-bearing walls. Another unusual feature is the widening of the windows near the top to avoid a tapering effect. From inside there is direct access to the public transport system.

Elf Tower. – Similar in height to its neighbour the Fiat Tower, the impressive Elf building is by the same team of architects. The three glass curtained towers of varying height are a blue colour which changes with the light.

Opposite the Fiat tower stand the fortress-like **Winthertur** and **Franklin** towers (the latter comprises two abutting structures), with their severe architectural style and dark glazed façades, designed by the same team. They are partly hidden by the Scor Tower in the form of a tripod. A white marble sculpture 'Dame Lune' by Julio Silva can be seen between the Atlantique and Crédit Lyonnais towers; further to the right, the pyramid-like **Défense 2000**, and to the left, the white elliptical outline of the **Eve** tower south of the Villon quarter contrast with the decorative aluminium façade and vivid colours of the **Générale** tower.

On the esplanade, the monumental **fountain by Agam** plays with music and illuminations *(Wednesdays and weekends, 3pm; in summer Fridays and Saturdays, 10.30pm)*.

Opposite the Esso building, the underground **Galerie** holds art exhibitions.

In the square, a stairway *(signpost)* in front of the Agam fountain leads down to the gallery where is displayed Moretti's Monster, a sculpture featuring different textures and symbolising the artist's artistic experiments *(open noon to 5pm except Sundays and Mondays; 3F; ☎ 47.76.18.84)*.

Bear left on the esplanade and pass round a small building to reach the **Place des Corolles** named after a sculpture, *'Les Corolles du Jour'*, adorning the copper fountain by Louis Leygue. A ceramic fresco, *'Le sculpteur de Nuages'*, by Attila ornamenting a low wall adds its dreamlike quality and vivid colours to the concrete environment.

The **Reflets** terrace is adorned with a sculpture by Philolaos, *L'Oiseau mécanique'*, depicted with its great steel wings tucked in.

Beyond the Vision 80 tower, built on stilts, is the **Place des Reflets** overlooked by the shimmering **Aurore** Tower, the rose-coloured Manhattan Tower and the green GAN Tower. Note the work by Derbré entitled 'La Terre'.

Manhattan Tower. – This is one of the most original structures of the whole complex in terms of shape, colour and materials used. The building attracts the eye with its undulating design, its smooth glazed façade harmonising with the colour of the sky, and its pure, elegant lines.

The S-shaped plan comprises two adjoining structures with the concrete pillars of the framework placed away from the façade to avoid any projections which would break the harmony. Each storey is made up of 4 000 transparent, reflecting glass panes.

GAN Tower. – This green tower in the form of a Greek cross, houses a group of insurance companies. This metallic structure with a reinforced concrete core has 42 storeys soaring 166 m – 545 ft above the podium. Black aluminium rails make a delicate pattern on the glazed façade.

Standing opposite is the **PFA Tower** in the form of a triangle.

A passageway above the ring road leads to the **les Miroirs** building.

On the way note the unusual Assur Tower, shaped like a three-pronged star, designed by Pierre Dufau.

The Aigle passageway leads down to the Pont de Neuilly.

Roussel-Nobel Tower. – This attractive blue-green, steel and glass tower was the first to be built (1967) at La Défense.

In the square, Napoléon I at the foot of the Neptune Tower, is a plaque commemorating the landing of Napoleon's remains at Courbevoie after the long sea voyage from St. Helena. The imperial eagle came from the railings of the Tuileries.

ADDITIONAL
WALKS AND SIGHTS

Listed alphabetically

(Photo R. Maillard/Vloo)

Buttes-Chaumont Park

THE ARSENAL

Michelin plan 🗺 - folds 33 and 45: K 17
Métro Station: Sully Morland – Entrance: 1 Rue de Sully

From 1352 the site was occupied by a Benedictine community, the Celestines. Proximity to royal residences such as the Hôtels St-Paul *(p 83)* and des Tournelles *(p 84)* brought considerable patronage. The monastic church accumulated great riches, in particular works of art and royal tombs. The latter are now in St-Denis or at Versailles.

In 1512, despite strong opposition from the Celestines, the city requisitioned the riverside stretch of land for the purpose of manufacturing cannon. Henri II purloined the workshops and founded a royal arsenal. Gun powder was one of the products and the famous explosion of 1563 was heard as far afield as Melun to the south. Philibert Delorme rebuilt the arsenal and it was here that Sully, Grand Master of Artillery, established his residence. Under Louis XIII the manufacture of cannon was discontinued and the production of gun powder was transferred to the Salpêtrière.

Fouquet's Trial. – In 1631 Richelieu established the Arsenal as a court for special hearings. It was the scene of the three year trial for embezzlement of Fouquet, Louis XIV's finance minister. Colbert energetically packed the magistrate's court, but the verdict was only banishment (1664). Displeased Louis XIV changed the sentence to life imprisonment and banished the chief offending magistrate to his estate.

The Poisoner's Court. – Following the affair of the notorious poisoner the Marquise de Brinvilliers *(p 87)* who dispatched her father and two brothers, the art of poisoning became extremely popular in the capital. A certain La Voisin masterminded the dealings in the lethal potions commonly known as the 'inheritance powder'. In the face of a growing scandal the Arsenal court became the Poisoners' court in 1680. On being questioned La Voisin implicated many, princesses, duchesses... Her fate was quickly sealed by burning at the stake.

The Library. – *Guided tours Wednesdays at 2.30pm; closed 1 to 15 September; 6F. Time: 1 hour. Apply to the Reception Desk on the first floor. ☎ 42.77.44.21.*

The library, created in 1757, was established as a public library in what remained of the Arsenal building in 1797. In the 19C it became the early meeting place of the Romantics, Lamartine, Hugo, Vigny, Musset, Dumas... The library possesses more than a million and a half volumes, 15 000 MSS, 120 000 prints and a large collection on the history of the theatre, which belongs to the National Library.

The building also includes rooms and an oratory with fine 17C paintings and ceilings and 18C salons. On the doors of the 18C music room are drawings of Bouchardon's low reliefs decorating the sides of the Four Seasons Fountain in Rue de Grenelle *(p 136)*.

As you walk along the Boulevard Morland note the cannon and mortar of the roof-top balustrade, recalling the early role of the building.

The statue in the square is to the 19C poet, Arthur Rimbaud by Ipousteguy.

The barracks, **Caserne des Célestins,** stand on the site of the convent gardens.

AUTEUIL

Michelin plan 🗺 - folds 26, 27, 38 and 39: K 4, K 5 - L 4
Distance: 4 km – 2 1/2 miles – Time: 1 1/2 hours (excluding Radio-France House). Buses nos 70, 72 and 52.

During the Second Empire Auteuil became part of the city of Paris but it was only at the turn of the century that the last vineyards disappeared. Many of the houses of this desirable residential area have retained good sized gardens.

On the midstream island, below the Pont de Grenelle, is a smaller version of Bartholdi's Statue of Liberty, which stands at the entrance to New York harbour.

The towers on the far bank of the Seine are part of the Front de Seine *(p 161)* urban renewal project.

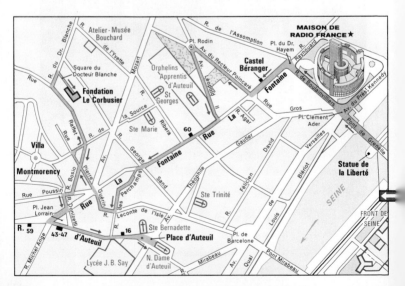

Radio-France House★. – *Guided tours of museum, 10 to 11.30am and 2 to 4.30pm; closed Mondays. Time: about 1 hour; 7.50F; ℡ 42.30.21.80.*

One concentric building 500 m – 547 yds – in circumference and a tower 68 m tall – 223 ft – covering in all 2 ha – 5 acres – go to make up Radio-France House. It was designed and erected by Henry Bernard in 1963 and is the biggest single construction in France. It is here in the 60 studios and the main auditorium (studio 104) that the programmes of French radio stations are produced.

A **museum** traces the technical evolution of radio and television.

On leaving the Radio-France House take the Rue de Boulainvilliers.

Rue La Fontaine. – The street takes its name from the spring which supplied the village of Auteuil. Here as in Rue Agar, there are several buildings by Hector Guimard, the famous *art nouveau* architect. His best known block of flats, **Castel Béranger**, is at no 14.

Take the Avenue du Recteur-Poincaré to reach the calm of Place Rodin, the setting for *The Age of Bronze*. Return by Avenue Léopold-II. The building at the junction with Rue La Fontaine is an orphanage (Orphelins Apprentis d'Auteuil).

Turn right. No. **60** another work by Guimard was built in 1911.

Having passed the Rue George-Sand turn left into Rue des Perchamps. Before taking the Rue Leconte-de-Lisle to the right, glance at the elegant rear façade of what was once one of Auteuil's finest mansions, the Hôtel de Puscher.

Take the Rue Pierre-Guérin. Beyond Rue de la Source, this dead-end street retains the aspect of a village lane.

Via Rue Raffet make for Rue du Dr.-Blanche.

Le Corbusier Foundation. – *8-10 Square du Dr.-Blanche. Open 10am to 12.30pm and 1.30 to 6pm (5pm on Fridays); closed weekends, holidays and in August; 5F. ℡ 42.88.41.53.*

Two buildings, namely Villas La Roche and Jeanneret, dating from 1923 serve as a documentation centre for the work of the famous architect, Le Corbusier. There is a permanent exhibition, a library and photographic collection.

Retrace your steps. To the right is the exclusive **Villa Montmorency** which was laid out on the site of the park of the former Hôtel de Montmorency. One notable owner was the Comtesse de Boufflers, mistress of the Prince de Conti and fervent admirer of Rousseau.

Rue Donizetti leads to Place Jean-Lorrain. The modern building at no **59** Rue d'Auteuil marks the site of a literary salon of a certain Madame Helvetius, but better known as 'Notre-Dame d'Auteuil'. The salon was frequented by philosophers and writers in the period from 1762 to 1800.

Rue d'Auteuil. – Follow the narrow Rue d'Auteuil with its many shops.

At nos **43-47** is an 18C mansion.

At no 11 bis a 17C château is now occupied by a school.

Admire at No **16** the main front of Hôtel de Puscher.

Place d'Auteuil. – The church of Notre-Dame is a Romano-Byzantine pastiche. The obelisk opposite the Ste-Bernadette Chapel is the last remaining tomb from the onetime cemetery. The monument commemorates the chancellor Aguesseau and his wife (1753).

To phone Great Britain from France, dial 19-44.

BASTILLE, Place de la

Michelin plan ⑩ - fold 33: J 17 - K 17 – *Métro Station: Bastille*

The vast crossroads, scene of the historic events of 1789, is dominated by the July Column.

Construction of the Bastille. – The first stone of the Bastille, which was intended to provide Charles V with a fortified residence, was laid in 1370 and the last in 1382. Its history is far from heroic: besieged seven times in periods of civil strife it surrendered six times.

The prison regime. – Prisoners were usually detained under the notorious *lettre de cachet* or royal warrant, and included the enigmatic Man in the Iron Mask and Voltaire. In 1784 *lettres de cachet* were abolished: the Bastille was cleared and its demolition planned.

The Taking of the Bastille. – In July 1789 trouble broke: the popular minister, Necker, was dismissed by the king: the Exchange closed and the militant crowd marched first on the Invalides to capture arms *(p 71)*, then on the Bastille. By late afternoon the Bastille had been seized and the prisoners – only seven in number – symbolically freed.

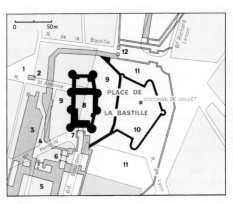

Site of the Bastille in the 18th century

1 Former Place de la Bastille	7 Main drawbridge
2 Guardroom	8 Great Courtyard
3 Barracks	9 Bastille defence ditches
4 Outer Courtyard	10 Bastion
5 Arsenal	11 Paris perimeter ditches
6 First drawbridge	12 St-Antoine Gate

155

Demolition. – The fortress was immediately demolished, 83 of its stones being carved into replicas and sent as dire reminders of the evil of despotism to the provinces.

The Square Today. – Paving stones mark out the ground plan of the Bastille on the square which was modified in appearance by the opening of the Rue de Lyon in 1847, the Boulevard Henri-IV in 1866 and the building of the station in 1859 (converted into an exhibition hall in 1970 and demolished in 1984). The station site is reserved for a second Opera House *(completion date: 1989)*.

The **July Column** (Colonne de Juillet) a bronze column 52 m high – 171 ft – crowned by the figure of Liberty, stands in memory of Parisians killed in July 1830 and 1848.

St. Martin's Canal★. – The canal dug at the Restoration, flows under the Place de la République, to reappear at the Arsenal basin.

THE BOTANICAL GARDENS★★
(Jardin des Plantes)

Michelin plan 🔟 - folds 44 and 45: L 16, L 17 – *Métro Station: Gare d'Austerlitz.*

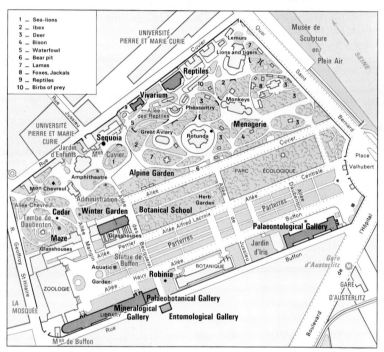

In 1626 Hérouard and Guy de la Brosse, physicians to Louis XIII, obtained permission, firstly, to establish in the St. Victor suburb, the Royal Medicinal Herb Garden which had previously been on the Ile de la Cité *(p 62)* and subsequently, to found a school of botany, natural history and pharmacy. In 1640 the garden was opened to the public.

After Fagon, Louis XIV's first physician, the botanist Tournefort, and the three Jussieu brothers journeyed widely to enrich the Paris collection.

It was during the curatorship of Buffon from 1739-1788, assisted by Daubenton and Antoine-Laurent de Jussieu, nephew of the earlier brothers, that the garden was at its greatest. Buffon's 36 volume *Natural History* was equalled by his expansion of the garden to the banks of the Seine, planting of lime trees along the avenues, creation of the maze, amphitheatre and museum galleries... so great indeed, was his prestige that a statue was erected to him in his lifetime.

The National Natural History Institute. – At the Revolution the garden's name was changed to that to Natural History Institute and a menagerie was created by transporting the royal animals from Versailles. This enabled Parisians to see for the first time such wild animals as elephants (brought from Holland in 1795), bears (all the animals which have occupied the pit have been called after the first one which was known as Martin), giraffes (1827) etc. In 1870, however, when Paris came under siege, the citizens' hunger exceeded their curiosity and most of the animals were slaughtered for food. With Geoffroy-Saint-Hilaire, Lamarck, Lacépède, Cuvier, Becquerel and many other great names, the institute won international recognition in the 19C which it maintains today through its teaching and research.

Tour. – In the 17C a tall mound built up from public waste was converted by Buffon into a **maze**. At the summit is a small kiosk overlooking the rest of the garden and the mosque. A column nearby marks the grave of Daubenton, naturalist and Buffon's collaborator.

The famous cedar of Lebanon, planted by Bernard de Jussieu in 1734 on the hillside facing the Seine was brought back, so the story goes, by the scientist from Syria on a sailing ship – he was said to have kept it in his hat, moistening it daily from his water ration. In fact, he was given it by Kew Gardens and only carried it across the Channel!

Near Cuvier's house, can be seen a cross-section of the trunk of an American sequoia tree more than 2 000 years old. It is inlaid with tablets describing events contemporary to its growth. The oldest tree in Paris, a Robinia or false acacia planted here in 1635, can be seen near the Allée des Becquerel.

Winter Garden (Jardin d'Hiver). – *Open 1.30 to 4.50pm; closed Tues. and holidays; 9F.*
The garden contains a large collection of tropical plants.

Alpine Garden (Jardin Alpin). – *Open 1 April to 30 September, weekdays 10 to 11.30am and 12.30 to 5.30pm; Sundays 2am to 6pm; closed Tuesdays and holidays; 9F.*
It includes plants from mountain and polar regions.

Menagerie, vivarium, reptiles. – *Open 9am to 6pm (5pm in winter). Closed holidays.* ℡ *43.36.19.09. 15F.*
Big reptiles, birds and beasts are shown in an old fashioned setting in which they nevertheless appear contented and their presence adds interest to the garden.

Botanical School (École de Botanique). – *Open 1.30 (10.30am on Sundays) to 4.30pm; closed Tuesdays and holidays.*
The garden contains more than 10 000 classified plants. Rising above everything is the Corsican Pine grown from seeds brought from the isle, by Turgot in 1774.

Palaeontological Gallery. – *Open weekdays 1.30 to 4.50pm; Sundays 10am to 4.50pm; closed Tuesdays and holidays; 15F.*
Models of prehistoric and earlier animals, fossils, etc.

Palaeobotanical Gallery. – *Open 1.30 to 4.50pm; closed Tuesdays, holidays; 11F.*
Evolutionary trends and specimens of fossil plants.

Mineralogical Gallery★. – *Same visiting days and hours as above; 15F.*
Minerals, meteorites and precious stones.

Entomological Gallery. – *Open 2 to 4pm. Closed Tuesdays and holidays; 11F.*
Selection of insects from all over the world.

BOUCHARD STUDIO AND MUSEUM

Michelin plan **ⅠⅠ** - fold 26: J 4 – *Métro Station: Jasmin*
25 Rue de l'Yvette. Open Wednesdays and Saturdays 2 to 7pm; 15F. ℡ *46.47.63.46.*

The sculptor, Henri Bouchard's (1875-1960) work varies from medals and statuettes to imposing memorials. Stone and bronze were his favourite materials. The studio display includes the plaster cast of *Apollo (p 49)*, the monumental bronze in front of Chaillot Palace, and the materials used in the creation of low reliefs, in particular those of the Church of St-Pierre de Chaillot *(p 138)*.

BUTTES-CHAUMONT PARK★

Michelin plan **ⅠⅠ** - fold 22: D 19, D 20 – E 19, E 20 – *Métro Station: Buttes Chaumont.*

Until 1864-1867 when Napoleon III and Haussmann converted the area into a park, Paris' first open space to the north, Chaumont, the bare or bald *(chauve)* mound, was a sinister area of quarries and rubbish dumps.

Haussmann took full advantage of the differences in ground level and of the quarries to dig a lake, fed by the St. Martin's Canal, in which he massed part natural, part artificial rocks 50 m – 150 ft – high. Two bridges lead to the island which he crowned with a temple commanding an extensive view of Montmartre and St-Denis.

At the corner of Rue Manin and Avenue Mathurin – Moreau stands the A.-de-Rothschild Ophthalmic Foundation, home of the French eye bank.

The Rue Georges-Lardennois affords an attractive view of Montmartre.

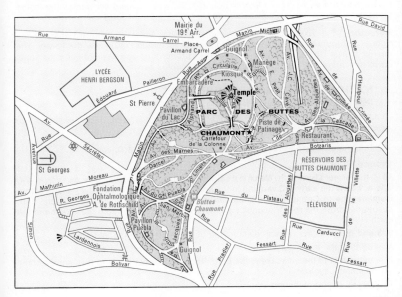

THE CATACOMBS★

Michelin plan ▥ - fold 42: N 12 – *Métro Station: Denfert-Rochereau.*

In the middle of **Place Denfert-Rochereau** is a small bronze version of Bartholdi's *Lion* in commemoration of Colonel Denfert-Rochereau's successful defence of Belfort in 1870-71. The two elegantly proportioned buildings adorned by sculpted friezes are examples of Ledoux' city gates and tollhouses *(p 16),* which punctuated "the wall walling in Paris".

Tour. – *Entrance: 1 Place Denfert-Rochereau. Open Tuesdays to Fridays, 2 to 4pm; Saturdays and Sundays, 9 to 11am and 2 to 4pm; closed Mondays; time: 1 hour; 12F.* ☎ *43.22.47.63.*

In 1785 it was decided to turn the disused parts of the quarries formed by excavation since Gallo-Roman times at the bases of the three "mountains" – Montparnasse, Montrouge and Montsouris – into ossuaries. Several million skeletons from the Innocents' and other cemeteries were thereupon transported to Montrouge where the bones were stacked against the walls, the skulls and crossed tibias form a macabre decoration.

On the liberation of Paris in August 1944 it was found that the Resistance Movement had established its headquarters within the catacombs.

CERNUSCHI MUSEUM★

Michelin plan ▥ - fold 17: E 10 – *Métro Station: Monceau or Villiers.*

7 Avenue Vélasquez. Open 10am to 5.40pm; closed Mondays and holidays; 7F. Sundays free (except during exhibitions). ☎ *45.63.50.75.*

The banker Henri Cernuschi donated to the City of Paris, on his death in 1896, his house and extensive collection of Oriental art. The museum is devoted to ancient Chinese art and includes Neolithic terracottas, bronzes, jade, ceramics, funerary statuettes and ink drawings. A 5C stone Bodhisattva and an 8C Tang painting on silk, *Horses and their Grooms,* are outstanding.

On the first floor temporary exhibitions alternate with showings of traditional Chinese painting.

(Photo Lauros-Giraudon)

The Horseman Han.

CONSERVATOIRE NATIONAL DES ARTS ET MÉTIERS★★

Michelin plan ▥ - fold 32: G 15, G 16

Métro Station: Réaumur-Sébastopol or Arts et Métiers

The Conservatory, an institution for technical instruction, a considerable industrial museum and a laboratory for industrial experiment, has incorporated in its present buildings the old church and refectory of the St. Martin in the Fields priory which once stood on the site. This Benedictine priory had developed around the original Chapel to St. Martin erected in the 4C. In 1273 the precincts were enclosed by a fortified wall, parts of which can still be seen if you continue round to the Rue du Vertbois (watch tower). The Conservatory, created by the Convention in 1794, was installed five years later in the priory.

Refectory★★. – *To visit apply in writing to the curator.* Enter the courtyard where on the right is the former monks' refectory by Pierre of Montreuil (13C), now the library. The interior is true Gothic with pure lines, perfect proportions and seven slender columns down the centre. On the right is a door with delightful carvings.

■ NATIONAL TECHNICAL MUSEUM★★
(MUSÉE NATIONAL DES TECHNIQUES)

292 Rue St-Martin. Open 1 to 5.30pm, Sundays 10 to 5.15pm; closed Mondays and holidays; 10F (free Sundays). ☎ *42.71.24.14, extn 375.*

The museum displays technical progress in industry and science.

Ground Floor:

10 – the former **Church of St. Martin in the Fields★** (St-Martin-des-Champs – *exterior: p 174*) where, below the early 12C vaulting in the ambulatory showing clearly the transition from Romanesque to Gothic – are exhibits on locomotion – cycles, cars, aircraft, etc. and, suspended from the roof, Foucault's pendulum which demonstrated the rotation of the earth (19C);

9, 8 and 5. – railways: steam, electric and diesel; numerous model trains

4. – agricultural machinery

2. – at the foot of the staircase is the Echo Room with apparatus and mementoes of the 18C chemist, Lavoisier

21. – weights and measures

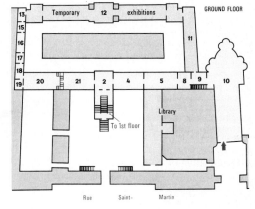

20. – mathematics, astronomy, geodesy: examples of Pascal's arithmetic machine, early instruments (astrolabes, globes, sun dials, pendulums, chronometers...)

19 to 15. – horology: fine collection with a particularly good 18C section

13. – automata: Marie-Antoinette's clockwork dulcimer – playing puppet of 1784

11 to 12. – *temporary exhibition area*

Return to gallery 2. The double flight staircase is by the 18C architect of the Mint, Antoine.

First Floor:

23. – in the stateroom at the top of the stairs: models based on the Encyclopaedia (late 18C)

24. – energy: mills to turbines

26 and 27. – physics and electricity: Charles the physicist's and other early scientific instruments

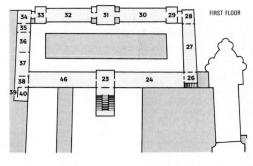

28 and 29. – glass from the greatest European glassworks

30. – optics: microscopes, spectacles

31. – music: experimental and early instruments

32. – mechanics: machine tools, gears

33 to 37. – radio, television, electronic acoustics: telecommunications systems for transmitting signals, images, sound, including the techniques of today radar, laser and satellite; the transmitting station from the Eiffel Tower

38 to 40. – photography, cinema: cameras of Niepce, Daguerre and Edison; the magic lantern used by the Lumière brothers *(p 80)*

46. – graphic arts (printing) and technology of everyday life (heating, elevation, lighting, domestic equipment).

EXPIATORY CHAPEL (Chapelle Expiatoire)

Michelin plan ⌷⌷ - fold 18: F 11 – *Métro Station: St-Augustin*

Square Louis XVI (entrance: 29 Rue Pasquier)
Guided tours 10am to 5.30pm; closed holidays; time: 1/2 hour; 10F April to September; 6F the rest of the year; children: 3F.

A small cemetery, opened in 1722, was used as burial ground first for the Swiss Guards killed at the Tuileries on the 10 August 1792 *(p 40)* and then for the victims of the guillotine which stood in the Place de la Concorde *(p 43)*. These last numbered 1 343 and included Louis XVI and Marie-Antoinette. Immediately on his return to Paris, Louis XVIII had the remains of his brother and sister-in-law disinterred and transported to the royal necropolis at St-Denis (21 January 1815 – *p 182*). Between 1816 and 1821 the chapel was erected to the plans of Fontaine.

The cloister occupies the site of the old burial ground. Charlotte Corday, who stabbed Marat in his bath to avenge the Girondins, and Philippe-Égalité are buried on either side of the steps leading to the chapel in which two marble groups show Louis XVI and an angel (by Bosio) and Marie-Antoinette supported by Religion symbolized by a figure with the features of Madame Elisabeth, the king's sister (by Cortot). The crypt altar marks the place where Louis XVI's and Marie-Antoinette's bodies were found.

THE FAUBOURG ST-ANTOINE

Michelin plan ▥ - folds 33, 34 and 46: K 18, K 19

Distance: 3 km – 2 miles – Time: 1 3/4 hours – Start from the Bastille métro station.

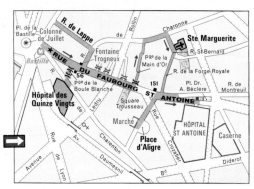

The community grew up round the fortified Royal Abbey of St. Anthony, founded in 1198. Louis XI added to the abbey's privileges by giving it power to dispense justice locally and allowing the craftsmen in the vicinity to work outside the established powerful and highly restrictive guilds. The cabinet-makers of St-Antoine thus became free to design furniture and, from the 17C, copied or adapted pieces from the royal workshops and began to employ mahogany, ebony, bronze, and produce marquetry.

By the time of the Revolution, workshops had developed in size, in the case of Réveillon, populariser of painted wallpapers, to 400 employees. The sheer numbers were a cause for social unrest and in April of 1789 the factory, at **31** Rue de Montreuil, was the scene of rioting and Réveillon was obliged to flee.

In October 1783 **Pilâtre de Rozier** made the first aerial ascent from Réveillon's factory yard in a balloon of paper made on the spot, inflated with hot air and secured by a cable.

The Revolution abolished the guilds thereby reducing the local craftsmen's advantage which suffered further with 19C mechanisation. Small workshops, nevertheless, abound. With the abolition of the national workshops in June 1848 the faubourg was the setting for the erection of numerous barricades.

Rue du Faubourg St-Antoine*. – The street is lined with furniture shops and honeycombed with courts and passages, often with picturesque names, where timber is matured and carpenters and cabinet-makers can be seen at work.

The Passage de la Boule Blanche at no 50 opens onto the entrance (No. 28) of the **Quinze Vingts Hospital** in Rue de Charenton. St Louis founded the hospital for 300 (15 × 20) blind persons and located it in the vicinity of the Louvre *(p 98)*. It was later transferred to these 18C buildings a onetime barracks by Robert de Cotte. At the far end of the courtyard of No. 56, the stairway G has a fine oak banister.

At the corner with Rue de Charonne is the Trogneux Fountain (1710). Continue up this side street until you reach the picturesque **Rue de Lappe** on the left, a centre of wrought iron manufacture and Auvergne shops. Return to the main street ; the Main-d'Or Passage at No 133, typical of the old quarter, comes out onto the Rue de Charonne.

St. Margaret's Church. – *Closed Sundays noon to 6pm.* Built in the 17C and enlarged in the 18C, the interior is disparate in style, the nave low and plain with basket handle arching, the chancel tall and light. The marble *pietà* (1705) behind the high altar is by Girardon; the false relief frescoes (1765) in the Souls in Purgatory Chapel, left of the chancel, are by Brunetti. The transept chapels contain 18C paintings which originally came from the Lazarus House *(p 168)*.

The small cemetery *(not open)* is presumed to be the burial place of Louis XVII who is said to have died in the Temple in 1795 *(p 175)*.

From St. Margaret's to the St. Anthony Hospital. – Return to the main street by the Rue de la Forge Royale. **Place d'Aligre** is the site of a daily market *(mornings only)*.

At No. 184 is the St Anthony Hospital on the site of the old abbey which gave the quarter its name. Adjoining these 18C buildings is the modern building (1965), the work of the architect Wogenscky. *Not open.*

FLEA MARKET* (Marché aux Puces)

Michelin plan ▥ - fold 7: A 13, A 14 – Métro Station: Porte de Clignancourt.

Open Saturdays, Sundays and Mondays.

The market developed from the casual offering of their wares by hawkers to the curious at the end of the 19C, to an established trading centre in the 1920's. A lucky few picked up masterpieces from the then unknowing sellers; now more than 2 000 stalls attract a motley throng to pick over every imaginable type of object.

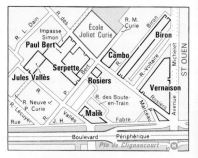

The stalls are grouped:

Vernaison: period furniture, ornaments.
Biron: antiques and valuables.
Cambo: furniture, paintings.
des Rosiers: furniture, ornaments, paintings.
Serpette: country furniture, antiques, ornaments.
Paul-Bert: secondhand goods, bronzes.
Jules-Vallès: country furniture, curios.
Malik: secondhand clothes, spectacles, records.

A variety of less permanent stalls is to be found in the neighbouring streets: Rue J.-H.-Fabre, Rue des Rosiers, Rue Voltaire, and Avenue Michelet.

FOCH, Avenue ★

Michelin plan 🔟 - folds 15 and 16: F 5, F 6 and F 7
Métro Station: Charles-de-Gaulle-Étoile

Avenue Foch radiating from the Étoile to the Place du Maréchal-de-Lattre-de-Tassigny is one of Haussmann's most magnificent roadways. This 120 m – 393 ft wide thoroughfare was laid out in 1854 as the Avenue de l'Impératrice and quickly became adopted by fashionable society as the way to the Bois de Boulogne. Today lawns and trees separate the avenue from the parallel side roads which are overlooked by elegant mansions. On the death of Marshal Foch in 1929 the avenue was renamed.

Armenian and Ennery Museums. – *At no 59 Avenue Foch.*

Armenian Museum. – *Ground floor: open Sundays 2 to 5pm; closed in August and holidays.* ☏ 45.56.15.88. The collection includes Armenian jewels, religious and folk art objects.

Ennery Museum. – *First floor: open Thursday afternoons and Sundays 2 to 5pm;* ☏ 45.53.57.96. The rich collections of the dramatist and librettist, Adolphe d'Ennery are displayed in their original Second Empire setting. Chinese and Japanese furniture, ceramics, bronzes, lacquerwork, jade and several hundred **netsuke ★** (small carved wood, ivory or bone belt ornaments) are displayed in show cases inlaid with mother of pearl.

Counterfeit Museum (Musée de la Contrefaçon). – *Open 8.30am to 5pm; closed at weekends and holidays and 1 to 2pm in July and August;* ☏ 45.01.51.11. The Manufacturers' Syndicate at 16 Rue de la Faisanderie have organised this small but interesting exhibition of commercial forgeries and non-copyright publicity material.

THE FRONT DE SEINE ★

Michelin plan 🔟 - folds 27 and 39: K 6 - L 5, L 6
Métro Station: Charles-Michels or Javel.

The area bordered by the Avenue Émile-Zola, the Rues St-Charles, Rouelle, Emeriau and du Docteur Finlay and the embankment is another urban renewal project. The plan integrates high rise flats, office towers, public buildings and a shopping centre, **Beaugrenelle.** A vast concrete podium, above the road network, ensures a traffic free zone which is given over to spacious gardens and children's playgrounds.

Paris was not built in a day...

Unlike Rome and New York but like London, no one knows when Paris was founded.

Julius Caesar sighted Lutetia in 53 BC and made the first written reference

to the town in his Commentaries.

In 1951 Paris officially celebrated its second millenium.

THE GOBELINS QUARTER

Michelin plan 🔟 - folds 44 and 56: N 15 - P 15
Distance: 2,5 km – 1 1/2 miles – Time: 2 hours – Start from the Place d'Italie métro station.

This walk takes you from the Place d'Italie via La Butte-aux-Cailles to the famous Gobelins' Tapestry Factory.

Place d'Italie. – The square marks the site of one of the city gates built by Ledoux and is today on the edge of an area of high rise buildings. From the Avenue des Gobelins there is a good view of the Pantheon.

La Butte-aux-Cailles. – On 21 November 1783, having taken off from the vicinity of La Muette, the physicist **Pilâtre de Rozier** landed his hot air balloon on this mound, then occupied by several solitary windmills. This was the first free flight *(p 166).*

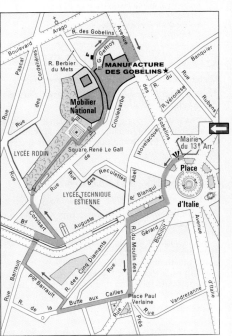

Today the district is one of surprising contrasts although the small houses and cobbled streets are slowly giving way to modern blocks of flats. A new quarter is growing out of the old village. In the Place Paul-Verlaine turn right into the Rue de la Butte-aux-Cailles. The Rue des Cinq-Diamants has retained a certain old-world charm. The peaceful Passage Barrault and then the street of the same name lead to Boulevard Auguste-Blanqui.

From La Butte-aux-Cailles to the Gobelins' Tapestry Factory. – On the far side of the boulevard take Rue Corvisart then cross the park, Square René-Le-Gall. The far end of the park is overlooked by Auguste Perret's 1935 building, the **National Furniture Storehouse** (Mobilier National).

The river **Bièvre** flows under the Rue de Croulebarbe and the Rue Berbier-du-Mets. Ice taken from the marshes was packed into wells and well covered with earth. This activity gave the district its name La Glacière (ice house). Up to the 17C this willow bordered stream was of sparkling clear water but dyeing, tanning and bleaching soon turned it into a murky evil smelling stream. In 1910 the stream was covered in.

A plaque on the wall of an old house, opposite the Mobilier National, recalls the famous 15C Gobelins dyeworks.

Take to the right the narrow but twisting Rue Gustave-Geffroy. At no 4 stands the old **Hôtel de la Reine-Blanche** which was no doubt named after Philippe VI's widow, Blanche d'Evreux. According to the chronicler Juvénal des Ursins, it was here in 1393 that Charles VI was almost burnt alive at one of the many festivities organised on his physicians' orders to attempt to cure his insanity. His hairy costume caught fire with near dire results! The house rebuilt in the 16C was taken over by the Gobelins in the 18C and today it is a dismal looking industrial building.

Gobelins' Tapestry Factory★ (Manufacture des Gobelins). – *42 Avenue des Gobelins*. In about 1440 the dyer, Jean Gobelin, who specialised in scarlet, set up a workshop beside the Bièvre which was to be used by his descendants until the reign of Henri IV when it was taken over by two Flemish craftsmen, summoned by the king. Colbert, charged by Louis XIV with the reorganisation of the tapestry and carpet weaving industry, grouped the Paris and Maincy shops around the Gobelin workshops thus creating, in 1662, the Royal Factory of Tapestry and Carpet Weavers to the Crown. At the group's head he placed the artist, Charles Le Brun. Five years later the group was joined by the Royal Cabinet-Makers. The greatest craftsmen, including also gold and silversmiths, were therefore working side by side and in an atmosphere propitious to the evolution of the Louis XIV style *(see the Louvre p 39)*.

In the last 300 years more than 5 000 tapestries have been woven at the Gobelins factory after cartoons by the greatest painters – Le Brun, Poussin, Mignard, Boucher, Lurçat, Picasso...

The former royal **Savonnerie** (1604-1826) and **Beauvais** (1664-1940) carpet and tapestry factories have, over the years, been incorporated to form the present single unit.

Guided tours of the workshops, Tuesdays, Wednesdays and Thursdays from 2.15pm; last tour 3.30pm; 15F; ☎ 48.87.24.14.

The factory, although in a modern building, has retained 17C methods: warp threads are set by daylight, the colours being selected from the factory's range of 14 000 tones. Weavers, working from mirrors, complete from 1 to 8 m^2 – 1 to 8 sq yds – each a year depending on the design. All production goes to the state.

The four great French Tapestry workshops

Aubusson: producing less fine hangings for the lesser 17 and 18C aristocracy and bourgeoisie; floral and plant, animal, Classical fable and, later, landscape designs. Chinoiseries and pastoral scenes (after Huet) were the most used motifs.

Beauvais: very finely woven in the 18C often with vividly dyed silks which, unfortunately, have faded. Motifs include grotesques, Fables after La Fontaine (by Oudry), Boucher's Italian Comedy, Loves of the Gods, Chinoiseries, and pastoral scenes (after Huet). 18C designs continued into 19C.

Felletin: coarser weave hangings with rustic motifs.

Gobelins: sumptuous quality hangings often with gold interwoven. Renowned for originality, series include The Life of the King, The Seasons and Elements, Royal Residences, Louis XV at the Chase. Motifs also after Oudry and Boucher (Loves of the Gods – p 39). Neilson, a Scot, became the most influential weaver in late 18C.

GRAND ORIENT LODGE MUSEUM

Michelin plan ⓫ - fold 19: F 14 – *Métro Station: Cadet.*

16 Rue Cadet. Open 2 to 6pm; closed Sundays and holidays and the 2nd week in September. ☎ 45.23.20.92 extn 303.

The museum occupies a vast hall in the modern premises of the Grand-Orient Lodge, an association of French provincial lodges. Documents, emblems and portraits retrace the history of this Grand Lodge and its freemason members.

HENNER MUSEUM

Michelin plan ⓫ - fold 17: D 9 – *Métro Station: Malesherbes.*

43 Avenue de Villiers. Open 10am to noon and 2 to 5pm; closed Mondays; 10F. ☎ 47.63.42.73.

Paintings, drawings and sketches by the Alsatian artist Jean-Jacques Henner (1829-1905) are the subject of this museum. An audio-visual display describes the artist's work and its evolution.

During a trip to Italy Henner was greatly influenced by the works of both Titian and Correggio and following this visit his landscapes were to include figures of nymphs and naiads. In his numerous portraits he employed a very vigorous brushwork technique.

Look at the maps on pp 4-7 for an idea for your next walk.

JEWISH ART MUSEUM

Michelin plan ⬜ - fold 7: C 14 – *Métro Station: Lamarck-Caulaincourt.*

42 Rue des Saules. Open 3 to 6pm; closed Fridays and Saturdays, in August and on Jewish holidays; 10F. ☎ 42.57.84.15.

On the third floor of the Montmartre Jewish Centre, this small museum contains in addition to devotional objects, works by Chagall and other contemporaries. Models of Polish and Lithuanian synagogues give some idea of the architectural styles current in the 17 and 18C in those countries.

THE LUTETIA ARENA (Arènes de Lutèce)

Michelin plan ⬜ - fold 44: L 15 – *Métro Station: Jussieu*

The exact date of the Gallo-Roman arena remains unknown. This is one of two Parisian monuments of this period, the other being the Cluny public bath house. The arena, destroyed in 280 by the Barbarians, lay buried for fifteen hundred years before being rediscovered by accident when the Rue Monge was laid in 1869. Only since the beginning of this century has the site been methodically excavated and restored.

The arena was constructed for circus and theatrical presentations, although many of its stone tiers have now vanished, the stage and wings remain.

Standing against a wall in Square Capitan are the engraved stones which indicated the seats of notables of the period.

MINERALOGICAL MUSEUM★★
(Musée de Minéralogie)

Michelin plan ⬜ - fold 44: K 16   – *Métro Station: Jussieu*

4 Place Jussieu: tower 25, ground floor, take the lift; open Wednesdays and Saturdays 3 to 5pm; closed during university vacations; 10F

The Place Jussieu is lined by the modern façades of the Pierre and Marie Curie University (Paris VI and VII) buildings built on the site of the former wine market. Inside the museum presents in a most attractive fashion its collections of minerals. Here in dazzling array are cut and uncut gemstones.

MONCEAU PARK★

Michelin plan ⬜ - fold 17: E 9, E 10 – *Métro Station: Monceau*

This elegant quarter includes one of Paris' rare green open spaces.

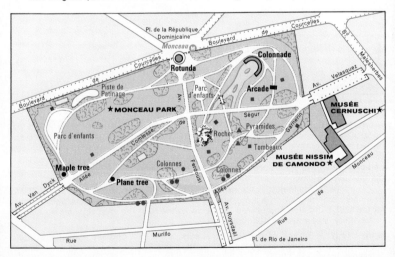

In 1778 the Duke of Orleans, the future Philippe-Egalité, commissioned the painter-writer Carmontelle to design a garden on the Monceau Plain, then rich in game.

The artist produced a land of dreams, scattered with follies and landscaped after the fashion of the English and German gardens of the time. He constructed a pyramid and a pagoda, a Roman Temple, feudal ruins, Dutch windmills, a Swiss farm, naumachia and mounds, linked by a network of rising and falling paths. Some still remain.

At the Revolution, Monceau Park – in which Garnerin, the first parachutist, had landed on 22 October 1797 – passed to the lawyer and statesman Cambacérès. It returned briefly to the Orleans before, in 1852, the financier, Pereire, sold part of the park for the building of luxurious houses. In 1869, the engineer Alphand laid out a farther area after the style of an English park.

The rotunda at the entrance, known as the Chartres Pavilion, was originally a tollhouse in the Farmers-General perimeter wall and has fine wrought iron gates. The many statues in the park take second place to the trees. The oval **naumachia basin** is modelled on the Roman pools constructed for the simulation of naval battles; the colonnade brought to adorn it was from the never completed mausoleum of Henri II at St-Denis while the nearby Renaissance arcade stood before the Hôtel de Ville.

MONTSOURIS PARK and
UNIVERSITY RESIDENTIAL CAMPUS★

Michelin plan □□ - fold 55: R 13 - S 13, S 14
Métro Station: Porte d'Orléans or RER Station: Cité Universitaire.

Together the Montsouris Park and the Paris University Residential Campus form a large green open space in the south of the city, which is highly appreciated by Parisians.

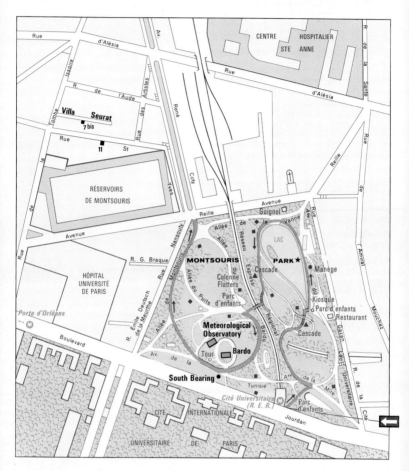

Montsouris Park★. – Haussmann began, work on this nondescript area, which was undermined by quarries and capped by dozens of windmills in 1868. By 1878 he had turned it into a park: the 16 ha – 50 acres – had been landscaped and paths constructed to climb the mounds and circle the cascades and large artificial lake (the engineer personally involved in the construction committed suicide, on the lake's suddenly drying out on opening day).

The park is dominated by the **south bearing** of the old Paris meridian *(plan p 132)* and even more emphatically by a reproduction of the Bardo (the Bey of Tunis' palace) made for the 1867 Exhibition and offered to the city by the Bey. The municipal meteorological observatory is in a nearby building.

In the vicinity. – Several of the smaller streets, some still cobbled, retain a peaceful aspect of former times, notably Rue des Artistes and Rue St-Yves with at No. **II** Cité du Souvenir.

Painters, attracted by the park's peace and proximity to Montparnasse at the beginning of the century, left their mark on the area, as, for instance, the Douanier Rousseau and Georges Braque who had a studio (west of the park) in a street, which now carries his name.

During the inter war period some of the most famous residents of the **Villa Seurat** were the artist Gromaire, Lurçat, Orloff the sculptor, Dali and Soutine. No. **7 bis** is the work of Auguste Perret.

The grass covered sides and rooftops of the Montsouris reservoirs overlook the Avenues Reille and René Coty. The waters of the Vanne, Loing and Lunain collect in these 100 year old reservoirs.

Paris University Residential Campus★ (Cité Internationale Universitaire de Paris). – *Main entrance: 19-21 Boulevard Jourdan.*

The "city" on the edge of Monsouris Park, spreads over an area of 40 ha – 100 acres – housing 5 500 students from 120 different countries in its 37 halls of residence. Each hall forms an independent community, reflecting in its architecture an individual character, frequently inspired by the country which founded it.

164

The first hall, the **E.-and-L.-Deutsch-de-la-Meurthe Foundation** was opened in 1925. The **International Hall** (1936) with a swimming pool, theatre and vast rooms was presented by John D. Rockefeller Jr; the **Swiss Hall** and **Franco-Brazilian Foundation** were designed by Le Corbusier. The **Persian Foundation**, one of the latest (1968), is interestingly modern.

The **Sacred Heart Church** (Sacré-Cœur – *open Sunday mornings*) stands on the far side of the ring road and is reached by a footbridge. Built between 1931 and 1936 in Neo-Romanesque style, it is plain with preponderantly blue stained glass windows.

MOREAU MUSEUM

Michelin plan 🔟 - fold 19: E 13 – *Métro Station: Trinité*

14 Rue de La Rochefoucauld. Open 10am to 12.30pm and 2 to 5pm; closed Mondays, Tuesdays and holidays, except Easter; 15F; 8F Sundays; ☎ 48.74.38.50.

On his death the artist Gustave Moreau (1826-1898) left his house and collection of some 11 000 paintings, drawings and water colours, to the nation. Moreau, influenced by Delacroix and his master Chassériau, delighted in lending a touch of fantasy to Biblical and mythological subjects.

On the third floor note *The Triumph of Alexander the Great* (opposite the spiral staircase) dated 1890 where the countries traversed by the conqueror are overpainted in black and one of his last works *Jupiter and Sémélé* (1895).

THE MOSQUE★

Michelin plan 🔟 - fold 44: L 15, L 16 - M 16 – *Métro Station: Monge*

Entrance: Place du Puits-de-l'Ermite, Guided tours 9am to noon and 2 to 6pm; closed Fridays and Moslem holidays; 6F; ☎ 45.35.97.33.

The white buildings overlooked by a minaret, making one feel far from home, were erected between 1922 and 1926.

Three holy men supervise the enclave: the *muphti,* lawyer, administrator and judge; the *iman* who looks after the mosque; the *muezzin* or cantor who calls the faithful to prayer twice a day from high up in the minaret.

Native craftsmen from the Mohammedan countries have contributed to the decoration of the halls and courts with Persian carpets, copper from North Africa, cedarwood from Lebanon, a dais from Egypt, etc. A Hispano-Moorish style courtyard has a garden at its centre surrounded by arcades – a symbol of the Muslim Paradise. At the heart of the religious buildings is a patio, inspired by that of the Alhambra in Granada. The prayer chamber is outstanding for its decoration and magnificent carpets.

Some decorative features and structures adorning the Paris streets are typically French and very popular with tourists:

Morris pillars introduced in 1869 when advertising posters came into use (some 300 original ones remain standing)

Wallace drinking fountains donated to the city of Paris in 1872 by Sir Richard Wallace (some 70 can still be seen throughout the city)

gas street lamps

wrought iron grilles of métro stations etc.

THE MUETTE QUARTER
AND RANELAGH GARDENS

Michelin plan ⅠⅠ - folds 26 and 27: H 4, H 5 - J 4, J 5

Distance: 1.5 km – 1 mile – Time: approx. 45 mins (excluding the Marmottan Museum) – Start from the Muette métro station.

The original Muette Estate was developed as an elegant quarter and today enjoys the green open space of the Ranelagh Gardens with the added attraction of the Marmottan Museum with its rich collections.

La Muette. – Take the Chaussée de la Muette. It was here that Charles IX had a hunting lodge where he kept his falcons when in moult (french *en mue*) hence the name Muette. This name was also used for the replacement château built by Philibert Delorme and set in a park extending to the Bois de Boulogne.

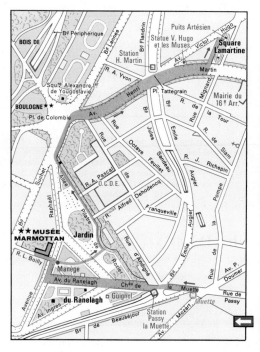

The château had a succession of royal owners from Queen Margot, first wife of Henri of Navarre, Louis XIII to the Duchesse de Berry. It was here, knowing her days to be numbered, that she lived up to her motto 'short and sweet' dying aged 24. Both Louis XV and the Marquise de Pompadour appreciated the château as a clandestine meeting place. The future Louis XVI and Marie-Antoinette spent the first years of their married life here.

At the Revolution the estate was subdivided and in 1820 the piano maker Sébastien Erard purchased the château and part of the park which adjoined Ranelagh. A century later the property was sold off as building lots.

Continue to Avenue du Ranelagh.

Ranelagh Gardens (Jardin du Ranelagh). – The gardens, on the far side of Avenue Raphaël, date from 1860 when they were laid out on the site of an earlier garden and café of high revelry. This had been established in 1774 and called in the spirit of Anglomania of the time, after the gay London pleasure gardens established by Lord Ranelagh.

Cross Avenue Raphaël. The statue at the corner is of the 17C French poet La Fontaine. At his feet the sculptor, Correia, has depicted two of the famous animal characters from his *Fables*.

Marmottan Museum★★ (Musée Marmottan). – *2 Rue Louis Boilly. Open 10am to 6pm; closed Mondays, 1 May and 25 December; 18F; ☏ 42.24.07.02.*

In 1971 the Marmottan Museum was transformed by an outstanding bequest by Michel Monet, of 65 paintings by his father. The museum had developed from the bequest in 1932 by the art historian, Paul Marmottan, of his house and Renaissance, Consular and First Empire collections to the Academy of Fine Arts. The Donop de Monchy legacy in 1950 added works by Claude Monet including the famous *Impression – Sunrise (stolen 1985)* which gave the Impressionist Movement its name. The majority of the Monet paintings, acquired in 1971 and for which a special underground gallery has been built, were painted at the artist's Normandy home at Giverny. They form a dazzling series of water lily, wistaria and garden scenes and with canvases by Renoir, Sisley, Pissarro, make a perfect complement to the Jeu de Paume and Orangery Museums *(p 42).*

A small gallery houses the 13-16C illuminated MSS of the Wildenstein Bequest.

From the Marmottan Museum to Square Lamartine. – Cross the Ranelagh Gardens and Avenue Prudhon to reach Allée Pilâtre-de-Rozier, named after the hot air balloonist who made his first free flight from here on 21 November 1783. This alley skirts a park. The Rue André-Pascal is marked after the pen name of the banker cum author Baron Henri de Rothschild and builder of the adjacent sumptuous mansion. Since 1948 the mansion has been international territory as the seat of the Organization for European Cooperation and Development (in French the O.C.D.E.); *not open to the public.*

The marble relief at the end of the alley by Victor Hugo is entitled *The Poet's Vision.*

Cross Place de Colombie, overlooked by the statue of Peter I of Serbia and his son Alexander I of Yugoslavia, before turning right into the Avenue Henri Martin, formerly the Avenue de l'Empereur. Once over the Auteuil railway the Avenue Victor Hugo is on the left. The monumental statue is Rodin's *Victor Hugo and The Muses.*

The calm **Square Lamartine** is the site of the Passy artesian wells (600 m – 1970 ft deep). Residents came for a supply of sulphur rich water at a temperature of 28 °C (82°F).

MUSICAL INSTRUMENTS MUSEUM★
(Conservatoire National Supérieur de Musique)

Michelin plan ⑩ - fold 18: E 11 – *Métro Station: Europe.*

Sarrette, a captain in the National Guard, established a school to form military musicians. The National Institute of Music, officially founded in 1795 at the time of the Convention, was originally in the Faubourg Poissonnière. The conservatory moved to the present premises in 1911.

Musical Instruments Museum. – *14, rue de Madrid. Open Wednesdays to Saturdays 2 to 6pm; closed on holidays; 7F.* ☎ *42.93.15.20, extn 370.*

The collection comprises some 4 000 European musical instruments dating from the Renaissance to the present. In addition to the stringed, wind and percussion instruments, there are such historical items as Berlioz' guitar, Beethoven's clavichord and the piano on which Rouget de Lisle, on arriving in Paris, played his own composition which came to be known as the *Marseillaise.*

NATION, Place de la★

Michelin plan ⑩ - fold 47: K 21 - L 21 – *Métro Station: Nation*

The square was originally named the Throne Square in honour of the state entry made by Louis XIV and his bride, the Infanta Maria-Theresa, on 26 August 1660, when a throne was erected at which the king received due homage. It was renamed, by the Convention in 1794, the Square of the Overturned Throne when they placed a guillotine upon it and it was renamed a third time, on 14 July 1880, during the first anniversary celebrations of the Revolution. The bronze group by Dalou illustrates the **Triumph of the Republic ★** and was originally intended for the Place de la République *(p 171).*

The columns on either side of Avenue du Trône, supporting statues of Philippe Auguste and St Louis, and the pair of tollbooths were by Ledoux *(p 16).*

The **Throne** or **Gingerbread Fair** was held on the nearby Cours de Vincennes for over 1 000 years. The fair recalls the concession obtained in 957 by the monks of St Anthony's Abbey to sell a rye, honey and aniseed bread in memory of their saint in Holy Week. The piglet-shaped breads were a reminder of St Anthony's faithful companion in the desert. The present day funfair is held in the Bois de Vincennes *(p 149).*

NISSIM DE CAMONDO MUSEUM★

Michelin plan ⑩ - fold 17: E 10 – *Métro Station: Monceau or Villiers*

63 Rue de Monceau. Open 10am to noon and 2 to 5pm. Closed Mondays, Tuesdays, and holidays; 12F. ☎ *45.63.26.32.*

In 1936 Count de Camondo presented his house and 18C art collection to the nation in memory of his son Nissim, who had died in the 1914-1918 War. The house built in 1910 stands in grounds adjoining Monceau Park *(p 163).*

The mansion presents an elegant Louis XVI interior with panelled salons, furniture made by the greatest cabinet-makers, Savonnerie carpets and Beauvais tapestries *(p 162),* paintings by Guardi and Hubert Robert and gold and silver ornaments. Among the outstanding pieces are tapestries of the *Fables* of La Fontaine after cartoons by Oudry and a splendid Sèvres porcelain service, known as the Buffon service, in which every piece is decorated with the design of a different bird.

PALAIS DES CONGRÈS★

Michelin plan ⑩ - fold 15: E 6 and plan p 141 – *Métro Station: Porte Maillot.*

The Paris Conference Centre, situated near the Bois de Boulogne on the Champs-Élysées-Défense axis, provides a modern conference centre (Palais des Congrès) in addition to other business and recreational facilities and hotel accommodation.

On several floors around the main conference hall there are exhibition halls *(1st floor),* other smaller conference and meeting rooms, business suites and offices and around 80 shops lining the Rue Basse and the Rue Haute. In addition there are restaurants, cinemas, a discotheque, an air terminal, parking space and on the seventh floor spacious kitchens, restaurants and function rooms can cater for over 4 000 guests at a time. The terraces on the 5th and 7th floors afford fine views of the Bois de Boulogne and La Défense.

The **Main Conference Hall ★★** *(to see the inside you must go to a performance)* within the centre is unique in Europe. This dual purpose hall for conferences and entertainment has a convertible stage and a seating capacity of 3 700. The decorative forms of the walls, the specially designed seats, and the roof ensure acoustic uniformity.

Concorde-La Fayette Hotel. – Dominating the centre is the 42 storey hotel, Concorde-La Fayette. This 1 000 room hotel communicates directly on the ground floor with the conference centre. On the top floor there is a panoramic bar *(open 11 am to 2am, access is reserved for customers only)* which affords an extensive **view★** of Paris, the Bois de Boulogne and at the far right La Défense.

Join us in our never ending task of keeping up to date.
Send us your comments and suggestions, please.

Michelin Tyre Public Limited Company
Tourism Department
Lyon Road — HARROW — Middlesex HA1 2DQ.

PALAIS OMNISPORTS DE PARIS BERCY

Michelin plan 🔟 - fold 46: M 9 – *Métro Station: Bercy*

On the eastern side of the capital, this new sports complex was built to stage international indoor sporting events. From the outside the appearance is somewhat surprising with grass-covered walls sloping away at 45 degrees. The glass roof is sheathed by a network of girders. The project was the result of collaboration between the architects Andrault, Parat and Guvan.

Sport takes first place with facilities catering for 22 different activities, but the centre's versatility is such that it can stage a variety of entertainments from opera, theatre and ballet to rock concerts. In addition to the adaptable main arena there are two multi-purpose halls and two warming-up or rehearsal halls.

PARADIS, Rue★

Michelin plan 🔟 - fold 20: E 15 - F 15, F 16 – *Métro Station: Gare de l'Est*

The street is known today for its shops of beautiful tableware, the chief points of sale of the French glass, china and porcelain factories.

The group of buildings at Nos. 30-32, houses the International Tableware Centre (trade members only) which regroups the best known names in porcelain and glass making.

At no 30 bis is **Baccarat** the glassmakers who have supplied royal palaces and state residences throughout the world for the last 150 years.

Glass Museum★ (Musée du Cristal). – *Exhibition and shop on the first floor. Open 9am to 6pm; closed weekends and holidays;* ☎ *47.70.64.30.*
Some of the workshops' finest pieces are on display.

Poster Museum (Musée de la Publicité). – *No 18. Open noon to 6pm; closed Tuesdays; 16F;* ☎ *42.46.13.09.*
This small museum is located in the former Choisy-le-Roi China and Porcelain house. Go through the small **courtyard★** decorated with pictorial multicoloured tiles and up the stairs to the museum where, by changing exhibitions, some 50 000 posters are shown.

■ THE QUARTER

Maison St-Lazare. – *107 Rue du Faubourg St-Denis.* In the Middle Ages this was the capital's leper house. St Vincent of Paul the founder of the Priests of the Mission (known today as Lazarists) died here in 1660.

At the time of the Revolutionary troubles the building became a prison and the poet André Chénier, one of its most industrious inmates, prior to his execution. Changed to a women's prison it once again became a hospital in 1935.

St-Laurent Church. – *68 Boulevard de Magenta.* The belfry is all that remains of the 12C sanctuary. The nave was rebuilt in the 15C and the church altered in the 17C (chancel sculpture and woodwork). The west front and spire date from the Napoleon III period.

The **St-Laurent Fair** was held for over 600 years in the grounds of what is now the Gare de l'Est railway station. Over a hundred stalls and booths offered their goods duty free. It was on one of these make-shift stages that the first presentation of the new dramatic form, comic opera took place around 1720.

St-Vincent-de-Paul Church. – *Place Franz-Liszt.* The church is the work of the architect Hittorff (1824-1844) who was also responsible for the final decoration of the Place de la Concorde. Basilical in form, the church has a columned portico and two tall towers. Inside Flandrin's fresco runs round the nave dividing the elevation in two. The bronze calvary by Rude stands on the high altar.

PASSY

Michelin plan 🔟 - fold 27: H 5, H 6 - J 5, J 6

Distance: 2 km – 1 1/4 miles – Time: approx. 1 1/2 hours (excluding the museums) – Start from the Trocadero métro station.

In the 13C Passy was a woodcutters' hamlet; in the 18C it became known for its ferruginous waters and in 1859 it was incorporated in the city of Paris.

The "Fellows of Chaillot" or *bonshommes* was the familiar name by which the Minim Friars, whose monastery stood on the hill until the Revolution, were known, presumably because of the red wine produced by the community and still recalled in the names of the Rue Vineuse and Rue des Vignes.

Today the houses in their own gardens that used to make up the peaceful residential quarter are being replaced by large blocks of flats.

Make your way from the Place du Trocadéro et du 11-Novembre *(p 49)* along the Rue Franklin.

Clemenceau Museum (Musée Clemenceau). – *8 Rue Franklin. Open 2 to 5pm; closed Mondays, Wednesdays, Fridays, and August; 10 F.* ☎ *45.20.53.41.*
The great man's apartment is as it was on the day of his death in 1929. Mementoes in a gallery on the first floor recall his career as a journalist and statesman: the Montmartre mayoralty, the Treaty of Versailles and the premiership.

Continue down the Rue de l'Alboni, to the right of the high level métro station, and, bearing right, turn into the Rue des Eaux, at the end of which are a small street and square named after Charles Dickens.

No. **5** Rue des Eaux marks the original entrance to the quarries. Under the Empire they were converted into France's first sugar beet refinery. The underground galleries now house a **wine museum** (musée du vin) *(open 2 to 6pm; closed Mondays, 1 January, 1 May and 25 December; tour and wine tasting: 20F; ☏ 45.26.63.28)* with waxwork figures and implements recalling the days of the wine producing monks.

Allée des Cygnes. – Continue along the Rue des Eaux and over Bir-Hakeim Bridge to the islet which divides the Seine at this point. The Allée des Cygnes, or Swans' Walk, which was built up on the riverbed at the time of the Restoration, makes a pleasant stroll

with a good view of the Radio-France House *(p 155)* on the right and of the Front de Seine *(p 161)* on the left. The figure of *France Renaissante* at the upstream end of the island is by the Danish sculptor, Wederkinch (1930).

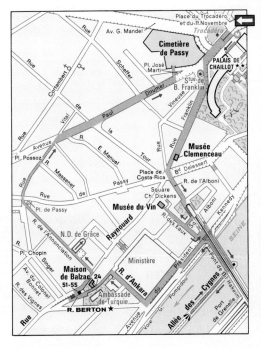

Rue d'Ankara. – The former château park of Marie-Antoinette's devoted friend, the Princess of Lamballe, at the end on the left, is now occupied by the Turkish Embassy and private houses. In the 19C it belonged to Doctor Blanche, a specialist in mental illnesses who converted it into a home for the insane.

Rue Berton★. – The Rue Berton, on the left, is one of the most unexpected in Paris – its ivy covered walls and gas brackets giving it an old country town atmosphere. No **24** was the back entrance to Balzac's house *(see below)*.

Rue Raynouard. – This street is full of historical interest. Many famous people have lived in this street named after an obscure academician of the Restoration: Louis XIV's powerful financier, Samuel Bernard, the Duke of Lauzun, Jean-Jacques Rousseau, the song writer, Béranger and Benjamin Franklin, when in France negotiating an alliance for the new republic of the United States with Louis XVI. It was at this time that he erected over his house, No 66, the first lightning conductor in France. The modern blocks of flats in reinforced concrete at Nos **51** to **55** are by Auguste Perret who died here in 1954.

No 47, half-hidden in its garden, was **Balzac's house** (Maison de Balzac) from 1840 to 1847 *(open daily; closed Mondays and holidays; 10am to 5.40pm; 7F, free Sundays, except during exhibitions; ☏ 42.24.56.38)*. Manuscripts, caricatures and engravings in the house reflect the Human Comedy described in his novels which can be seen in an adjoining museum-library.

Turn left into the Rue de L'Annonciation, the former name of the 17C chapel, much restored and now known as Our Lady of Grace. Cross the square and Rue de Passy, the old village main street, to go along the Rue Vital and Avenue Paul-Doumer, on the right.

Passy Cemetery (Cimetière de Passy). – The cemetery above Trocadero square, contains, amidst burgeoning greenery, the remains of many who have died since 1850 from the world of literature (Croisset, Tristan Bernard, Giraudoux), painting (Manet, Berthe Morisot), music (Debussy, Fauré), aviation (Henry Farman) and films (Fernandel).

PASTEUR INSTITUTE

Michelin plan ⑪ - fold 41: M 10 – *Métro Station: Pasteur*

25 Rue du Docteur-Roux. Museum and crypt open Mondays to Fridays 2.30 to 5pm; closed in August; Film and lecture on the Institute available on appointment, same hours, ☏ 45.68.80.00, extn 8273.

This internationally famous Institute has laboratories for pure and applied research *(p 178)*, lecture theatres, a vaccination centre, a hospital for the treatment of infectious diseases and a serum and vaccination production plant (at Louviers-Incarville).

The Institute and its Lille, Lyons and other auxiliary institutes abroad continue the work of Louis Pasteur (1822-1895), whose tomb is in the crypt and whose apartment has been converted into a museum.

PÈRE-LACHAISE CEMETERY★★

Michelin plan 🔟 - folds 34, 35: H 20, H 21 – *Métro Station: Père Lachaise*

Open 7.30am to 6pm, 16 March to 5 November; 8am to 5.30pm, 6 November to 15 March; Saturdays open from 8.30am; Sundays and holidays 9am, closing time established according to the season. Main entrance: Boulevard de Ménilmontant.

In 1626 the Jesuits bought in this country area, a site on which to build a house of retreat. This became a frequent visiting place of Louis XIV's confessor, Father La Chaise, who gave generously to the house's reconstruction in 1682. The Jesuits were expelled in 1763. Forty years later, the city acquired the property for conversion to a cemetery.

The cemetery was the scene of the Paris Commune's final and bloody stand on 28 May 1871. The last insurgents were cornered and attacked on the night of the 27th, fierce fighting taking place among the graves. At dawn the 147 survivors were stood against the wall in the southeast corner – the **Federalists' Wall** (Mur des Fédérés) – and shot. They were buried where they fell in a communal grave which remains a political pilgrimage for many.

Paris' largest cemetery, designed by Brongniart, is on rising and falling ground. Only some of the tombs of the famous are marked on the plan. A sculpture by Paul Landowski in the basement of the **Columbarium** is noteworthy.

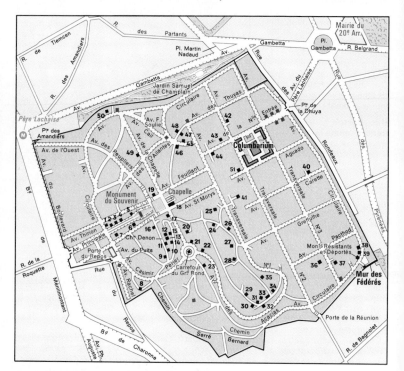

1 Colette	21 Monge	37 Edith Piaf
2 Rossini (cenotaph)	22 Champollion	38 Henri Barbusse
3 A. de Musset (in the shade of a willow, as he requested)	23 Auguste Comte	39 Paul Eluard, Maurice Thorez
4 Baron Haussmann	24 Gay-Lussac	40 Oscar Wilde
5 Generals Lecomte and Thomas	25 Corot	41 Sarah Bernhardt
6 Félix Faure	26 Molière and La Fontaine	42 Marcel Proust
7 Arago	27 Alphonse Daudet	43 Guillaume Apollinaire
8 Abélard and Héloïse *(p 54)*	28 Hugo family *(p 84)*	44 Allan Kardec (founder of spiritualist movement – the tomb is always a mass of flowers)
9 Gustave Charpentier	29 Bibesco family (Anna de Noailles)	
10 Chopin *(p 82)*	30 Marshal Ney *(p 132)*	45 Delacroix *(p 108)*
11 Cherubini	31 Beaumarchais *(p 89)*	46 Michelet
12 Boïeldieu (cenotaph)	32 Larrey	47 G. de Nerval
13 Bernardin de St-Pierre	33 Marshals Davout, Masséna, Lefebvre	48 Balzac and the Countess Hanska
14 Grétry. – 15 Bellini	34 Murat and Caroline Bonaparte	49 Georges Bizet
16 Branly	35 David d'Angers	50 Georges Méliès
17 Géricault. – 18 Thiers	36 Modigliani *(p 127)*	51 Simone Signoret
19 David. – 20 C. Bernard		

PICPUS CEMETERY

Michelin plan 🔟 - fold 47: L 21, L 22 – *Métro Station: Nation or Picpus.*

35 Rue de Picpus. Guided tours 2 to 6pm (4pm 1 October to 14 April); closed Mondays holidays, 4 July and in September; ☎ 43.42.24.22.

In 1794 the guillotine on the Place de la Nation fell on the heads of 1 306 people including André Chénier and 16 Carmelite nuns whose bodies were thrown into two communal graves. The ground, known as the Martyrs' Field, was later enclosed by a wall and an adjoining cemetery opened in which relatives of those guillotined on the square could be buried. At the far end of the cemetery the Martyrs' Field can be seen through a gate.

POPULAR ARTS AND TRADITIONS,
National Museum of **

Michelin plan ▢▢ - fold 14: E 4 – *Métro Station: Les Sablons*
6 Route du Mahatma-Gandhi.
Open 10am to 5.15pm; closed Tuesdays; 15F (8F Sundays); ☏ *47.47.69.80.*

Two galleries give a glimpse of day to day life in pre-industrial France.

The **Cultural Gallery** *(ground floor)* evokes man's environment, the technical progress made by man to enable him to exploit the natural resources and the institutions he created for community living.

The **Study Gallery** *(basement)* has displays concerning agriculture, husbandry, domestic life, crafts, local beliefs and customs, games, music and local folklore.

An audio-visual show and slides add interest to the visit.

RENAN-SCHEFFER MUSEUM

Michelin plan ▢▢ - fold 19: E 13 – *Métro Station: Pigalle or St-Georges*
16 Rue Chaptal. Open 10am to 5.40pm; closed Mondays; 7F. ☏ *48.74.95.38.*

This was the charming house where Ary Scheffer (1795-1858) lived and worked for nearly 30 years. The painter of Dutch origin was much favoured by Louis-Philippe. His home was the meeting place for a group of painter and literary friends (Delacroix, Ingres, Listz, Beranger, Lamartine, Chopin, George Sand and Ernest Renan). The permanent section *(ground floor)* includes paintings, jewellery and drawings of George Sand. Upstairs changing exhibitions cover the literary and artistic life of the 19C.

RÉPUBLIQUE,
Place de la

Michelin plan ▢▢ - fold 33: G 17
Métro Station: République

The original square was named Place du Château-d'Eau. On it stood the Théâtre Historique, built in 1847, by Alexandre Dumas as a setting for his historical dramas – it opened with his *Queen Margot* for which crowds queued for seats for two days and nights.

In 1854 Haussmann decided to replace the small square with the present vast expanse as part of his anti-revolutionary street planning scheme. The diorama built in 1822 by Daguerre, of daguerreotype fame, was knocked down in favour of a barracks for 2 000 soldiers and wide avenues cut through turbulent areas – the Boulevard Magenta, Avenue de la République, Boulevard Voltaire and Rue de Turbigo, The Boulevard du Crime was razed.

The square was completed by 1862 and the **Statue to the Republic** by Morice erected in 1883. The best part is the base by Dalou *(p 167)* on which are bronze low reliefs of the

(Photo Revault/Pix)

Statue to the Republic.

great events in the history of the Republic from its inception to 1880 when the 14 July was celebrated as a national holiday for the first time in the Place de la Nation.

ST ALEXANDER NEWSKY CATHEDRAL

Michelin plan ▢▢ - folds 16 and 17: E 8, E 9
Métro Station: Courcelles or Ternes – 12 Rue Daru
Guided tours on Wednesdays and Fridays between 3 and 5pm.

This, the Russian Orthodox Church of Paris, was erected in 1860 in the Russian Neo-Byzantine style with a typical Greek cross plan. The main features of the exterior are gilded onion shaped domes while the interior is decorated with frescoes, gilding and icons. The services are magnificently sung in the tradition of Holy Russia.

ST AUGUSTINE'S CHURCH

Michelin plan ▢▢ - fold 18: E 11 – *Métro Station: St Augustin*

Both the church and imposing 1927 building of the Cercle Militaire border the Place St-Augustin with in the centre a replica of the statue of Joan of Arc by Paul Dubois. The original is in Reims.

Baltard, the architect of the old covered market (the Halles), who designed this church in 1860, employed for the first time in such a building a metal girder construction which enabled him to dispense with the usual buttressing. The triangular shape of the site dictated the church's unusual form, widening out from the porch to the chancel.

ST MARTIN'S CANAL★

Michelin plan ⏛ - folds 21 and 33: E 17 to K 17 – *Métro Station: Jaurès or République.*

The peaceful, old-fashioned reaches of the 4.5 km – 2 3/4 mile – canal, dug at the time of the Restoration to link the Ourcq Canal with the Seine, are still navigated by numerous barges. The embankments where the water course is above the surrounding plain, the nine locks and bordering trees, make an unusual landscape.

(Photo J.-P. Bourret, Pitch)

St. Martin's Canal.

Rotonde de la Villette. – *Place de Stalingrad.* The rotunda, another of Ledoux' tollbooths *(p 16)* serves as a storehouse for archaeological finds.

Follow the Quai de Jemmapes between Place de Stalingrad and Square Frédéric-Lemaître.

Montfaucon Gallows. – The canal and the Rues Louis-Blanc, de la Grange-aux-Belles and des Écluses-St-Martin delimit an area that was the site of the gallows notorious for being able to hang sixty condemned at once. Various finance ministers died by it, notably Marigny, the builder, during the reign of Philip the Fair, Montaigu, the repairer, and the unlucky Semblançay who had nothing whatsoever to do with it. Following the assassination (1572) of Admiral Coligny his body was displayed here. Although already in disuse during the 17C it was 1760 before the gallows were dismantled.

St-Louis Hospital. – *Entrance: Rue Bichat.* One of the oldest Parisian hospitals. St-Louis specialises in dermatology. The brick and stone buildings, reminiscent of the Places des Vosges and Dauphine with their steeply pitched roofs and dormer windows, are divided by flower lined courts.

The canal disappears in Frédéric-Lemaître Square (beyond the Quai Valmy) to flow underground and reappear beyond the Place de la Bastille as the Arsenal Basin. The basin followed the line of the moat skirting Charles V's ramparts and has been developed as a pleasure boat harbour the **Arsenal Marina** (Port de Plaisance de Paris-Arsenal) to accommodate over 200 boats. The quaysides have been landscaped as terrace-gardens.

Boat trips. – *Half day excursions between the Place de Stalingrad and the Seine. For further information apply to Guiztour, 19 Rue d'Athènes, Paris 9th,* ☏ *48.74.75.30 or Canauxrama 4 Villa Blanche, 92200 Neuilly-sur-Seine.* ☏ *46.24.86.16.*

THE ST-MÉDARD QUARTER★

Michelin plan ⏛ - fold 44: L 15 - M 15
Distance: 2 km – 1 1/4 miles – Time: 1 hour. Start from Censier-Daubenton métro station.

The beautiful Church of St Medard marks the opening of the unique Rue Mouffetard.

St. Medard's. – St. Medard's was originally the parish church of a small market town on the River Bièvre. Its patron, Saint Medard, counsellor to the Merovingian kings of the 6C, was also the author of the delightful custom of giving a wreath of roses to maidens of virtuous conduct. The church, started in the mid 15C, was completed in 1655.

The "Convulsionnaires". – In 1727 a Jansenist deacon with a saintly reputation died at the age of 36 of mortification of the flesh and was buried in the St. Medard churchyard beneath an upraised black marble stone. Sick Jansenists came to pray before the tomb, to lie upon and underneath it giving rise to a belief in miraculous cures which led to massive scenes of collective hysteria.

In 1732, Louis XV decreed an end to the demonstrations; the cemetery was closed; an inscription nailed to the gate:

> *By order of the King, let God*
> *No miracle perform in this place!*

Tour. – *Open Tuesdays to Saturdays 8.30am to noon and 2.30 to 7.30pm; Sundays 4 to 7pm. Closed Mondays*. The exterior is interesting. From the front with the great Flamboyant window overlooking the Rue Mouffetard, continue right, along the narrow and picturesque Rue Daubenton where at No **41** a gate and passage lead to a small side entrance to the church. The famous cemetery surrounded the apse.

Return to the façade by way of the Rues de Candolle and Censier.

The Flamboyant Gothic nave has modern stained glass; the unusually wide chancel is Renaissance influenced with unsymmetrical semicircular arches and rounded windows. In 1784 the pillars were transformed into fluted Doric columns. There are paintings of the French school, a remarkable 16C triptych *(behind the pulpit)* and, in the second chapel to the right of the chancel, a *Dead Christ* attributed to Philippe de Champaigne.

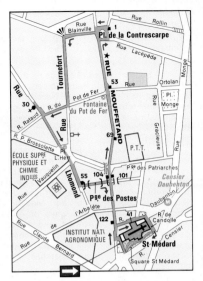

Rue Mouffetard ★ . – The Rue Mouffetard, downhill, winding, lined with old houses and crowded with life, is one of Paris' most original streets. The bustle is greatest in the morning particularly at the lower end where the street climbs between small domestic shops distinguished by painted signs which date from far back and are sometimes picturesque as "At the clear Spring" at No. **122** where a well has been carved on the façade, and No. **69** where a tree in relief surmounted the now vanished sign of the Old Oak.

Nos. **104** and **101,** on opposite sides of the street, mark the entrances to quiet passages – Postes and Patriarches. The Iron Pot Fountain – Pot-de-Fer – at the corner, like others in the district, runs with the surplus water from the Arcueil Aqueduct which Marie dei Medici had constructed to bring water to the Luxembourg Palace. Its Italian style bossages are reminiscent of the Medici Fountain *(p 122)*.

When No. **53** was demolished in 1938, a cache was discovered in the ruins of 3 350 gold coins bearing the head of Louis XV, placed there by Louis Nivelle, the king's bearer and counsellor. An inscription at No. **1 Place de la Contrescarpe** recalls the Pinecone cabaret – Pomme-de-Pin – described by Rabelais.

Other streets in the vicinity. – During the Middle Ages the area abounded in student colleges. One of the rare examples is the **Scottish College** *(p 114)*.

Continue along the Rue Blainville (glance to the right at the Pantheon dome) and left down the old and quiet **Rue Tournefort**. Turn right into the Rue du Pot-de-Fer then left into the **Rue Lhomond** which descends the Montagne Ste-Geneviève (the steps beside the road indicate the mound's original height). The richly decorated chapel at No **30** was built by Chalgrin in 1780. Turn up by No. **55**, into the picturesque **Passage des Postes**, to return to the Rue Mouffetard and St. Medard's Church.

THE SALPÊTRIÈRE HOSPITAL ★

Michelin plan ▥ - fold 45: M 17 – *Métro Station: St-Marcel*
Entrance: Square Marie-Curie.

The hospital has all the grandeur of the Grand Siècle. In the time of Louis XIII a small arsenal on the site manufactured gun powder from saltpetre. In 1656 Louis XIV established a General Hospital for the Poor of Paris in the saltpetre works in the hope of clearing the capital's streets of beggars and the more vicious characters – fifty-five thousand beggars were known to exist in Paris at the time.

By 1662, 10 000 pensioners had been taken in, but following the cleaning up of the Courts of Miracles *(p 126)* in 1667, the buildings had to be enlarged – a project undertaken by Le Vau and Le Muet. In 1670, a chapel was added, designed by Libéral Bruand at the same time as he was building the Invalides *(p 71)*.

Gradually the hospital began to take in indiscriminately the mad, the infirm, the orphaned and prostitutes – the hospital, in fact, became a prison with all subject to the same harsh regime. At last, at the end of the 18C, one of the doctors, Philippe Pinel (1745-1826) began the work on a reformed treatment for the insane which was to win him and the hospital wide acclaim, a century later Professor Charcot, under whom Freud came to study, was to further the hospital's reputation with research and treatment in advanced neuro-psychiatry.

Tour. – A formal garden precedes the central wing of the immense, austere and majestic edifice which has a certain family resemblance to the Invalides.

At the centre is the octagonal dome of the **St-Louis Chapel** surmounted by a lantern. The chapel ground plan is unusual with a rotunda encircled by four aisles forming a Greek cross and four chapels at the angles of the crossing. Eight areas were thus formed in which the inmates could be placed separately: women, girls, the infectious, etc.

The ensemble, with the exception of one of the chapels which is still used by the hospital, now serves as a cultural centre.

THE SEITA MUSEUM

Michelin plan 📖 - fold 29: H 9 – *Métro Station: Invalides*

12 Rue Surcouf. Open 11am to 6pm; closed Sundays and holidays. ☎ *45.55.91.50 extn 2069.*

The building at No 12 stands on the site of France's first cigarette factory which dated from 1845. The museum traces the history of the tobacco habit from its original medicinal use as snuff, then through the various modes of being chewed, snuffed and smoked.

The tobacco trade flourished between the old and new continents and outward cargoes of this American plant were paid for by return loads of manufactured goods. The French Ambassador to Portugal, Jean Nicot introduced Marie dei Medici to snuff taking. The various ways of enjoying tobacco are illustrated and accompanied by a variety of pipes, tobacco pouches and pots, snuff boxes, cigarette cases, holders, lighters, matches, cigar cutters...

(Photo Musée-Galerie de la Seita)

French tobacco shop sign, late 19C.

THE SEWERS (Les Égouts)

Michelin plan 📖 - folds 28 and 29: H 8, H 9 – *Métro Station: Alma-Marceau*

The Paris sewer system was initially the giant undertaking of the engineer Belgrand at the time of Napoleon III. 2 100 km – 1 305 miles of underground tunnels, some passing under the Seine, channel sewage towards Achères, Europe's largest biological purification station or to the treatment plants (Achères, Pierrelaye and Triel) on the outskirts of Paris.

Tour. – *Entrance: corner of Quai d'Orsay and Pont de l'Alma. Mondays, Wednesdays and last Saturday of the month from 2 to 5pm; closed holidays and days before and after holidays. No tours during storms, after a heavy rainfall or when the Seine is in flood.* ☎ *43.20.14.40; 8F.*

The sewer system, its layout and operation, are explained with the help of a historical display and audio-visual presentation. The tour with audio-guides, includes an overflow outlet, sand filtering basins, a secondary conduit and holding and regulating reservoirs. The larger mains also contain pipes for drinking and industrial water and telephone and telegraph cables.

THE TEMPLE QUARTER★

Michelin plan 📖 - folds 32 and 33: G 15 to G 17

Distance: 2 km – 1 1/4 miles – Time: 2 1/2 hours – Start from the République métro station.

This quarter was the domain of Knights Templar and Benedictines from St. Martin's.

Place de la République to St Nicholas in the Fields

At 195 Rue du Temple stands **St Elizabeth's** *(closed Sundays)*, a 17C convent chapel now the Church of the Knights of St. John of Malta and outstanding for the hundred 16C Flemish **low reliefs★** of biblical scenes round the ambulatory.

Turn left in the Rue de Turbigo to approach the former **St-Martin-des-Champs★** with its Romanesque east end (1130-restored), fine capitals, belfry of the same period and Gothic nave.

Turn right into the Rue St-Martin.

Conservatoire National des Arts et Métiers★★. – *Description p 158.*

St Nicholas in the Fields★ (St-Nicolas-des-Champs). – The church, built in the 12C by the priory of St. Martin in the Fields for the monastery servants and neighbouring peasants, was dedicated to one of the most popular mediaeval saints, Nicholas, 4C Bishop of Myra in Asia Minor and patron of children, sailors and travellers. It was rebuilt in the 15C and enlarged in the 16 and 17C. The Revolution rededicated it to Hymen and Fidelity.

The façade and belfry are Flamboyant Gothic, the south **door★** Renaissance (1581).

Inside, the nave is divided into five by a double line of pillars; the first five bays are 15C; the vaulting in the aisles beyond the pulpit rises in height, semicircular arcs succeed pointed arches; the sides of the pillars towards the nave have been fluted. The chancel and chapels contain a considerable number of mostly French 17, 18 and 19C paintings; the twin sided high altar is adorned with a retable painted by Simon Vouet (16C) and four angels by the 17C sculptor, Sarrazin. The best point from which to see the forest of pillars and double ambulatory is the Lady Chapel (Adoration of the Shepherds by Coypel).

The typically Parisian organ is 18C; the organist was for a time Louis Braille *(p 112)*.

From St. Nicholas to Place de la République

Continue left down the Rue St-Martin and along to the Temple Square. On the way you pass No. **51** Rue de Montmorency, the oldest house (1407) in Paris, once the **house of Nicolas Flamel,** legal draughtsman to the university and bookseller who made a fortune copying and selling manuscripts. He used the proceeds in good works, including setting up above his shop (now a restaurant) an "almshouse" in which the high rent charged for the lower floors allowed the upper rooms to be given rent free to the poor who were asked, in an inscription above the old shop fronts, to say a prayer for their benefactor.

Turn left in the Rue Beaubourg, scene of street fighting in 1834, and right into the old Rue au Maire. Off this, at No. **3** Rue Volta, is a **house**, dating from the 17C, which reveals a timbered façade (gable now gone).

Continue along the Rue au Maire before turning left into the narrow Rue des Vertus. This, in turn, leads to the Rue Réaumur and the Square du Temple.

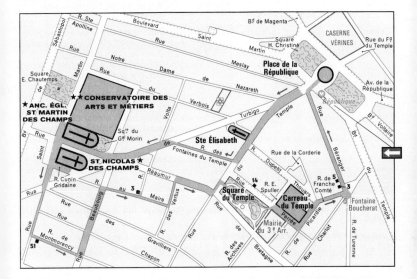

The Former Templar Domain. – In 1140 the religious and military order, founded in 1118 in the Holy Land by nine knights to protect pilgrims and known as the Order of Knights Templar, established a house in Paris. By the 13C the order had achieved great power with 9 000 commanderies throughout Europe and an unrivalled international banking system. In France the knights had become independent of the crown and had acquired possession of one quarter of the land area of Paris – including all the Marais quarter.

The Templars fortified their domain and its keep became a refuge for local peasants and those fleeing royal jurisdiction. Craftsmen also congregated, exempt from guild taxes, until there were 4 000 within the walls where even kings were known to seek shelter.

Philip the Fair decided to suppress this state within a state and one day in 1307 had all the Templars in France arrested; the order dissolved; the leader and fifty-four followers *(p 62)* burnt at the stake and the property divided between the crown and the Knights of St. John of Jerusalem, later known as the Knights of Malta.

The Templar Prison. – The Knights of Malta were suppressed in their turn at the Revolution and the Temple Tower, as it is known, was used as a prison for Louis XVI, Marie-Antoinette, the king's sister Madame Elisabeth, the seven year old Dauphin and his sister, on their arrest on 13 August 1792 *(see Carnavalet Museum, p 87)*.

The king was held in the tower and it was from here, therefore, that he went to the guillotine on 20 January 1793 following his trial and conviction by the Convention. The following July the Dauphin was separated from his mother, who, in August, was transferred with her sister-in-law to the Conciergerie *(p 61)* which she was to leave only to go to the guillotine on 16 October. Two years later, on 8 June 1795, a young man in the Temple Tower died and the mystery arose which has never been solved, of whether he was Louis XVII, the son of Louis XVI or who he was. In 1808 the tower was razed to prevent Royalist pilgrimages and the domain converted into an open air secondhand clothes market known as the Carreau du Temple or Temple Stones. In 1857 Haussmann laid out the covered market, the town hall, on the other side of Rue Perrée, and the present square.

Square and Carreau du Temple. – Cross the square where, on the left at No. **14**, is the Assay Office (Hôtel de la Garantie) for precious metals. At the far end, left of the town hall, is the Carreau, still lined, like the surrounding Picardie, Corderie and Dupetit-Thouars streets, with clothes, costume and fancy clothes shops and stalls *(market except Mondays: 9am to noon)*.

Continue along the Rue de Franche-Comté and, leaving the 1699 Boucherat Fountain on your right at the end of the street, turn left up the Rue Béranger. At Nos. **3** and **5** there is an 18C hôtel where in 1857 the poet and writer of popular songs, Béranger, died.

The Rue Béranger leads to Place de la République.

Place de la République. – *Description p 171.*

La VILLETTE

Michelin plan 🔟 - fold 10: B 20, C 20 – *Métro Station: Porte de la Villette (N) or Porte de Pantin (S).*

La Villette, another of Paris' important inner city development projects, lies on the north eastern periphery of the capital, between Porte de la Villette and Porte de Pantin.

The original village with its peaceful air and numerous country retreats, rapidly changed its aspect with the building of the various waterways (Canal de l'Ourcq, Canal St Denis and Canal St Martin) in the early 19C. This in turn brought the railways, industrialisation and in 1867 the creation of the new slaughter houses and livestock markets at La Villette.

The project. – The redevelopment plan for the 55 hectare - 136 acre site includes in addition to the Centre for Science and Industry *(see below)*, the Great Hall (Grande Hall, 1867), one of three original livestock markets to be retained and transformed into an exhibition centre, a theatre (Théâtre Paris-Villette) in the 19C exchange and Le Zénith a pop and rock concert hall. The Lion Fountain, near the south entrance, was part of the 19C project. A final phase will include the building of a Music Centre and the landscaping of a 30 hectare - 74 acre park.

Centre for Science and Industry (Cité des Sciences et de l'Industrie). – *Open 2pm (10am as from September 1986) to 10pm; closed Mondays; 40F ℡ 40.05.72.72. Various parts of the centre will not be open until the end of 1986.*

The transformation of the unfinished slaughter house into a futuristic building encircled by water filled moats was the work of the French architect, Adrien Fainsilber.

The permanent exhibition, Explora *(1st, 2nd and 3rd floors),* with the help of the latest computer and audio-visual techniques elucidates four main themes: the planet earth and the universe, man and the environment, matter and the work of man and languages and communication. In addition there is a planetarium *(2nd floor),* an inventorium *(main floor)* with discovery workshops for children, an industrial exhibition area *(2nd underground level),* an information centre on the regions of France *(1st underground level)* and a multimedia library *(1st underground level).*

When approaching the centre from the south the landscape is dominated by the polished steel spherical form of **La Géode.** The sphere with a diameter of 36 m - 118 ft houses a unique cinema with a hemispherical screen.

ZADKINE MUSEUM

Michelin plan 🔟 - fold 43: L 13 – *Métro Station: Vavin or Port Royal (R.E.R.)*

100 bis, Rue d'Assas. Open 10am to 5.50pm; closed Mondays and holidays; 7F (free on Sundays). ℡ 43.26.91.90.

Russian by birth and French by adoption, the sculptor Ossip Zadkine (1890-1967) came to Paris in 1909, after a stay in London. His works in wood and stone expressed his anguish and anxiety. This house, now presented as a museum, was his home from 1928 to his death.

Amongst the works on display note in particular the *Woman with a Fan,* from his Cubist period, the elm wood sculpture of *Prometheus* and the model of his memorial to the destruction of Rotterdam *(The Destroyed City).* Van Gogh is the subject of the last room which includes several busts and portraits of the artist as well as the plaster cast of the statue in Auvers-sur-Oise.

A variety of sculptures stand in the garden.

EXCURSIONS

Listed alphabetically

(Photo J.N. Reichel/Top)

The Palace of Versailles – Garden Façade

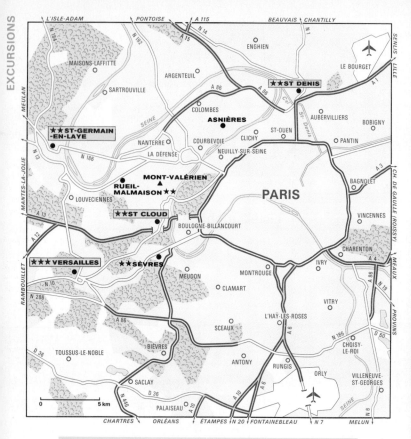

The places shown with a yellow background each have a more detailed plan.

ASNIÈRES

Michelin map 101 - fold 15 — Pop 71 220
3 km – 2 miles from Porte d'Asnières. Métro Station: Gabriel-Péri.

This suburb to the north west of Paris is known for its Dogs' Cemetery.

Dogs' Cemetery. – *4 Pont de Clichy. Open 9 to 11.45am and 2 to 5.45pm (5pm October to February); closed Sunday mornings and holidays; 12F.*
More than 100 000 pets (dogs, cats, rabbits, birds, racing horses and even the odd lion and monkey) have been laid to rest in this island cemetery since 1899. The tomb stones, monuments and epitaphs are at times surprising.

MOUNT VALÉRIEN (Le Mont Valérien)

Michelin map 101 - fold 14
3.5 km – 2 miles from Porte Maillot. RER station: La Défense then bus 360.

Ever since the Middle Ages the slopes rising from the Seine have been vine-clad and the village of **Suresnes** has acquired a reputation for its slightly acidic wine. The vineyard was replanted in 1965 *(grape harvest festival: first Sunday in October)*. The local **museum** *(Avenue Charles de Gaulle; open 15 September to 30 June on Wednesdays and week-ends 3 to 6pm; closed holidays; ☎ 47.72.38.04)* in addition to other historical exhibits has a section on the vineyard.
Going up Boulevard Washington, on the left is the American Military Cemetery. A terrace to the right affords a wide panorama of Paris beyond the Bois de Boulogne.

Mount Valérien. – Already a sacred place in Gallic times by the 17C it had acquired a Stations of the Cross and a popular pilgrimage chapel. Parisians came by their hundreds via the Suresnes ferry and often completed the final climb on their knees.
A fort was built during the reign of Louis-Philippe and it played an important part in 1870-71 in the defence of Paris. Between 1940 and 1944, 4 500 men of the Resistance were shot on its slopes.

Memorial to Fighting France. – *Guided tours 10am to noon and 2 to 7pm (5pm from 1 October to 31 March). Time: 20 mins. Dress appropriately.* The memorial decorated across its wide façade with a stone frieze showing the Cross of Lorraine and the struggle for liberty, was opened on 18 June 1960 by General de Gaulle. The flame of remembrance is rekindled annually on the 18 June. In the crypt are the tombs of 16 soldiers and an urn containing the ashes of unknown victims. In a clearing the commemorative chapel to the men of the Resistance can be made out from the fort.

RUEIL-MALMAISON★★

Michelin map ⬛⬛⬛ - folds 13 and 14 — Pop 64 545
9 km – 5 1/2 miles from Porte Maillot. RER station: La Défense then bus 158A.

Rueil-Malmaison lies encircled by a bend in the Seine to the west of Paris. Its claim to fame is the Malmaison Château Museum, treasure house of Napoleonic souvenirs.

Malmaison in Napoleon Bonaparte's time. – Josephine Tascher de la Pagerie, born in 1763, widow of General de Beauharnais, beheaded during the Terror, married General Bonaparte in 1796. Three years later she bought the château and 260 ha – 640 acre park of Malmaison where she was to pass the happiest years of her married life with Napoleon. As First Consul, Bonaparte was already residing officially at the Tuileries but he paid frequent visits to the château, built in 1622, where he could live completely informally and Josephine was gay, elegant, extravagant and capricious.

Josephine alone at Malmaison. – After his coronation as Emperor, Napoleon frequented only the official residences of the Tuileries, St-Cloud and Fontainebleau but Josephine kept her affection for Malmaison and whenever possible, hastened to her own château and its glorious rose garden.

After the divorce Josephine returned to Malmaison which Napoleon had given her together with the Elysée Palace and a château near Evreux. She continued to receive guests such as the King of Prussia. She caught cold during the reception given for the Tsar Alexander I at the Château of St-Leu and died a few days later on 29 May 1814.

Napoleon's Farewell. – Napoleon returned three times to Malmaison after Josephine's death: firstly on his escape from Elba, secondly at the end of the Hundred Days when he sought refuge with his sister-in-law, the beautiful Hortense, and her young son, the future Napoleon III, and finally, when he remained largely in his personal apartments on the first floor, during the period between Waterloo and his departure for St. Helena.

■ MALMAISON MUSEUM★★

Guided tours 1 April to 30 September, 10am to 12.30pm and 1.30 to 5.30pm; the rest of the year, 10am to 12.30pm and 1.30 to 5pm; closed Tuesdays; 16F; 8F Sundays; 16F combined ticket with Bois-Préau. ☎ 47.49.20.07.

On Josephine's death, the château passed to her son, Prince Eugène de Beauharnais, but when he died it was sold, passing from hand to hand until it returned to the family under Napoleon III. His wife, Empress Eugénie, then had the idea of converting Malmaison into a museum – a project, however, not fully realized until 1906.

The museum, which is devoted entirely to Josephine and Napoleon Bonaparte, consists of items donated or purchased which were originally in the château or at the Tuileries, St-Cloud or Fontainebleau.

Ground Floor. – 1) Vestibule in the Antique style; busts of the imperial family.

2) Billiard room: the room retains its original furniture.

3) The Gold Salon: furniture, Josephine's tapestry frame. Beautiful mantelpiece flanked by two paintings by Gérard and Girodet inspired by the poems of Ossian.

4) The Music Room: the furniture by the Jacob brothers, the Empress' harp and Queen Hortense's piano.

5) Dining Room: the walls are decorated with mural paintings of dancers.

6) Council chamber: the room has been decorated to make it appear as though it were the interior of an army campaign tent. The chairs are from St-Cloud.

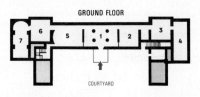

GROUND FLOOR

COURTYARD

7) The Library: furniture, books and maps from Malmaison and the Tuileries.

1st Floor. – It was in this set of rooms that the Emperor spent most of his time after Waterloo, before going to St. Helena.

8) The Emperor's Drawing Room: portraits by Gérard of the imperial family.

9) Napoleon's Bedroom: the canopied bed of Prince Eugène and personal objects are from the Tuileries.

10) Marengo Room: paintings of Napoleon's victories in the field by Gérard and Gros. On display are a ceremonial sword and sabre.

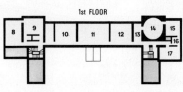

1st FLOOR

11) Josephine's Room: mementoes and portraits of Josephine, Sèvres china and a precious porcelain table showing the Emperor surrounded by the victorious generals of the Battle of Austerlitz (1805).

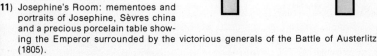

12) Exhibition Gallery: a mural frieze in the Antique style from the First Consul's house in the Rue Chantraine, Josephine's dressing table and two busts by Chinard.

13-17) Josephine's Apartments: portraits and personal objects in profusion including her jewels, perfumes and her huge dress bills – at her death she had debts amounting to three million francs!

2nd Floor. – One of the rooms contains a selection of clothes worn at court.

Another room is devoted to Queen Hortense: furniture and personal mementoes. Mementoes of Prince Eugène de Beauharnais and other frequent visitors to Malmaison. The last room has a display on the history of the château and estate.

RUEIL-MALMAISON ★★

Pavilions. – The Osiris Pavilion contains mementoes of the principal donors: antiquities and *objets d'art* collected by Mr. Osiris who bequeathed the property to the nation in 1904 and a selection of other objects all relating in some way to the Napoleonic legend. The central area is dominated by Gérard's full length portrait of Tsar Alexander I.

The **Carriage Pavilion** includes some of the imperial coaches and the landau used by Blücher at Waterloo.

Park. – In the 6 ha – 15 acre park look for the cedar planted to commemorate the Victory at Marengo on 14 June 1800 and visit the rose garden. At the far end of the avenue of century-old limes stands the **summer house,** where Napoleon often used to work.

On leaving the estate walk to the right along Avenue Marmontel and you will soon see on the left the mausoleum of Napoleon III's son, the Prince Imperial who was killed by the Zulus in 1879. The statue of the young prince with his dog is a replica of the Carpeaux original in the Louvre.

(Photo Musées Nationaux)
Rueil-Malmaison
General Bonaparte – by David

Bois-Préau Château★. – *Same times as Malmaison; 8F; 4F on Sundays; 16F for combined ticket with Malmaison.*

The château, bought by Josephine in 1810 and rebuilt in 1855 was bequeathed the following century by the Americans, Mr and Mrs Edward Tuck, to the French, for use as a Napoleonic museum. The exhibits are devoted to Napoleon's exile on St Helena from 1815 to his death (1821) and the return of his body to the Invalides *(p 71).*

ST-CLOUD ★★

Michelin map **101** - folds 14 and 24 – Pop 28 760
3 km – 2 miles from Porte de St. Cloud. Métro Station: Boulogne-Pont de St. Cloud.

St-Cloud on the south bank of the Seine is one of the capital's more desirable residential suburbs. The town's main attraction is the park of the onetime royal residence.

Monastic beginnings. – Clovis' grandson, Clodoald was spared the unhappy fate of his brother princes, massacred through family strife. He became the follower of the hermit Severin *(p 115)* and founder of a monastery where he died in 560 AD. His tomb became a pilgrimage centre and shortly afterwards the village, then known as Nogent, took the name of St-Cloud. The Bishops of Paris inherited the titles and estates of Clodoald, which they retained until 1839.

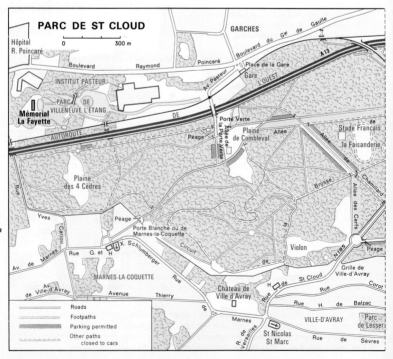

Assassination of Henri III. – It was while besieging Paris (1589), with his newly found ally, the protestant Henri of Navarre, that Henri III was attacked by a young Jacobin monk, Jacques Clément. The king died two days later and Henri of Navarre succeeded.

Monsieur's Residence. – In 1658 the episcopal seat passed to the Duc d'Orléans, Louis XIV's brother better known as Monsieur. It was here that his first wife and cousin, Henrietta of England died suddenly in 1670 amidst rumours of poisoning. His second wife was Princess Elizabeth-Charlotte of the Palatinate. Monsieur extended the estate from the original 12 ha – 30 acres to 590 ha – 1 457 acres and commissioned J. Hardouin-Mansart to build on a sumptuous scale. Le Nôtre designed the park and gardens with the famous Grand Cascade as the centrepiece. In 1780 Marie-Antoinette acquired the château which became state property at the Revolution.

Overthrow of the Directory. – Following his victorious campaign in Egypt (1798) Napoleon was generally acclaimed as the man to restore peace and order. On the 18 Brumaire, Year VIII (9 November 1799) the seat of the legislative councils was transferred to St-Cloud.

Next day the Five Hundred, under the presidency of Lucien Bonaparte, deliberated in the Orangery. Napoleon is met by protestations and only saved from a manhandling by his brother who ordered Murat to expel the assembled. Thus ended the Directory and began the Consulate.

Imperial Residence. – Napoleon was nominated Consul for life in 1802 and St-Cloud became his favourite official residence. Following his divorce with Josephine *(p 179)*, the civil wedding ceremony (1810) with Marie-Louise took place at St-Cloud while the religious service was held in the Louvre.

The Prussian Marshal Blücher took up residence in 1814 and wreaked great vengeance on the furnishings with his spurs.

Charles X precipitated his downfall and compromised the Bourbon restoration by signing at St-Cloud the July 1830 ordinances. Opposition became revolution and Charles left for exile, part of which he spent in the Palace of Holyroodhouse, Edinburgh. Louis-Napoleon was proclaimed Emperor as Napoleon III on 1 December 1852. For the Great Exhibition of 1867 62 monarchs were received at the château.

Ironically the council which declared war on Prussia on 15 July 1870 was held in the château, which three months later was to be fired. Demolition followed in 1891.

■ THE PARK★★

Open: March, April, 7 am to 9pm; May to August, 7am to 10pm; September, October 7am to 9pm; November to February 7am to 10pm.

Admission: free for pedestrians; those with bicycles 6F; motorcycles: 8F; cars: 9F; Restricted parking.

The park, which extends some 450 ha – 1 100 acres – over a hillside dominating the Seine, was landscaped by Le Nôtre and contains fine vistas, viewpoints, expanses of water, woods and shrubberies.

The lodge, a former guard house, beside the main gates *(entrance toll booth-péage)* contains a **historic museum** (musée historique) which evokes the history of the estate and its famous owners *(guided tours Wednesdays, Saturdays, Sundays and holidays 2 to 6pm; time: 1 hour; ☎ 45.66.57.89).*

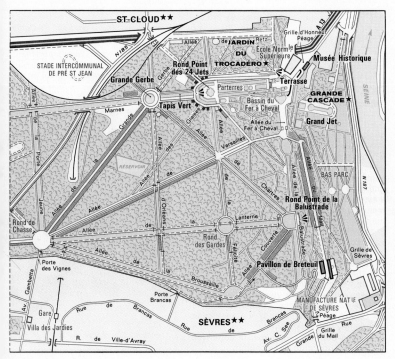

Grand Cascade★ and Fountains. – This typically elaborate 17C fountain with allegories of the Seine and the Marne was designed by Lepautre. Jules Hardouin-Mansart extended it by building a second basin. The waters tumble from basin to basin down to the lower pool, covering in the process 90 m – 295 ft. The **fountains★★** *(May to September, 2nd and 4th Sundays of the month, 4 to 5pm)* provide a splendid display.

Alongside the cascade is the Grand Jet, the most powerful fountain in the park. When playing its waters reach a height of 42 m – 138 ft.

Terrace. – The exact site of the château is indicated by yew trees and marble paving. The château surrounded by its formal privy garden provided the focal point for the Tapis Vert and its continuation the Allée de Marnes.

Trocadéro Garden★. – This garden at a slightly higher level was laid out at the Restoration in the English style, a harmonious combination of trees, flowers and water. The garden also has an aviary. The terrace affords a fine panorama of the privy garden below and the Artois Pavilion (now the prestigious state-run teacher's training college the École Normale Supérieure).

Tapis Vert. – This stretch of lawn between the Grande Gerbe pool and the pool with 24 fountains (Rond Point des 24 Jets) offers a fine perspective over the formal gardens (parterres) to Paris beyond.

Rond Point de la Balustrade. – At this spot Napoleon built a monument incorporating a lantern which was to be kept lit whenever he was in residence at the château. The Prussians destroyed the monument.

From the terrace there is a splendid **panorama★★** of Paris from the Bois de Boulogne right across to the Bois de Meudon.

Breteuil Pavilion. – *Not open to the public.* This 18C pavilion is now the seat of the International Weights and Measures Bureau.

La-Fayette Memorial. – *At the west end of the park. Boulevard Raymond-Poincaré (N 307) in the park, Parc de Villeneuve l'Etang.* The La-Fayette Memorial in the park, was raised by an American foundation in honour of the 209 American voluntary aviators who joined the La-Fayette squadron in the First World War. The monument consists of an arch and a colonnade reflected in a pool. The crypt beneath the terrace contains the bodies of the 67 pilots killed in action including the fighter ace, Lufbery.

Nearby is the Pasteur Institute *(p 169)* where Pasteur himself died in 1895. His former flat now houses a museum *(open 2 to 6pm, 5.30pm on Fridays; closed week ends and holidays; 15F; ☎ 47.01.15.97)* on applied research.

The construction of Notre-Dame, which began after that of St-Denis and Sens in about 1140, heralded the age of great Gothic cathedrals in France: Strasbourg (c 1176), Bourges (c 1185), Chartres (c 1194), Rouen (1200), Reims (1211), Amiens (1220), Beauvais (1247).

Early English, the corresponding period in England, lasted until the end of the 13C and included in whole or in part the cathedrals of Wells (1174), Lincoln (chancel and transept: 1186), Salisbury (1220-1258), Westminster Abbey (c 1250) and Durham (1242).

ST-DENIS★★

Michelin map ⬛⬛⬛ - fold 16 – Pop 91 275.
10 km – 6 miles from Porte de la Chapelle by the motorway; Métro Station: St-Denis-Basilique (line 13).

St-Denis, a dormitory town of more than 100 000 has but one tourist interest for a foreigner, the famous cathedral, necropolis of the kings and queens of France. The town's cultural activities include the Gérard-Philipe Theatre and the organisation of an annual music festival in summer.

"Monsieur St-Denis". – St. Denis, 3C evangelist and first bishop of Lutetia, continued on his way after having been decapitated in Montmartre *(p 76)*, bearing his head in his hands. He was finally buried where he fell by a pious woman. In due course an abbey was erected over the tomb of this man, commonly known as Monsieur (Monseigneur) St. Denis. Such is the legend. Fact, at least, is that a Roman town, Catolacus, commanding both the Paris - Beauvais road and the river, stood on the site from 1C; that it was in a nearby field that Denis and his two companions would appear to have been martyred and that a pilgrimage chapel has existed in the area from the time of Constantine.

The first large church was built in 475, possibly at the instigation of St. Genevieve; this was pillaged in 570; rebuilt by Dagobert I and the bodies of the martyrs interred within it on 24 February 636. Finally a Benedictine community was established to look after the ever more popular pilgrimage. In about 750 Pepin the Short rebuilt the church.

(J. Feuillie/© C.N.M.H.S./S.P.A.D.E.M. 1983)

St. Denis – Louis X effigy (detail).

Abbot Suger. – The basilica we see today is essentially the edifice erected by Suger, Abbot of St-Denis in the 12C, and of Pierre of Montreuil, architect to St. Louis in the 13C.

Suger, the son of poor parents, was "given" at the age of 10, to the abbey where his gifts greatly influenced his fellow novice, the future Louis VII. In 1122 Suger, by now one of the most learned men of his time, was elected Abbot of St-Denis, Louis VII appointed him minister and regent during his absence on the 2nd Crusade when the abbot's wisdom and care for the public good made the king, on his return, name him "father of the nation". Suger's personal flag, a red and gold oriflamme, became the military standard of France.

The Lendit Fair. – The fair, inaugurated by the abbey in 1109, attracted merchants and crowds from all parts of France and many countries abroad for the 600 years

(Photo J. Feuillie/© C.N.M.H.S./S.P.A.D.E.M. 1983)

St. Denis-interior.

during which it flourished on the St-Denis plain. The University of Paris used to purchase from among the 1 200 stallholders the parchment required by its scholars.

The Royal Necropolis. – For twelve centuries, from Dagobert to Louis XVIII, all French kings apart from three Merovingians and a few Capetians, were buried at St-Denis. In 1793 the Convention decreed the destruction of the mausoleums; the coffins were exhumed, the bodies thrown pel-mel into unnamed graves; the tombs, however, were saved as the archaeologist Alexandre Lenoir, had removed them some time previously and placed them in a specially created museum. The tombs were returned to the basilica under Louis XVIII.

■ **THE CATHEDRAL★★** *Time: 1 hour*

The church is a landmark in French architecture: as the first great Gothic edifice it became the inspiring prototype for late 12C cathedral architecture, notably Chartres.

From abbey church in the 13C to basilica with special privileges the church was raised to cathedral status as an episcopal seat in 1966.

Construction. – Under Suger, construction took place of the façade and the first two bays of the nave (1136-1140), the chancel and the crypt (1140-1144), and the Carolingian nave, provisionally conserved, was repaired and refaced (1145-1147). At the beginning of the 13C, the north tower, which had been struck by lightning, was given a magnificent stone spire; the chancel and transept were enlarged and work begun on the nave. In 1247 St. Louis commissioned Pierre of Montreuil to take over the task which was, in fact, to continue until 1281, long after the architect's death in 1267. Immense wealth, amassed by the abbey, can be seen, in part, at the Louvre in the Apollo Gallery *(p 38)*.

Decadence. – There followed centuries of neglect and, finally, depredation during the Revolution when the lead roofing was stolen. Napoleon ordered repairs and restored the church to worship in 1806.

Restoration. – In 1813 the architect, Debret, took charge of the building and for thirty-three years worked on it with a total lack of understanding of mediaeval architecture and devastating results. Viollet-le-Duc took his place in 1847 and, after patiently collecting all the relevant early documents, began, in 1858, to restore the church to its original design. By his death in 1879 the cathedral looked much as it does now. Excavations in the crypt have uncovered walls of the Carolingian martyrium, a rich late 6C Merovingian necropolis (sarcophagi and jewels) and the foundations of five earlier sanctuaries.

Exterior. – The cathedral has a strangely fortified appearance with crenelations and four massive buttresses and a general air of dissymmetry, lacking as it does, a north tower and with both pointed Gothic and rounded Romanesque arches included in the main façade. Above the round arched doors are stained glass windows, blind arcades, a gallery of statues and a rose window – the first in any church and a feature which was, from the 13C, to form an integral element in the design of every Gothic cathedral. The tympana over the central, right and left doorways (restored and recarved respectively) illustrate the Last Judgment, St. Denis' last communion, the death of the saint and his two companions. At the doorway shafts are the Wise and Foolish Virgins (centre), the labours of the months (right) and the signs of the zodiac (left).

On the north side double tiered flying buttresses strengthened the nave. The design of the transept included a fine rose window and two towers (the church was to have six in all). The latter never materialized as building never went beyond the first floor level.

Interior. – *Guided tours 10am (noon on Sundays) to 5.30pm; 1 October to 31 March 10am to 3.30pm; Sundays noon to 3.30pm. Closed 1 January, 1 May, 1 and 11 November, 25 December; time: 1 hour; 20F.*

In the following description the tombs are numbered according to their chronological order.

The cathedral, although slightly smaller than Notre-Dame, has the impressive dimensions of length 108m – 354 ft, width at the transepts 39 m – 128 ft and height 29 m – 95 ft.

The northern of two bays is still supported on massive pillars and pointed arches, dating from Abbot Suger's time. Further within, Pierre de Montreuil has given the nave and adjoining aisles, the chancel, an architectural lift and lightness that are almost ethereal. The transept triforium, even at this date, was glazed with stained glass. The lower windows of the nave have modern glass.

The Tombs★★★. – The kings of France, their queens, the royal children and a few great servants of the crown – Du Guesclin (1) – lay in St-Denis, 79 figures in all, until the Revolution. Now the tombs are empty and the statuary is therefore, virtually, a great museum of funerary sculpture.

Until the Renaissance, tomb sculptures consisted only of **effigies** – among such are the 12C copper filleted cloisonned mosaics of Clovis (2) and Frédégonde (3) from St-Germain-des-Prés *(p 106)*. In about 1260 St. Louis had effigies carved of all his ancestors going back to the 7C. These are purely symbolic and of little interest except for King Dagobert (4) founding the basilica, Charles Martel (5), Pepin the Short (6) and a recumbent figure in Tournai marble (7). From the death of Philippe III, the Bold

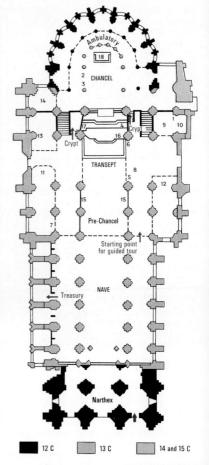

| ■ 12 C | ▨ 13 C | ▨ 14 and 15 C |

(8), in 1285 more care was taken to make a true likeness. It became usual from the mid-14C for notables to commission their tombs while still alive and thus Charles V (9), Charles VI and Isabela of Bavaria (10) are true portraits.

At the Renaissance funerary stones were replaced by **mausoleums** – their two tiers presenting a pathetic contrast: above the king and queen appear kneeling in full regalia: below as naked cadavers. Outstandingly ornate are Louis XII and Anne of Brittany (11), François I and Claude of France (12) by Philibert Delorme and Pierre Bontemps. Catherine dei Medici, who died thirty years after Henri II, had time to erect her husband's tomb but when she saw her own traditional style effigy, she fainted in horror and substituted a figure asleep – the visitor can compare the two versions, the first by Il Primaticcio (13) the second by Germain Pilon (14).

The chancel. – The beautiful pre-Renaissance stalls (15) carved with biblical scenes are from the Normandy castle of Gaillon; the polychrome Romanesque **Virgin★** on her throne (16) is 12C and from St-Martin-des-Champs *(p 174)*; the episcopal seat (17) is a reproduction of Dagobert's throne *(original: p 95)*.

A modern shrine, behind the chancel, contains relics of St. Denis, St. Rusticus and St. Eleutherius (18). The early Gothic **ambulatory★** dates from the time of Abbot Suger and forms a striking contrast to the high 13C nave and chancel.

The Crypt★★. – The lower ambulatory, built in the Romanesque style by Suger in the 12C, was greatly restored by Viollet-le-Duc. In the centre, is the vaulted chapel of the abbot, Hilduin where a stone covers the tomb of the Bourbons, in which are buried Louis XVI, Marie-Antoinette *(p 159)* and Louis XVIII, and in the north transept, a communal grave excavated in 1817, which received the bodies of some 800 Merovingians, Capetians, Orleans and Valois.

MICHELIN *publications for your stay in Paris*

PARIS and environs Hotels and Restaurants
(red annual booklet – extract from the Guide FRANCE)

Plan de PARIS 10 *scale 1:10 000*

PARIS Atlas 11 *practical information, useful addresses, street index, public transport (métro, bus, car)*

Map 101 *Outskirts of PARIS*

to cross Paris rapidly, to find your way in the suburbs, to avoid Sunday evening bottlenecks

ST-GERMAIN-EN-LAYE★★

Michelin map ⅢⅪⅪ - fold 12 – Pop 40 829
14 km – 9 miles from Porte Maillot; RER station: St-Germain-en-Laye.

The lovely old town, with its Renaissance château, park, great terrace and nearby St-Germain and Marly woods, is a most attractive excursion.

The Old Castle. – Louis VI, in the 12C, erected a castle commanding the Seine on St-Germain Hill to which St. Louis added a chapel in 1230. The castle, but not the chapel, was destroyed in the Hundred Years War, and rebuilt by Charles V in 1368. François I rebuilt the castle entirely in 1539 with the exceptions of the chapel and Charles V keep.

The New Château. – Henri II, son of François I and born in the castle, found the place stark and commissioned Philibert Delorme to erect him a country seat. It was completed by Henri IV. The royal diversions of the time – dancing, theatrical performances and recitals – were given added spice by the construction of fountains in the grounds which Henri IV delighted to turn on his guests. Louis XIV had similar fountains at Versailles *(p 188).* Like Henri II, Charles IX and Louis XIV were born at St-Germain – the cradle and Bourbon lily of the latter being incorporated in the town's arms. Louis XIII died there.

Last Years. – The Old Castle and New Château were both used by the court – Louis XIV getting Jules Hardouin-Mansart to convert the five towers into living pavilions, Le Nôtre to lay out the park and terrace before he finally left for Versailles in 1682.

The New Château passed to the future Charles X who demolished and never rebuilt it. Such parts as remained and the Old Castle furnishings were sold by the Revolution. Finally the Old Castle was converted into the museum of National Antiquities by Napoleon III in 1867. The treaty of peace concluded between the Allies and Austria was signed in the château in 1919.

Associations with Britain. – St-Germain's royal associations with Britain, besides the Black Prince, are several. Mary Stuart, later Mary Queen of Scots, lived in the castle from the age of six to her marriage ten years later in 1558 with the Dauphin, the future, shortlived, François II, son of Henri II. The wife of Charles I, Henrietta, daughter of Henri IV, lived there from 1645-1648 with her daughter during part of the Civil War and in 1689, James II, deposed from the throne, arrived to live in moody retirement until his death in 1701. His tomb is in St-Germain Church opposite the castle.

ST-GERMAIN-EN-LAYE

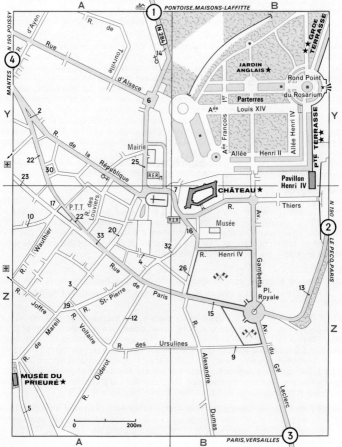

EXCURSIONS

■ THE CHÂTEAU★ *Time: 3 1/2 hours*

The château, an irregular pentagon in which the feudal substructure, watchpath and machicolations can be clearly seen even now, is given an added military aspect by the towers at each of its five corners. That to the left of the main entrance on the Place Charles de Gaulle is the Charles V keep which François I had capped by a turret which Louis XIV, in turn, had converted into an observatory where he installed Cassini *(p 132)*.

The flat roofs, the first in France, are edged by a vase ornamented stone balustrade and dominated by tall chimney stacks.

Museum of National Antiquities★★ **(Musée des Antiquités nationales).** – *Open 9.45am to noon and 1.30 to 5.15pm; closed on Tuesdays and holidays; 12F.*

This museum contains rich archaeological collections from France's earliest inhabitants (Palaeolithic) to the Middle Ages which are attractively displayed.

Mezzanine Floor (Prehistoric to Gallic Period). – The show cases on the right contain the various raw materials (silex, quartz, bone and horn) used to manufacture the primitive tools of the Palaeolithic period which dates back to 1 000 000 BC. On the same side are hand and foot prints of prehistoric man, from the sites of Gargas and Aldène respectively. Archaeological finds are arranged chronologically down the left side. The masterpieces of Palaeolithic art are often quite small and here include the figurine of the Brassempouy Woman (*c* 20 000 BC) the oldest known representation of the human face; the bison from La Madeleine (*c* 16 000 BC); the Bruniquel baton in the form of a jumping horse (*c* 13 000 BC) and the horse's head from le Mas-d'Azil (*c* 10 000 BC).

During the Neolithic Period, with its geographical origins in the Near East (8 000 BC), man lived in settled communities and turned to crop growing and stock raising and was proficient in the making of pottery. Jadeite and other hard stones were worked and polished to produce arms and tools.

In the Bronze Age which was marked by the gradual dominance of metals over stone there appeared a variety of small objects in copper then bronze (mixture of copper and tin): daggers, curved axes, bracelets decorated with geometric motifs, twisted torque-necklaces, sickles and fibulas. Note *(in case)* jewellery in solid gold or sheets of beaten gold. Characteristic of the early Iron Age are the richly furnished graves of the Hallstatt (*c* 750-450 BC) culture, called after a famous Austrian site. The graves of princes were distinguished by the presence of a large iron sword. Also included (in the graves) were fibulas (clasps or brooches), pottery and furniture as in the tomb at Magny-Lambert in the Côte-d'Or or even a four-wheeled wagon and harness. The La Tène culture which followed has left evidence of trade contacts between the civilized Mediterranean world and Champagne and Burgundy: a variety of fibulas, amber necklaces, glass and enamel pendants, Greco-Italian pottery and Celtic arms. The Gallic tribes still placed two-wheeled chariots in the graves (see the reconstruction of such graves from Berru and La Gorge-Meillet), worked gold (case of jewellery) and struck coins. The arrival of Caesar in 52 BC and the taking of Alesia (model of the camp) marked the end of this culture.

The reconstitution of the Cave of the Bulls from the vicinity of Montignac in the Dordogne is impressive. The cave, not far from Lascaux, touk its name from the vigorous drawings and wall sculptures of a group of black bulls.

First Floor (Gallo-Roman and Merovingian Periods). – The long *Pax Romana* and the tolerance of the invaders, allowed the expression of an original art which is well illustrated here through funerary and mythological statues and everyday objects (dishes, glassware and red pottery). There is a rich collection of early grave headstones.

The turmoil of the Merovingian period (3-8C), marked by the invasions, has left few remains other then graves rich in objects of all sorts: swords and battle-axes, *cloisonné* jewellery, S-shaped fibulas and bronze buckles with fantastic decoration.

The ballroom with its decorative stone ribbed vaulting and fireplace emblasoned with François I's salamander has a comparative archaeological section. This display allows the visitor to compare the artifacts from different continents, cultures and prehistoric periods. Take the back stairs.

After visiting the museum go through to the inner court, where François I's emblems can once again be seen on the upper balustrade, to reach the chapel.

Sainte-Chapelle★. – The chapel, built in 1230 by St. Louis, ten years before the Sainte-Chapelle in Paris *(p 60)*, is undoubtedly by the same architect, Pierre of Montreuil. The tall windows, however, were too early to be glazed with the brilliant glass which makes the Paris chapel a medieval jewel and the beautiful rose window has been blinded by other constructions. On the arch keystones are carved heads which may well be portraits of St. Louis, his mother Blanche of Castile, his wife and other close associates. These are probably the earliest royal portraits.

Parterres (BY). – An iron grille opens onto the gardens from the château which in this façade includes a loggia approached by a formal staircase. The moat now contains reconstituted megaliths and copies of Roman monuments such as Trajan's and Nero's columns.

Henri IV Pavilion (BY). – *Not open to the public.* The brick and domed pavilion along with the Sully Pavilion *(not open)* slightly lower down, are all that remain of the New Château. Inside is Louis XIII's oratory where the newly born Louis XIV was hurriedly baptised on 5 September 1638. In 1836 the pavilion became a private mansion and later in the century was famous as a meeting place of artists, politicians and men of letters. Here Alexandre Dumas wrote two of his historical novels *The Count of Monte Cristo* and *The Three Musketeers*, Offenbach composed *The Drum Major's Daughter* and Léo Delibes the ballet *Sylvia*. The statesman and president Thiers died here in 1877.

Terrace★★ (BY). – The Grande Terrasse – beyond the Petite Terrasse on which there is a viewing table – is one of Le Nôtre's masterpieces. It is 2 400 m long – 2 500 yds – bordered with lime trees and took four years to lay out, being completed in 1673. Beyond lies a landscaped garden★.

■ ADDITIONAL SIGHT

Priory Museum★ **(Musée du Prieuré)** **(AZ)**. *Open 10am to 5.30pm (6.30pm Sundays and holidays); closed on Mondays, Tuesdays and holidays; 20F.*

The hospital founded by Madame de Montespan became a priory before it was finally transformed into a home by the artist Maurice Denis (1870-1943). Surrounded by his extensive family, he delighted in entertaining fellow members of the Nabis group (Bonnard, Vuillard, Ranson...).

The two former dormitories, linked by a majestic staircase are now arranged as a museum, which traces the origins of the Nabis group and illustrates the importance they attached to the decorative and pictorial in various domains (painting, posters and glass work). Ranson is well represented as it was his studio which served as a meeting place for the group. The portrait of Mrs Ranson is by M. Denis. Auguste Perret designed the **studio** for his friend Denis who was working on the decoration of the Champs-Élysées Theatre. Denis also redecorated the **chapel** in an unusual blue colour scheme.

SÈVRES★★

Michelin map **101** - fold 24 – Pop 20 255
3.5 km – 2 miles from Porte de St-Cloud. Métro Station: Pont de Sèvres.

The name of this small town is known all the world over for its brillant multicoloured porcelain.

SÈVRES PORCELAIN

Porcelain is a ceramic material, which when fired in the piece undergoes vitrification, emerging as an extremely hard, translucent product when finally moulded (as opposed to the opacity of china).

Soft-paste porcelain. – For a long time porcelain imported from the Orient was the only kind known in Europe. In early attempts to emulate this mystery substance potters produced soft-paste ware by combining a very fine grained marl (clay) and glass and then vitrifying.

Soft-paste ware was produced in 1738 at Vincennes. The factory received a royal warrant in 1753 and three years later transferred to Sèvres where it became crown property. The royal cypher of interlaced L's (Louis) was used from this period as the factory mark. Sèvres soft porcelain was originally known for its natural sprigged flowers, before specialising in tableware, statuettes and panel decoration of gallant scenes. The pieces were magnificent; the prices prohibitive.

Hard-paste porcelain. – At the beginning of the 18C Johann Friedrich Bottger was the first European to make porcelain at his factory in Dresden (1708). His secret was the use of kaolin. Although the secret of the manufacturing process leaked from Saxony to France

(Photo Musées Nationaux)
Sèvres porcelain – The Thesmar Vase.

it was only in 1769, when a deposit of kaolin was discovered in the Limousin, that the new product could be manufactured. From the Empire onwards the Sèvres production consisted exclusively of hard-paste ware. Hard-paste porcelain, using kaolin and firing at a high temperature (1 400 °C – 2 550 °F), had remarkable strength although it was more difficult to decorate. Only a limited range of colours was suitable for high temperature firing. These included the famous coloured grounds royal or Sèvres blue *(bleu de Sèvres)* which had already been used on soft-paste ware under the name of *beau bleu*.

Colours suitable for low temperature firing like pink had the disadvantage that they did not sink into the glaze, as was the case with soft-paste ware.

In the early years the factory retained the exclusivity of gilding and even today all Sèvres pieces are gilded – with a few rare exceptions for technical reasons.

Biscuit ware, generally figures and groups, was left unglazed to avoid altering the graceful forms of these pieces.

National Porcelain Museum★★ **(Musée National de Céramique)**. – *Open 10am to noon and 1.30 to 5pm. Closed Tuesdays and holidays; 12 F (6 F on Sundays); ☎ 45.34.99.05.*

The museum, founded in 1824, contains china and porcelain from all parts of the world including the Orient and the Middle East, and all the major factories of Europe from Sèvres itself and all other centres in France to Meissen, Berlin, Copenhagen, Delft, Vienna, St-Petersburg, England (Wedgwood)...

The sales room, to the left of the entrance, has a display of the **factory's** present day production of traditional and modern pieces.

An audio-visual display explains the various processes (turning, firing, moulding, decoration...) involved in porcelain making. Each piece passes through the hands of 20 craftsmen. If it does not pass the test of perfection it is destroyed. *There are demonstrations on the first and third Thursdays of the month (except in July and August) at 1.15pm; 2pm; 2.45pm and 3.30pm; time: 1 1/2 hours.*

VERSAILLES★★★

Michelin map ⭐⭐⭐ - fold 22 – Pop 95 240
13 km – 8 miles from Porte d'Auteuil. Access also by train: Gare des Invalides to Versailles Rive-Gauche.

The French monarchy reached its zenith in Versailles – to build a Versailles became the ambition of every king and princeling in Europe and echoes, therefore, of the château architecture and style, the gardens, the Trianons, are to be found in palaces and mansions in almost every country in the West whether they were friendly or opposed to Louis XIV.

The town grew up in the shadow of the palace, never emerging in its own right and, like the palace, remains much as it was in the 17 and 18C.

HISTORICAL NOTES

Louis XIII's Château. – At the beginning of the 17C, Versailles was a village surrounded by marsh and woodland. Game abounded and Louis XIII, who enjoyed hunting, bought a local manor farm which, in due course, he had reconstructed by Philibert le Roy (1631-1634). The resulting small rose brick and stone château consisting of a main building and two wings can still be seen with the Marble Court at its centre. Gardens surrounded the château.

The palace enlarged. – Louis XIV came to the throne at five and achieved majority at twenty-three in 1661. In the intervening years he had grown attached to his father's château and determined to enlarge it and also to outstrip in grandeur the country mansion at Vaux-Le-Vicomte of Fouquet, his finance minister. To this end he commissioned the three who had been working for Fouquet – Le Vau as architect, Le Brun as decorator, Le Nôtre as garden designer, to reconceive the château at Versailles.

Louis XIII's construction was too small to be enlarged: the land was too wet to grow plants satisfactorily and there was insufficient water for the fountains which were an integral part of any 17C garden. Such details meant little to the king! Soil was shifted, land was drained, building began – and although construction was to continue for a further half century, by 1664 the first of the many celebrations that one associates with Versailles were being held there to the satisfaction of king and court.

The palace of palaces. – In 1678, Jules Hardouin-Mansart, then aged 31, took over as project architect – a post he was to occupy until his death thirty years later. By 1685, 22 000 workmen with 6 000 horses were engaged on the palace site under the direction of Mansart, Le Brun and Le Nôtre. Such numbers are understood when it is appreciated that the installation of 1 400 fountains (today 600), necessitated the diversion of the River Bièvre and 16 000 h – 37 000 acres – of land being drained; bedding plants numbered 150 000 a year; there were 3 000 orange, pomegranate, myrtle and rose-laurel trees to be moved seasonally into the orangery. 100 statues were commissionned by Le Brun for the gardens alone.

Life at Court. – The court numbered 3 000. In addition there were thousands of soldiers billetted in the town and servants housed in the palace annexes. Nobles and their servants lived in the palace itself while the lesser nobility frequented the precincts in the hope of recognition by the king from whom favours, riches, position, everything depended. Louis encouraged this attraction as a means of keeping his nobles under his eye and control, encouraged also their rivalries in place-seeking, fashion, gambling to distract their attention from political dissension. Life at court was carefully regulated and all was gaiety until 1684 when the influence of Mme de Maintenon became paramount.

On the death of the Sun King in 1715, the court returned to Paris. In 1722, however, Louis XV moved back to Versailles though not to live in the public style of Louis XIV – it was during his reign that certain palace rooms were converted into private apartments and the Petit Trianon was built.

Since 1789, Versailles has ceased to be a royal residence.

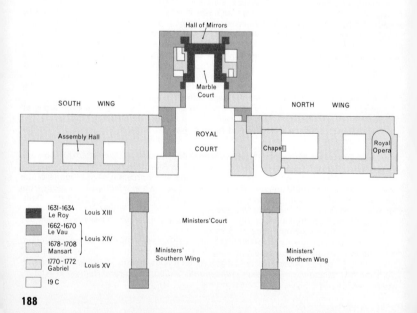

To the glory of France. – The execution of Louis XVI on 21 January 1793 marked the start of Versailles' spoliation: the furniture was auctioned, the fine art removed to the Louvre, the palace itself allowed to fall into disrepair, the gardens were abandoned.

The rot was only stopped by Louis-Philippe who gave 23 million francs from his personal fortune towards the palace's rehabilitation and conversion into a museum "to the glory of France". Restoration has continued ever since, particularly after the 1914-1918 war with the assistance of a munificent gift by John D. Rockefeller and since 1950.

Restoration. – Since 1950 an important programme of restoration has been undertaken. Following the installation of central heating and electric lighting, and general refurbishing other landmarks include the restoration of the Royal Opera, King's Bedroom and Hall of Mirrors all to their original splendour. Many of the hangings and curtains have been rewoven to the original patterns.

Phases of construction and other notable events

1631	Building of Louis XIII's château.
1643	Death of Louis XIII. The five year old **Louis XIV** succeeds. The Regent Anne of Austria and Mazarin rule.
1661	Louis XIV comes of age. On the death of Mazarin, the king assumes full control and dispenses with the services of a Prime Minister.
1664	The first of many sumptuous celebrations to be held in the gardens of the as yet unfinished palace.
1666	The fountains play for the first time.
1668	Louis Le Vau enlarged the existing palace.
1671	Interior decoration begins, directed by Charles Le Brun.
1674	The king resides in the palace for the first time.
1682	The courtiers and other officials take up residence.
1683	Death of Marie-Therese of Austria. Louis XIV marries Madame de Maintenon in secret.
1684	The Hall of Mirrors is completed.
1687	The Marble Trianon replaces the Porcelain Trianon.
1710	Birth of Louis XV great grandson of Louis XIV.
1715	Death of Louis XIV. Again a five year old prince, **Louis XV,** succeeds. Philippe d'Orleans is Regent. The court leaves Versailles for Paris.
1722	The court returns to Versailles.
1729	Birth of the Dauphin, father of Louis XVI, Louis XVIII and Charles X.
1745	Madame de Pompadour becomes Louis XV's favourite a position she is to occupy for 15 years.
1754	Birth of Louis XVI.
1770	Marriage of the 16 year old prince with Marie-Antoinette.
1774	Death of Louis XV. **Louis XVI** is the successor.
1783	Signing of the Treaty of Versailles under which the independence of the 13 States was recognised.
1789	The Estates General assemble in the town. The royal family leaves Versailles for good.

THE PALACE★★★

Open *(1).* – *The courtyards, palace and Trianon gardens and park (9F per car) are open daily from dawn to dusk (2).*

Palace and Trianons	Visiting times	Prices
Closed on Mondays and holidays (also on Easter Sunday. Whitsun and Ascension Day)		
Free Visit *(Entrance C)*		
Chapel	*Visible only from the doorways of the lower and upper vestibules*	*16F*
State Apartments	*9.45am to 5pm*	
Grand Trianon................	*9.45am to 5pm*	*12F*
Petit Trianon	*2 to 5pm*	*8F*
Guided Tours only *(Entrances A and B) (maximum no. of persons per group: 30)*		
King's Suite and Royal Opera	*9.45am to 3.30pm*	*additional: 18F*
Madame de Maintenon's Suite and the Queen's Private Suite	*Tuesdays-Fridays 3.30pm*	*additional: 18F per tour*
King's Private Apartments: Madame de Pompadour's and Madame du Barry's Suites	*Tuesdays-Fridays 2pm*	*additional: 18F per tour*

(1) The following information is given as a general indication only and therefore with all reserve.
(2) For information on the fountains and illuminations see p 196

One day tour:

Morning: the palace (exterior and State Apartments)

Afternoon: King's Suite and Opera Royal, the gardens following the main perspective down to the Apollo Basin and Grand Canal as well as the groves to the south of this.

By car: from the Grand Canal to the Trianon – for access by car see the map on p 196

The Grand Trianon (exterior) and gardens of the Petit Trianon
The Parterres du Nord of the Palace (park the car on Avenue de Trianon or Boulevard de la Reine).

Two day tour:

Day 1 – Morning: Tour of the palace as above

Afternoon: Complete tour of the palace gardens and boat trip on the Grand Canal

Day 2 – Morning: King's Suite and Opera Royal

Afternoon: Complete tour of the Trianon (châteaux and gardens)

■ **THE PALACE EXTERIOR** *Quick tour: about 1 hour*

Place d'Armes Façade. – The square, as vast as the Place de la Concorde and the meeting point of three avenues each wider than the Champs-Élysées – the Avenue de St-Cloud, Avenue de Paris and Avenue de Sceaux – serves as a forecourt to the magnificent **royal stables ★** (now a barracks) designed by Jules Hardouin-Mansart to house Louis XIV's 2 500 horses and 200 carriages, and simultaneously to emphasize Versailles' massive expanse.

The courtyards. – Beyond the wrought iron gates are three courts: the **Ministers' Court,** lined by wings of the palace formerly occupied by ministers and government officials; the **Royal Court,** beginning where the equestrian statue of Louis XIV erected in 1837 now stands and formerly separated from the outer court by a grille through which none but the royal family, princes and peers, might pass and with three gilded grilles marking the entrances to the state apartments beyond the north and south arcades; and, finally, the **Marble Court ★★**, surrounded on three sides by the old Louis XIII Château and now upraised to its original level and paved in black and white marble. It was Le Vau and Hardouin-Mansart who altered these brick façades by adding busts and at roof level a balustrade punctuated by statues and vases. The gilded balcony at first floor level fronts the windows of the King's Bedroom.

Garden Façade ★★★. – Pass through the façade, decorated with columns and statues, to the gardens and park. This façade – 680 m long – 733 yds – overall, is divided into three, the centre being well in advance of the north and south wings on either side. Monotony has been avoided by the lines of windows, uniform at each of three levels, and the horizontal lines of balcony balustrade, cornice and roof balustrade being broken respectively by projecting pilasters, columns and, at the higher levels, by ornamental vases and great trophies.

Marking the royal apartments at the centre of the main façade and the focal point from the gardens, are statues of Apollo and Diana, symbolizing the king and queen, surrounded by the months of the year.

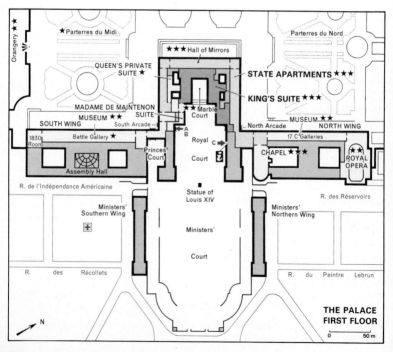

THE PALACE
FIRST FLOOR

0   50 m

The palace terrace, the major viewpoint of the gardens, is adorned with two magnificent grand **vases★** by Coysevox and Tuby on War and Peace respectively. The terrace affords good views of: the Water Terrace (Parterres d'Eau) and beyond the grand perspective which terminates at Grand Canal; the Parterres du Midi *(see below)* to the left and Parterre du Nord and second perspective focussing on the Neptune Basin, to the right.

Parterres du Midi★. – The windows of the Queen's Apartments overlook the Parterres du Midi, formal box edged flowerbeds. From these there is a **view★** over the Orangery down to the **Pièce d'Eau des Suisses** (Swiss Lake) with the wooded slopes of Satory in the distance.

Orangery★★. – Mansart took advantage of this downward slope when designing the Orangery: the roof of the central building is level with the parterres, the projecting wings on either side of the court, in which stand orange and palm trees in summer, end in the **Great Staircases of 100 Steps** (Escaliers des Cent-Marches).

Return to the Marble Court via an opening in the South Wing which leads to the Princes Court.

■ THE PALACE INTERIOR

(First floor: see plan p 193)
Restoration work is indicated only when it necessitates the closing of a gallery.

Go through from the ground floor entrance A to the vestibule *(ticket office)* then up the circular stairway to the upper vestibule (**a**). Alternatively you may come through the 17C galleries of the Museum of French History.

THE CHAPEL★★★

The Chapel, dedicated to St. Louis (Louis IX), harmoniously ornate in its white and gold decoration, remains one of Hardouin-Mansart's masterpieces although it was only completed in 1710 after his death, by his brother-in-law, Robert de Cotte. The pillar and arcade sculpture are by Van Cleve, Robert Le Lorrain and G. Coustou: the organ loft is by Robert de Cotte; the marble altar with bronze gilt ornament by Van Cleve and the Resurrection in the apse by La Fosse.

Louis XIV attended mass daily and, although still surrounded by the court, it was while the Sun King was in chapel that any subject had the right to petition him.

The Chapel was the setting for all the religious occasions of the Court: baptisms, weddings. The marriage of the Dauphin (the future Louis XVI) and Marie-Antoinette, daughter of Francis I and Maria-Theresa of Austria, was celebrated here on 16 May 1770.

THE HERCULES SALON★★

The salon, on the site of an earlier chapel, was created in 1712 and was named after the huge fresco of Hercules, 312 m^2 in area – 3 390 sq ft – painted on the ceiling between 1733 and 1736 by François Lemoyne. The artist committed suicide not long after completing this work.

The room's original rich decoration by Robert de Cotte was enhanced by the two Veronese paintings, *Eliezer and Rebecca* over the marble mantlepiece and **Christ at the House of Simon the Pharisee,** the latter given by the Venetian Republic to Louis XIV.

THE GRAND APARTMENT★★★

Access to this suite of six reception rooms was formerly by the Ambassadors' Staircase which was destroyed in 1752.

This suite reflects the style of Louis XIV in all its sumptuous magnificence – only the finest multicoloured marbles were used, bronze was everywhere sculptured and gilded, craftsmen from none but the most reputed workshops were employed.

Furnishings were limited to the few stools, supplemented when necessary by folding chairs, pedestal and console tables.

The six salons, opening one out of another, were built by Le Vau (1668) and their decoration is by Le Brun. Each is named after the paintings decorating the ceilings and it was in these rooms that Louis XIV held court between 6 and 10pm on three evenings each week.

Abundance Salon (b). – When Louis XIV held court the drinks were laid out in this room. The green velvet hangings are the winter set. The four royal portraits are by Rigaud and Van Loo.

The two following salons were originally vestibules for the Ambassadors' Staircase, and their marble lined walls provided a highly suitable decor for what must have been a busy passageway.

Venus Salon (c). – This first of the planetary salons has a ceiling compartmented by heavy gilt stucco.

Diana Salon (d). – In the time of the Sun King this served as the billiard room. Admire the famous **bust of Louis XIV** by Bernini.

Mars Salon (e). – Originally a guard room it was used during Louis XIV's time for gaming and dancing. The musicians' galleries were on either side of the fireplace. The paintings include *Darius' Tent* by Le Brun, the *Pilgrims of Emmaüs* after Veronese, *Louis XV* by Rigaud, *Maria Leczinska* by Van Loo and above the fireplace one of Louis XIV's favourite paintings, Domenichino's *King David.*

The ceiling paintings all have a martial theme.

Mercury Salon (f). – Originally an antechamber, it then became one of the state suites and was used for gaming on the evenings when Louis XIV held court. It was also where the Sun King lay in state for one week after his death in 1715.

Apollo Salon (g). – The former throne room, is the most sumptuous of the planetary series. Louis XIV saw Apollo as his ideal, the god of wisdom and prophecy, of light and the arts – and took as his personal symbol Apollo's attribute, the sun. On the ceiling of this salon La Fosse painted *Apollo in a Sun Chariot attended by the Seasons*. At the end were the silver throne and canopy at which Louis received ambassadors.

Beyond, the Hall of Mirrors and adjoining War and Peace Salons occupy the entire length of the garden front.

THE WAR SALON★

This salon is decorated with a great oval medallion, carved in relief by Coysevox, of the king riding in triumph over his enemies and being crowned by the goddess of war.

THE HALL OF MIRRORS★★★

The most famous hall in the palace must have been fantastic when the king and queen in full dress moved among their court, beneath lighted chandeliers. It is 75 m long by 10 m wide – 246 × 33 ft; light from the 17 windows is reflected in the 17 mirrors of equal size on the wall opposite. Le Brun painted the ceiling in glorification of the Sun King's early reign from 1661-1678, although he reigned until his death in 1715.

The hall was the setting for the greatest occasions: princely marriages such as that of Marie-Antoinette and the future Louis XVI, receptions and splendid festivals...

Then the silver chandeliers would be lit, flowers and orange trees in silver tubs disposed, Savonnerie carpets laid and all would appear in their finery. Originals and copies of the gilded candelabras ordered by Louis XV now stand in the hall, as well as crystal chandeliers.

Stripped of furnishings the hall became the scene in 1871 of Bismarck's proclamation of the King of Prussia as Emperor of Germany and on 28 June 1919 of the signing of the Versailles Treaty which ended the First World War.

From the central windows there is a superb **vista★★★** of the Grand Perspective.

THE PEACE SALON★

Counterpart of the War Salon this was used as an annexe to the Queen's Suite towards the end of Louis XIV's reign. The salon contains a painting by Lemoyne of *Louis XV bringing peace to Europe*.

THE QUEEN'S SUITE★★, CORONATION ROOM

This suite of rooms overlooking the flowerbeds of the south garden (Parterres du Midi) form the counterpart of the king's state apartments.

Queen's Bedroom (h). – The bedroom restored as it was in 1787, was designed for the Infanta Maria Theresa, bride of Louis XIV. She was succeeded by her daughter-in-law, Maria-Anna of Bavaria, wife of the Grand Dauphin, then Marie-Adélaïde of Savoy, Duchess of Burgundy and mother of Louis XV, Louis XV's wife Maria Leczinska, and finally by Marie-Antoinette. It was in this room that the queen spent her last night at Versailles before escaping from the mob on the morning of 6 October 1789. In all nineteen royal children were born in the room.

The decoration of the panelling and the ceiling was the work of Gabriel for Maria Leczinska while the fireplace, jewel chest, sphinx shaped andirons and fire screen were for her successor Marie-Antoinette. The silk has been rewoven to the original pattern.

The Peer's Salon (k). – In this onetime antechamber the Queen recieved ambassadors and held her circle. It also served as the lying in state room for queens and dauphines. Of the original decor only Le Brun's ceiling remains as Marie Antoinette commissioned Mique to refurbish the room. It has been reconstituted to look exactly as it did in 1789 with almond green furnishings and Riesener's commodes and corner cupboards.

Antechamber (m). – Transformed from a guardroom it was here that Louis XVI and Marie-Antoinette ate in public. The family group by Madame Vigée-Lebrun shows Marie-Antoinette with her children (1787): second from the left is the future Louis XVII; the boy pointing to the empty cradle (symbolising his sister Sophie who died young) was the Dauphin who himself died 2 years later.

Queen's Guard Room (n). – The decor by Le Brun is pure Louis XIV in style. The marble panels were taken from the present War Salon, or Jupiter Salon as it was then known, when the Hall of Mirrors was created. It was into this room that the revolutionaries burst on 6 October 1789 and stabbed to death one of Marie-Antoinette's bodyguards.

Coronation Room. – Chapel from 1676 to 1682 this former guardroom also served as meeting place for the parliament when administering justice. Louis Philippe made alterations to accommodate several immense paintings commissioned for Napoleon I's coronation. On the left of the entrance hangs the second version of David's *Napoleon's Coronation* (1808-22). The original is in the Louvre.

1792 Room. – The room is hung with portraits of soldiers and battle scenes. Cogniet in his work *The Paris National Guard leaves for War* portrayed Louis Philippe in the uniform of a Lieutenant-General.

On leaving the Queen's Suite go down the Princes' Stairs to the court of the same name. If the visitor is to continue the tour with a visit to the King's Suite then pass through the arcade towards the gardens then turn sharp right taking the South Arcade.

Guided tour: King's Suite, Private Suite and Royal Opera.

■ **KING'S SUITE★★★** *(First floor)*

Guided tours only, groups are limited to a maximum of 30 people. The tour starts at the ticket office at the bottom of the Queen's Staircase; enter by the South Arcade (entrance A). For times and prices see p 189

Between 1684 and 1701 Jules Hardouin-Mansart redesigned for the king the apartments in the Louis XIII château overlooking the Marble Court. The decoration epitomised the Louis XIV style: ceilings, no longer compartmented, are surrounded by heavy friezes, panelling has replaced marble on the walls, large mirrors surmount the fireplaces.

Queen's Staircase. – This staircase was the formal palace approach to the royal apartments and with its multicoloured marble decor it is typical of Le Brun's work.

A guardroom (**1**) and first antechamber (**2**) lead to the Bull's Eye Salon.

Bull's Eye Salon (**3**). – The salon is so called after the false window in the form of a bull's eye (Œil-de-Bœuf) over the chimneypiece. Originally two rooms, Mansart and Robert de Cotte created the present chamber which makes a good comparison with those decorated at the beginning of Louis' reign. The style is all together lighter and more elegant. Three busts decorate the salon, *Louis XIV* by Coysevox, *Louis XV* by Gois and *Louis XVI* by Houdon. On the walls are royal family portraits and Nocret's rather strange family group, with above on the coving a delightful freize of children at play.

The courtiers assembled in this antechamber while awaiting the lever ceremony.

King's Bedroom (**4**). – This became the Sun King's bedroom in 1701. The King's Bedchamber is as it was under Louis XIV. The royal bed, in the exact centre of the palace and turned towards the east, was the centrepiece of the morning and evening ceremonies which took place daily at 8am and midnight from 1701 to 1789 when the reigning monarch rose and retired before the assembled members of his court. It was also amid these sumptuous surroundings, which date structurally from 1689, and in this same bed, that at 77, Louis XIV, still surrounded by courtiers, died of gangrene poisoning on 1 September 1715.

Behind the gilded balustrade stands the sumptuous canopied bed with hangings of gold and silver embroidered brocade. The six religious scenes are by Valentin de Boulogne and Lanfranco while the portraits above the doors are by Van Dyck and Caracciolo.

Council Chamber (**5**). – This was transformed by Louis XV in 1755 when it was given its present dimensions and decoration of gold and white Rococo panelling. It was in this room that the decision was taken to engage France in the American War of Independence.

THE KING'S PRIVATE SUITE

The State Apartments which were entirely public were duplicated from the time of Louis XV by the informal private suite transformed by Gabriel.

King's Bedchamber (**6**). – The King's Bedchamber is the room where Louis XV died of smallpox on 10 May 1774. Although the king had continued the ritual rising and retiring in the state bedroom throughout his reign, he used to slip away to this warmer and more comfortable room!

Above the doors are portraits of Louis XV's three daughters: two of Madame Elisabeth, Madame Henriette and Madame Adélaïde.

Pendule or Clock Cabinet (**7**). – The room is so called after the astronomic clock made by Passemant and Dauthiau in 1754 which marks the hours, the days of the week, the date in the month, the months, the years and phases of the moon.

The equestrian statue of Louis XV, or the Well Beloved as he was known, is a copy by Vassé of Bouchardon's statue which originally graced the Place de la Concorde. The statue was toppled when the square was renamed Square of the Revolution in 1792 and the obelisk now takes its place.

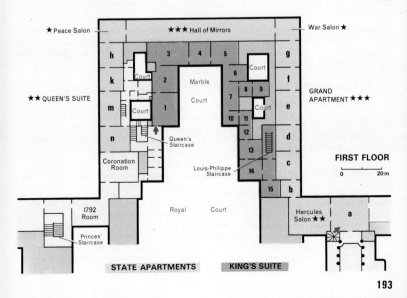

Dogs' Antechamber (8). – Used as a passageway to and from the stairs, the room has Louis XIV wooden panelling which is noticeably different from the preceding rooms.

Hunters' Dining Room (9). – As of 1750 this was where the King dined with courtiers after the hunt. Note the beautiful Sèvres porcelain plaques representing hunting scenes by Oudry ordered by Louis XVI for the China Salon.

Corner Room (10). – Completely transformed for Louis XV by Gabriel and the wood carver Verberckt the room is a masterpiece of 18C craftsmanship and of the Rococo style. The precious Oeben and Riesener roll top secretaire is one of the rare royal pieces which was not dispersed at the Revolution. On the chest-medal cabinet is the candelabra which commemorates the role played by France during the American War of Independence. The set of chairs by Foliot are dated 1774 and the corner cupboards by Joubert, 1755.

In 1785 in the presence of Marie-Antoinette, Louis XVI informed the Cardinal de Rohan of his impending arrest for his implication in the Necklace Affair.

Pass through the Inner Cabinet (11) where both Louis XV and Louis XVI kept their secret political and diplomatic documents and granted private audiences.

Madame Adélaïde's Cabinet (12). – Overlooking the Royal Court, this room was redecorated with rich panelling with musical, fishing and gardening motifs in 1753 by Louis XV for his favourite daughter. It was in this room that Mozart at the age of seven during the winter of 1763-64 is said to have played the clavichord before members of the royal family.

Louis XVI's Library (13). – The ageing Gabriel's elegant white and gold designs were ably executed by the wood carver, Antoine Rousseau: the ensemble is a very successful example of the Louis XVI style (1774). Note the Riesener table.

China Salon (14). – Under Louis XVI this room with its white and gold designs, served as the Hunters' Dining Room.

Louis XVI's Gaming Room (15). – Admire from the doorway the Riesener corner cupboards (1774), the carved and gilded chairs by Boulard and fine brocade curtains.

Take the Louis-Philippe Staircase down to leave by the North Arcade (the passageway leading to the park). In the ground floor room under the staircase is a model of the Ambassadors Staircase. Ask permission to view.

■ **THE ROYAL OPERA★★** *(Ground floor)*

In 1768 Jacques-Ange Gabriel began to construct the opera-house which was opened two years later at the wedding of the Dauphin, the future Louis XVI, and Marie-Antoinette.

The interior was built of wood – with excellent acoustic results – and painted to look like green and rose marble. Ornament lies in the gilded low reliefs and medallions and vases coloured blue to pick up the colour of the sky on the ceiling painting, the deep blue seating and light blue curtain scattered with gold *fleurs de lys*. It took five years to restore the Opera to its present splendour. In 1957 the opening performance was attended by Queen Elizabeth II and Prince Philip.

■ **THE QUEEN'S PRIVATE SUITE★** *(First floor: see plan p 190)*

The queens of France retreated to this rather cramped suite of rooms which overlook the inner courts. Unlike the king's suite where he lived, these were only a daytime retreat. The 18C decor and layout was arranged for Marie-Antoinette.

Gold Cabinet. – The panelling by Rousseau is rich in antique motifs. The chandelier is in bronze and the commode is by Riesener. It was here that the Queen sat for Madame Vigée-Lebrun.

Library. – This was essentially a passageway. The drawer handles are in the form of a double headed eagle, the Habsburgs emblem.

Meridienne Room. – The small octagonal boudoir was used as a rest room by Marie-Antoinette. Mique redecorated it in 1781 on the birth of the dauphin and the furnishings include blue silk hangings and Georges Jacob furniture. The clock was given to the queen by the city of Paris and the table was a present from her sister.

■ **MADAME DE MAINTENON'S SUITE** *(First floor: see plan p 190)*

Madame de Maintenon, Louis XIV's morganatic wife, lived in this suite of rooms during the last 32 years of Louis' reign. The suite without furnishings is now part of the Museum of French History.

In the Grand Cabinet, decorated with red wall hangings, Mme de Maintenon entertained the royal family and Racine declaimed his latest tragedies.

■ **KING'S PRIVATE APARTMENTS★** *(Second and third floors)*

Louis XV disliked the public life-style adhered to by his great-grandfather the Sun King. He rearranged a more intimate series of rooms overlooking the inner courts and in the attics to which he, his mistresses and inner circle of close friends could escape. The king came to read, work, indulge in his favourite hobbies or eat in the tiny roof top gardens with their aviaries. The decor and the occupants changed regularly.

For those who appreciate the 18C decorative styles these suites are a must. Compare the multicoloured woodwork of the rooms overlooking the Stag Court with the more refined Rococo work of those around the Marble Court.

Madame de Pompadour's Suite. – *Third floor.* Louis XV's mistress lived in these apartments between 1745 and 1750. Carved woodwork by Verberckt and delicate 18C furniture constitute the sumptuousness of the Grand Cabinet.

Madame du Barry's Suite. – *Second floor.* This suite installed all around the Stag Court also has rooms overlooking the Marble Court. The suite includes a bathroom, a dining room, a bedchamber (*gouache* by Gauthier Dagoty representing Mme du Barry being waited on by her little black boy Zamore), a corner salon from which Louis XV used to admire the view over the town and surrounding hillsides and a library.

■ THE MUSEUM OF FRENCH HISTORY★★

Since 1984 various sections of the museum have been closed for restoration, apply in advance for further details: ☎ *49.50.58.32, extn 316.*

The outstanding feature of this Museum of French History from the 16 to the 19C, is that the thousands of portraits are seen in their contemporary settings and, in most cases, are of people who were associated with the palace.

17C Galleries. – These occupy most of the ground floor and first floor of the north wing. One of the ground floor galleries is devoted to Henri IV, the first to discover Versailles, and to Louis XIII, who built the first château. The Louis XIII and early Louis XIV reigns are portrayed by Vouet, Philippe de Champaigne, Deruet and Le Brun. The kings and queens, their children and favourites are shown on great state occasions and also informally. The Versailles Gallery shows the palace in construction.

On the first floor the portraits include members of the royal family, Louis XIV's successful generals, the favourites, Mme de Montespan and Mme de Maintenon, portraits of Louis XIV's children, legitimate and illegitimate, and such great men of the time as Racine, Molière, La Fontaine, Le Nôtre, Couperin, Colbert...

18C Galleries★★★. – The galleries occupy the ground floor of the central wing and start historically, from the Queen's Staircase. Pictures in the **Dauphine's suite** show Louis XIV's immediate successors: the Regent and Louis XV, at the age of five, by Rigaud. Next come a six-panel Savonnerie screen, pictures of the mariage of Louis XV and Marie Leczinska, a portrait of Mme de Pompadour, delightful allegorical portraits by Nattier of Louis XV's daughters, Mme Adélaïde as Diana and Mme Henriette as Flora. The furniture, fine commodes and carved, silk upholstered chairs, contribute to the original atmosphere.

In the **Dauphin's suite** the former library is still beautifully panelled. The Grand Corner Room is hung with further pictures by Nattier of Marie Leczinska and her daughters. The decoration of the Dauphin's bedroom dates from 1747, the chimney-piece being one of the finest in the palace.

The antechamber to the gallery below the Hall of Mirrors, is hung with pictures of battle scenes, while the **Gallery** has portraits of the members of the royal family.

The antechamber to **Mme Victoire's suite** fourth daughter of Louis XV, was previously Louis XIV's bathroom and was then equipped with a marble piscina and two baths. The fine Grand Cabinet or corner room retains its original chimney-piece and panelling by Verberckt.

The former bedroom of Mme Victoire has furniture of an exceptional quality (lacquerwork) and summer wall hangings. The final galleries document the great festivals and political occasions of the century.

The heavy Ambassador's Staircase, removed by Louis XV in 1752, led formerly to the **Ambassador's Salon,** a room of impressive architectural proportions, false relief painting and marble paving, where the most precious item is a clock designed by Claude Siméon Passement in 1754 illustrating the creation of the world. A model of the Ambassadors' Staircase can be seen in the antechamber.

The next gallery or guardroom is devoted entirely to the American War of Independance and the Treaty of Versailles of 1783 under which the independance of the 13 States was recognised.

The final galleries illustrate the last days of the monarchy and the approach of the Revolution.

Consulate and Empire Galleries★. – These periods are evoked on the first floor (Coronation Room and Battle Gallery) and on the second floor in the vast south attic above, as well as in the Chimay Attic above the Queen's Suite.

To visit the first floor galleries start from the Queen's Suite or the Queen's Staircase. Documents, drawings, engravings, furniture and furnishings bring the Napoleonic era to life once more: in the **Coronation Room,** the former Guardroom, hang David's famous paintings: *Napoleon's Coronation* and *The Distribution by Napoleon of Eagle Standards on the Champ-de-Mars in 1804* as well as Antoine-Jean Gros' *Battle of Aboukir.* Between the windows looking on to the gardens, there are two portraits of Napoleon, each is surmounted by a medallion of his wife at the time. On the ceiling is Callet's painting, *The Allegory of 18 Brumaire,* commemorating the overthrow of the Directory. The medallions depict the glorious episodes in the life of Napoleon.

The **Battle Gallery★** was created in the former princes' suites in 1836. The gallery takes its name from the 33 paintings representing the great French victories from Tolbiac (496) to Wagram (1809). The series was commissioned by Louis-Philippe and includes works by Horace Vernet (Bouvines, Friedland), Eugène Delacroix (Taillebourg) and Antoine-Jean Gros (Austerlitz).

The second floor galleries *(access: Escalier de Stuc)* evoke the First Italian campaing (Bagetti's *gouaches,* Gros' *Bonaparte on the Bridge at Arcole)* the Egyptian and second Italian campaigns. Portraits present notable people of the period by Gérard; the Imperial family, artists and writers. The last rooms show the marriage of Napoleon to Marie-Louise, the Russian campaign and the end of the Empire (Waterloo).

19C Galleries. – *Second floor, North attic, temporarily closed for restoration.*

THE GARDENS★★★

Time: about 3 hours – See plan below.

The gardens at Versailles, extending over some 100 ha – 250 acres – provide not so much a setting to the palace as an open-air architectural extension. The gardens were planned architecturally first by Le Vau, Le Brun and Le Nôtre and later by Mansart; axes, vistas, viewpoints were designed always with an architectural or statuesque point of focus and trees, shrubs and plants were used to provide background, mass and sometimes colour to pavilions, pools, fountains and statues. There is a remarkable sense of pattern and formality. The garden's style evolved over the years from Baroque to Classical and on to the picturesque in statuary, fountains and buildings.

A lot of the colour disappeared with the reduction in bedding plants from the 150 000 a year of Louis XIV's time to the more modest quantities under later monarchs. Mass and silhouette changed as trees grew to majestic heights.

The basic idea from which the garden design evolved, however, has never been altered – this is that there should be two axes, one north to south extending the line of the palace terrace in either direction, the other due west from the same terrace centre. Symmetry, and therefore monotony, is avoided – in its place is balance.

Fountains★★★. – *The fountains – the Grandes Eaux – play by daylight from 3.30 to 5pm three Sundays a month from May to September. The fountains at the Neptune Basin do not play when there is a floodlit performance – Fêtes de Nuit – the same evening. For full details apply to the Tourist Information Centre (see below).*

When the fountains are in operation access to the gardens (8 am to 5pm; 12F) is by the following entrances only: Princes Court, the Great Staircase of 100 steps, the two gates beside the Grand Canal and the Dragon Gate at the far end of Rue de la Paroisse. Leaflets showing the itinerary to follow are available.

The fountains are in operation for only a limited time. Arrive promptly, start at the Water Terrace (Parterres d'eau) overlooking the Latona Basin, and keep walking or they may end before you have completed the tour! Do not miss the Ballroom and Apollo's Bath groves which are only open on fountain playing days. The final display *(at 5.20pm for 10 minutes)* takes place at the Neptune and Dragon Basins. Here 99 fountains play together with some rising to a height of 42 m – 138 ft.

Illuminations★★★. – *The dates are fixed in advance for the season. For further details apply to the Office de Tourisme; 7, Rue des Réservoirs. ☏ 39.50.36.22.*

These evening displays occur four times a year at the Neptune Basin, they are followed by a fireworks display.

■ **THE GRAND PERSPECTIVE**

Water Terrace★★ (**Parterres d'eau**). – The palace is reflected in the waters of these two vast basins, decorated with bronze allegorical statues of the rivers of France and groups of children and water nymphs. From the terrace there is another admirable **vista★★★** right down the main or Sun axis and over the gardens.

Fountains. – To the left and right of steps leading down to the Latona Basin are the **Dawn** (**1**) and **Diana★** (**2**) **Fountains**. The statues are among the finest works in the gardens.

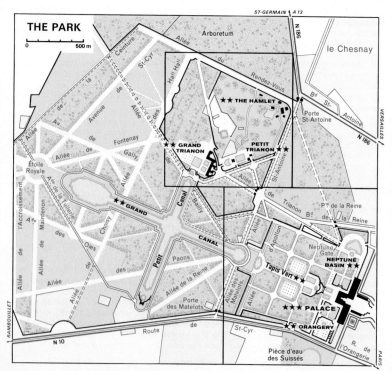

Latona Basin★. – This group of Latona and her children: Diana and Apollo is a copy of Marsy's original. Latona who was insulted by the Lycian peasants demanded justice from Jupiter who turned them into lizards and frogs.

At the bottom of the slope is the delightful **Nymph with a Shell (3)** a modern copy of Coysevox' work in the Louvre.

Tapis Vert★★. – This long avenue (translation: Green Carpet), offers fine perspectives of the palace and Grand Canal. It is lined with vases and statues such as the **Richelieu Venus (4)**, beside the Allée du Midi. For this sculpture Le Gros was influenced by an Antique work belonging to Richelieu.

Leave the Tapis Vert to explore the groves to the south.

■ THE GROVES SOUTH OF THE GRAND PERSPECTIVE
(BOSQUETS DU MIDI)

Ballroom Grove★ (5). – *Open only when the fountains play (p 196)*. This delightful grove is part of the original scheme. Arranged around what was once a circular marble dance floor are the tiers of grassy banks to serve as seating and the steps of the formalised cascade.

Bacchus or Autumn Basin (6). – Marsy's work shows Bacchus, at the centre of a group of Satyrs, with grapes and vine leaves, representing autumn. In Le Brun's original scheme the groups symbolising the four seasons, recently regilded and painted, were placed at the junctions of the main avenues *(see also nos 9, 12 and 13)*.

Queen's Grove (7). – *Closed in winter*. This grove laid out on the site of a maze during the 1775 replanting of the park, is now decorated with busts and statues (Aphrodite, the Fighting Gladiator, replicas of Greek and Roman statues).

Water Mirror Basin (8). – This is one of a pair which once encircled the Royal Island. Louis XVIII replaced the larger one when it started to silt up, with an English style garden called the King's Garden. The Water Mirror Basin is adorned with statues.

King's Garden★. – *Closed in winter*. This should be seen in summer when it is in full flower and a mass of colour. The whole is enhanced by a central lawn and fine trees.

Saturn or Winter Basin (9). – A winged god surrounded by cherubs amidst ice flows and shells by Girardon, represents winter.

Colonnade★★. – *This group is usually closed but can be seen well enough through the railings*.

Mansart erected the circular colonnade in 1685 in conjunction with fifteen other sculptors. The charm of the monument lies in the variety of marble: blue, red, mauve and white. Two fine masques adorn the keystones with children's games on the spandrels.

■ APOLLO BASIN★

In the middle a massive group by Tuby shows the Sun God in his chariot rising from the sea among monsters of the deep, to light the world.

The esplanade between the basin and the Grand Canal is bordered by statues some of which are Greek or Roman antiquities.

■ GROVES NORTH OF THE GRAND PERSPECTIVE
(BOSQUETS DU NORD)

Dôme Grove (10). – *Open only when the fountains play*. This grove takes its name from two lodges by Mansart, which were demolished in 1820.

The low reliefs running round the basin depict the arms of the period and show all the customary elegance and delicacy of a work by Girardon.

Enceladus Basin★ (11). – Marsy's all too realistically violent work contrasts with the other groups in the garden. Only the head and arms of Enceladus are visible above the engulfing rocks of Mount Olympus by which the Titans had hoped to reach the sky.

Obelisk Basin. – Mansart designed this basin encircled by stone steps and lawns. The fountain shows to advantage when full on and the water rises in the shape of an obelisk.

Flora or Spring Basin (12). – Another of the four statues of the seasons by Tuby.

Ceres or Summer Basin (13). – Regnaudin was responsible for this last in the seasons series.

Apollo's Bath Grove★ (14). – *Open only when the fountains play*.

This was part of the Anglo-Chinese garden created by Hubert Robert at the beginning of Louis XVI's reign. Marie-Antoinette greatly favoured this style which was employed at the Petit Trianon.

The **Apollo Group★** now appears in a lakeside grotto with a setting of greenery which would have been quite unimaginable in the 17C. The weary Apollo is attended by a group of nymphs (by Girardon and Regnaudin). On either side tritons groom the horses. (Marsy and Guérin).

Philosophers' Crossroads (15). – From this point flanked by large terms there is an unusual sideways **view★★** of the palace beyond the Parterres du Nord.

Look down the alley to the right which is bordered by statues, including winter by Girardon, and a double row of yew trees.

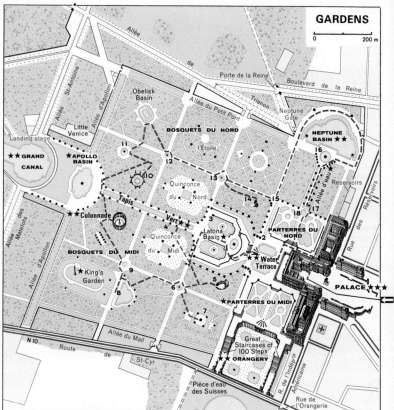

■ NEPTUNE AND DRAGON BASINS

Closed on the afternoons when there are illuminations in the evening.

Neptune Basin★★. – This closes the main axis, Allée d'eau, running to the north. The largest in the park, this basin was designed by Le Nôtre but only acquired its final appearance in 1741 with the addition of the elaborate lead group by Adam, Lemoyne and Bouchardon depicting the Sea God, dragons and cherubs.

Dragon Basin (16). – The victory over the monsters of the deep symbolises the mastering of the troubles of the Fronde, which remained an unpleasant memory with Louis XIV. Only the dragons are original, the rest was recast in 1889.

■ PARTERRE DU NORD

At the north end of the terrace, this was originally overlooked by the King's Suite and Louis XIV had expressed the wish that childhood be one of the themes. The Neptune Basin closes the vista in this direction and the sea and its creatures are another theme for the overall design.

Water or Children's Alley. – The alley is lined by twenty-two small white marble basins in which stand bronze groups of three children holding aloft even smaller pink marble basins.

Basin of the Nymphs of Diana (17). – All around the basin are Girardon's graceful 17C low reliefs★ which inspired many an artist in later years, particularly Renoir.

Lower Terrace★★. – To the north and west are statues and terms representing the continents, seasons, poetry...

The **Pyramid Fountain★ (18)** is a lead group by Girardon after Le Brun's designs, a most graceful composition incorporating tritons, dolphins and shrimps.

At the top of the steps leading to the water terrace are two superb bronzes the **Knifegrinder**, a replica of the antique by Foggini (original in Venice) and **Venus on a Tortoise** by Coysevox (original in the Louvre).

■ GRAND CANAL★★

Boats and bicycles are for hire at the near end of the canal on the right.

In the form of a cross, the Grand Canal measures 1 650 m long by 62 m wide – 1850 × 68 yds, the Petit or Small Canal 1 070 m – 1 170 yds.

In Louis XIV's time the waters were alive and gay with brilliantly decorated gondolas manoeuvred by gondoliers who lived in the Little Venice (Petite Venise), nearby. *There are plans to make this into a visitors' centre.*

THE TRIANONS★★ *See map below*

Access for pedestrians. – *From the Neptune Gate straight along the Avenue de Trianon or alternatively by the avenue from the head of the Grand Canal.*

Access by car. – *See the map on p 196*

Fountains. – *At the Grand Trianon these take place on five Sundays between May and September from 4 to 5pm.*

Bicycle hire. – *Bicycles are available at the entrance Boulevard de la Reine, to the north of the palace's formal gardens.*

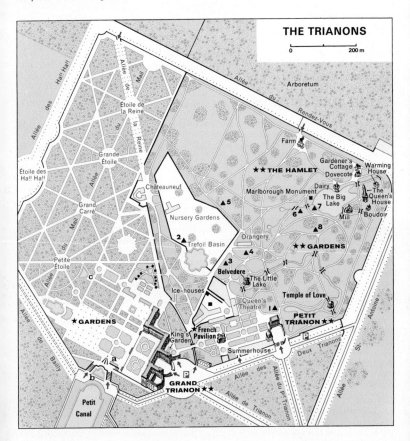

THE TRIANONS

0   200 m

■ THE GRAND TRIANON★★ *time: 2 hours*

From 1670 to 1687 there existed on the site a small château known as the Porcelain Trianon from its facing both outside and in with Delft blue and white tiles. Louis XIV enjoyed retiring to the peace of the small domain with his intimates, particularly Mme de Montespan. With time, however, she lost the king's favour and the château fell into disrepair! In due course the king replaced the earlier building designed by Mansart to which he returned with the new favourite, Mme de Maintenon. On the king's death, this second Trianon gradually fell into disuse, his successors preferring the Petit Trianon when this was built.

Finally at the Revolution the furniture was dispersed and all seemed at an end until Napoleon, after his marriage to Marie-Louise of Austria, decided to refurnish it. Louis Philippe had it restored as did General de Gaulle in 1962 with the intention of using it on state occasions.

The château★★. – Well proportioned wings with multicoloured pink marble pilasters border the main courtyard and are linked at their far end by a peristyle of predominantly rose-coloured marble columns through which can be seen the gardens beyond. At the roof edge, above the single storey, is a regular balustrade. There is an extension *(not open to the public)* away to the right which is not visible from the courtyard.

The peristyle overlooking both the courtyard and the gardens was designed by Robert de Cotte and adopted in spite of Mansart's reservations.

The apartments. – The rooms have been restored to their Louis XIV decor although the furniture dates from the First Empire and the Restoration. The families of both Napoleon I and Louis-Philippe resided here.

The attractive Mirror Room, in the left wing, was formerly the Council Chamber. The Empire furniture and silk curtains, rewoven to patterns originally chosen by Marie-Antoinette, are attractive elements of this noble room.

The bedroom retains the bed ordered by Napoleon for the Tuileries and which Louis-Philippe later had modified. The former Empire Salon beyond was once a separate room.

Louis-Philippe rearranged the right wing reception rooms in a more intimate manner. The paintings are mostly by French masters of the 17C. In the former Music Room note the shutters which enclose the musicians' loggias. Further reminders of the princesses appear in the Grand Salon where the table drawers are marked to indicate where each of Louis-Philippe's daughters kept her embroidery.

The Malachite Salon is named after the green malachite candelabra and other pieces presented by the Tsar Alexander I to Napoleon. The cool salon with its northerly exposition has four canvases portraying the original palace. Beyond, the **gallery** ★ lit by four massive Empire chandeliers, contains 24 illustrations commissioned by Louis XIV of the Versailles and Trianon gardens in the 17C. At the far end of the gallery the Garden Salon has a fine set of chairs from the château at Meudon.

Gardens ★ . – From the terrace (**a**) overlooking the steps and Horseshoe Pool (**b**) there is a good view over the Small Canal (Petit Canal). Beyond the formal garden the woodland area is criss-crossed by a network of alleys. The basin Buffet d'Eau (**c**) by Mansart has in Neptune and Amphitrite the only mythological sculpture in this garden.

On the far side of the château is the King's Garden.

To reach the Petit Trianon cross the Reunion Bridge built by Napoleon I.

■ THE PETIT TRIANON *time: 1 1/2 hours*

Louis XV, who enjoyed looking at both animals and flowers, established a model farm and a botanical garden, directed by Jussieu, in the Trianon domain. Both were later dispersed. The king also commissioned Gabriel to design him a summerhouse, the French Pavilion and, at the end of his reign, the Petit Trianon.

The Petit Trianon was given by his successor, Louis XVI, to Marie-Antoinette who delighted in it, visiting it frequently, accompanied by her children and sister-in-law, Madame Elisabeth. There, the queen, who already felt free from the stifling etiquette of the 18C court, increased the feeling of informality even further, by ordering her architect, Richard Mique, and the painter, Hubert Robert, to modify the gardens and, in imitation of the countryside of her native Austria, build the celebrated Hamlet. It was when Marie-Antoinette was at the Petit Trianon that she received the news on 5 October 1789 that the Revolutionaries were marching on Versailles. The queen left immediately never to return.

Neither Pauline Bonaparte, Napoleon's sister, nor his wife, Marie-Louise, paid more than fleeting visits to the Petit Trianon and it was only with the Empress Eugénie, who felt considerable sympathy for Marie-Antoinette, that interest revived. The Empress' enthusiasm was such that by 1867 the château had returned, in part, to its former appearance and been largely refurnished with period pieces, including some which had belonged to the former queen.

French Pavilion ★ . – Set in a formal garden between the Grand and Petit Trianons, this is considered Gabriel's greatest small scale masterpiece. The pavilion was designed as a summerhouse for Louis XV and Madame de Pompadour. Look in through the french windows to get some idea of the delicacy of the interior decoration. Note at cornice level the animal freize, a reminder of the menagerie established nearby. (This can only be visited during one of the more detailed tours of the Petit Trianon.)

To the south stands the cool **summerhouse** which was rebuilt in 1982.

Château ★ ★ . – The façade overlooking the entrance courtyard is sober, but that on the garden reflects all Gabriel's mastery of the 18C Neo-Classical style. Four colossal columns on either side of three tall windows, rise from ground level to the cornice over the first floor; above is a low balustrade matching that of the terrace fronting the façade and the central double stairway leading to the former gardens.

Inside a stone staircase decorated with a wrought iron banister in which Marie-Antoinette's initials are used as a decorative motif, leads to a series of rooms.

First Floor Apartments. – A series of rooms are open to the public. Note in particular the delicately detailed **panelling** ★ ★ by Guibert in the dining and reception rooms. The pale green background colour of the dining room has banished the habitual Trianon grey of the 19C. In the formal salon redecorated in the 19C is Riesener's remarkable astronomical writing desk (1771).

Gardens ★ ★ . – Anglo-Chinese in style, the garden with its river, lakes and majestic trees and enchanting follies was the combined effort of Mique and Hubert Robert to the plans of an amateur.

Some of the trees which have reached the venerable age of 150-200 years, belonged to Jussieu's original botanical collection. The oldest is without doubt the pagoda tree (**1**) planted at the north east corner of the Petit Trianon during the reign of Louis XV.

Belvedere. – Also known as the Music Room this delightful Neo-Classical pavilion by Mique overlooks the Little Lake. Inside all is elegance and refinement.

Leave for a moment the winding paths of the English style garden to reach Charpentier's Garden, go into the grounds of the Grand Trianon to discover a magnificent cedar of Lebanon (**2**), beside the Clover Basin and behind, two 17C ice-houses (reconstructed). Return to Charpentier's Garden with its many exceptional trees: two sequoia big trees (**3**) and a fastigiate (**4**). Going further left beyond the Orangery is a very old Siberian elm (**5**). Returning towards the hamlet, standing beside the lake is a tulip tree (**6**) and two groups of bald cypresses (**7**).

The Hamlet ★ ★ . – *Interiors not open.* Scattered around the Big Lake (Grand Lac) are 10 thatched cottages replicas of those at Chantilly.

The monument to Marlborough recalls the nursery rhyme popularised at Louis XVI's court by the Dauphin's nurse.

On the path to the Temple of Love is a remarkable plane tree (**8**).

Temple of Love. – There, on a small island, is the temple with at its centre, Bouchardon's statue of Cupid cutting his Bow from the Club of Hercules (original in the Louvre).

INDEX

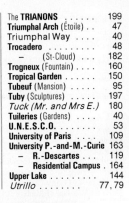

Antiquities

Louvre ★★★ p 27; **Museum of National Antiquities** ★★, St-Germain-en-Laye p 186

Army

Army Museum ★★★ p 73; **Museum of the Order of Liberation** ★★ p 74

Art

Louvre ★★★ p 27; *African:* **African and Oceanian Art Museum** ★ p 149; **Armenian Museum** p 161; **Decorative Arts:** see below; *European:* **Cognacq-Jay Museum** ★★ (18C) p 80; **Jacquemart-André Museum** ★★ p 93; **Nissim de Camondo Museum** ★ (18C) p 167, **Orsay Museum** (19C) p 135 opening scheduled late 1986; **French Monuments** ★★ p 50; *Impressionism:* **Jeu de Paume Museum** ★★★ (transferring to Orsay 1986) p 42; **Marmottan Museum** ★★ p 166; **Palais de Tokyo Museums** ★ (preview of Orsay Collections) p 137; **Jewish Art** p 163; *Modern Art:* **Palais de Tokyo** p 137, **National Museum of Modern Art** ★★★, Beaubourg p 104; *Nabis:* **Priory Museum** ★, St-Germain-en-Laye p 187; **Naive** p 77; *Oriental:* see below; *Popular:* **National Museum of Popular Arts and Traditions** ★★ p 171.

Artists; Sculptors

Bouchard p 157; **Bourdelle** ★ p 128; **Delacroix** p 108; **Henner** p 162; **G. Moreau** p 165; **Picasso** p 89; **Renan-Scheffer** p 171; **Rodin** p 136; **Zadkine** p 176

Books, MSS, Prints, Maps, Posters

Bibliothèque Nationale ★ p 95; **Forney Library** (Posters) p 90; **Poster Museum** p 168

Coins, Medals, Orders

Army Museum ★★★ p 73; **Bibliothèque Nationale** ★ p 95; **Legion of Honour Museum** ★ p 135; **The Mint** ★ p 139

Costume, Fashion

Costume and Fashion Museum, p 98; **Palais Galliera** p 138

Decorative Arts

Gobelins' Tapestry Factory ★ p 162; **Hotel de Cluny Museum** ★★ (Middle Ages) p 118; **Museum of Decorative Arts** ★★ p 98

History

of Paris: **Hotel Carnavalet Museum** ★★ p 87; **Hotel de Cluny Museum** ★★ (Middle Ages) p 118; **Hotel de Lamoignan** (Historical Library) p 87; **Montmartre Museum** p 79
of France: **Museum of French History** ★★, Versailles p 195; **Museum of National Antiquities** ★★, St-Germain-en-Laye p 186; **Historical Museum of France** ★★ p 88

Maritime

Maritime Museum ★★ p 50

Miscellaneous

Bricard Museum (Locks p 88); **Counterfeit Museum** p 161; **French Office for Modern Methods of Teaching** p 131; **Grand Orient Lodge Museum** (Free masonry) p 162; **Magic World of Automata** p 105; **Museum of the Chase and of Nature** p 88; **Police Museum** p 114; **Postal Museum** ★★ p 129; **SEITA Museum** (Tobacco) p 174; **Social Service Museum** p 65

Music

Conservatoire Superieur National de Musique ★ (Musical Instruments) p 167; **Charles Cros Museum** (Phonographs) p 95; **Musical Instruments Museum** (Mechanical Reproducers of music) p 105; **Opera** (Library and Museum) p 81

Oriental Art

Cernuschi Museum ★ (Chinese) p 158; **Ennery Museum** (Chinese and Japanese) p 161; **Guimet Museum** ★★ p 138

Personalities

Balzac p 169, **Clemenceau** p 168, **Victor Hugo** p 86, **Napoleon**, Malmaison p 179, **Pasteur** p 169

Porcelain, Glass

Glass Museum ★ p 168; **National Porcelain Museum** ★★ p 187

Science

Anthropology: **Museum of Mankind** ★★ p 51; *Astronomy:* **the Observatory** ★ p 132, **Palais de la Découverte** ★★ p 46, *Holography:* **Holography Museum** p 100; *Medicine:* **Val de Grace Museum** p 131; *Mineralogy:* **School of Advanced Mining Engineering** ★★ p 132, **Botanical Gardens** p 157, **Mineralogical Museum** ★★ p 163; *Natural History:* **Botanical Gardens** p 156; *Radio and Television:* **Radio France House** p 155; *Science:* **Cité des Sciences et de l'Industrie** p 176, **National Technical Museum** ★★ p 158, **Palais de la Decouverte** ★★ p 46; **Sea and Water Centre** p 132

Theatre, Cinema

Arsenal Library (Theatre Collection) p 154; **Dramatic Arts Museum**, Colbert Arcade (window displays only) p 95; **Henri Langlois Cinema Museum** ★ p 51; **Kwok-On Museum** (Oriental Theatre) p 91

Waxworks

Grevin Museum ★ p 124; **Grevin's Forum Annexe** ★ p 99; **Historial Museum** p 77